Civil Liability for Defective Premises

Civil Liability for Defective Premises

J H Holyoak BA (CANTAB)
of Gray's Inn, Barrister,
Lecturer in Law, University of Leicester,
Part-time Lecturer in Law, Loughborough University of Technology

David K Allen MA (OXON), LLM (McGILL)
of the Middle Temple, Barrister,
Lecturer in Law, University of Leicester

London
Butterworths
1982

England	Butterworth & Co (Publishers) Ltd
London	88 Kingsway, WC2B 6AB
Australia	Butterworths Pty Ltd
Sydney	271–273 Lane Cove Road, North Ryde, NSW 2113
	Also at Melbourne, Brisbane, Adelaide and Perth
Canada	Butterworth & Co (Canada) Ltd
Toronto	2265 Midland Avenue, Scarborough, M1P 4S1
New Zealand	Butterworths of New Zealand Ltd
Wellington	33–35 Cumberland Place
South Africa	Butterworth & Co (South Africa) (Pty) Ltd
Durban	152–154 Gale Street
USA	Butterworth (Publishers) Inc
Boston	10 Tower Office Park, Woburn, Mass. 01801

ISBN   0 406 23340 3

Typeset by Colset Pte Ltd, Singapore and printed in Singapore by Tien Wah Press

Preface

The purpose of this book is to provide a comprehensive coverage of the rules and principles governing civil liability for defective premises. This comprehensive coverage is designed to reflect, on the one hand, the need to examine separately the potential liability of the different categories of likely defendants, and, on the other hand, the need to describe and analyse the considerable impact that the law of negligence has had on such liability in the last decade.

The book is primarily intended to be of assistance to the practitioner whose client, whether as plaintiff or defendant, is faced with a possible claim for civil liability for defective premises. It is also hoped that academics and their students will find the book helpful in considering the contextual application of contractual and tortious rules; we feel that the area of premises liability is especially important in view of the far-reaching recent developments which have stemmed from premises cases.

Chapter 1 explains what, for the purposes of this book, is meant by 'civil liability for defective premises', and also explains the structure of the work which, it is hoped, will assist the practitioner in advising a client as quickly and easily as is possible. Chapters 2 to 7 describe and analyse the law relating to the various categories of person, such as the builder, architect, vendor etc. who may be liable in damages as a result of their responsibility for defective premises, and chapter 8 discusses the law concerning the public control of defective premises. Chapter 9 is concerned with those cases where more than one person is liable, and discusses the law relating to joint liability and contribution.

The law, as we understand it to be, is stated as at 31 July 1981. We have, however, updated the text at proof stage so as to provide references to *Yianni v Edwin Evans & Sons* and *Eames London Estates Ltd v North Hertfordshire District Council* that were not available to us earlier. Unfortunately it has not been possible to incorporate discussion of the decisions in *Solloway v Hants County Council* (1981) 79 LGR 449 (nuisance), *Balcomb v Wards Construction (Medway) Ltd* (1981) 259 Estates Gazette 765 (engineers' liability), *Perry v Sidney Phillips & Son* (1981) 260 Estates Gazette 389 (surveyors' liability), *London and South of England Building Society Ltd v Stone* (1981) Times 19 November (surveyor's liability), *Crump v Torfaen Borough Council* (1981) Times 3 August (local authority liability) and *Walker v Boyle* (1981) Times 10 October (vendor's liability). In addition, the Building Research Establishment Digest 251, published in July 1981, entitled 'Assessment of

Damage in Low-rise Buildings', is of particular importance to all concerned in the provision, survey and valuation of premises, and also their legal advisers.

Jon Holyoak
David Allen
30 *November* 1981

Acknowledgments

We have received advice and assistance from a number of people in connection with this book and it is our pleasant task to record our grateful thanks to them. Several of our colleagues in the Faculty of Law at the University of Leicester have commented on and discussed with us various aspects of the book, but we owe especial thanks to Professor Graham Barnsley, Jackie Minor, Peter Handford and Robin White. In addition Roger Farley of Municipal Mutual Insurance, Donald Harmer of Grundy and Harmer, Mr Small, Mr Hoare and Mr Morell of Barlow, Lyde and Gilbert, Thomas Akroyd, and Mr Mayes, the Chief Solicitor of the London Borough of Merton and several of his colleagues have all been extremely generous with their time and advice, and we are most grateful to them. Liability for any defects in the book remains exclusively ours, however.

In addition we are grateful to the Solicitors' Law Stationery Society Ltd, the copyright owners of the National Conditions of Sale and of their form of Enquiries before Contract, for permission to reproduce extracts from the National Conditions of Sale and the Enquiries, and we are equally grateful to the Law Society for permission to quote extracts from their Conditions of Sale.

We are also grateful to the Research Board of the University of Leicester for a grant which assisted in defraying the expenses incurred in researching and writing the book.

We should also like to express our thanks to Barbara Goodman, Christine Driver, Anne Folwell, Gladys Hurst, Christine Stanger and especially Barbara Harris, in the Faculty of Law office, for their skilful typing and powers of decipherment. In addition, we should like to thank our publishers for preparing the Tables and Index, and for coping with our dilatory ways.

Finally, but by no means least, David Allen would like to thank his wife and daughter for their help and encouragement.

Contents

Table of statutes

References in this Table to *Statutes* are to Halsbury's Statutes of England (Third Edition) showing the volume and page at which the annotated text of the Act will be found.

Table of cases

R

Chapter 1

Introduction

1.1 The purpose of this chapter is threefold. Firstly, certain remarks as to the scope of the work are made. Secondly, the structure of the book is explained. Thirdly, consideration is given to certain general features of the law of civil obligations which underpin the detailed discussion in many of the subsequent chapters.

The scope of the work

1.2 This book is only concerned with civil actions. This primarily includes the action for damages, where so much recent change in the law has occurred, and associated claims for injunctive or ancillary relief. This also includes public law remedies, such as prerogative orders; however, no reference is made (other than in passing) to any criminal liabilities that arise.

1.3 The book covers liability for premises which are defective. In our view, defective premises are those which have in them some physical shortcoming, whether latent or patent, which either renders them (or is likely in the future to render them) a danger to their users or neighbours, or to other premises, or else renders the premises less valuable in themselves. Any of these factors renders premises defective; more than one will be present in a number of cases.

1.4 For the purpose of this book, liability for defective premises arises in two different ways. Normally, liability will be imposed on the person who has caused the defect, by building the premises carelessly, designing them badly or failing to maintain them to the appropriate standard, among many other examples. However, liability can also arise in relation to defective premises, where the effect of one person's breach of a duty, imposed on him in respect of premises, is to cause another to live or work in defective premises. Examples may make this clearer – we will discuss the liability of the surveyor whose report carelessly fails to disclose the existence of defects in the property he has surveyed, and the liability of the local authority which does not perform an inspection of premises adequately. It should be noted that only liability under the law of England and Wales is covered in this book.

1.5 We regard the book as covering within the term 'premises', all land and all structures on the land. The coverage also extends to other property which the law in a specific area of liability treats in the same way as land and structures thereon. For example, ships are regarded as falling within the scope of the Occupiers' Liability Act 1957, but on the other hand the principles we discuss concerning the sale of defective premises are clearly inapplicable to sales of defective ships. Highways are not regarded as premises for the purposes of this book.

The structure of the book

1.6 We have considered that the topic is most usefully and coherently expounded by separate consideration of the potential civil liability of the various categories of person or institution likely to be the defendant in a claim concerning defective premises. Such persons range from those directly liable for the defect, for example the architect who makes a negligent design, or the builder whose workmanship is faulty, to those whose responsibility is only indirect, such as those who provide careless advice concerning the state of premises, for example the surveyor whose examination of premises carelessly fails to disclose the existence of dry rot, or the local authority whose building inspector fails to inspect, or to inspect adequately, the foundations dug by a builder. Each ensuing chapter, subject to necessary cross-referencing and reference to the general discussion in the third part of this chapter, is designed to provide complete coverage of the potential and actual civil liability of the category discussed in that chapter, for defective premises. Inevitably this has led to a degree of repetition which can be discerned if the book is read as a whole; no apology is made for this, as the book is primarily designed for the professional adviser who, it is assumed, would prefer to have ready access in a discrete chapter to the law concerning the liability of, for example, the architect whom his client is contemplating suing, even though this may mean he finds an element of repetition should he turn to the chapter concerning the local authority whose liability may also be in issue. A separate chapter discusses public law controls which impose duties both on local authorities in respect of premises, and on the owners or occupiers thereof. In cases where there is more than one defendant, questions of apportionment of liability as between defendants and contribution are clearly highly important, and these issues are examined in a further separate chapter.

General features of the law of civil obligations

1.7 It is to minimise the repetition as between the various chapters that we choose to discuss certain aspects of the law of civil obligations which are a foundation for many of the specific rules relating to defective premises. In this chapter there will be found a general account of these particular aspects of both contract and tort, while the especial significance of these aspects for individual categories of potential defendants is considered in the appropriate chapters that follow. As an example, questions of limitation of liability are obviously relevant to all the categories of potential defendant and detailed discussion of specific points which arise in the context only of one particular Act of Parliament or in relation to only one group of potential defendants are considered in that context; this chapter, however, may be seen as a common denominator, providing a discussion of the principles of limitation generally.

1.8 The following general matters are considered in the remainder of this chapter:

(a) Measure of damages;
(b) Remoteness of damage;
(c) Claims for economic loss;
(d) Limitation periods;
(e) Misrepresentations; and
(f) Exclusion of liability.

A Measure of damages[1]

1.9 The purpose of an award of damages, whether in contract or in tort, is to compensate the plaintiff for the loss or damage that he has suffered. The measure of damages, as defined by Lord Blackburn in *Livingstone v Rawyards Coal Co*[2] is 'that sum of money which will put the party who has been injured, or who has suffered, in the same position as he would have been in if he had not sustained the wrong for which he is now getting his compensation or reparation'. This statement is as true for contract as for tort, but there is a fundamental distinction between the basis on which damages are assessed in contract and the basis on which they are assessed in tort which the statement does not indicate, and which requires elaboration. In contract the basic purpose of the award of damages is to put the plaintiff 'so far as money can do it ... in the same situation ... as if the contract had been performed',[3] for in contract, as McGregor explains,[4] 'the wrong consists not in the making but in the breaking of the contract and therefore the plaintiff is entitled to be put into the position he would have been in if the contract had never been broken'. Contract therefore looks to the future rather than the past and, being mainly concerned with commercial matters, compensates basically[5] for loss of expectation. Tort, however, looks rather to a restoration of the position prior to the tortious act, a *restitutio in integrum*, seeking to put the plaintiff in the position he was in before the tort was committed. Loss of bargain is generally[6] not in issue. The classic statement is that of Lord Wright in *Liesbosch Dredger v SS Edison (Owners)*,[7] who stated that the plaintiff is said to be entitled to recover 'such a sum as will replace [him], so far as can be done by compensation in money, in the same position as if the loss had not been inflicted on [him]'.

1 See generally *McGregor on Damages* (14th edn), especially paras 572–580; Ogus *The Law of Damages* (1973).
2 (1880) 5 App Cas 25 at 39. See also *Victoria Laundry (Windsor) Ltd v Newman Industries Ltd* [1949] 2 KB 528 at 539, [1949] 1 All ER 997 at 1002.
3 Per Parke B in *Robinson v Harman* (1848) 1 Exch 850 at 855.
4 *McGregor* para 573.
5 But by no means exclusively. See, inter alia, Atiyah *The Rise and Fall of Freedom of Contract* (1979); Atiyah (1978) 94 LQR 193; *Ogus* ch 8.
6 Though not always; e g deceit, see, for example, *Doyle v Olby (Ironmongers)* [1969] 2 QB 158, [1969] 2 All ER 119. However, even though the fraud of the defendant may have caused loss to the plaintiff, compensation will be based on *restitutio in integrum*; though the plaintiff may have suffered loss of bargain this will not be compensated in the action for deceit.
7 [1933] AC 449 at 459.

1.10 Until comparatively recently the implications of this distinction were minimal. However, the increasing interrelationship of contract and tort,[1] evidenced by such developments as the expansion of tortious liability in areas such as professional negligence[2] and the nature of the law of misrepresentation, in which contract and tort have become thoroughly intertwined,[3] has led to a corresponding increase in the importance of the distinction between the two measures. Insofar as, in a particular case, the effect of the distinction is to render one cause of action more potentially profitable to a would-be plaintiff he will naturally seek to bring his claim within that cause of action, and the law will now permit him so to do.[4]

1 See e g Fridman (1977) 93 LQR 422.
2 See paras 4.41 ff, below.
3 See paras 1.46 ff, below.
4 See e g *Esso Petroleum Co Ltd v Mardon* [1976] QB 801, [1976] 2 All ER 5.

1.11 When it will be advantageous for a plaintiff to sue in one form of action rather than the other is a difficult question to answer in any manner other than a very generalised one. Much depends on the relevant tests of foreseeability, as well as the rules concerning measure. A claim in contract is generally regarded as having a narrower ambit;[1] however, in cases involving claims for qualitative defects and pure economic loss, or where there has been disclosure of specific information, beyond that reasonably or remotely foreseeable, from one party to the other, a claim in contract is likely to produce results that are more advantageous to the plaintiff than a claim in tort.

1 See *Koufos v C Czarnikow Ltd, The Heron II* [1969] 1 AC 350 at 385, [1967] 3 All ER 686 at 691.

1.12 An important issue concerning measure of damages in cases of liability for defective premises is whether the cost of repair of the premises or their diminution in value should form the basis of the award of damages, for clearly, as e g in *Philips v Ward*[1] where the difference between cost of repair and diminution in value was £3,000, there may be a significant difference. No obvious answer to the question is provided by the different tests for measure of damages in contract and tort, and indeed Widgery LJ in *Harbutt's 'Plasticine' Ltd v Wayne Tank and Pump Co Ltd*[2] said, 'the distinction between those cases in which the measure of damage is the cost or repair of the damaged article, and those in which it is the diminution in value of the article is not clearly defined. In my opinion each case depends on its own facts.' As will be seen below in later chapters, different answers to this question have been provided by the courts depending upon the cause of action and the particular nature of the defendant's obligation as well as the circumstances of the case, and these are considered in their particular contexts below, so no general answer can be offered at this stage.

1 [1956] 1 All ER 874, [1956] 1 WLR 471.
2 [1970] 1 QB 447 at 472–473, [1970] 1 All ER 225 at 240.

1.13 An associated and equally important question concerns the date at which damages are assessed. In *Philips v Ward*[1] the Court of Appeal stated that damages should be assessed at the date when the damage occurred, for sterling was taken to be constant in value. This fell to be reconsidered in the recent decision of the Court of Appeal in *Dodd Properties (Kent) Ltd v Canterbury City Council.*[2] As a result of pile-driving operations carried out by the defendants, serious structural damage was caused to a garage belonging to the plaintiffs. The plaintiffs did not carry out any repairs prior to the hearing, although repairs would have been technically possible in 1970, eight years before the hearing. They claimed that to have carried out repairs at that time would have caused them financial stringency, and in any event, as the defendants denied liability until shortly before the hearing in 1978, it would not have made commercial sense for them to repair the building before they were sure of recovering the cost from the defendants. Overruling the decision of Cantley J[3] (who followed *Philips v Ward*) the Court of Appeal held that the damages were to be assessed as at 1978 rather than 1970 prices (the difference between an award of £11,375 and £30,327). Sterling could no longer be taken to be constant in value according to *Miliangos v George Frank (Textiles) Ltd*,[4] where it was also stressed that the general principle that the date of breach was the usual date for assessing damages was not a universal rule. Megaw LJ said,[5] 'the true rule is that where there is a material difference between the cost of repair at the date of the wrongful act and the cost of repair when the repairs can, having regard to all the relevant circumstances, first reasonably be undertaken, it is the latter time by reference to which the cost of repairs is to be taken in assessing the damages'. The financial stringency that the plaintiffs would have suffered if they had repaired the garage in 1970 was a relevant circumstance which, together with other factors made it only sensible commercially to delay the repairs. In effect the duty incumbent upon the plaintiff to act reasonably can be equated with the duty owed by the victim of a breach of contract to mitigate his losses.

1 [1956] 1 All ER 874, [1956] 1 WLR 471.
2 [1980] 1 All ER 928, [1980] 1 WLR 433. See Feldman (1980) 43 MLR 708.
3 [1979] 2 All ER 118, [1980] 1 WLR 433 at 437.
4 [1976] AC 443, [1975] 3 All ER 801.
5 [1980] 1 All ER 928 at 933, [1980] 1 WLR 433 at 451.

1.14 As regards building contracts, the House of Lords had to consider the date at which damages on a cost of repair basis should be assessed, in *East Ham Corporation v Bernard Sunley & Sons Ltd*[1]. The House did not agree that damages should be assessed as at the date of the breach, at which time, it was argued, the supervising architect ought to have noticed the breach. It was held that damages must be assessed at the time when the defects were discovered and put right, for it must have been in the contemplation of the parties that there might be defects in the building which would not be revealed by a reasonable examination in the defects liability period. In the important decision of the Supreme Court of New Zealand in *Bevan Investments Ltd v Blackhall and Struthers (No 2)*[2] a situation strongly parallelling the state of affairs in *Dodd* fell to be considered. A structural engineer was in breach of contract to design a recreation centre. A modified scheme could have been carried out, but the plaintiffs, largely for reasons of financial difficulty, refused to go ahead with the scheme.

1 [1966] AC 406, [1965] 3 All ER 619.
2 [1978] 2 NZLR 97. See Duncan Wallace (1980) 96 LQR 101.

1.15 On the basis that it followed from the *East Ham* case that a building owner is to be compensated for the actual cost of work in a case where he acts with reasonable promptitude after discovering the defect, and has repairs done, the trial judge[1] held that, as the plaintiff had at no time acted unreasonably but had done his best to mitigate the loss, the damages were to be assessed as at the date of trial. The Supreme Court agreed with this. The likely cost of the modified scheme, the plaintiff's depleted resources, the reluctance of the plaintiff's bank to advance money for repair work and the lack of any assurance from the structural engineer as to coming to terms were all factors rendering the conduct of the plaintiff reasonable. Thus, in cases where the cost of repair is the basis upon which the damages are assessed, the earlier of the date of repair and the date of the trial is likely to be the date at which damages are assessed, both in contract and tort, subject to the duty to mitigate.[2]

1 [1973] 2 NZLR 45 (Beattie J).
2 Though Donaldson LJ suggested in *Dodd*, above, at 939 and 458, that there might even be cases where the court would have to assess the costs at some future time as being the reasonable date of repair, but such is likely to be an exceptional case. See Feldman (1980) 43 MLR 708.

1.16 Ultimately it may be that the courts will accept the argument that, provided no physical increase in the damage is caused by delays in repairing, it should not be necessary to give reasons justifying the delay, for 'the defendant has had the use of the money during the period he has not had to pay the damages, and it is unrealistic to suppose that his assets or income are laid out or regulated in such a way as to remain static in the face of inflation'.[1]

1 *Hudson's Building and Engineering Contracts* (10th edn) p. 592. See also Feldman and Libling (1979) 95 LQR 270.

1.17 Will the position be different where diminution in value rather than cost of repairs is taken as the basis for assessing damages, for example in a case where premises are destroyed or so severely damaged that the cost of repairs would be so high as to make repair uneconomic? Donaldson LJ in *Dodd* was of the view[1] that in normal circumstances the general principle that damages are assessed at the date when the cause of action arises would apply where diminution in value was the relevant measure of damages. It might appear somewhat anomalous to hold a plaintiff whose premises are destroyed by the defendant's negligence to the diminution in value measure assessed at the date of the negligent act, whereas if the damage were less serious and repairs were feasible, a possibly larger sum might be awarded on the basis of cost of repair at the date of the trial. Certainly the award of interest would in theory compensate the plaintiff receiving diminution value damages, but in practice, as the *Dodd* case shows, this may well not be the case. The total award of damages made by Cantley J at first instance[2] to the first and second plaintiffs (the second plaintiffs were the lessees of the first plaintiffs) was £22,974, including £7,491 interest. The total award made by the Court of Appeal was £42,278. Much, of course, will depend upon the circumstances of the case and, in particular, in a case such as *Philips v Ward*,[3] where diminution in value is taken as the measure of damages in a situation where repairs are feasible, the duty to mitigate, but subject to that there is a strong case for assessing damages, in cases where the measure of those damages is the diminution in value, on the basis of value at the date of the trial, thereby assimilating the rule to cases where the cost of repair basis is used.

1 [1980] 1 All ER 928 at 939, [1980] 1 WLR 433 at 458.
2 [1979] 2 All ER 118, [1980] 1 WLR 433 at 437.
3 [1956] 1 All ER 874, [1956] 1 WLR 471.

B Remoteness of damage[1]

1.18 As with measure of damages, there are differences which may be of more than semantic importance between the contractual and tortious tests concerning remoteness of damage. For the last twenty years the generally accepted test in the law of negligence has been that laid down by the Judicial Committee of the Privy Council in *The Wagon Mound*,[2] whereby the defendant is liable for all the consequences that a reasonable man would foresee at the time the tort was committed, disapproving of the earlier test applied in *Re Polemis*,[3] by which the defendant was liable for all damage directly caused by his act. The law of contract takes a more subjective approach and considers rather the question whether the loss is, in the words of Lord Reid in the leading modern authority,[4] 'of a kind which the defendant, when he made the contract, ought to have realised was not unlikely to result'. Lord Reid went on to say,[5] 'the crucial question is whether, on the information available to the defendant when the contract was made, he should, or the reasonable man in his position would, have realised that such loss was sufficiently likely to result from the breach of contract to make it proper to hold that the loss followed naturally from the breach, or that loss of that kind should have been within his contemplation. The modern rule of tort is quite different and it imposes a much wider liability. The defendant will be liable for any type of damage which is reasonably foreseeable as liable to happen even in the most unusual case, unless the risk is so small that a reasonable man would in the whole circumstances feel justified in neglecting it.' Lord Reid went on to explain the rationale behind this difference; the fact that in contract a party has the opportunity before the contract is made to protect himself against potential risks which he, but not the other party, may consider possible by drawing them to that other's attention; whereas in tort the absence of such advance protection justifies the broader remoteness test in that branch of the law.

1 See *McGregor on Damages* (4th edn) ch 6 and paras 578–580; Treitel *The Law of Contract* (5th edn) pp. 713–722; *Winfield and Jolowicz on Tort* (11th edn) pp. 114–132.
2 *Overseas Tankship (UK) Ltd v Morts Dock and Engineering Co Ltd (The Wagon Mound)* [1961] AC 388, [1961] 1 All ER 404.
3 *Re Polemis and Furness, Withy & Co Ltd* [1921] 3 KB 560.
4 *Koufos v C Czarnikow Ltd, The Heron II* [1969] 1 AC 350 at 382–383, [1967] 3 All ER 686 at 690. The decision comments on and refines the doctrine established by and developed in *Hadley v Baxendale* (1854) 9 Exch 341 and *Victoria Laundry (Windsor) Ltd v Newman Industries Ltd* [1949] 2 KB 528, [1949] 1 All ER 997.
5 *The Heron II*, above, at 385–386 and 691–692.

1.19 However, in the recent decision of the Court of Appeal in *H Parsons (Livestock) Ltd v Uttley Ingham & Co Ltd*[1] Lord Denning MR sought to assimilate the test of remoteness in contract to that in tort where the plaintiff's claim was for physical damage rather than economic loss, but this argument was not accepted by his colleagues. The logic of Lord Denning's argument, that it was 'absurd that the test for remoteness of damage should, in principle, differ according to the legal classification of the cause of action', was accepted by Scarman LJ (as he then was),[2] who also agreed that the law does not differentiate between contract and tort except in cases where the agreement, or the factual relationship between the parties, requires such differentiation in the interests of justice, but he did not agree that the case law justified the making of a distinction between loss of profit and physical damage as proposed by Lord Denning. 'Of course (and this is a reason for refusing to draw the distinction in law) the type of consequence, loss of profit or market or physical injury, will always be an important matter of fact in determining whether in all the circumstances the loss or injury was of a type which the parties could reasonably be supposed to have in contemplation.'[3] It is hard to be precise as to the impact of these divergent principles. Much will of course depend upon what was contemplated by the contracting parties, and it is difficult to disagree with McGregor's conclusion[4] that 'the scope of the protection afforded to the plaintiff is sometimes wider in tort and sometimes wider in contract, depending upon the voluntary factor in contract, varying from agreement to agreement, of the contemplation of the parties'.

1 [1978] QB 791, [1978] 1 All ER 525. See Hadjihambis (1978) 41 MLR 483.
2 Ibid at 805 and 535.
3 Ibid.
4 *McGregor on Damages* (14th edn) at p. 88, para 580. See also paras 577–579.

C Claims for economic loss

1.20 The question of what types of loss are recompensed by damages in the tort of negligence is not one that admits of an easy answer. Unlike the law of contract, where obligations are specified in advance of any breach, and where it can consequently be generally assumed that damages are payable for breach of those obligations, subject to the rules on remoteness of damage, the law of tort, and in particular negligence, cannot generally have recourse to examining a previous course of dealings between the parties as a means of regulating the duties owed and as a means of determining what aspects of the damage caused to the plaintiff may be the proper subject of a claim, so the question of duty is left to be considered by the court. It is suggested that the fact that the duty in a negligence case falls to be decided upon by the court, and the increasingly policy-orientated approach of the courts in negligence cases,[1] and also the fact that the question of remoteness is ultimately a factual question to be decided upon by the court, have all combined to obfuscate the precise approach of the law of negligence towards claims for economic loss i e where there is no physical damage, or where physical damage does not represent the whole loss. This is now an area of very great complexity. It is proposed to consider firstly when the law will award compensation in a negligence action for economic loss, and then proceed to discuss the related issue of precisely what the courts regard as economic loss.

1 *Home Office v Dorset Yacht Co* [1970] AC 1004, [1970] 2 All ER 294.

1.21 Traditionally the law of negligence has, since *Donoghue v Stevenson*,[1] imposed liability for negligent acts which cause personal injury or property damage, provided the plaintiff is able to establish that the defendant owed him a duty of care which was breached. However, since *Cattle v Stockton Waterworks Co*[2] the courts have resolutely set their faces against compensation for pure economic loss caused by a negligent act. Thus, in *Spartan Steel and Alloys Ltd v Martin & Co (Contractors) Ltd*,[3] as a result of the negligence of the defendant's servants an electricity cable, the property of the electricity board, was damaged, so that the power supply to the plaintiff's factory was cut off for a number of hours. In consequence the plaintiff suffered three separate financial losses, the depreciation in value of the 'melt' which was at that time in the furnace, the loss of profit on that melt and the profit that would have been made from other melts which could have been carried out had the power not been cut off. They claimed damages for all three, and the decision of the court illustrates the often difficult distinction between damages for financial loss consequential upon physical loss, which may be recovered, and pure economic loss, which may not. Damages under the first two heads were awarded, but not under the third. As Cane explains:[4] 'Loss of profit on the sale of the ruined contents is a causal consequence of the damage to those contents, loss of profit due to lost production is not the consequence of physical damage to anything.' Usually the courts have denied liability for pure economic loss on the basis that no duty was owed; less often on the basis that the damage was too remote.[5]

1 [1932] AC 562.
2 (1875) LR 10 QB 453. See also *Weller & Co Ltd v Foot and Mouth Disease Research Institute* [1966] 1 QB 569, [1965] 3 All ER 560; *SCM (UK) Ltd v WJ Whittall & Son Ltd* [1971] 1 QB 337, [1970] 3 All ER 245; *Spartan Steel and Alloys Ltd v Martin & Co (Contractors) Ltd* [1973] QB 27, [1972] 3 All ER 557. See also Atiyah (1967) 83 LQR 248; Craig (1976) 92 LQR 213; Cane (1979) 95 LQR 117.
3 [1973] QB 27, [1972] 3 All ER 557.
4 Cane, above, at 120.
5 See *Rivtow Marine Ltd v Washington Iron Works* (1973) 40 DLR (3d) 530 at 551, per Laskin J.

1.22 However, where pure economic loss is caused by negligent words, as opposed to acts, the possibility has existed since 1964 of a successful claim for damages,[1] provided that there exists a 'special relationship'[2] between the maker of the statement and the person who suffers loss in consequence of his reliance upon the statement. The House of Lords in *Hedley Byrne v Heller*[3] was concerned to avoid imposing a full, *Donoghue v Stevenson* duty of care upon the maker of a negligent misstatement. Lord Pearce said,[4] 'negligence in word creates problems different from those of negligence in act. Words are more volatile than deeds. They travel fast and far afield. They are used without being expended and take effect in combination with innumerable facts and other words . . . If the mere hearing or reading of words were held to create proximity, there might be no limit to the persons to whom the speaker or writer could be liable. Damage by negligent acts to persons or property on the other hand is more visible and obvious; its limits are more easily defined.' Lord Reid said,[5] 'the law must treat negligent words differently from negligent acts . . . The most obvious difference between negligent words and negligent acts is this. Quite careful people often express definite opinions on social or informal occasions even when they see that others are likely to be influenced by them; and they often do that without taking that case which they would take if asked for their opinion professionally or in a business connection . . . But it is at least unusual casually to put into circulation negligently made articles which are dangerous . . . Another obvious difference is that a negligently made article will only cause one accident, and so it is not very difficult to find the necessary degree of proximity or neighbourhood between the negligent manufacturer and the person injured. But words can be broadcast with or without the consent or the foresight of the speaker or writer.'

1 *Hedley Byrne & Co Ltd v Heller & Partners Ltd* [1964] AC 465, [1963] 2 All ER 575.
2 The nature of which is discussed in para 4.70, below.
3 [1964] AC 465, [1963] 2 All ER 575.
4 Ibid at 534 and 613–614.
5 Ibid at 482–483 and 580.

1.23 Though their Lordships regarded these factors as sufficient justification for refusing to impose a normal duty of care upon the maker of the misstatement, they were prepared to accept that once the existence of a special relationship had been established liability even for pure economic loss could be imposed.[1] Lord Devlin could find 'neither logic nor common sense'[2] in distinguishing between cases where the loss was physical and those where it was economic. However, the effect of the case law is that such a distinction is drawn: where the consequent damage is physical, liability may be imposed whether the negligence was manifested by a statement or an act; where pure economic loss is suffered, liability may only be imposed if caused by a negligent misstatement, and only then if the safety valve of a special relationship (designed to prevent the risk of 'liability in an indeterminate amount for an indeterminate time to an indeterminate class')[3] is present. Quite apart from the question as to why whether or not a duty is owed should be determined by reference to the type of loss suffered,[4] it may well be asked whether the distinction between acts and statements will even in the ordinary course of events be so clear cut as to justify this differentiation. For example,[5] does the careless or non-existent inspection in a case such as *Dutton v Bognor Regis UDC*[6] constitute a negligent act or a negligent misstatement on the part of the building inspector? Would there really be any sense in finding an architect who prepared a defective design not liable in negligence for pure economic loss but liable for such loss if in addition to providing the design he assured the person who relied upon it that it was free from defect?

1 Even prior to *Hedley Byrne v Heller* it had been established that liability could be imposed under the ordinary principles of negligence for a negligent misstatement which caused physical injury: see *Clayton v Woodman & Son (Builders) Ltd* [1962] 2 QB 533, [1962] 2 All ER 33.
2 [1964] AC 465 at 517, [1963] 2 All ER 575 at 602.
3 Per Cardozo CJ in *Ultramares Corpn v Touche* 174 NE 441 (1931) at 444.
4 See Craig (1976) 92 LQR 213.
5 See Cane (1979) 95 LQR at 121, n. 18.
6 [1972] 1 QB 373, [1972] 1 All ER 462. See para 1.30, below.

1.24 No clear solution to the difficult problem of the extent to which pure economic loss can or should be compensated in the law of negligence has yet emerged, but the cases do provide some guidance. In *Ministry of Housing and Local Government v Sharp*[1] a landowner, having been refused permission to develop his land, obtained statutory compensation from the plaintiff Ministry and notice of this compensation was duly registered in the local land charges register of the local authority. Later the landowner reapplied for planning permission and was successful. Intending purchasers of the land from him caused a search to be made in the register; the search was negligently carried out by a clerk employed by the second defendants and a certificate omitting reference to the compensation notice was issued to the purchasers. The Ministry applied for repayment of the compensation as statute entitled it to do, but was forced to concede that the clear certificate which the purchasers were able to show entitled them to resist repayment. The Ministry claimed damages in negligence against the local authority on the grounds that they were vicariously liable for the negligence of their clerk.[2]

1 [1970] 2 QB 223, [1970] 1 All ER 1009. See also *Ross v Caunters* [1980] Ch 297, [1979] 3 All ER 580, discussed at para 1.29, below.
2 Damages for breach of statutory duty were claimed from the first defendant, the clerk to the local authority.

1.25 As Salmon LJ recognised,[1] 'the present case does not precisely fit into any category of negligence yet considered by the courts'. The negligent statement made by the clerk was not made to a person who suffered loss in reliance on it; in fact it benefited the representees; the person who suffered loss was the Ministry which lost the right to enforce a charge on the land. Lord Denning MR nevertheless considered that the case fell completely within the principles of *Hedley Byrne v Heller*, essentially on the basis that the duty arose 'from the fact that the person making it knows, or ought to know, that others, being his neighbours in this regard, would act on the faith of the statement being accurate. The duty is not only owed to the person to whom the certificate is issued . . . but it also is owed to any person whom he knows, or ought to know, will be injuriously affected by a mistake, such as the incumbrancer here.'[2]

1 [1970] 2 QB 223 at 278, [1970] 1 All ER 1009 at 1027.
2 Ibid at 268–269 and 1019.

1.26 Salmon LJ was of the view that there was as close a degree of proximity between the council and the incumbrancer as existed between the plaintiff and the defendant in *Donoghue v Stevenson*. He said,[1] 'So far . . . as the law of negligence . . . is concerned, the existence of a duty to take reasonable care no longer depends upon whether it is physical injury or financial loss which can reasonably be foreseen as a result of a failure to take such care'. He seemed therefore to base his finding of liability upon *Donoghue v Stevenson* rather than *Hedley Byrne v Heller*. Cross LJ with considerable doubt agreed with his colleagues, and his judgment expresses no clear preference for *Donoghue v Stevenson* or *Hedley Byrne v Heller* as the basis of liability.

1 [1970] 2 QB 223 at 278, [1970] 1 All ER 1009 at 1027.

1.27 At least one member of the Court of Appeal was therefore apparently prepared to base liability for pure economic loss on *Donoghue v Stevenson* principles rather than having recourse to the narrower 'special relationship' basis of *Hedley Byrne v Heller*. There was of course only one person, the Ministry, who could be injured by the clerk's negligence, and therefore the menace of unlimited potential plaintiffs did not exist in the circumstances. If, however, the number of persons who suffer pure economic loss as a result of a negligent act or statement is great then, if it is accepted that there are sound policy reasons for restricting their number in some way, the courts might find it necessary to impose restrictions. In discussing the ways in which the courts have restricted liability in negligence for pure economic loss, Laskin J (as he then was) in his notable dissenting judgment in *Rivtow Marine Ltd v Washington Iron Works*[1] said: 'this restriction on liability has in it more of a concern to avoid limitless claims for economic loss from any kind of negligence than a concern for the particular basis upon which . . . liability for negligence rests'. It matters not, therefore, whether recovery for economic loss is limited by means of a denial of duty or an assertion that the damage suffered was too remote. However if it is accepted that some restriction is necessary, there must exist the means of effecting that restriction.

1 (1973) 40 DLR (3d) 530 at 551, Supreme Court of Canada.

1.28 The question is essentially one of policy, but establishing general principles to determine the class of person to whom a duty not to cause pure economic loss is owed is far from easy. A variety of possible tests was expounded by the High Court of Australia in *Caltex Oil (Australia) Pty Ltd v The Dredge 'Willemstad'*.[1] One approach was to require that the defendant must have been in a position to foresee that the plaintiff individually and specifically would suffer pure economic loss as a result of the defendant's negligence. This test would clearly be workable in a number of cases, for example, the *Ministry of Housing and Local Government v Sharp* case discussed above. The difficulty, as Cane[2] notes, would be in defining the limited class to which potential plaintiffs would have to belong, and almost of necessity this could only be determined by examining the facts of each case as it arose. Another suggested test was to determine whether or not the damage suffered was too remote by means of an examination of the facts of the case, bearing in mind policy issues such as whether a finding of liability would open the floodgates; thus if the results of a finding of liability would not offend policy considerations, pure economic loss would be deemed to be sufficiently proximate. This, like the further suggestion that liability for all loss caused by negligence should be imposed unless acceptable reasons of public policy militated against recovery, is open to the criticisms of excessive vagueness and uncertainty. The final suggested test, that liability be imposed where the loss is a result of the 'physical effect' on the plaintiff's property, may be criticised on the grounds that it suggests a new concept without defining it; it really does little more than provide a name for the classes of case in which liability will be imposed without providing any clearer guidance to the nature of those cases that is to distinguish them from cases in which liability is not imposed.

1 (1977) 11 ALR 227. See Cane (1977) 93 LQR 333.
2 Cane, above, at 335.

1.29   In his recent decision in *Ross v Caunters*[1] Megarry VC reviewed the case law on recovery for pure economic loss and concluded:[2] 'If the general *Donoghue v Stevenson* basis is applied at large to cases of purely financial loss, the problems of indeterminate liability are bound to occur. Cases of negligent misstatements already have the restrictive test of liability that was laid down in *Hedley Byrne*. For other cases the question is what modification or form of application of the *Donoghue v Stevenson* basis must be applied in order to meet it.' He did not find it necessary in that case to lay down a test or tests; sooner or later this would be possible when enough decisions existed from which a general principle or general principles could be drawn; it sufficed to say that whatever test was ultimately developed it would be broad enough to allow the plaintiff in that case (a legatee whose husband had attested the relevant will; the testator's solicitors had failed to warn him that attestation of the will by a beneficiary's spouse would invalidate a gift to the beneficiary) to succeed.

1 [1980] Ch 297, [1979] 3 All ER 580.
2 Ibid at 320 and 597–598.

1.30   The courts' awareness of the difficult problems attaching to liability for pure economic loss has also been manifested in cases where some doubt exists as to whether the loss suffered by the plaintiff is physical or economic, which has especially been an issue in defective premises cases. In *Dutton v Bognor Regis UDC*[1] the plaintiff was the second purchaser of a house which, shortly after she moved in, developed serious defects in its internal structure. It was discovered that this was due to the unsoundness of the internal foundations which had been built on the site of an old rubbish tip. A careful inspection by the local authority's building inspector would have revealed this. Lord Denning MR did not accept the argument that the damage suffered was economic loss; it was, he said, physical damage to the house. Sachs LJ agreed:[2] 'If physical damage is, contrary to my view, a *sine qua non* before a cause of action can arise against a builder or a building owner, then it seems to me to have occurred in the present case.' He went on to suggest that it was correct, in cases involving the exercise of powers and duties by public authorities, to determine whether particular damage was recoverable by deciding what was the range of damage that the proper exercise of the power was designed to prevent, rather than considering whether it was physical or economic damage. Whether this reasoning can be extended beyond public bodies to other potential defendants is a difficult question posing problems very much akin to the issues discussed in the *Caltex* case, but the tenor of Sachs LJ's judgment very much favours the imposition of liability in building cases for pure economic loss in negligence claims, though with no consideration of any limiting factors that might be necessary. Stamp LJ, like Lord Denning, based liability upon *Donoghue v Stevenson* rather than *Hedley Byrne v Heller* principles. He was prepared to accept that the claim was for economic loss, but he did not suggest any ways of avoiding the possibility of unrestricted liability and extensive litigation that might ensue where, in Craig's words,[3] 'the type of duty involved is derived from *Donoghue v Stevenson*, while the reason for allowing recovery for economic loss is based upon *Hedley Byrne*'.

1 [1972] 1 QB 373, [1972] 1 All ER 462.
2 Ibid at 404 and 481.
3 Craig (1976) 92 LQR 213 at 225.

1.31   *Dutton v Bognor Regis UDC* was followed by the House of Lords in *Anns v London Borough of Merton*.[1] This case again concerned the liability of a local authority for a negligent (or non-existent) inspection of foundations by their building inspector. The leading judgment was delivered by Lord Wilberforce, who characterised the damage caused to a block of maisonettes as a result of being constructed upon inadequate foundations as 'material physical damage'.[2] The *Anns* case (which applies beyond local authorities to all other persons concerned with the production of buildings or structures[3]) restricted liability to damage which constituted a present or imminent danger to the health or safety of occupiers who are such when the damage occurs. The House of Lords did not thus appear to be prepared to accept that damages could be awarded for pure economic loss in this context (though it has been argued[4] that even if the damage in *Anns* were classified as financial loss it could arguably be recovered, following *Spartan Steel and Alloys Ltd v Martin & Co (Contractors) Ltd*,[5] as being consequential upon physical damage). Even if this argument is not accepted, on policy grounds it would be quite acceptable for the damage to the maisonettes to be classified as pure economic loss, on the basis that, as Lord Wilberforce himself indicated,[6] restricting the right of action to an owner or occupier who is such when the damage occurs avoids the problems of an endless, indeterminate class of potential plaintiffs, thus introducing a safety valve, whose effect is similar to that of the 'special relationship' in negligent misstatement cases.

1 [1978] AC 728, [1977] 2 All ER 492.
2 Ibid at 759 and 505.
3 See *Hudson's Building and Engineering Contracts* (1st supplement to 10th edn) pp. 65–75. See also *Batty v Metropolitan Property Realisations Ltd* [1978] QB 554, [1978] 2 All ER 445.
4 See Cane (1979) 95 LQR 117 at 123–124.
5 [1973] QB 27, [1972] 3 All ER 557.
6 [1978] AC 728 at 758, [1977] 2 All ER 492 at 504.

1.32   It has been cogently argued[1] that the physical damage in such cases as *Dutton* and *Anns* is damage to the property itself, and the damage relates to the financial cost of repair to the houses. It had previously been generally assumed that the principle of *Donoghue v Stevenson* did not extend to compensation for damage to the defective product itself, and therefore by analogy to the defective building itself, but was restricted to compensation for damage caused by the defective product (or building). In such cases the damages awarded go beyond the manifestations of physical damage (cracking, etc.) and essentially compensate for the cost of removing the threat to health or safety. Indeed, as can be seen from the decision of the Court of Appeal in *Batty v Metropolitan Realisations Ltd*[2] the existence of physical manifestations of damage may be at best minimal.

1 See Duncan Wallace (1978) 94 LQR 60.
2 [1978] QB 554, [1978] 2 All ER 445. See Duncan Wallace (1978) 94 LQR 331.

1.33 In that case (involving liability of a builder and a developer to purchasers of a house built upon unstable land, the house was doomed to collapse within the next decade), Megaw LJ regarded the manifestation of damage (damage caused to the garden not the house) as incidental to the main issue: that liability exists from the time when there is present or imminent danger to the health or safety of occupiers. Actual physical damage would therefore appear to be irrelevant. If, for example, in a case like *Batty*, it could be established that the house was destined to collapse some time within the next few years, as a result of a slip of the natural strata of the hillside upon which the house was built (these were the facts of *Batty*), whether this was manifested by cracks on the Batty's land or on a neighbour's land would be immaterial; as long as the present or imminent danger is established a cause of action can arise.[1] The rationale behind the characterisation of such damage as physical damage is presumably that if one waits for long enough the *Anns* maisonette or the *Batty* house will collapse, probably causing personal injury and property damage, and it seems preferable to allow a claim at the earlier date, when a real threat can be said to exist, even though the physical damage is potential rather than actual. As we have indicated, however, there is no policy reason why such damage should not be characterised as pure economic loss.

1 And the limitation period will begin to run. See para 1.36, below.

1.34 A degree of uncertainty will exist in all cases where liability is based essentially upon future rather than actual damage, over questions such as the meaning of 'imminent', and the type of 'danger' involved. Cane[1] sums up the likely attitude of the courts as follows: 'It would seem, therefore, that the degree of likelihood that the danger will materialise required to justify recovery of preventive damages will vary according to how imminent the danger is and to the nature of the damage threatened, i e personal or property. Such flexibility is needed where the aim of the award of damages is not merely to compensate for things which have occurred but to prevent certain occurrences in the future.'

1 Cane (1979) 95 LQR 117 at 135.

D Limitation periods[1]

1.35 Questions concerning the time at which damage is deemed to have taken place clearly have implications for limitation periods. Sections 2 and 5 of the Limitation Act 1980, provide that actions founded on tort or on simple contract shall not be brought after the expiration of six years from the date on which the cause of action accrued, and by section 8(1) the relevant period is twelve years where the contract is under seal. It should be noted that where there is a continuing wrong the limitation period beings to run afresh each time the wrong is committed.

1 See *Emden's Building Contracts and Practice* (8th edn) ch 17.

1.36 In breach of contract cases the cause of action is the breach, and the limitation period will begin to run from that time.[1] The occurrence of damage is not necessary in order to prove a breach of contract, and hence the fact that the plaintiff suffers damage within six years of the claim being brought will not avail him if the breach of contract occurred before that six year period. When time begins to run will in tort cases depend upon whether damage is an essential element of the tort in question. Damage must be established in negligence claims, the claims with which we are concerned here, and hence the cause of action will accrue when damage takes place.

1 See e g *Bagot v Stevens, Scanlan & Co* [1966] 1 QB 197, [1964] 3 All ER 577.

1.37 In *Dutton v Bognor Regis UDC*[1] Lord Denning MR stated that the damage was done when the foundations were badly constructed and consequently the limitation period began to run from the time of construction. This was followed by Mars-Jones J in *Higgins v Arfon Borough Council*,[2] as a result of which the plaintiff was time-barred in a case where, following a careless inspection by the local authority building inspector, wet rot, due to inadequate ventilation of the underfloor area, was discovered. However, Lord Denning recanted the views he had expressed in *Dutton* on the question of the time from which the limitation period begins to run, in the following year in *Sparham-Souter v Town and Country Developments (Essex) Ltd.*[3] Again the case concerned liability of a local authority for the negligence of their building inspector in passing a building. Lord Denning decided that in cases where building work was badly done and covered up, the cause of action did not accrue, and time did not begin to run, until the time when the plaintiff discovered that the building work had done damage or ought with reasonable diligence to have discovered it. Roskill LJ took the view that the earliest time at which a plaintiff in the position of first or subsequent purchaser could be said to suffer damage was when, by agreeing to purchase the premises, he acquired an interest in the property. However, he did not necessarily suffer damage then; indeed he might sell the property without the defects ever emerging; and consequently Roskill LJ considered that the plaintiff suffered the damage when the defective state of the premises first appeared. Geoffrey Lane LJ agreed that 'it is the emergence of the faults, not the purchase of the house, which has caused him the damage',[4] and thought the potential indefinite postponement of the period of limitation was preferable to the deprivation of a house owner of a cause of action which began to run before the damage could ever be detected.

1 [1972] 1 QB 373, [1972] 1 All ER 462.
2 [1975] 2 All ER 589, [1975] 1 WLR 524.
3 [1976] QB 858, [1976] 2 All ER 65.
4 Ibid at 880 and 80.

1.38 This clearly effected an important change, and caused concern about the problems that would ensue from such an 'extended' limitation period not only to local authorities but to builders, architects and surveyors, all of whom would potentially be affected. The sound basis for such concern was amply demonstrated by the decision of the House of Lords in *Anns v London Borough of Merton*[1] which, as we have seen, applies to all concerned with the provision of premises where they have been negligent and as a result there is a threat to health or safety of owners or occupiers. Lord Wilberforce, delivering the leading judgment, agreed with the Court of Appeal in *Sparham-Souter* in discarding the notion that the cause of action arose on conveyance of the defective premises, and stated that the cause of action 'can only arise when the state of the building is such that there is a present or imminent danger to the health or safety of persons occupying it'.[2]

1 [1978] AC 728, [1977] 2 All ER 492. See para 1.31, above.
2 Ibid at 760 and 505.

1.39 This test raises a potential inconsistency with the *Sparham-Souter* test for the state of a building may well constitute a present or imminent danger to the health or safety of occupiers without the occupier having discovered the damage or, because of the lack of manifestation of damage, without it being reasonable to expect him to have discovered the damage. Given the approval expressed by the House of Lords in *Anns* for Lord Denning's judgment in *Sparham-Souter* it is suggested[1] that problems can best be avoided by reading the *Anns* test in the light of *Sparham-Souter*. Thus time would begin to run when the plaintiff occupier realises, or should realise, that the state of the building constitutes a present or imminent danger to health or safety. Otherwise cases might well occur where time was running without it being possible for the occupier to realise damage had occurred, the very contingency that was anathema to the Court of Appeal in *Sparham-Souter*, and it is suggested that the support expressed in *Anns* for that decision[2] and the absence of any disagreement in the speeches of Lords Wilberforce, Diplock, Simon and Russell with the rationale behind *Sparham-Souter*, makes the case for running the two tests together in the way outlined above a strong one.

1 See *Emden's Building Contracts and Practice* (8th edn) p. 509.
2 Even by Lord Salmon, who held that it was when the damage occurred that time began to run, irrespective of when the plaintiff comprehended the existence of damage.

1.40 Some support for this can be derived from the recent decision of Judge Fay QC in *Eames London Estates Ltd v North Hertfordshire District Council*.[1] He held (in a case involving liability in negligence of a developer, builder, local authority and architect for defective premises) that with defective buildings the limitation period begins to run upon the occurrence of the later of two events: the date when the plaintiff first acquires an interest in the property or when he first learns of the damage. For the period to run, the plaintiff has to be aware not only of the symptoms, but also the disease. It may perhaps be assumed, to be consistent with the earlier authorities, that if the plaintiff is aware of symptoms that would lead a reasonable man to investigate their cause, then time will begin to run from then, though in the particular case, the failure of two of the plaintiffs, who had been made aware of the existence of cracks when they took their tenancy to have the building surveyed did not count against them for the purposes of the commencement of the limitation period.

1 (1980) 259 Estates Gazette 491. See para 3.102, below.

1.41 In certain breach of contract cases, a not dissimilar test concerning the time from which the limitation period will begin to run exists. Section 32 of the Limitation Act 1980[1] provides that:

(1) Subject to subsection (3) below, where in the case of any action for which a period of limitation is prescribed by this Act, either—
    (a) the action is based upon the fraud of the defendant; or
    (b) any fact relevant to the plaintiff's right of action has been deliberately concealed from him by the defendant; or
    (c) the action is for relief from the consequences of a mistake;
  the period of limitation shall not begin to run until the plaintiff has discovered the

fraud , concealment or mistake (as the case may be) or could with reasonable diligence have discovered it.

References in this subsection to the defendant include references to the defendant's agent and to any person through whom the defendant claims and his agent.

1 See *Emden's Building Contracts and Practice* (8th edn) pp. 499–503; *Hudson's Building and Engineering Contracts* (1st supplement to 10th edn) pp. 368–370. These discuss Limitation Act 1939, s. 26, the broadly similar predecessor of s. 32.

1.42 The case law in the area of building law gives some idea of how the courts have interpreted fraud. Thus, in *Clark v Woor*,[1] bricks of a different type and quality from those required in the specification were used by a builder. Eight years after they went into occupation of a bungalow built with the bricks, the plaintiffs noticed that the bricks were beginning to flake. It was held that they were entitled to rely upon section 32 in their subsequent breach of contract action. The builder knew that the plaintiffs were inexperienced in building matters and were relying on him to perform the contract honestly (no architect had been employed to supervise the work) and consequently the builder's conduct was unconscionable and amounted to concealment of the plaintiffs' right of action by fraud within section 32; thus they were not time-barred.

1 [1965] 2 All ER 353, [1965] 1 WLR 650.

1.43 In *Applegate v Moss*[1], a case concerning liability of a developer for a house constructed on defective foundations, Lord Denning MR stated[2] that section 32 'applies wherever the conduct of the defendant or his agent has been such as to hide from the plaintiff the existence of his right of action, in such circumstances that it would be inequitable to allow the defendant to rely on the lapse of time as a bar to the claim. Applied to a building contract, it means that if a builder does his work badly, so that it is likely to give rise to trouble thereafter, and then covers up his bad work so that it is not discovered for some years, then he cannot rely on the statute as a bar to the claim.' It appears from the later decision of the Court of Appeal in *King v Victor Parsons & Co*[3] that, in order for section 32 to apply, the defendant must have known of the existence of his breach of contract or recklessly have disregarded its possibility.[4] The defendants in *King v Victor Parsons & Co* were estate agents who had acquired a site and instructed builders and, as in *Applegate v Moss*, it was held that the builder was the defendants' agent and thus his knowledge was their knowledge.[5]

1 [1971] 1 QB 406, [1971] 1 All ER 747.
2 Ibid at 413 and 750.
3 [1973] 1 All ER 206, [1973] 1 WLR 29.
4 In his unreported decision in *Street and Street v Sibbasbridge and Stratford-on-Avon District-Council* (1980) 6 August, Judge Fay QC held that an honest blunder by a builder did not amount to concealed fraud, and hence his conduct was not unconscionable and the plaintiff was time-barred.
5 *Emden's Building Contracts and Practice* (8th edn) p. 503.

1.44 The most recent reported decision on section 32 is *Lewisham London Borough v Leslie & Co Ltd*[1] which is of particular interest in that it establishes that, in a case involving appropriate facts, even a plaintiff amply provided with architects to supervise building work will not be barred from claiming that concealed fraud has been committed by builders whom he employs. Lord Denning said:[2] 'It seems to me that there is no difference in principle between a small house and a small building-owner and a great tower block and a great council, even though it does employ architects and supervisors. It only requires a little imagination to think of circumstances in which workmen may do their work badly, leaving defects – which the architect or supervisor would not discover, even by using reasonable diligence.' Consequently the plaintiffs' appeal against

the decision of Judge Fay QC striking out their statement of claim succeeded, for the architects and supervisors might have been misled, or the work might have been done while they were absent for some good reason.
1 (1978) 250 Estates Gazette 1289.
2 Ibid at 1290.

1.45 As Lord Denning also noted, a parallel cause of action may in any event exist in such cases in negligence, when, on Lord Denning's interpretation of the present rule concerning the time from which the limitation period begins to run, 'in the case of a defective building when the cracks or other signs of damage appear, or the defects could, with reasonable diligence, have been discovered'.[1] Inevitably the implications of these developments for those civilly liable for defective premises are considerable, and these implications are considered in the appropriate context below.
1 (1978) 250 Estates Gazette 1289 at 1290.

E Misrepresentation

1.46 Relevant aspects of the law on misrepresentation are considered in detail in the appropriate chapters of the book and consequently it is not proposed to provide a general description of the relevant rules at this point; for the most part misrepresentation is best considered in the context of the particular defendant under discussion.[1] However, the measure of damages for misrepresentation raises general problems which, at least in the case of liability under the Misrepresentation Act 1967, are not solved by the case law pertaining to the particular categories of defendant discussed below, and hence merit discussion in this chapter.
1 See paras 4.70 ff, 4.91 ff and 6.15 ff, below.

1.47 Liability for negligent misstatement at common law under *Hedley Byrne & Co v Heller & Partners*[1] has not posed particular problems. The action is clearly a tortious one, with *restitutio in integrum* the object of the award of damages.[2] The main importance of the action is that damages are available for pure economic loss once the existence of a special relationship[3] between representor and representee has been established, though damages for personal injury which results from the negligent misstatement may also be awarded (as indeed had been established prior to *Hedley Byrne v Heller*)[4].
1 [1964] AC 465, [1963] 2 All ER 575.
2 See para 1.9, above.
3 See paras 4.70 and 6.17 ff, below.
4 See *Clayton v Woodman & Son (Builders) Ltd* [1962] 2 QB 533, [1962] 2 All ER 33.

1.48 Greater difficulties have arisen in relation to the Misrepresentation Act 1967. The relevant section provides as follows:

2. Damages for misrepresentation.—(1) Where a person has entered into a contract after a misrepresentation has been made to him by another party thereto and as a result thereof he has suffered loss, then, if the person making the misrepresentation would be liable to damages in respect thereof had the misrepresentation been made fraudulently, that person shall be so liable notwithstanding that the misrepresentation was not made fraudulently, unless he proves that he had reasonable ground to believe and did believe up to the time the contract was made that the facts represented were true.
(2) Where a person has entered into a contract after a misrepresentation has been

made to him otherwise than fraudulently, and he would be entitled, by reason of the misrepresentation, to rescind the contract, then, if it is claimed, in any proceedings arising out of the contract, that the contract ought to be or has been rescinded, the court or arbitrator may declare the contract subsisting and award damages in lieu of rescission, if of opinion that it would be equitable to do so, having regard to the nature of the misrepresentation and the loss that would be caused by it if the contract were upheld, as well as to the loss that rescission would cause to the other party.

(3) Damages may be awarded against a person under subsection (2) of this section whether or not he is liable to damages under subsection (1) thereof, but where he is so liable any award under the said subsection (2) shall be taken into account in assessing his liability under the said subsection (1).

1.49 Dealing first with section 2(1), it is far from clear what is the measure of damages where liability for negligent misrepresentation is established under the subsection.[1] Prima facie, given the reference to fraud, it would appear that the damages are tortious. Also, as McGregor points out,[2] there was a wealth of pre-1967 case law concerned with distinguishing representations from contractual terms,[3] and to assess damages under section 2(1) on a contractual basis would be to ignore this background. However the decided cases have been far from unequivocal on this issue.

1 For detailed discussion of this issue see especially *McGregor on Damages* (14th edn) paras 1482–1489; Treitel *The Law of Contract* (5th edn) pp. 267–268; Atiyah and Treitel (1967) 30 MLR 369 at 373–374; *Chitty on Contracts* (24th edn) para 377.
2 *McGregor on Damages* (14th edn) para 1482.
3 See e g para 6.16, below.

1.50 Thus, in *Watts v Spence*[1] the defendant represented that he was the sole owner of a house and thereby induced the plaintiff to enter into a contract to purchase the house from him. In fact the house was owned jointly by the defendant and his wife, and she refused to consent to the sale. Damages for loss of bargain were not recoverable in a contractual action because of the rule in *Bain v Fothergill*[2] which precludes the award of such damages where a vendor is unable to convey because of a defect in title. The court held that this did not prevent damages for misrepresentation under section 2(1) from being awarded on the basis of loss of bargain,[3] as represented by the difference between the value of the house at the time of the contract and at the time of completion. Though it has been doubted whether this accurately reflects the true contractual measure of damages,[4] the inference from the use of the term 'loss of bargain' is that the court at least envisaged that the measure of damages under section 2(1) was contractual. This conclusion is supported in certain dicta,[5] but more recently, in *Andre & Cie SA v Ets Michel Blanc & Fils*[6] Ackner J has stated unequivocally that the measure of damages under section 2(1) is tortious.[7] The fact that damages for loss of bargain could not be awarded for breach of contract because of *Bain v Fothergill* may well have motivated the court in *Watts v Spence*, and in *Andre v Michel Blanc* only nominal damages could have been awarded if the contractual measure had been employed, whereas more substantial compensation was available on the tortious basis. Perhaps the courts are likely to prefer to treat each case on its own merits and award the damages that seem most appropriate in the circumstances, but the weight of authority seems to support a tortious basis, if a choice has to be made.

1 [1976] Ch 165, [1975] 2 All ER 528.
2 (1874) LR 7 HL 158.
3 See Crane (1975) 39 Conv (NS) 361.
4 See Treitel *The Law of Contract* (5th edn) p. 268.

5 See e g *Jarvis v Swans Tours Ltd* [1973] QB 233 at 237, [1973] 1 All ER 71 at 73, per Lord Denning MR; *Davis & Co (Wines) Ltd v Afa-Minerva* (EMI) [1974] 2 Lloyd's Rep 27 at 32, per Judge Fay QC.
6 [1977] 2 Lloyd's Rep 166.
7 The learned judge derived comfort from the concurrence of the authors of *Cheshire and Fifoot, Treitel, Chitty,* and *McGregor on Damages* in this view. More recently this view is also supported in *Howard Marine and Dredging Co Ltd v A Ogden & Sons (Excavations) Ltd* [1978] QB 574 at 595, [1978] 2 All ER 1134 at 1144, per Bridge LJ. See also *F and H Entertainments Ltd v Leisure Enterprises Ltd* (1976) 120 Sol Jo 331, where it was held that the measure of damages under s. 2 was the same as in an action for deceit, and that all expenditure properly incurred by the plaintiff could be recovered. This happy state of consensus is described by Tettenborn (1979) 123 Sol Jo 669 as 'the accepted orthodoxy'.

1.51 In some cases, however, it may not be possible to establish that the defendant was negligent; for example he may be able to demonstrate the reasonableness of his belief in the truth of the misrepresentation and the continuation of such reasonable belief up to the time when the contract was made. Nevertheless, as a result of his statement, the plaintiff may have been misled and may have suffered loss. The only remedy available prior to the enactment of the Misrepresentation Act 1967 in such a case was rescission of the contract,[1] thereby restoring the parties to the status quo, plus, where appropriate, an indemnity whereby the plaintiff was compensated in respect of obligations necessarily created by the contract.[2]

1 See Treitel *The Law of Contract* (5th edn) pp. 274–291; *Chitty on Contracts* (24th edn) paras 392–408.
2 E g *Whittington v Seale-Hayne* (1900) 82 LT 49 where the plaintiff who had been induced to take a lease of the defendant's premises as a result of an innocent misrepresentation was allowed an indemnity for rent and rates paid and repairs done under the lease, but not for matters such as loss of profit.

1.52 Section 2(2) provides for the case where the court may deem rescission inappropriate (for example because it would necessitate the unscrambling of a number of transactions) and gives the court a discretion to grant damages in lieu of rescission. It has tended to be assumed that the subsection will apply to cases of innocent (i e non-negligent, non-fraudulent) misrepresentation, though the wording of section 2(2) only excludes fraudulent misrepresentations from its ambit. However, if the misrepresentation is negligent, the damages will fall to be considered under section 2(1) and therefore the 'damages in lieu of rescission' which section 2(2) empowers the court to award will in effect be those applicable to a totally innocent misrepresentation. Again there is uncertainty concerning the measure of these damages, and the case law is silent on the point. It has been suggested[1] that if it is true that the correct measure of damages under section 2(1) is tortious, it would appear unlikely that the contractual measure will be employed under section 2(2), given the wording of section 2(3), providing that damages awarded under section 2(2) shall be taken into account in assessing section 2(1) damages, and arguably, therefore, section 2(2) damages are likely to be less than section 2(1) damages. This is either on the basis that section 2(1), being based on fraud, incorporates the deceit rules on remoteness of damage[2] and is therefore wider than negligence liability, or that section 2(1) damages are negligence damages, and section 2(2) damages do not compensate for consequential loss. The question may be primarily an academic one, but it is suggested that section 2(2) damages are to be assessed on the basis of compensating the plaintiff, in the particular case, for the loss of his right to rescind. This is developed by McGregor, who concludes[3] 'the damages will be held to the difference between the value transferred and the value received, with the value

20

received arrived at in the light of the obligations taken on, so that this will represent not only the normal measure but the only measure of damages with no recovery being possible for consequential losses'.

1 See e g *Chitty on Contracts* (24th edn) para 390; Treitel *The Law of Contract* (5th edn) p. 270.
2 See e g *Doyle v Olby (Ironmongers) Ltd* [1969] 2 QB 158, [1969] 2 All ER 119.
3 *McGregor on Damages* (14th edn) para 1492.

F Exclusion of liability[1]

1.53 Particularly in the light of the Unfair Contract Terms Act 1977, it has seemed appropriate to deal with exclusion[2] of liability in some detail, as it applies to the particular potential defendants discussed in this book, in the relevant chapters.[3] However, a brief general outline by way of background will not be out of place. Initially it is important for a person seeking to rely upon an exclusion clause to ensure that the clause is incorporated in the contract, whether as a result of the signing of a contractual document by the other party,[4] reasonable notice of the existence of the clause given to the other party,[5] or as the result of a regular course of dealing between the parties.[6]

1 For detailed discussion of exclusion clauses generally, see, inter alia, Yates *Exclusion Clauses in Contracts* (1978); Treitel *The Law of Contract* (5th edn) pp. 152–195; Coote *Exception Clauses* (1964). On the Unfair Contract Terms Act 1977 see Thompson *Unfair Contract Terms Act 1977*; Lawson *Exclusion Clauses after the Unfair Contract Terms Act*; Coote (1978) 41 MLR 312; Sealy [1978] CLJ 15.
2 Hereafter 'exclusion' is deemed to include 'limitation of liability'.
3 See paras 2.25–2.31, 3.32–3.45, 3.109, 4.100–4.109, 6.30–6.39, 7.28, below.
4 See e g *L'Estrange v F Graucob Ltd* [1934] 2 KB 394.
5 E g *Parker v South Eastern Rly Co* (1877) 2 CPD 416; *Chapelton v Barry UDC* [1940] 1 KB 532, [1940] 1 All ER 356; *Thornton v Shoe Lane Parking Ltd* [1971] 2 QB 163, [1971] 1 All ER 686.
6 E g *Hardwick Game Farm v Suffolk Agricultural and Poultry Producers' Association* [1969] 2 AC 31, [1968] 2 All ER 444.

1.54 Even though the clause is incorporated into the contract, the traditional hostility of the courts towards exclusion clauses is manifested by a number of rules of construction which the clause must satisfy in order to be upheld. The clause must be clear[1] and unambiguous;[2] it will be construed strictly *contra proferentem*, i e against the person seeking to rely upon it. Insofar as, as a result of the Unfair Contract Terms Act 1977, it is still possible to exclude liability for negligence, clear words must be employed to do so.[3]

1 E g *Hollier v Rambler Motors (AMC) Ltd* [1972] 2 QB 71, [1972] 1 All ER 399.
2 E g *Houghton v Trafalgar Insurance Co Ltd* [1954] 1 QB 247, [1953] 2 All ER 1409.
3 E g *White v John Warrick & Co Ltd* [1953] 2 All ER 1021, [1953] 1 WLR 1285; *Rutter v Palmer* [1922] 2 KB 87.

1.55 The courts were especially offended by clauses which sought to exclude liability for particularly serious breaches of contract. The doctrine of breach of a fundamental term was developed, whereby certain terms in any contract were deemed to be so fundamental that their breach constituted a total non-performance of the contract, and they could not be affected by any exclusion clause. Thus if under a contract to deliver peas a party delivered beans instead, this would be breach of a fundamental term.[1] Associated with this principle was the doctrine of fundamental breach, whereby if the manner of the breach of contract or the effects of the breach were fundamental then again an exclusion clause would be ineffective.[2] As regards the nature of fundamental breach (by which general title we shall refer to the two principles together), it was said by

Pearson LJ in *UGS Finance Ltd v National Mortgage Bank of Greece*[3] that the application of an exemption clause to a fundamental breach was only a matter of construction, based upon the intention of the parties to the contract. Hence, depending upon the parties' intention, an appropriately worded clause was capable of excluding liability even for a fundamental breach. The House of Lords agreed with this view in *Suisse Atlantique Societe d'Armement Maritime SA v NV Rotterdamsche Kolen Centrale.*[4] Difficulties were caused by the later decision of the Court of Appeal in *Harbutt's 'Plasticine' Ltd v Wayne Tank and Pump Co Ltd*[5] where it was held that the defendants could not rely upon an exclusion clause which on its true construction covered the loss that they had caused to the plaintiffs, because they had committed a fundamental breach. However, this decision was overruled by the House of Lords in *Photo Production Ltd v Securicor Transport Ltd*[6] in which it was held that as a matter of construction the wording of the exclusion clause on which they sought to rely relieved the defendants from their liability to the plaintiff. The notion that as a matter of substantive law an exclusion clause cannot apply where the party seeking to rely upon it has committed a fundamental breach is clearly untenable; it will always be a question of construction of the parties' intention and the wording of the clause.[7]

1 See *Chanter v Hopkins* (1838) 4 M & W 399 at 404, per Lord Abinger.
2 On this difficult topic see inter alia, Guest (1961) 77 LQR 98; Reynolds (1963) 79 LQR 534; Lord Devlin [1966] CLJ 192; Treitel (1966) 29 MLR 546; Coote [1970] CLJ 221.
3 [1964] 1 Lloyd's Rep 446.
4 [1967] 1 AC 361, [1966] 2 All ER 61.
5 [1970] 1 QB 447, [1970] 1 All ER 225.
6 [1980] AC 827, [1980] 1 All ER 556. See Guest (1980) 96 LQR 324.
7 See also s. 9 of the Unfair Contract Terms Act 1977, which provides that effect may be given to a term that satisfies the requirements of reasonableness laid down in s. 11 of that Act, even though the contract has been terminated (s. 9(1)); and also that the requirement of reasonableness is not excluded where a contract that has been breached is affirmed (s. 9(2)).

1.56 Of major importance to exclusion clauses is the Unfair Contract Terms Act 1977, which outlaws certain exclusion clauses (and non-contractual notices) and subjects many others to a test of reasonableness. Detailed discussion of the Act is contained, where appropriate, in the ensuing chapters.

1.57 A final point to note at this stage is the principle that in general it is not possible to exclude liability to a third party by means of a contract term.[1] However, certain exceptions, of varying merit and acceptability to the courts, exist; for example agency,[2] *volenti non fit injuria*,[3] and indemnity and promise not to sue,[4] and any of these may conceivably be relevant to civil liability for defective premises.

1 See Treitel *The Law of Contract* (5th edn) pp. 471–477; Battersby (1975) U 25 Toronto LJ 371, (1978) 28 U Toronto LJ 75.
2 E g *New Zealand Shipping Co Ltd v A M Satterthwaite & Co Ltd* [1975] AC 154, [1974] 1 All ER 1015; *Port Jackson Stevedoring Pty Ltd v Salmond and Spraggon (Australia) Pty Ltd* [1980] 3 All ER 257.
3 E g per Lord Denning in *Scruttons Ltd v Midland Silicones Ltd* [1962] AC 446 at 448–449, [1962] 1 All ER 1 at 19–20 (however, the other members of the House of Lords disagreed with Lord Denning); see Battersby (1975) 25 U Toronto LJ 371 at 372–378.
4 See Battersby (1975) 25 U Toronto LJ 371 at 381–382. See also Treitel *The Law of Contract* (5th edn) pp. 475–476 and *Snelling v John G Snelling Ltd* [1973] QB 87, [1972] 1 All ER 79.

Chapter 2

The occupier

2.1 This chapter concerns itself with the civil liabilities of the occupier of premises purely in his capacity as occupier. Specific rules apply to govern certain incidents of occupation, e g the occupier who builds upon his premises or the occupier who lets his property to tenants, and these specific instances will be dealt with in the appropriate parts of the chapters that follow.

2.2 The law relating to the civil liability of the occupier *qua* occupier comes from several sources. Most obviously there is the Occupiers' Liability Act 1957, but there are analogous common law duties of care in circumstances not covered by the Act,[1] and there are also relevant duties imposed by the tort of nuisance, the rule in *Rylands v Fletcher*[2] and by various modern statutes. However, this chapter will commence with an examination of the Occupiers' Liability Act and the duties imposed thereby.

1 See paras 2.37 ff, below.
2 (1868) LR 3 HL 330, below.

Occupiers' Liability Act 1957

2.3 The law relating to the civil liability of the occupier of premises was never encompassed within the general principles of negligence laid down by the House of Lords in *Donoghue v Stevenson*.[1] Indeed, the highly technical common law rules had already developed at that stage, governing occupiers' liabilities with respect to injuries carelessly caused to persons on their property. The complexity of these rules gave rise to increasing dispute, the House of Lords being called upon to intervene on several occasions,[2] and invidious comparisons could be drawn between the ease with which the general principles of negligence had been incorporated into the law and developed by the courts, and the mounting difficulty and confusion pervading the rules relating to occupiers' liabilities. Thus reform was widely demanded, the issue was referred to the Law Reform Committee and their report,[3] issued after lengthy consideration of the topic, led to the enactment of the Occupiers' Liability Act 1957. The Act purports to replace (and generally succeeds in replacing[4]) all common law rules[5] concerning the liability of the occupier to his lawful visitors with a new statutory framework, but equally does not enact anything analagous to a complete code, leaving certain aspects to be explained with reference back to the case law. Amongst such matters is the key issue of the legal meaning of 'occupier'.

1 [1932] AC 562.

2 North *Occupiers' Liability* p. 3, n. 9.
3 Cmd 9305 (1954).
4 See para 2.36, below.
5 S. 1(1).

2.4   Who, then, in English law, is the occupier? The Occupiers' Liability Act
does not attempt a definition; although section 1(2) refers to duties arising from
'a person's occupation or control of premises', the subsection goes on to explain
that the common law as to the persons on whom a duty is imposed is unaltered,
and the old definitions in occupiers' liability cases are still relevant. Equally, it is
reasonably clear that definitions of 'occupier' from other areas of the law e g
rating, taxation, are irrelevant.[1] The best approach seems to centre on the
concept of control of premises, as implied by section 1(2). This is a commonsense
approach; only those with any real control of premises have any effective
responsibility for their condition and it therefore is only realistic to make them,
and them alone, legally responsible for defects in those premises which render
them unsafe. However, within this broad principle, many difficult cases have
arisen, well exemplified by the leading decision of the House of Lords in *Wheat
v Lacon*.[2] This case concerned an accident in a public house owned by the respondent brewery. The manager of the public house was in sole day-to-day
control of the premises, but the defendants had reserved certain rights of entry,
and the agreement between the brewery and the manager did not (purportedly)
create a legal tenancy. The appellant was staying in an upper part of the
property, as paying guest of the manager, and was fatally injured while des-
cending the staircase, which was in darkness and had inadequate handrails. On
whose shoulders should responsibility fall? The House rejected the respondents'
arguments that they had divested themselves of the occupation of the whole
public house as a result of the degree of control delegated to their manager;
rather, they felt that the respondents had, by reserving sufficient rights over the
property and by specifically permitting guests such as the appellant to stay in
the premises, put themselves in the position of being (at the very least) joint
occupiers of the premises and could thus be held liable for the appellant's
accident. Great emphasis was placed on the flexibility of the concept of 'control'
permitting, for example, two or more persons to have control of the same premises and thus be deemed occupiers. However, such general principles do not
particularly aid the consideration of the position of particular types of potential
occupier, and a more rigorous analysis will now be attempted.

1 *Wheat v Lacon* [1966] AC 552 at 577, [1966] 1 All ER 582 at 593, per Lord Denning; cf Viscount
   Dilhorne at 573 and 590.
2 [1966] AC 552, [1966] 1 All ER 582.

2.5   (1) *The owner of premises*. Obviously, if in possession, the owner of premises will count as the occupier. If he is not in possession, the position is more
complicated. In general, much will depend on the extent to which the owner
retains any active control of the land and this in turn will often depend on the
precise terms of the grant from the owner permitting the creation of the rights to
possession. Thus, if an owner lets part of his property, but retains ownership of
other parts, including the common areas, he will be regarded as continuing as
occupier of those parts, e g where the owner of an office block does not let the
entrance hall, stairs and lift,[1] or where a local authority erects a block of flats but
only lets the individual flats and retains full rights over the staircase.[2] In
addition the owner may be liable, though not in possession, merely because he
reserves certain rights of entry having granted a licence,[3] though this does not

suffice in cases where a full and formal tenancy agreement has been entered into.[4]

1 *Richards v Land Revenue Trust Ltd* (1966) 198 Estates Gazette 29.
2 *Moloney v Lambeth London Borough Council* (1966) 64 LGR 440.
3 *Wheat v Lacon*, above.
4 See ch 7, below.

2.6 (2) *Lessees and licensees of premises.* Lessees and licensees will normally also be regarded as occupiers, and it is clear from *Wheat v Lacon*[1] (and many older cases) that the fact that the owner of the same property is regarded as an occupier is no bar to a finding that the lessee or licensee is also an occupier of those premises. In practice, of course, this is of relative unimportance, since the lessee or licensee is often the injured party and will wish to sue the landowner,[2] while in other cases it is a visitor to the lessee or licensee who is injured and who may wish either for personal or financial reasons only to sue the owner of the property. However, the principle is clear that in almost all cases the lessee or licensee will have sufficient factual control over the premises in question, albeit not exclusive control, to be legally labelled an occupier.

1 [1966] AC 552, [1966] 1 All ER 582.
2 E g *Wigzell v Verigood Investments Ltd* (1968) 207 Estates Gazette 531.

2.7 (3) *Contractors working on premises.* Several cases have arisen wherein the liability *qua* occupier of persons carrying out construction work or repair on another's premises has been discussed, and there is ample authority for the proposition that such persons may be regarded as occupiers. In *Savory v Holland and Hannen and Cubitts (Southern) Ltd*[1] the plaintiff was employed by subcontractors of the defendants who were engaged in the excavation of the site of a new factory for a major manufacturing company. The plaintiff was injured on a muddy bank, and the Court of Appeal held that the defendants were the occupiers of the site because of the degree of control they held over it (though they were held not to be in breach of their duties as occupier since the injury was a result of a risk which could be foreseen by the plaintiff). Similarly, it has been held that repairers working on a ship in dry dock are occupiers of the ship at that time.[2] Again, it will be an issue of fact as to whether or not a particular contractor is regarded as an occupier or not, depending on the exact degree of control exerted by that contractor. This is well illustrated by *Smith v Vange Scaffolding and Engineering Co Ltd*[3] where the plaintiff's employers were sub-contractors on the site of a new oil refinery, under the overall control of the principal contractors. The site was unduly untidy and the plaintiff was injured while on his way across the site; the dangerous untidy state of the site was caused by the principal contractors but was known to the sub-contractors. Mackenna J held that only the principal contractors could be held liable under the Occupiers' Liability Act; the sub-contractors, though negligent, were not occupiers; they clearly had no responsibility for the general condition of the site.

1 [1964] 3 All ER 18, [1964] 1 WLR 1158.
2 *Hartwell v Grayson, Rollo and Clover Docks Ltd* [1947] KB 901.
3 [1970] 1 All ER 249, [1970] 1 WLR 733.

2.8 (4) *Vicarious occupation.*[1] An employer, especially where a company, may be held liable as an occupier through occupation of the premises in question by his employees, though consideration of whether either or both employer or employee are occupiers may be a complex matter, with regard having to be paid to the factual and contractual responsibilities assumed by both. Thus, in some cases, the employer will exert such a high degree of control over the premises that the employee may not be personally liable;[2] in other cases, both employer and employee may be regarded as occupiers simultaneously.[3]

1 See North *Occupiers' Liability* pp. 26–28.
2 *Wheat v Lacon* [1966] AC 552 at 574, [1966] 1 All ER 582 at 591, per Viscount Dilhorne.
3 Ibid at 585 and 598.

2.9 The foregoing illustrates the main instances where a defendant's status as occupier may be discussed, but obviously it is not a fully comprehensive list. Further, no attempt has yet been made to identify precisely the level of control which has to be satisfied to show that anyone is an occupier. In essaying this, a general principle for use in all cases should emerge. Formerly, it had been suggested[1] that a landlord was not the occupier because he had no right to regulate the admission of others onto the demised premises, and the fact that the landlord had agreed to repair the premises was of no consequence. This connotes a relatively high level of control. Later cases have expanded this by reference to such concepts as responsibility[2] for the premises, and now care should be taken not to over-emphasise the aspect of regulation of entry. As we have seen, many landlords can be held liable, even though they cannot have any real control over entry to the premises, and thus a broader formulation is necessary. The problem was fully faced in the case of *Nicholls v Lyons*[3] where a tenant sued her landlord for injuries sustained on a common stairway. The New Zealand Court of Appeal held that the landlord was liable since, having regard to the relevant contractual terms, the landlord had as a result of retaining certain rights of occupation and control, full opportunity of observing the state of the premises. This case followed comments made in prior English cases such as *Greene v Chelsea Borough Council*,[4] where the local authority requisitioned a house and were in practice responsible for its upkeep, and had done work on the house, though they were merely empowered to repair and were under no such duty. Denning LJ stated that in practice, 'they had control of the house for the purpose of repairs', and were therefore under a tortious duty of care. Thus whether someone is an occupier or not does not merely depend on the relevant legal entitlements, but also depends on the facts of each case. So, in *Whiting v Hillingdon London Borough Council*[5] a local authority were under a statutory duty to maintain a footpath, but James J held that the occasional brief inspection which fully satisfied that duty would not amount to a sufficient degree of control for the local authority to be regarded as occupiers for the purposes of an action against them brought, under the 1957 Act, by an injured pedestrian. On the other hand, the most recent case in this area, *Harris v Birkenhead Corporation*,[6] concerned a local authority who merely by issuing a notice of entry, consequent upon having made a compulsory purchase order, were held to have become occupiers. Megaw LJ reasoned that the council could expect the house to become empty after their assertion of a right of entry, and would be regarded as the occupiers from that time, actual possession not being necessary.[7] In other words the legal and factual background merged so as to render the local authority the sole possible 'controller' of the premises, and thus the occupier of them.

1 *Cavalier v Pope* [1906] AC 428.
2 *Hartwell v Grayson, Rollo and Clover Docks Ltd*, above.
3 [1955] NZLR 1097.
4 [1954] 2 QB 127, [1954] 2 All ER 318.
5 (1970) 68 LGR 437.

2.10 To summarise, the question of occupation, whether under the 1957 Act or not, is a complex one. There may be more than one occupier of premises in any particular case, and the traditional test of occupation – who has control – though helpful, does not go all the way to giving an answer. In each case, an occupier must be legally entitled to control the premises (or part thereof) in question, and must either have done something by way of control, or clearly established a right to control, with due regard being had to whether or not there is anyone else who is controlling the premises – if there is, the burden of occupation may be shared with, or even transferred to, that person.

2.11 The occupier's duties,[1] created by the Act, are only owed to his lawful visitors and this therefore confines the ambit of the Act to persons coming onto the occupier's premises, in a capacity other than that of trespasser[2] i e as an invitee or licensee. No distinction is now drawn between these two categories, in terms of the duty owed to entrants in each class, and between them they cover a wide range of persons, such as persons entering premises after an express or implied invitation by the occupier or a person entering the premises so as to conduct business with the occupier – a full list is impossible, such is the comprehensive range of entrants onto premises covered by the general definition of 'lawful visitor'.

1 See paras 2.20 ff, below.
2 Occupiers' Liability Act 1957, s. 1(2).

2.12 Certain specific categories of visitor do however call for more detailed discussion. The traditional categories of licensee and invitee do not include persons entering premises under contractual rights but they are not without protection under the Occupiers' Liability Act, since section 5(1) lays down that in the absence of any specific terms of the contract, it will be implied into the contract that the occupier shall owe the visitor an analogous duty of care to that owed to licensees or invitees. Thus, a workman carrying out repairs on an occupier's premises, or a visitor to a sports arena, will be within the ambit of the 1957 Act.

2.13 Special care also needs to be taken when considering persons entering premises under general legal rights rather than by personal permission of the occupier. The principal rule is contained in section 2(6) of the Act whereby it is provided, inter alia, that 'persons who enter premises for any purpose in the exercise of a right conferred by law are to be treated as permitted by the occupier to be there for that purpose'. Thus, anyone entering premises in pursuance of a legal right, whether a general right open to all e g persons entering public parks or libraries, or a specific statutory right giving the individual a right to enter premises e g members of the fire brigade or police force in the execution of their duties, will come within the definition of a 'lawful visitor', and thus within the protection of the Act, subject to one major limitation, well illustrated by *Greenhalgh v British Railways Board*.[1] The plaintiff was utilising a public right of way across a railway bridge when, in consequence of the poor state of repair of the bridge, she fell and was injured. The Court of Appeal unanimously held that persons utilising public (or private) rights of way were not, at common law, licensees or invitees,[2] and therefore not within the category of 'lawful visitors'

27

for the purposes of the 1957 Act, and that although the situation was apparently covered by the words of section 2(6), in fact that subsection was only relevant to other parts of the same section,[3] and therefore was only concerned with the extent of duties owed, and did not extend the categories of persons to be regarded as visitors. So the plaintiff could not claim under the Occupiers' Liability Act. Whether the common law position was as clear as the Court of Appeal stated is a little uncertain.

1 [1969] 2 QB 286, [1969] 2 All ER 114.
2 Following *Gautret v Egerton* (1867) LR 2 CP 371 at 373.
3 The subsection is prefaced, 'for the purposes of this section'.

2.14 The common law is clear, as the court correctly perceived in *Greenhalgh*, that the person using a highway or other public right of way cannot complain, as against the occupier of the land over which the highway runs, of a failure by the occupier to maintain that highway. The leading case illustrating this is *Gautret v Egerton*[1] where the plaintiff, who was using a footpath over a canal bridge, fell in and was drowned, allegedly due to the defendants' failure to maintain their premises properly. The Court of Common Pleas stated that this disclosed no cause of action since the defendants' 'gift'[2] of access should not be penalised by making them liable for mere failure to maintain their land. However, it was conceded that a positive wrongful act might ground liability, as in *Corby v Hill*,[3] where the defendant was held liable for injury caused by a stack of slates left on a road on his land; this case would seem to be outside the scope of *Greenhalgh v British Railways Board*,[4] and thus still represents good law. Where the common law seems less clear is where the problem is that of a person injured while using a private right of way, such as an easement, over another's land. Is such a person within the scope of the Occupiers' Liability Act? The best that can be said is that while there was no intention to bring such persons within the Act,[5] this depended on the view that they were not within any category of persons owed duties by occupiers under the common law. The present position does seem clear[6] that the owner of the land is not under any general duty to ensure the enjoyment of an easement over his land; any duty to repair will only be as a result of express contractual stipulation. So only the victim of some wilful default will be able to sue the occupier in respect of injuries incurred while passing along any public or private right of way. Special provisions apply to persons entering land in consequence of an access agreement made under the National Parks and Access to the Countryside Act 1949.[7] Such persons, though lawfully on the land, are not regarded as visitors and are not owed the occupier's usual duty of care.[8]

1 (1867) LR 2 CP 371.
2 Ibid at 373, per Willes J.
3 (1858) 4 CB NS 556.
4 [1969] 2 QB 286, [1969] 2 All ER 114.
5 The Law Reform Committee's view is endorsed by *Thomas v British Railways Board* [1976] QB 912,]1976] 3 All ER 15.
6 *Gale on Easements* (14th edn) p. 47.
7 S. 59.
8 Occupiers' Liability Act 1957, s. 1(4).

2.15 Reference is also necessary to the fact that some visitors may only be lawfully on the land as a result of implied permission from the occupier and the scope of the concept of implied permission falls to be discussed. Its roots lie in the traditional difference between the rights of lawful visitors and the rights of trespassers. As will be seen[1] trespassers have until recently had no rights whatsoever against occupiers, irrespective of the culpability of the occupier, and in response to this seemingly harsh principle, the courts from time to time endeavoured to extend the categories of persons deemed to be lawfully on premises. Thus, an occupier's continuing acquiescence in allowing persons to cross his land, though without his direct or explicit permission, has been held to amount to a grant of implied permission, rendering those persons lawful visitors. This clearly means that anyone intending to call on an occupier will be a lawful visitor, unless the occupier has specifically withdrawn permission to enter, and will remain a lawful visitor until the permission to enter has been specifically abrogated. In *Phipps v Rochester Corporation*[2] the defendants were unsuccessful in their argument that the plaintiff, a young child, could not sue simply on the ground that she had no permission to enter the premises. Rather, said Devlin J,[3] the fact that the defendants had never chased anyone from their land, and took no steps to show that they objected to the intrusions onto their land, meant that children as a class were licensed to play on the open space where the accident occurred (though he finally held that this particular child was so young that her presence on the land, unaccompanied by a responsible companion, could not have been anticipated). In *Lowery v Walker*,[4] even verbal objections by the landowner could not prevent a finding that the continuing use of a route over his land by the public meant that those persons had an implied licence to use the land. The respondent had never taken any legal action to prevent the use of his land, and this, combined with the fact that the continuing usage was known to him, rendered him liable to the appellant, who suffered injuries when he was attacked by a savage horse placed in the field by the respondent.

1 See paras 2.63 ff, below.
2 [1955] 1 QB 450, [1955] 1 All ER 129.
3 Ibid at 456 and 133.
4 [1911] AC 10.

2.16 Whether an implied permission has been granted is of course primarily a question of fact, though in the cases that have arisen it would seem that there is a tendency for the courts to be more inclined to allow children to be given implied permission to enter,[1] while there are equally few cases of general application where an adult has been able to take advantage of this principle. This may partly be due to the realisation that adults are better placed to understand and appreciate their true entitlement to be on land than are children, but is also to some extent due to the operation of the doctrine of allurement in favour of children. This stems initially from the case of *Lynch v Nurdin*[2] where a child was injured whilst playing in an unattended cart with horse attached. The court refused to hold that the child was trespassing, and preferred to find that the child was tempted by the obvious attractions of the horse and cart, and that this was the defendant's fault. The doctrine has gradually been developed alongside the notion of the implied license to enter premises. In *Cooke v Midland Great Western Railway Co of Ireland*[3] a child was injured whilst playing on a railway turntable. The railway company were held liable since they knew (or ought to have known) of the regular intrusions onto their property and yet had done nothing notwithstanding that, in the words of Lord Atkinson,[4] 'every person must be taken to know that young children and boys are of a very inquisitive and frequently mischievous disposition and are likely to meddle with whatever happens to be in their reach'. Thus the railway company were effectively held to have created an attraction for the local children and by ignoring their intrusions were held to have granted them implied permission to enter. Later in *Glasgow Corporation v Taylor*[5] where a child died after eating berries taken without express permission from a bush in a park, it was held that the appellants were liable. They had created a dangerously tempting allurement, an attractive though poisonous plant, and were held liable for the inevitable consequences although they did not intend or permit that the berries be eaten. Again, the application of this doctrine of allurement will primarily be a question of fact, though it is clear from such cases as *Perry v Thomas Wrigley Ltd*[6] that only particularly enticing objects, the dangers of which were not obvious, could be classified as allurements, and any ordinary hazard (such as the large hole in a road into which the plaintiff fell) would not be an allurement. Thus, lawful entrants include persons in whose favour permission to enter is impliedly granted, and within that general category, in particular, implied permission to enter may be deemed in favour of a child in consequence of the presence of an allurement.

1 E g *Cooke v Midland Great Western Railway of Ireland* [1909] AC 229 and *Glasgow Corpn v Taylor* [1922] 1 AC 44; cf *Edwards v Railway Executive* [1952] AC 737, [1952] 2 All ER 430.
2 (1841) 1 QB 29.
3 [1909] AC 229.
4 Ibid at 237.
5 [1922] 1 AC 44.
6 [1955] 3 All ER 243n., [1955] 1 WLR 1164.

2.17 It is however to be noted that since the foregoing rules clearly developed in response to the former rigours of the law where trespassers were concerned, such attempts to shift the boundaries between the categories of lawful entrant and trespasser are now less necessary, since trespassers can now obtain some redress against a culpable occupier and, indeed, this kind of distinction ought to be discouraged in view of its artificiality and unpredictability. In *British Railways Board v Herrington*[1] Lord Reid[2] summarised the then state of the law by saying that persistent attempts had been made to extend protection to some child trespassers beyond that envisaged in the leading House of Lords decision confirming that trespassers could not sue the occupier,[3] and that the whole area of the law needed re-examination; Lord Diplock[4] stated that 'the "licence" treated as having been granted in such cases was a legal fiction employed to justify extending to meritorious trespassers, particularly if they were children, the benefit of the duty which at common law an occupier owed to his licensees'. Thus, it is suggested, fewer cases will need to use such ideas as implied permission or allurement to ensure success, and these clearly artificial and arguably over-extended notions are likely to become of lesser importance in due course.

1 [1972] AC 877, [1972] 1 All ER 749.
2 Ibid at 896 and 756 respectively.
3 E g *Robert Addie & Sons (Collieries) Ltd v Dumbreck* [1929] AC 358.
4 *British Railways Board v Herrington*, above, at 933 and 789.

2.18 Other cases have arisen where the issue is whether a lawful visitor has gone beyond the limits of the permission to enter given to him. Again, this is primarily a question of fact in each case, but the general principle is clear. When anyone is invited onto premises, it is not the case that that invitation is a licence to do anything anywhere on the premises. The invitation will always be restricted, perhaps with reference to time – the grounds of a stately home may be open to the public until 5 p.m. – or with reference to a particular area of the premises – visitors to a stately home would doubtless not be allowed into the private quarters – or with reference to a particular purpose – entry may be allowed solely so as to deliver mail or collect laundry. Cases abound on this topic; in *Gould v McAuliffe*[1] the plaintiff was at a public house and, in search of the lavatory, went into a part of the grounds where the public were not permitted and was there savaged by a dog owned by the landlord. It was held that the plaintiff's claim could succeed since the defendants had not sufficiently clearly indicated the boundaries of the plaintiff's licence to enter and there was no general reason why she should have realised that she was stepping into forbidden territory. On the other hand, in *Periscinotti v Brighton West Pier Co Ltd*[2] where the plaintiff was injured having dived from the defendants' pier into shallow water, it was held that his claim should not succeed since by stepping over a chain and two railings designed to prevent entry to the diving platform he must have realised that he was stepping beyond the boundaries of his permission to enter. Much may depend on the precise action taken by the landowner himself to indicate the limits of the permitted entry. This was the view adopted by Lord Greene MR in *Pearson v Coleman Bros*,[3] an unfortunate case concerning a child who wandered away from a circus performance in search of a toilet and was injured when she crawled into what turned out to be a lion's tent. He stated, 'in my opinion, if a landowner is minded to make part of his land a prohibited area, he must indicate this to his invitees by appropriate means'[4] and it was held that the steps taken by the occupiers in this case were inadequate and thus they were held liable for the plaintiff's injuries. It will also, however, often be necessary to consider the reasonableness or otherwise of the plaintiff's own conduct – he must use his own common sense in assessing the implied limits of his rights to entry, or else lose the protection afforded by the status of lawful visitor.

1 [1941] 2 All ER 527.
2 (1961) 105 Sol Jo 526.
3 [1948] 2 KB 359, [1948] 2 All ER 274.
4 Ibid at 375 and 280.

2.19 Before the Occupiers' Liability Act can be applied to a situation, one further prerequisite has to be satisfied, viz the premises on which the incident has occurred must be within the Act's ambit. There is no full definition of 'premises' in the Act and thus the common law rules must be our starting-point. Land and permanent buildings thereon are clearly premises at common law, as are builders' ladders,[1] scaffolding[2] and other less permanent structures. However, the Act does extend this somewhat by section 1(3), which states that the rules in the Act governing the occupation of premises also apply to regulate 'the obligations of a person occupying or having control over any fixed or moveable structure including any vessel, vehicle or aircraft'. Thus the Act has been used in a case where a crew-member was injured while disembarking from a car ferry on an inadequately secured gangway,[3] where collapsing cargo has injured stevedores in a ship's hold,[4] or where a workman was injured by a large, slow-moving digging machine's rollers whilst the machine was engaged in constructing a new tunnel.[5] So far, then, no major practical difficulties have arisen and the broad meaning ascribed to 'premises' will be helpful to plaintiffs in cases framed under the Act.

1 *Woodman v Richardson and Concrete Ltd* [1937] 3 All ER 866.
2 *Pratt v Richards* [1951] 2 KB 208, [1951] 1 All ER 90n.
3 *Jolliffe v Townsend Bros Ferries Ltd* [1965] 2 Lloyd's Rep 19.
4 *Catton v British India Steam Navigation Co Ltd* [1965] 2 Lloyd's Rep 344.
5 *Bunker v Charles Brand Ltd* [1969] 2 QB 480, [1969] 2 All ER 59.

2.20 Now we can move to the heart of any discussion of the Occupiers' Liability Act – given the presence of an occupier and lawful visitor on appropriate premises, what duty of care is owed by the occupier? The simple answer is provided by the Act itself by section 2(1): 'an occupier of premises owes the same duty, the common duty of care, to all his visitors'. However, there is no precise explanation as to what constitutes the 'common duty of care'. Section 2(2) states that it is 'a duty to take such care as in all the circumstances of the case is reasonable to see that the visitor will be reasonably safe in using the premises for the purposes for which he is invited or permitted by the occupier to be there', but this takes us little further on the crucial question of the level of care imposed on persons with duties under the Act. In fact, there is little mystery, as is evidenced by *Ward v Hertfordshire County Council*.[1] In this case, the infant plaintiff tripped whilst running in an unsupervised school playground and fell against its boundary wall which was primarily composed of flints set in mortar, injuring himself seriously. The trial judge, Hinchcliffe J, said that the duty under the Act was really the same as the ordinary common law duty not to be negligent i e to take reasonable care with regard to the safety of the children in the playground. The same approach was adopted (though with differing results) by the Court of Appeal. No other case seems to have approached the issue so directly, but it is suggested that the view of Hinchcliffe J is correct bearing in mind the problems and difficulties that would arise if there were to be slightly differing tests in ordinary negligence and Occupiers' Liability Act cases, given the overlap that exists between them.[2] This approach also seems consistent with the range of cases that have applied the 1957 Act. The approach of the court to foreseeability of injury in *Simms v Leigh Rugby Football Club Ltd*[3] (where a rugby football player crashed into a wall 7 feet beyond the touchline), to acts of third parties in *Sawyer v H and G Simonds Ltd*[4] and to the dangers of excessive imposition of liability in *Lee v Blue Star Line Ltd*[5] (all cases under the 1957 Act) in each case seems identical to the approach that would be adopted in a traditional negligence action. The usual rules in relation to economic loss also apply to cases under the 1957 Act.[6] Thus, old distinctions between the precise level of duty owed to various classes of visitors are swept away, and one duty, a clearly identifiable one, is owed to all lawful visitors.[7] So, in the well-known case of *White v Blackmore*,[8] the guard ropes at a jalopy-racing site were so tied as to engender greater danger to spectators when the ropes were struck by a car – clearly this was (and was held to be) a breach of the common duty of care. On the other hand, in *Wood v Morland & Co Ltd*[9] the plaintiff failed in his action against a hotel-owner who had not cleared snow from his forecourt. The plaintiff fell on the snow and was injured but could not succeed in a claim under the Act since any steps taken to remove the snow would, in all probability, have only increased the danger and thus (by inaction) the defendants had fulfilled their duty to the plaintiff to enable him to be reasonably safe. It is a testimony to the improvements wrought by the 1957 Act that the number of reported cases in this area has substantially declined, strongly implying that settlement of claims is now much simpler.

1 [1969] 2 All ER 807, [1969] 1 WLR 790; revsd on appeal (1969) 114 Sol Jo 87.
2 See paras 2.36 ff, below.
3 [1969] 2 All ER 923.
4 (1966) 197 Estates Gazette 877.
5 [1962] 1 Lloyd's Rep 440.
6 *AMF International Ltd v Magnet Bowling Ltd* [1968] 2 All ER 789 at 807–808, [1968] 1 WLR 1028 at 1050–1051.
7 The duty clearly covers personal injury and associated property damage (see below where

property damage alone is incurred).
8 [1972] 2 QB 651, [1972] 3 All ER 158.
9 (1971) 115 Sol Jo 569.

2.21 Where property damage alone is incurred, the application of the Act is less clear. By section 1(3) of the 1957 Act, it is provided that the duty of the occupier extends, inter alia, to cover property damage incurred on the premises to the same extent that the common law would. So, the common duty of care will be relevant in cases where property alone is damaged while lawfully on premises other than those of its owner, though the occupier will, as before, not be liable if the goods are stolen.[1] There is some difficulty as to the precise extent of the pre-existing common law liability, however. If a visitor is uninjured, some authorities indicate that he cannot claim for property damage,[2] but it is submitted that the better view is that such an action is permissible,[3] so long as the usual requirements of foreseeability are met. Where property owned by a third party is brought onto the defendant's land by a lawful visitor, no problem seems to arise insofar as section 1(3)(b) of the 1957 Act specifically refers to the common duty of care extending to cover a third party's property, but this must be read in the light of the fact that section 1(3) only acts to extend the duty of care to property where the common law would do so. No clear solution to this problem appears, given the dearth of case law in the area; however, it is suggested that a third party has a perfectly adequate claim under the ordinary rules of negligence in most cases and the reference in section 1(3)(b) to 'the property of persons who are not themselves his visitors' may be construed narrowly, perhaps covering persons who are not visitors at the present time but were when the property was left on the premises and perhaps also covering property of a principal whose agent lawfully entered with the article in question, but not covering a third party's property which without his express permission is carried onto the defendant's premises. Thus, the occupier's own property is probably within the scope of the common duty of care, but that of a third party such as a car hire firm whose car is driven onto the defendant's premises and there carelessly damaged, should not be within the Act's ambit.

1 *Edwards v West Herts Group Hospital Management Committee* [1957] 1 All ER 541, [1957] 1 WLR 415.
2 *Tinsley v Dudley* [1951] 2 KB 18 at 25, [1951] 1 All ER 252 at 255–256, per Lord Evershed MR.
3 *Lancaster Canal Co v Parnaby* (1839) 11 Ad & EL 223 at 243. See North *Occupiers' Liability* p. 95 for a further discussion and a different conclusion.

2.22 An additional guide to those involved in cases of occupiers' liability is provided by section 2(3) of the 1957 Act which initially states that the character of the particular visitor in question will be relevant to the question of the standard of care owed to him by the occupier. Thus, obviously, greater care needs to be taken if blind persons are expected to use the premises, or, perhaps, foreign tourists who may well be unable to understand English warning signs. The subsection goes on to give two particular examples of specially relevant circumstances, firstly, 'an occupier must be prepared for children to be less careful than adults',[1] secondly, 'an occupier may expect that a person, in the exercise of his calling, will appreciate and guard against any special risks ordinarily incident to it, so far as the occupier leaves him free to do so'.[2] Turning first to the ever-present problem of children in the law of occupiers' liability, the Act endorses the long-standing principle, recognised by the common law, that a child cannot look after himself so well as an adult – he will not have the intelligence or the experience of life fully to appreciate when he is in fact walking into danger, and so the occupier must, if he knows, or ought to know, of the presence of children on his premises, take greater care to prevent the children suffering injuries. The relatively recent case of *Moloney v Lambeth London Borough Council*[3] illustrates the extra care which may have to be taken; the defendant local authority were regarded as the occupiers of the common parts of a block of flats, including a staircase which had what in normal circumstances would be an adequate guardrail. However, the plaintiff was a child, aged four, and he accidentally tripped and fell through the rail, and it was successfully argued that the council should have known that children used the staircase and could fall through the rail, and that measures could easily be taken to prevent such accidents. Thus, the council were held liable. Also, in *Reffell v Surrey County Council*[4] a local authority was held to be at fault in installing thin glass in the windows of school corridor doors, which was incapable of resisting the pressure of a child's hand in certain circumstances. Veale J was clearly of the view[5] that the glass had to be capable of resisting normal horseplay amongst schoolchildren. The cases already cited[6] on the doctrine of allurement also show that occupiers must sometimes take greater care with respect to infant visitors – what is alluring to a child, for example an attractive but poisonous fungus or berry, will be clearly perceived as potentially dangerous by adult visitors, and therefore the occupier will have no need to do anything to protect adult visitors. It seems clear that the younger a child visitor is, the more care needs to be taken; extreme youthfulness must be a relevant feature of character. Again here the Act is not substantially different in its effect from the common law.[7]

1 S. 2(3)(a).
2 S. 2(3)(b).
3 (1966) 64 LGR 440.
4 [1964] 1 All ER 743, [1964] 1 WLR 358.
5 Ibid at 747 and 363.
6 See para 2.16, above.
7 E g *Latham v R Johnson & Nephew Ltd* [1913] 1 KB 398.

2.23 The second example given concerns the expert visiting premises who will, thanks to his calling, be more aware of the potential and actual dangers than the ordinary occupier. In many ways, this example is the opposite of that of the child who is inherently less aware of dangers arising from premises. The leading case here is *Roles v Nathan*.[1] Here, two chimney sweeps were asphyxiated while working on an old boiler after having been warned that dangerous carbon monoxide fumes were emanating from it when lit. In the subsequent action under the Fatal Accidents Acts it was contended that the occupier of the premises containing the boiler was liable under the 1957 Act, but this view was rejected by the Court of Appeal. Lord Denning MR took the view that, as experienced chimney sweeps, the two deceased should have been aware of the possibility of the fumes and their inherent danger and the occupier was entitled to rely on their presumed specialist knowledge, while Harman LJ stated that the risks from this particular gas were risks which were ordinarily incidental to the chimney sweep's trade and of which the deceased had stated they were fully aware, and therefore the occupier successfully resisted the claim. This is again similar to the previous position at common law.[2] It is supported by *Clare v L Whittaker & Son (London) Ltd*,[3] another Fatal Accidents Acts claim, brought by the dependants of a workman killed while working on a roof, through which he fell, at least in part due to the non-provision of 'crawling-boards'. The claim failed since, as an experienced roof-worker, the deceased knew that crawling-boards were available and usable, and the defendants were entitled to rely on his judgment as to whether they were needed, and were under no duty to ensure that they were used. However, not all cases are, in their result, unfavourable to the claimant. The principle exemplified by section 2(3)(b) only applies to dangers which the visiting expert is uniquely qualified to observe; more general dangers are still the responsibility of the occupier, as is shown by *Bird v King Line Ltd*[4] where the plaintiff was injured whilst working on a ship. The evidence showed that he had slipped and fallen on a bottle left lying on the deck. It was held that while the plaintiff should, as a result of his regular work on ships, have been aware of the dangers arising from ropes, cables, winches, etc. on deck, there was no reason for him to be aware of the possibility of there being a bottle left lying on deck, for this was a general danger in no way relateable to his particular expertise. His claim therefore succeeded. So, section 2(3)(b) only acts to hinder the expert plaintiff's claim where the danger is one uniquely observable by dint of his own expertise.

1 [1963] 2 All ER 908, [1963] 1 WLR 1117.
2 E g *General Cleaning Contractors v Christmas* [1953] AC 180, [1952] 2 All ER 1110.
3 [1976] ICR 1.
4 [1970] 2 Lloyd's Rep 349.

2.24 This seems an appropriate place to review the operation of these basic sections of the 1957 Act. It establishes a broad framework whereby a wide range of occupiers owe to all lawful visitors to their premises a duty of care which, if not totally clear, is at least readily identifiable as akin to the usual duty of care in negligence. The new rules build on the pre-existing common law principles, but successfully endeavour to remove many of the technicalities which formerly bedevilled this area of the law. In most cases it will be clear whether any given person is an occupier, using the test of the degree of control exercised. There will be no difficulties normally as to whether a visitor has lawfully entered on the land or not, and the application of the general duty of care to the specific circumstances in question will generally not be difficult – the condition of the premises will, in the nature of things, be normally readily ascertainable, the application of normal common law principles will bring into consideration all the surrounding circumstances, such as the premises being in darkness or a regular history of accidents on the premises, and the particular difficulties of child and expert visitors are covered by the particular provisions in the Act, and the pre-existing case law. The 1957 Act seems, notwithstanding initial mis-givings,[1] to be a sound framework for dealing with issues of occupiers' liability.

1 E g Newark (1958) 12 NILQ 203, Payne (1958) 21 MLR 359.

2.25 However, there remain several particular issues to be considered. Perhaps paramount amongst these are the related questions of the extent to which the occupier may limit or negate his liability by placing notices either warning of the dangers on the premises or purporting to exclude liability for injuries incurred on the premises. This is not an easy area of the law, since the common law was supplemented by provisions in the 1957 Act, while to this picture must now be added the effects of the Unfair Contract Terms Act 1977. The first question is as to the effect of warnings promulgated by the occupier addressed to the visitor, advising him of prospective perils on the land, such as a sign warning that a building is unsafe and about to be demolished, or a notice warning of high voltages attached to electricity pylons. The 1957 Act lays down the general principle applicable to such cases by section 2(4)(a), which states 'where damage is caused to a visitor by a danger of which he had been warned by the occupier, the warning is not to be treated without more as absolving the occupier from liability, unless in all the circumstances it was enough to enable the visitor to be reasonably safe'. The Act thus takes a more positive role towards warnings than may be expected, and the courts will be able to investigate not merely the existence but the character of any warning sign. So, in *Roles v Nathan*,[1] a clear warning given by an expert on heating systems was held sufficient to absolve the defendant occupier (the heating expert was held to be their agent) from liability. The warning contained enough information to enable the particular plaintiffs to comprehend and act on it, if they had so desired. On the other hand, in *Woollins v British Celanese Ltd*,[2] a notice advising that a roof was unsafe 'without special precautions' was placed behind a door so that anyone heading towards the roof would be unlikely to see it; this meant that the defendant occupiers were held liable to the plaintiff, a GPO engineer working on the roof. It is arguable, in any case, that this notice would also fall foul of the 1957 Act by being too vague to assist the visitor in remaining reasonably safe in giving no indication as to the precise defects of the roof, for section 2(4)(a) imposes an objective test. In *Bishop v J S Starnes & Sons Ltd and Macandrews & Co Ltd*,[3] the plaintiff was injured by gassing in a tank on a ship. His claim was resisted on the grounds that 'No Admittance' and 'No Smoking' signs had been posted, and there was some evidence that the ship's boatswain had made a general comment about fumes. These various warnings were held to be quite inadequate by Dunn J. He stated that the tank was a water-tank and far stronger warnings were needed to successfully negate liability for injuries due to fumes caused by a petrol-engine that had been used in the tank for some days previously. So, the less obvious and predictable a danger is, then, clearly, the stronger relevant warnings have to be. Indeed, it may well be that some obstructions or pitfalls can never be rendered safe by warnings alone, such as a steep-sided pool in the middle of a field where children regularly play. It should also be noted that section 2(4)(a) refers to warnings alone being adequate or otherwise; if any warning is coupled with some physical signal or genuine attempt to minimise the danger[4] then this will suffice.

1 [1963] 2 All ER 908, [1963] 1 WLR 1117.
2 (1966) 1 KIR 438.
3 [1971] 1 Lloyd's Rep 162.
4 Per Newark (1958) 12 NILQ 203 at 212.

2.26 In considering warning notices, it is also important to note the relevance of any other particular defences to negligence actions which apply equally here. The 1957 Act, by section 2(5), specifically preserves the defence of *volenti non fit injuria* in stating that the occupier owes no obligation in respect of risks willingly accepted by the visitor. The defence of contributory negligence is also available to an occupier, since the common duty of care is clearly a fault-based form of liability and thus within the terms of the Law Reform (Contributory Negligence) Act 1945. Thus, an occupier is able to reduce or negate his liability if a visitor has ignored a clear warning sign or a danger which he ought to have spotted.

2.27 In many cases, either associated with a warning notice or independently, the occupier will go further and attempt to exclude or limit liability for injuries occurred on the premises, but the general trend of opinion against exclusion clauses in recent years has affected the position. The principal common law decision on this topic is *Ashdown v Samuel Williams & Sons Ltd*,[1] where the plaintiff was injured by a train while taking a short-cut to work over the defendant's railway tracks. A notice claiming to exempt the defendants from liability in negligence stood at the entry to the short-cut – the principal issue was therefore whether this notice operated to affect the plaintiff's claim. The Court of Appeal unanimously held that the plaintiff's entry onto the premises was capable of regulation by notices of an appropriate character, and that the notice in the case was adequate[2] to render her entry subject to the conditions contained in it, including exemption from liability, irrespective of the fact that there was no contract between the parties. The case, notwithstanding substantial criticism by academic writers,[3] was effectively endorsed by the Act[4] which lays down that the common duty of care only applies in cases where there has been no (lawful) extension, restriction, modification or exclusion of that duty – in other words, under the Act, warning signs may irrespective of contract attach conditions to grants of permission to enter, or may amount to contractually binding exclusion clauses, since the subsection states that the exclusion etc., may be by agreement 'or otherwise'. The principal recent case in this area is *White v Blackmore*[5] where a competitor in a jalopy race was fatally injured whilst watching another event at the meeting. The organisers' defence to the ensuing claim was, inter alia, that the deceased was subject to various exclusion clauses in notices on the site and in the official programme. The Court of Appeal endorsed this view, but Lord Denning MR, dissenting, stated that *Ashdown's* case[6] only applied where entry to the premises was not regulated by a contract; here, there was a contract and (on the facts) he held the various exclusion clauses had not been properly incorporated into it. This dissenting view, though favourable to the occupier, is, it is submitted, not to be regarded as representing the law – an argument has been propounded[7] that since you are free to forbid entry, a partial permission to enter subject to conditions which are contractually binding (the visitor 'trades' his rights in exchange for permission to enter) is permissible, and this seems cogent. Professor Gower's view,[8] although endorsed by Lord Denning's dissenting judgment, seems fallacious; in saying that a licensor can, under *Ashdown's* case,[9] irrespective of contract, divest himself of the liabilities of a licensor, and that this is erroneous, he ignores the fundamental nature of the concept of the bare licence which is, as its name implies, a licence *all* the terms of which may be determined by the parties by contract or otherwise. Professor Gower admits that a ban on licensees entering premises with dogs is effective irrespective of contract; surely there is only a qualitative and not a legal difference between such a term and a term purporting to exclude liability. Thus it seems clear that there is no need for conditions imposed on a licensee's right of entry to be included in a contract. On the other hand, there seems to be force in Lord Denning's more general view that *Ashdown's* case cannot apply where a licence is created by contract; to permit non-contractual variation of the contractually agreed situation would be wrong. To sum up as far as the common law position is concerned, a contractually binding exclusion or limitation clause will be valid as against an occupier; in addition, a non-contractual clause will act as a condition on a licensee's right of entry, unless this right is founded on a contract.

1 [1957] 1 QB 409, [1957] 1 All ER 35.
2 The adequacy of the notice to be assessed in accordance with the method more normally used in questions of incorporation of contractual terms.
3 See especially Gower (1956) 19 MLR 532, (1957) 20 MLR 181.
4 S. 2(1).
5 [1972] 2 QB 651, [1972] 3 All ER 158.
6 [1957] 1 QB 409, [1957] 1 All ER 35.

7 *Winfield and Jolowicz on Tort* (11th edn) p. 207.
8 Above.
9 [1957] 1 QB 409, [1957] 1 All ER 35.

2.28 To this picture must be added the far-reaching impact of the Unfair Contract Terms Act 1977. A few general words are in order as to the ambit of this Act in the sphere of defective premises. The Act endeavours to control attempts to circumvent both contractual[1] and tortious[2] liability by means of contractual exemption clauses and non-contractual notices,[3] though does not cover clauses in contracts for the sale of land,[4] and only covers attempts to exclude liabilities incurred in the course of a business.[5] Within this framework, there are substantial repercussions on the liability of the occupier. The first point to note is that a breach of the common duty of care created by the 1957 Act is defined as 'negligence' by the 1977 Act.[6] This then means that section 2(1) of the Act operates in the sphere of occupiers' liability. This states: 'A person cannot by reference to any contract term or notice given to persons generally or to particular persons exclude or restrict his liability for death or personal injury resulting from negligence.' It is clear that both contractual and non-contractual attempts to limit liability are covered by the Act, since section 14 defines 'notice' as including written and other announcements, or any other (real or attempted) communication. It should also be noted that clauses will fall foul of the Act whether they purport to totally exclude liability or merely slightly limit it; this stems from section 13(1), whereby the exclusion or restriction of liability (the phrase used throughout the Act) includes any attempt to impose restrictive conditions on either the liability or its enforcement, or any attempt to limit the remedies available to the plaintiff. The effect of these comprehensive provisions is therefore that an occupier cannot avoid liability for death or personal injury occurring to his visitors by reference to notices on tickets, or at the point of ticket-sale, or by notices at the point of entry to premises, such as in *Ashdown's* case, if those notices have any adverse effects on the plaintiff's rights and their enforcement. This major protection for the lawful visitor is backed up by section 2(2) of the Unfair Contract Terms Act; this deals with cases where damage other than death or personal injury is caused, such as damage to the plaintiff's car while parked in the defendants' car park, or perhaps damage to clothing and effects accompanying a visitor's personal injuries. In such cases, there is no complete ban on exclusion clauses; rather, section 2(2) ordains that such clauses or notices are to be subjected to a requirement of reasonableness – only 'reasonable' contract terms or notices are to be given effect.

1 S. 3.
2 S. 2.
3 S. 2(1) and (2).
4 Sch 1, para 1(b).
5 S. 1(3). See para 2.32, below.
6 S. 1(1)(c).

2.29 Relatively little help is given by the Act in deciding whether a term or notice is a reasonable one; section 11(2) states that a contract term's reasonableness is to be assessed with regard to the circumstances which were known or ought reasonably to have been known to the parties when the contract was made, while by section 11(3) a non-contractual notice, to stand as reasonable, must be considered in the light of the circumstances when liability arose or (but for the notice) would have arisen. This is one of the less satisfactory aspects of the 1977 Act, with excessively vague and unhelpful definitions in a novel area of legislation where clear guidance would have been useful. The only substantial assistance given by the Act comes from section 11(4) which draws particular attention, in considering the question of reasonableness in cases where liability is limited to a specified sum, to the resources which a defendant could be expected to use to meet any liability and the extent to which he could have insured himself against that liability. Thus an impoverished occupier will stand a better chance of being able to rely on a clause limiting liability to a set figure in cases of property damage, especially if no insurance policy is available to cover the liability to an aggrieved visitor. Beyond this, however, the Act gives no help in deciding what is and what is not reasonable and it is unsurprising in these circumstances of uncertainty that as yet no bold plaintiff has taken a claim to the higher courts which would elucidate the concept of reasonableness. However, it must be that other circumstances are relevant to the issue of reasonableness, as sections 11(1) and 11(3) indicate, and it is therefore a matter of speculation as to what those other factors are. Certain additional factors to which regard must be had in sale of goods contracts[1] may presumably be utilised in other cases e g the relative bargaining power of the parties and whether the visitor receives any inducement (such as a reduction in entry fee) in exchange for his agreement to the exclusion clause. It must be arguable that other relevant factors in assessing reasonableness would include a consideration of the scope of the term or notice in question – a blanket exclusion attacking the very notion of responsibility for one's premises may be more likely to be unreasonable – and an assessment of the adequacy or otherwise of the way in which the term or notice was brought to the visitor's attention – a clause may notwithstanding the fact that it has been publicised adequately for the purposes of incorporation nonetheless be inadequately publicised for the purposes of reasonableness.

1 S. 11(2); Sch 2.

2.30 The implications of exclusion clauses in tortious actions are also covered. By section 2(3) of the 1977 Act a person's agreement to a contract term attempting to exclude or restrict[1] liability or his awareness of a notice attempting the same is not of itself to be taken as indicating his voluntary acceptance of any risk. This amounts to a new limitation on the doctrine of *volenti*, and it is difficult to assess how the doctrine will now operate in a typical occupier's liability case. If the occupier erects a clear notice restricting the visitor's rights to compensation which is read and understood by the visitor, and this awareness is not of itself to be evidence of his consent to the risk, it is difficult to see what other factors may be relevant to add in some way to the consent and permit the doctrine of *volenti* to operate. Arguably section 2(3) has the effect, intended or not, of preventing the doctrine operating in most cases where clauses restricting or excluding liability are being used, although of course this does not affect notices advising visitors of dangers, unless these are to be regarded as exclusions or restrictions of liability; while such notices could be construed as having the effect of restricting the occupiers' liability, this could result in occupiers not erecting such helpful signs (since they would have little effect thanks to the 1977 Act), with detrimental consequences. The better approach is to say that genuine warning signs prevent liability arising in the first place, and should not therefore be regarded as excluding or restricting liability.

1 See s. 13.

2.31   A brief comment is necessary on the principal limitation of the 1977 Act as applied to cases of occupiers' liability. By section 1(3), 'In the case of both contract and tort, sections 2 to 7 apply . . . only to business liability'. This key term is defined as 'liability for breach of obligations or duties arising: (a) from things done or to be done by a person in the course of a business (whether his own business or another's); or (b) from the occupation of premises used for business purposes of the occupier.' This is further elucidated by section 14, which gives a partial definition of 'business'; this is stated to include a profession and the activities of any government department or local or public authority. However, many cases are still unclear. Are universities or private schools to be viewed as businesses? Should homes opened to the public for charitable purposes be brought within the definition? One consideration could be whether an occupier is profiting financially from the visit, or is intending so to do; such a factor would ensure that any occupier deemed to be a business occupier should have the resources to meet the liabilities thus imposed; on the other hand, such a consideration would remove many large-scale enterprises such as public utilities and colleges from the categories of businesses, which would be detrimental to many visitors and might seem anomalous if seen alongside a very small but slightly profitable enterprise which would be treated as a business. Profit therefore seems a less than adequate criterion. Consideration of whether an enterprise is a 'business' or not on the grounds of its size and turnover would not be an invariably workable approach, but it is submitted that it does show the way forward. After all, any large enterprise can (and indeed should) insure its premises; any large enterprise ought to have the resources to ensure that its premises are reasonably safe. Therefore an analysis of whether a non-residential occupier is occupying in the course of a business or not should focus on the resources of the occupier, and an inevitably subjective appraisal of the character and size of the enterprise in which the occupier is engaged. Such an approach should enable an injured visitor to point to the financial and human resources of a university or public utility, and claim that they are sufficiently able to take care of their visitors that they should be regarded as businesses for the purposes of the Unfair Contract Terms Act 1977. It is conceded that the proposed approach is somewhat imprecise, though it should notwithstanding that be workable; it is also recognised that the approach is not directly alluded to by the Act, but the Act is so vague that the courts will surely have to formulate a more regular approach to the question. The proposed approach would also cover the problem of the stately home opened for charitable purposes; the charity is receiving a sum of money from this, and it seems not unreasonable to regard this as the resource from which liabilities can be met, or, preferably, insurance premiums paid. Thus the scope of the 1977 Act and its full impact cannot yet be precisely measured. While a large, profitable factory will clearly be regarded as a business bringing its occupiers within the Act's controls and a private householder will equally clearly not be regarded as a business, a large intermediate area will be enshrouded in doubt, at least until an appropriate case reaches the higher courts. Whether such cases are likely to be brought amidst such depths of uncertainty is an open question here, as in the earlier topic of the definition of 'reasonableness'; what at first sight seem to be sensible discretions left to the courts by Parliament can also be viewed as a great obstacle to those intended to benefit from the Act in their attempts to understand and utilise its provisions.

2.32   One major possible defence which plays a special role in occupiers' liability cases, and which needs to be discussed, is the extent to which occupiers of dangerous premises can shelter behind the fact that the danger in question was created and/or should have been prevented by an independent contractor on the premises. By section 2(4)(b) of the 1957 Act, regard is to be had, in cases where a visitor is harmed by the defective work of an independent contractor, to three issues: (1) whether it was reasonable for the occupier to delegate the work in question to a contractor; (2) whether appropriate care was taken in the choice of a contractor; and (3) whether it was necessary for the occupier to supervise the execution of the work. In cases involving any specialised knowledge not likely to be possessed by the occupier, it will be reasonable to appoint an independent contractor, as in the first instance decision in *Clayton v Woodman & Son (Builders) Ltd*[1] where the perhaps trite proposition was endorsed that it was reasonable to appoint an architect to advise on building operations, and such a delegation will be the first stage in the occupier's avoidance of liability. Then he must also show that he chose an appropriately qualified contractor – thus for complex electrical work an occupier could not escape liability by appointing an unqualified workman or an electrician with a known record of drunkenness and incompetence. Finally, the occupier may be under a duty to check that the work has been carried out. The basic principle is that the occupier should check the work for any obvious defects which the untrained eye ought to observe,[2] and while in cases of greater technicality the occupier may not have such a supervisory duty, there the occupier may be obliged to import an appropriate professional man in a supervisory role, as in *AMF International Ltd v Magnet Bowling Ltd*,[3] where the defendants constructed a bowling alley for the plaintiffs, whose equipment was damaged by rain entering the building before its completion. The defendants argued that they had fulfilled their duties as occupiers by entrusting the relevant work to reputable independent contractors but this was rejected, since they had not used their architects to examine and report on the satisfactory outcome (or otherwise) of the work, and, in the words of section 2(4)(b) had not 'taken such steps (if any) as he reasonably ought in order to satisfy himself that . . . the work had been properly done'.[4]

1]1962] 2 QB 533, [1961] 3 All ER 249; revsd on another issue [1962] 2 QB 533, [1962] 2 All ER 33.
2 E g *Coupland v Eagle Bros Ltd* (1969) 210 Estates Gazette 581.
3 [1968] 2 All ER 789, [1968] 1 WLR 1028.
4 See North *Occupiers' Liability* pp. 141 ff.

2.33 It should be noted that the burden of proof lies on the defendant in trying to establish that a danger on his premises is due to the default of an independent contractor.[1] Also anyone entering onto premises as a result of a contract to which he is not a party, who will normally have an action under the 1957 Act if injured,[2] will not succeed in his claim if the defect in the premises is due to the work of an independent contractor.[3] Thus the occupier's defence that defects in his premises are the responsibility of an independent contractor is an important defence, but one circumscribed to some extent, and one which can only be relied on in appropriate circumstances, as has been seen. Perhaps the major defect in this area of the law is that these circumstances are not as precisely defined as they could be, as a result of various shortcomings in the drafting of section 2(4)(b) not hitherto noted. North[4] points out that the paragraph only refers to work of 'construction, maintenance and repair' carried out by independent contractors, thus implying that demolition, storage of goods on premises or supervisory work is outside the scope of this paragraph. The best answer is provided by Browne J in *Mullis v United States Lines Co*[5] (where improperly secured cargo fell onto the plaintiff, a docker), in pointing out that section 2(4) states that warning notices[6] and the intervention of independent contractors are only examples of the factors to be borne in mind when considering whether an occupier has fulfilled his duty of care, and that therefore other factors than those noted in the ensuing paragraphs can be utilised; thus, the words in the paragraph are in no way an exclusive list. It may also be observed that, according to section 2(4)(b), the occupier is not to be held liable for the danger 'without more', if he has duly entrusted the work to an independent contractor; no clear interpretation of these words has yet been provided and their role is quite unclear. Overall though, the defence seems workable, and it is submitted that the right balance is struck between the occupier and the visitor, and apart from the technical difficulties of parts of the drafting, section 2(4)(b) forms a worthy successor to the common law, as embodied by such well-known decisions as *Haseldine v C A Daw & Son Ltd*[7] and *Woodward v Hastings Corporation*.[8]

1   *Christmas v Blue Star Line and Harland and Wolff Ltd* [1961] 1 Lloyd's Rep 94.
2   S. 3. See para 2.34, below.
3   S. 3(2).
4   *Occupiers' Liability*.
5   [1969] 1 Lloyd's Rep 109.
6   S. 2(4)(a), above.
7   [1941] 2 KB 343, [1941] 3 All ER 156.
8   [1945] KB 174, [1944] 2 All ER 565.

2.34   The 1957 Act makes specific provision for visitors who enter in consequence of contracts, although not parties to the contract. Section 3 seeks to alter the common law rule that all persons entering premises under a contract were bound by the terms of that contract, including exemption clauses, irrespective of whether they were privy to the contract or not. Thus, workmen entering premises by dint of terms agreed between the tenant of the premises and his landlord or a servant of a passenger carrying his master's luggage onto a cruise liner before departure could be adversely affected by such clauses, perhaps even without their knowledge or consent. The section affects this situation by preventing any diminution by a contract term of a visitor's rights below the common duty of care, so long as the visitor is a stranger to the contract. On the other hand, if the contract seeks to protect such visitors by giving them greater rights, then the section will have the effect of permitting the old common law rules to operate and the visitor will take the benefit of the extra protection offered.

2.35   The 1957 Act has therefore generally succeeded both in its overall aims and its detailed application. It seems almost churlish to point to defective drafting and interpretation in places when comparisons may be drawn with the complications and difficulties of many of the common law rules that formerly governed this area. Indeed, the new law of occupiers' liability is in some key essentials very similar to the old – the close relationship between the two duties has been already discussed and the major change must be the removal of the technicality from the law.

Negligence actions against occupiers

2.36   In some cases, of course, negligence is still the appropriate method of framing an action against the occupier of defective premises, since a few cases will still fall outside the ambit of the 1957 Act. The various definitions in the Act lead to some cases falling outside it; some premises may be sufficiently impermanent to be incapable of being regarded as premises as defined by the Act,[1] so that if a plaintiff is injured by the collapse of the defendant's holiday tent, the ensuing liability may be considered under the normal principles of negligence; similarly some persons who may be regarded as occupiers in the usual sense of the word may not possess a sufficient degree of control over premises[2] to be regarded as occupiers under the 1957 Act; so any liabilities owed to his visitors by a short-stay hotel guest who has carelessly damaged his room may again be dealt with outside the framework of the 1957 Act in accordance with the rules of negligence liability.

1 See para 2.19, above.
2 See paras 2.4–2.9, above.

2.37 It is of particular importance to note the potential distinction between occupation of premises, and liabilities arising therefrom, and the carrying out of work on premises, and the often very different set of liabilities which are thereby created. The first point to make is simply that in many cases a person carrying out work on premises will not be an occupier – most independent contractors will not possess the requisite degree of control – and if the work causes injury to visitors to the premises, with the actual occupier often being able to rely on the defence that he has appointed an appropriate independent contractor, the visitor's only redress will be against the contractor in negligence.[1] However, beyond this it must also be recognised that there is a clear division in the practical approach to cases stemming from mere occupation of premises and those arising from work being carried out on premises. If a workman is injured by a large, fixed machine on his employer's premises, the case would be capable of being framed within the Occupiers' Liability Act – the workman is a visitor to his employer's premises and their dangerous condition can be regarded as a breach of the common duty of care. However, such an action would not be framed under the 1957 Act but rather under the various common law and statutory duties of the employer. Similarly, if the occupier of a stately home chooses to drive along his private road at 80 mph on his motor-cycle, hitting and injuring the postman on his way to deliver the mail at the house, the ensuing action would also be framed within the common law principles of negligence and not under the 1957 Act, though seemingly capable of being fitted within its terms. There are two reasons for this; one is the straightforward point that there may be two partially overlapping tortious duties (i e in the latter example a duty not to drive carelessly, and a duty not to be careless on one's premises) and that the plaintiff may opt to use only one of these, the one which seems to fit the facts best; the other reason is more complex and stems from certain ambiguities concerning the precise scope of the common law rules which were replaced by the rules in the 1957 Act. There are clear arguments to suggest that not all the duties imposed on the occupier at common law were replaced by the 1957 Act. These arguments stem from the fact that, before the enactment of the legislation, inventive advocates propounded many methods whereby the old common law's technicalities could be circumvented and, in particular, the courts were persuaded that the duties of the occupier related solely to defects arising from the overall condition of his premises and did not extend to dangers stemming from activities being carried out on the land. Denning LJ perhaps provides the clearest expression of this view in *Dunster v Abbott*,[2] explaining that the then relevant distinction between invitees and licensees was unimportant in a case where the premises were not themselves found to be inherently defective and stating that 'that distinction is only material in regard to the static condition of the premises. It is concerned with dangers which have been present for some time in the physical structure of the premises. It has no relevance in regard to current operations . . . [where] the duty of the occupier – or the person conducting the operations – is simply to use reasonable care in all the circumstances.' These principles were subsequently employed to render liable a hospital management committee who were responsible for the careless polishing of a ward floor on which the plaintiff had slipped and injured herself,[3] and a private railway operator whose locomotive had struck and injured the plaintiff, a pedestrian taking a short cut through the defendant's tunnel,[4] in each case without regard to the technicalities of the then rules of occupier's liability.

1 E g A C *Billings & Sons Ltd v Riden* [1958] AC 240, [1957] 3 All ER 1; *O'Connor v Swan and Edgars Ltd* (1963) 107 Sol Jo 215.
2 [1953] 2 All ER 1572, [1954] 1 WLR 58.
3 *Slade v Battersea and Putney Group Hospital Management Committee* [1955] 1 All ER 429, [1955] 1 WLR 207.
4 *Slater v Clay Cross Co Ltd* [1956] 2 QB 264,]1956] 2 All ER 625.

2.38 As to the precise point – whether the 1957 Act does embrace within its scope such 'activity duties'[1] – no clear answer emerges. Section 1(1) of the Act states that the Act replaces common law rules 'in respect of dangers due to the state of premises or to things done or omitted to be done on them', which indicates fairly clearly that 'activity duties' are replaced by the statutory duties laid down by the Act. However, section 1(2) goes on to say that the statutory duties established by the Act apply so as to 'regulate the nature of the duty imposed by law in consequence of a person's occupation or control of premises', firmly implying a restriction to duties stemming from mere occupancy of premises alone. Opinion appears greatly divided as to the solution to this apparent clash;[2] the words of section 1(2) could be taken as limiting the broad ambit of section 1(1), restricting the statutory rules to cover duties arising narrowly from 'occupation or control of premises' alone, and therefore much depends on the precise interpretation of that phrase. Injury caused by activities which are part of the normal incidents of occupation, such as gardening or do-it-yourself repair work (e g a visitor may fall over a carelessly discarded garden rake or may be injured by a negligently replaced slate falling from a roof), could be regarded as being within the scope of the Act; while injuries caused by abnormal activities on the land are less clearly within the words of section 1(2), so a visitor injured by an occupier carelessly practising his golf swing in his garden may be outside the ambit of the Act. Even then, though, the argument could still be raised that the visitor is only injured because the occupier is playing golf on his property by dint of his occupation of it. Only an activity not carried out with any reference to that occupation is undoubtedly outside section 1(2) on this broader interpretation, and it is difficult to find any appropriate examples. It may therefore be suggested that, in cases of doubt, actions in respect of injuries caused by activities on premises may be framed under the 1957 Act, though it may well be that in cases where the activity is not particularly related to the occupation of the land an ordinary negligence action may alternatively be brought.

1 I e duties arising from operations carried out on premises.
2 See *Winfield and Jolowicz on Tort* (11th edn) p. 196, n. 59.

2.39 In one other major respect an occupier may be held liable other than under the 1957 Act; this is where the person affected by the defective condition of the premises is not a lawful visitor to those premises. If he is an unlawful visitor, then the occupier's liability to him (if any) will be considered with reference to the principles laid down in *British Railways Board v Herrington*.[1] Equally if the victim of the defective premises is an occupier of adjacent land any actions will be considered under the principles of the tort of nuisance.[2] If, however, anyone suffers as a result of defects in premises, and is neither a visitor or an adjacent occupier, then this is a final case whereby the general law of negligence liability can affect an occupier. The best illustration of this is in *Cunard v Antifyre Ltd*.[3] In this case, the defendants neglected to repair some guttering on their premises which in consequence became detached and fell through the (glass) kitchen roof of the adjacent property owned by the plaintiff, injuring his wife who was in the kitchen at the time. The wife's only possible cause of action lay in negligence since she had no interest in the property and was thus prevented from bringing an action in nuisance,[4] and it was duly held that she was a foreseeable victim of the defendants' negligence, and thus was successful in her action. Subsequently, in *Taylor v Liverpool Corporation*,[5] the defendants were held to be liable in negligence when their chimney fell onto tenants of the property while they were in the adjacent yard; this liability was irrespective of whether the yard was subject to the tenancy or not. Thus, the occupier clearly owes a duty to occupiers of adjoining premises not to be negligent, though this may be subject to particular rules. In the recent case of *Thomas v Gulf Oil Refining Ltd*,[6] the defendants were engaged in the construction of a railway line on their land and, in doing so, allegedly adversely affected the water-table under adjacent land, including the plaintiff's; his ornamental lake drained, as did his ponds for watering his cattle; however it was held that there was no liability in nuisance or negligence for interference with the undefined percolation of subterranean waters. Equally, claims may fail where the facts do not disclose a breach of duty, as in *Knight v Hext*,[7] where the defendant's tree fell onto the plaintiff's adjacent barn; the county court judge found that the defendant had been negligent in not heeding a prior warning about the state of the tree from the plaintiff, but the Court of Appeal noted that the period of eleven days between the warning and the accident included the Christmas holiday period and therefore concluded that there was nothing else the defendant could have been reasonably expected to do.

1 [1972] AC 877, [1972] 1 All ER 749.
2 See paras 2.46 ff, below.
3 [1933] 1 KB 551.
4 See para 2.46, below.
5 [1939] 3 All ER 329.
6 (1979) 123 Sol Jo 787.
7 (1979) 253 Estates Gazette 1227.

Liability under *Rylands v Fletcher*

2.40 However, the legal duties owed by occupiers to their neighbours, irrespective of those neighbours' legal status, does not end here. There is also a need to consider liability under the rule in *Rylands v Fletcher*;[1] this may shortly be described as the duty imposed on the occupier not to cause noxious and dangerous substances to escape from his premises, and is regarded as representing a stricter form of liability. This relative strictness is however to a considerable degree counter-balanced by the fact that this particular form of occupiers' liability is closely circumscribed in its application. The original rule was formulated as the judicial response to a case where the defendant constructed a reservoir on his premises and, due to the presence of old mine-workings, caused the plaintiff's nearby mine to become flooded. The defendants were not negligent, and the case was not founded on the principles of nuisance (which may have been appropriate) but rather on a separate principle which Blackburn J, in the Court of Exchequer Chamber (affirmed by the House of Lords), stated to be that 'the person who for his own purposes brings on his land and collects and keeps there anything likely to do mischief if it escapes, must keep it in at his peril, and, if he does not do so, is prima facie answerable for all the damage which is the natural consequence of its escape'. He went on to explain that Act of God or default of the plaintiff would be capable of being used as defences, but that otherwise the defendant should take the responsibility of having introduced onto the land something dangerous and (this was a gloss added by the House of Lords) non-natural in character. Such then is how the rule began; what we must now consider is its scope and relevance today.

1 (1866) LR 1 Exch 265; affd (1868) LR 3 HL 330, HL.

2.41 Firstly, there has to be a deliberate collection of things not normally on the land for an action to succeed; this will often prevent claims from succeeding as in *Seligman v Docker*,[1] where a spontaneous natural gathering of pheasants on the land as a result of abnormal weather conditions was held not to satisfy this test, since there was no intention on the landowner's part to attract them. Equally, in *Pontardawe RDC v Moore-Gwyn*,[2] where naturally weathering rocks fell from an outcrop on the defendant's land, there was no liability – this was an ordinary, natural rockfall and the defendant could not be said to have collected the rocks in any way. However, in *Crowhurst v Amersham Burial Board*,[3] the defendants were held liable for growing a yew tree, and allowing its branches with their poisonous berries to hang over an adjacent field to the detriment of the plaintiff's cattle therein; it was held not to be natural for a poisonous tree to be planted and allowed to grow in this fashion. This leads into a second consideration; for an action to succeed there must be a 'non-natural user' of the land. By this term, it is endeavoured to signify that the occupier is not liable for ordinary activities, but only special usages with an element of risk to others attached.[4] The problem that arises is that over the last century or so since these rules were formulated society's conception, and the courts' conception, of what is a special use has greatly changed. So, in the 1920s, the House of Lords could say[5] that an explosion at a munitions factory would cause liability to arise under the rule in *Rylands v Fletcher*, thus clearly connoting that the manufacture of explosives was a non-natural user of premises. After a further major war, however, the House had great difficulty in following the earlier case, and eventually merely avoided the issue, Lord Macmillan stating that he would hesitate to regard a munitions factory as being a non-natural user of land.[6] Therefore there seems little need to look at the many decisions (often controversial in their day) from the past on what amounts to a non-natural user of land. Rather, the correct approach must now be to consider what is an unnatural land use in the light of the circumstances in today's industrialised society, but with special regard to the amount and precise character of the allegedly dangerous substances and the character of the surrounding neighbourhood.[7] So, for example, a munitions factory in a predominantly residential area may still be a non-natural user; a particularly large accumulation of tyres might come within the rule if they caught fire, but a chemical works or oil refinery in an appropriate site, away from housing and major roads, would probably not be regarded as a non-natural user of land, notwithstanding the potentially serious consequences of an accident at the plant.

1 [1949] Ch 53, [1948] 2 All ER 887.
2 [1929] 1 Ch 656.
3 (1878) 4 Ex D 5.
4 See *Rickards v Lothian* [1913] AC 263 at 278–280.
5 *Rainham Chemical Works Ltd v Belvedere Fish Guano Co* [1921] 2 AC 465.
6 *Read v J Lyons* [1947] AC 156, [1946] 2 All ER 471.
7 *Mason v Levy Auto Parts of England* [1967] 2 QB 530, [1967] 2 All ER 62.

2.42 A third factor to be present before liability can be established under the rule in *Rylands v Fletcher* is that the cause of the incident must be inherently dangerous – 'likely to do mischief', in Blackburn J's words. This again poses difficulties, since it fudges the major distinction between latent and patent dangers, and between things dangerous in themselves and those dangerous only in combination with other materials. So, a stool with a leg missing may not be inherently dangerous, since only a fool would sit on it; however, a stool with a hidden defect in one leg would be highly dangerous. Equally, a substance such as sodium is of no great danger by itself, but produces an explosion if it comes into contact with water; a loaded gun with a safety catch is only dangerous if in the hands of an untrained child who may unwittingly fire the weapon. Perhaps the best example is water – a harmless substance normally but the very substance which caused liability to arise in *Rylands v Fletcher* itself. Blackburn J in that case gave some examples of how the new principle should work which are still instructive; he referred to escaping cattle harming a neighbour's crops, sewage entering adjoining cellars, or noxious fumes escaping from a nearby factory. It could be said that cattle are not inherently dangerous, but the point must be that cattle which are loose in a field of crops can be properly so regarded; fumes released into the atmosphere are not dangerous, but become so when in proximity to persons or animals. In other words, the situation after the substance or article in question has escaped is considered when the assessment of danger should be made.

2.43 This brings the discussion to the fourth key prerequisite of this form of liability – this is a simpler but still crucial point, viz that there must be an escape of the substance or article complained of from the defendant's premises. This was one of the factors preventing the plaintiff from successfully claiming in *Read v J Lyons & Co Ltd*[1] where she was working in the defendant's factory when a shell exploded, injuring her. The House of Lords emphasised that there was no escape from the defendant's factory; in other words, an action under the rule in *Rylands v Fletcher* would only have been appropriately brought by anyone injured on an adjoining road or in nearby premises. A further important requirement to be satisfied before the rule in *Rylands v Fletcher* can be used is that its application is confined to cases where a noxious substance or material escapes from the defendant's own premises. Thus only an occupier of premises can be liable in such cases. However, the definition of occupier does seem to be relatively wide-ranging for these purposes, covering virtually any interest in land, such as a statutory franchise or a person's licence to use the highway.[2] One question still unsolved by the decided cases is whether the rule in *Rylands v Fletcher* extends so as to allow the plaintiff to claim for his personal injuries. In *Read v Lyons*,[3] the House of Lords was divided on this question; the plaintiff had only suffered personal injuries and Lord Macmillan said that the rule derived from the obligations stemming from ownership of property[4] and therefore the action could not succeed on this ground also. However, the other four judges were not so clear in their view: two made no comment and the general view was that the extension of liability to include personal injuries would be a novel proposition. It seems likely that Lord Macmillan's view is incorrect as applied to an occupier who suffers personal injury,[5] who would certainly be able to claim in a similar or associated nuisance action, while in *Shiffman v Order of St John*,[6] a non-occupier plaintiff succeeded in claiming for personal injuries when the defendant's flagpole fell on him; Atkinson J found the defendants liable both in negligence and under the rule in *Rylands v Fletcher*.

1 [1947] AC 156, [1946] 2 All ER 471.
2 See *Winfield and Jolowicz on Tort* (11th edn) pp. 404–405.
3 [1947] AC 156, [1946] 2 All ER 471.
4 Ibid at 173 and 477.
5 *Hale v Jennings Bros* [1938] 1 All ER 579.
6 [1936] 1 All ER 557.

2.44 The availability of defences – Act of God[1] and default of plaintiff – has already been noted, but other defences have also been successfully utilised. Chief amongst these is the defence of 'common benefit'. In other words, if the alleged hazard exists so as to provide a benefit (in normal circumstances) for both plaintiff and defendant, can the plaintiff sue the defendant when problems arise? The most recent case on this is *Dunne v North Western Gas Board*[2] where a gas explosion occurred in a main for reasons unknown (thus preventing any successful negligence action being brought). The Court of Appeal stated that one of the main reasons why they would not uphold the plaintiffs' claims under the rule in *Rylands v Fletcher* was this very factor of common benefit. The plaintiffs were members of the community which the gas board had laid the pipes to serve. This seems harsh; the consumer only consents to the provision of gas in the absence of explosions, and the case does not stand easily alongside *Northwestern Utilities Ltd v London Guarantee and Accident Co Ltd*.[3] There, the Privy Council found the appellants liable under the rule in *Rylands v Fletcher* for an explosion of their gas which had destroyed a hotel, without reference to the notion of common benefit. The basis of the defence of common benefit is presumably that the plaintiff has consented to the presence of the hazard; perhaps, it is submitted, the best solution is to make the defendant liable in such situations merely for less foreseeable disasters to which the plaintiff has not, and would not have, if asked, consented. There are few other defences. If a third party creates the hazard which subsequently causes harm then it may be possible for the defendant occupier to escape liability. The main case on this is *Northwestern Utilities Ltd v London Guarantee and Accident Co Ltd*.[4] There the Privy Council stated clearly that third party intervention could amount to an excuse, but equally circumscribed its availability by stating that in many circumstances, including the instant case, the defendant might be under a duty to check and investigate the possibility of such intervention, and might be held liable in negligence for failure so to do; the defence therefore will apply only where the intervention and its consequences are beyond the actual or possible control of the occupier. Additionally, where a statute clearly mandates the presence of a potential hazard, this can act as a defence,[5] except in the case of reservoirs.[6] It should also be noted that there is a developing tendency to regard an absence of fault on the part of the defendant as a possible defence. *Dunne v Northwestern Gas Board*[7] is an excellent example of this; Sellers LJ giving the judgment of the Court of Appeal, distinguished *Rylands v Fletcher* itself on the basis that unlike the instant case there was negligence there, thus implying strongly that liability under the rule in *Rylands v Fletcher* can only arise in cases where fault is present. Perhaps in consequence of this clear statement, no case has yet been brought which would necessitate a court testing the validity of this view.

1 See *Greenock Corpn v Caledonian Rly Co* [1917] AC 556.
2 [1964] 2 QB 806, [1963] 3 All ER 916.
3 [1936] AC 108.
4 Ibid.
5 *Green v Chelsea Waterworks Co* (1894) 70 LT 547.
6 Reservoirs Act 1975, Sch 2.
7 [1964] 2 QB 806, [1963] 3 All ER 916.

2.45 The foregoing has been a very brief discussion of the principal tenets of liability under the rule in *Rylands v Fletcher*. This relative brevity is not accidental; the action is no longer of anything more than slight practical importance. In fact, no reported case has provided an example of a successful utilisation of the rule since at least 1945. While the rule does provide a stricter form of liability, in accordance with more recent developments elsewhere in the law of tort, this of itself has been not enough, given the very limited ambit which has been the rule's downfall. With ever-increasing levels of industrialisation, the concept of the 'non-natural user' of land has become increasingly artificial and restrictive and prospective plaintiffs have found it increasingly difficult to use the rule. Because large-scale industry is not regarded as a non-natural user, major explosions, such as that at the Flixborough chemical works in 1974 are unlikely to be covered by an application of the rule, although the kind of incident that may have been envisaged by its formulators in the nineteenth century. Similarly, cases may fall on the doctrine of common benefit as now widely formulated[1] and it may be difficult to sue any nationalised industry under the rule, even if they can be regarded as collecting material 'for their own purpose'.[2] One of the main rationales of the action was to provide in serious cases an action where proof of fault was not necessary, but this distinction has now become clouded and the action cannot be brought when there is no fault, if *Dunne v Northwestern Gas Board*[3] is correctly decided. In any case, many instances are now unlikely to be dealt with by an application of the rule in *Rylands v Fletcher*, but are covered by specific statutory intervention.[4] However, the importance of the availability of a strict liability remedy in certain cases currently within the ambit of *Rylands v Fletcher* is emphasised by the Pearson Report[5] which recommended[6] that, in view of the inadequacies and technicalities of the present rules, there should be created a statutory scheme whereby strict liability would be imposed on the controller of dangerous articles or activities in the event of death or personal injury being caused thereby. The proposal is that a list of prescribed articles and activities be drawn up through the medium of statutory instruments passed under a general enabling Act, with regard to the serious consequences of any incident involving them and to the degree of skill or supervision necessary for their adequate control. No action has yet been taken with regard to the implementation of this proposal.

1 See para 2.44, above.
2 See *Dunne v Northwestern Gas Board* [1964] 2 QB 806, [1963] 3 All ER 916.
3 Ibid.
4 See paras 2.75 ff, below.
5 Royal Commission on Civil Liability and Compensation for Personal Injury, Cmnd 7054 (1978).
6 Ibid, para 1651.

Nuisance

2.46 The condition of an occupier's premises may cause him to be held liable in the tort of nuisance if they affect neighbouring landowners, persons using adjacent highways or the community at large. All may be able to bring an action in nuisance, but there are several different kinds of nuisance action, based on somewhat different rules and principles. It is therefore important to distinguish between these three different potential plaintiffs or groups of plaintiffs. In considering the occupier's liability to neighbouring landowners we immediately enter the domain of the tort of private nuisance. For an action in private nuisance to be brought, the plaintiff must have an interest in land; the action essentially exists so as to protect such an interest, as explained in *Sedleigh-Denfield v O'Callaghan*.[1] There, a pipe on the respondent's land had been incorrectly laid without his consent, causing floodwater to spread to the plaintiff's own land. The respondent was held liable even though not responsible for placing the defective pipe in position since it was his land and responsibility would therefore fall on him for its condition insofar as it affected his neighbour. The action's derivation was explained by Lord Wright[2] as stemming from the old action on the case for nuisance which had as its basis the correlative duties arising from occupation or possession of neighbouring portions of land. Thus the occupier of defective premises need only fear an action in private nuisance from a limited range of other occupiers – landowners and tenants can obviously sue, as can owners of incorporeal hereditaments, as in *Nicholls v Ely Beet Sugar Factory Ltd*[3] where the defendants would have been held liable for damage caused by their effluent to the plaintiff's enjoyment of fishing rights further down the river, were it not solely for the plaintiff's failure to establish a causal link between the pollution and the harm suffered. Anyone with a reversionary interest in land can also claim if the nuisance is likely to affect the premises when they inherit them.[4] Others, however, seem to have no rights of action in private nuisance, for example licensees without possession including members of the occupier's household with no rights in the property, as in *Cunard v Antifyre Ltd*.[5] One further limitation that should be noted comes from *Bridlington Relay Ltd v Yorkshire Electricity Board*[6] where the defendant's power cable ran close to the plaintiffs' television mast threatening to interfere with its transmissions. The plaintiffs' attempts to preserve their business did not succeed, though this is not to say that the action in private nuisance does not extend to protect business interests, rather it was held that the ability of the population of Bridlington to enjoy clear television transmissions in their homes was, as a mere recreation, not enough to justify protection by an action in private nuisance and the plaintiffs' business was one too specially sensitive[7] to merit protection.

1 [1940] AC 880, [1940] 3 All ER 349.
2 Ibid at 902–903 and 363–364.
3 [1936] Ch 343.
4 *Jones v Llanrwst UDC* [1911] 1 Ch 393.
5 [1933] 1 KB 551. See also para 2.39, above.
6 [1965] Ch 436, [1965] 1 All ER 264.
7 See also *Robinson v Kilvert* (1889) 41 ChD 88.

2.47 Liability in private nuisance falls on the occupier who creates a nuisance irrespective of whether he still owns the land or not.[1] The creator of the nuisance will be liable invariably irrespective of whether the occupier is or not. In some cases, however, the occupier will seek to avoid liability by claiming that the nuisance was created by an independent contractor working on the premises. At least in cases where the nuisance is an inevitable consequence of the work being undertaken, the excuse will not succeed, as in *Matania v National Provincial Bank Ltd and Elevenist Syndicate Ltd*,[2] where the plaintiff, a music teacher, complained successfully about the interference caused by major redesigning work being carried out on the floor of a building below that which he occupied. Indeed, it may well be that the occupier will always be liable for his independent contractor, if *Spicer v Smee*[3] is correct. The parties owned adjacent wooden bungalows and when the defendant's bungalow caught fire, the plaintiff's was also destroyed. The fire was caused by defective wiring installed by an independent contractor. Atkinson J emphasised the owner's clear duty to be responsible for his premises and stated that the occupier would normally be liable for the default of his independent contractor in cases where nuisances were created: 'where danger is likely to arise unless work is properly done, there is a duty to see that it is properly done'.[4] One further case of relevance to this issue is *Salsbury v Woodland*.[5] The independent contractor negligently felled a tree and the trial judge found the occupier of the land on which the tree was growing liable for his defaults; the Court of Appeal overruled this and firmly reiterated the usual rule that the occupier was not liable for the negligence of the independent contractor in such a case as the instant one. So the extent to which the occupier can rely on the use of an independent contractor to avoid liability in nuisance is unclear, but clearly the level of reliance is more limited in nuisance cases than in others.

1 *Thompson v Gibson* (1841) 7 M & W 456.
2 [1936] 2 All ER 633.
3 [1946] 1 All ER 489.
4 Ibid at 495.
5 [1970] 1 QB 324, [1969] 3 All ER 863. On the facts, nuisance was held to be inappropriate.

2.48 On other occasions the nuisance may in fact be the result of a third party's intervention without the permission of the occupier, as in *Sedleigh-Denfield v O'Callaghan*.[1] There the blockage in the drainage pipes was apparently the result of negligent work carried out by the local authority though without the landowner's permission. However, it was held that the blockage had been there for such a long time (almost three years) that the occupier had effectively adopted the nuisance and was therefore liable for it. He had at least constructive knowledge of the nuisance. If of course he had had no reasonable opportunity to discover the actual or potential nuisance then he would not be liable; the liability would have fallen solely on the trespasser who had brought the state of affairs into being. More problematical has been the case where a nuisance has been created naturally, beyond the control of the occupier (i e by Act of God) and the extent to which he has to abate it. The leading case on this issue is now *Goldman v Hargrave*,[2] a decision of the Privy Council on appeal from Australia. A large redgum tree on the appellant's land was struck by lightning and caught fire and had to be felled, the fire then being left to burn itself out. A couple of days later the weather changed dramatically and hot, dry and windy conditions prevailed. Inevitably the fire rekindled itself and spread to the respondent's land. The question was whether the appellant was obliged to deal (and deal successfully) with the outbreak, and the issue was considered as a question in the law of negligence, not nuisance.[3] It was held that the occupier owned a general duty to his neighbours (in the physical sense) to remove or reduce naturally occurring hazards on his land, though whether the duty had been fulfilled in any given case would depend on a whole range of factors, including 'knowledge of the hazard, ability to foresee the consequences of not checking or removing it and the ability to abate it',[4] with due regard to the financial and physical resources of that occupier and his neighbours. The appellant was held liable, since the hazards of bush-fires were obvious and the fire could easily have been extinguished. More recently the case's obvious applicability to nuisance actions has led to the decision in *Leakey v National Trust*,[5] where it was explained[6] that the whole basis of the decision in *Goldman v Hargrave* involved issues of nuisance. In *Leakey*, O'Connor J was faced with an unusual set of facts; the defendants owned a small hill and the plaintiffs owned cottages at the foot of the slope and occasional minor falls of earth and rocks from the hill increased in frequency and size after the unusual weather conditions experienced in 1976–77. The plaintiffs' claim succeeded on an application of *Goldman v Hargrave*, the judge stating that the defendants knew of the condition of their land (the land itself was effectively defective) and the effect it would have on the plaintiffs' premises and so were responsible for the resulting damage, if reasonable steps were not taken; the defendants had taken no such steps. The Court of Appeal fully upheld the decision of the trial judge. It is submitted that there is now no doubt that an occupier may be held liable in private nuisance for naturally created hazards on his premises. A further instance where the occupier may seek to blame someone else for the condition of his premises is when the nuisance complained of is allegedly the creation of the previous owner or occupier of the premises in question. A clear answer to this problem is provided by *St Anne's Well Brewery Co v Roberts*.[7] The defendants owned part of the old city wall of Exeter which collapsed onto the plaintiff's inn, destroying the greater part of it. The cause of this collapse was some part excavation into the wall by persons unknown, but this only came to light after the collapse occurred. The defendants were held not liable since they could not have found the defect in their premises other than, perhaps, by a major excavation and it was therefore not reasonable to hold them responsible. This decision, in itself just, also seems capable of standing alongside *Goldman v Hargrave*.

1 [1940] AC 880, [1940] 3 All ER 349. See para 2.46, above.
2 [1967] 1 AC 645, [1966] 2 All ER 989.
3 Ibid at 656–657 and 991–992.
4 Ibid at 663 and 996.
5 [1978] QB 849, [1978] 3 All ER 234; affd [1980] QB 485, [1980] 1 All ER 17.
6 [1978] QB 849 at 858, [1978] 3 All ER 234 at 241.
7 (1929) 140 LT 1.

2.49   The other area of case law which the landowner may find useful when trying to avoid liability in private nuisance is that concerning the relative responsibility of landlord and tenant for nuisance. The owner will only be found liable for nuisance in certain circumstances when the premises are let to a tenant since he will not normally be an occupier for the purposes of the law of nuisance. The owner will be liable if he knew or ought to have known of the nuisance before the date of the letting,[1] and this will be the case even where the tenant has covenanted to repair – while the tenant may well be held liable, the landlord too may be held responsible for pre-existing nuisances, as in *Brew Bros Ltd v Snax (Ross) Ltd*.[2] If the landlord has undertaken to repair then he will have sufficient control to ground liability in nuisance, even if he does not actually know of the defect, unless it be due to hidden natural processes or the acts of trespassers.[3] Equally, if the landlord has expressly or impliedly[4] reserved rights of entry and/or repair then he may be found liable for nuisances on the premises (per

Wilchick v Marks and Silverstone[5]), though in these cases the tenant too may not be exempt from blame – it is a question of fact in each case. In *Wilchick v Marks and Silverstone*[6] both landlord and tenant knew of the defect and both were held liable. Finally, a landlord may also be held liable in nuisance if in the creation of the tenancy he has authorised the activity which may give rise to complaints of nuisance e g if land is let for the purpose of tipping rubbish onto it, the landlord will be liable in the event of the creation of a nuisance, unless he can show that it was uniquely the fault of the tenant and not a nuisance inherent in the usual operation of rubbish-tips. However a limitation is added by *Smith v Scott*[7] where a local authority were not held liable for nuisance created by a problem family to whom they had let one of their houses; it was held that the local authority had in no way authorised the nuisance created by the family to their neighbours. To sum up then, liability in nuisance can affect a potentially wide range of occupiers; indeed since the creator of a nuisance may always be held responsible for it, the question of whether he is an occupier or not does not arise, other than in the particular cases outlined above, where the occupier has the opportunity to blame another party for the creation of the nuisance.

1 *Todd v Flight* (1860) 9 CBNS 377.
2 [1970] 1 QB 612, [1970] 1 All ER 587.
3 *Wringe v Cohen* [1940] 1 KB 229, [1939] 4 All ER 241.
4 *Mint v Good* [1951] 1 KB 517, [1950] 2 All ER 1159.
5 [1934] 2 KB 56.
6 Ibid.
7 [1973] Ch 314, [1972] 3 All ER 645.

2.50 Now consideration must be given to the standard of care laid down for the occupier by the tort of private nuisance, and much judicial and academic time has been devoted to the formulation of general definitions of the appropriate standard to be adopted. The basic duty of the occupier is not to interfere unreasonably with his neighbour's enjoyment of land, or at least not to so interfere if damage is thereby caused, since nuisance is not normally a tort actionable per se,[1] but rather damage has to be proved. The various formulations of the duty which have been provided explain reasonably clearly what is meant by 'unreasonable interference'. It has been said that regard should be had to the 'ordinary usages of mankind living in a particular society',[2] while Bramwell B in *Bamford v Turnley*[3] spoke of 'rules of give and take, or live and let live'. It should not be forgotten that the English law of nuisance has developed in an increasingly crowded island and an increasingly industrialised society with high population densities in many parts, and there is nothing in English law to say that any person shall be free from 'nuisances'. It may well be that interference with another's enjoyment of land is the concept at the heart of the law of nuisance, but the only actionable nuisance is an unreasonable interference, an interference which goes beyond what may be normally expected in society. In the words of Erle CJ in *Cavey v Ledbitter*,[4] 'the affairs of life in a dense neighbourhood cannot be carried on without mutual sacrifices of comfort; and that, in all actions for discomfort, the law must regard the principle of mutual adjustment'. The issue of reasonableness or otherwise is to be decided with regard to the suffering of the victim of the nuisance, and not to the reasonableness or otherwise with which the activity in question is being conducted.[5]

1 Cf *Nicholls v Ely Beet Sugar Factory* [1936] Ch 343: nuisance was held actionable per se once causation was established (criticised (1936) 52 LQR 463).
2 *Sedleigh-Denfield v O'Callaghan* [1940] AC 880 at 903, [1940] 3 All ER 349 at 364.
3 (1860) 3 B & S 62 at 63.

4 (1863) 13 CBNS 470 at 476.
5 *Street on Torts* (6th edn) p. 226.

2.51 Beyond these generalities, however, the cases which have developed the law of nuisance over the years have pointed to particular factors which should be borne in mind in considering the issue of reasonableness. Perhaps the most important and obvious of these is the nature of the locality where the activity being complained of takes place. The leading case is *St Helen's Smelting Co v Tipping*.[1] Shortly after the plaintiff had purchased a large estate in Central Lancashire, a mile and a half away a large smelting works commenced operations and the fumes and pollution from the works affected the estate, in fact causing physical damage to the shrubs and trees thereon. In a famous dictum, Lord Westbury LC stated, 'If a man lives in a town, it is necessary that he should subject himself to the consequences of those operations of trade which may be carried on in his immediate locality which are actually necessary for trade and commerce and also for the enjoyment of property and for the benefit of the inhabitants of the town and of the public at large.'[2] Perhaps a more famous and certainly a more succinct formulation of this concept is provided in *Sturges v Bridgman*[3] where Thesiger LJ[4] stated, 'What would be a nuisance in Belgrave Square would not necessarily be so in Bermondsey.' While the overtones of this comment have been frequently criticised in recent times, it still encapsulates the essence of this part of the law of nuisance. However, the law clearly does distinguish between tangible and intangible injuries in assessing the appropriate standard of care. In cases where the nuisance causes actual physical damage to the plaintiff's property and that damage is anything beyond a mere trifle, sufficient to affect its value, then that in itself will render the nuisance actionable and regard need not be had to the locality.[5] Intangible injuries will only make a nuisance actionable if they amount to a substantial interference with enjoyment; what amounts in fact to a substantial interference will of course ultimately be a question for the judge, in his discretion, to decide e g *Thompson-Schwab v Costaki*,[6] where an interlocutory injunction was awarded when the plaintiffs complained of nuisances caused by the presence of a neighbouring brothel, and *Halsey v Esso Petroleum Co Ltd*,[7] where a claim succeeded in relation to noises and smells emanating from the defendants' oil storage depot in a heavily built-up area of London. More recently, in *Hubbard v Pitt*,[8] Lord Denning MR held that a peaceful picket in support of tenants' rights outside an estate agent's office was not a nuisance in the absence of actual obstruction, violence or intimidation, but the other two Lords Justice of Appeal held that the plaintiffs had established a prospect of succeeding in an action for nuisance, and therefore granted an interlocutory injunction. Many other factors may be relevant in a given case e g the duration of the nuisance,[9] or its temporary or intermittent character.[10] Another factor which falls to be considered in some nuisance cases is whether it was reasonable to expect the occupier to prevent the nuisance. If this could be done without undue expense, or without undue inconvenience, then that would be a factor which would render the continuation of the nuisance unreasonable. On the other hand if only expensive and awkward methods of abatement are apposite, this may assist the occupier in his defence.

1 (1865) 11 HL Cas 642.
2 Ibid at 650.
3 (1879) 11 ChD 852.
4 Ibid at 865.
5 *St Helen's Smelting Co v Tipping* (1865) 11 HL Cas 642.
6 [1956] 1 All ER 652, [1956] 1 WLR 335.

7[1961] 2 All ER 145, [1961] 1 WLR 683.
8[1976] QB 142, [1975] 3 All ER 1.
9*Matania v National Provincial Bank Ltd* [1936] 2 All ER 633.
10*Bolton v Stone* [1951] AC 850, [1951] 1 All ER 1078.

2.52 Particular cases have given rise to less obvious factors e g *Heath v Mayor of Brighton Corporation*,[1] where the plaintiff, a vicar, complained that the defendants' power station emitted noise and vibration detrimental both to his church and himself. When the evidence showed that only the vicar himself was irritated by the activities at the power station and there was no evidence that use of the church had in fact altered, it was held that the plaintiff's complaints, though genuine enough, could be ascribed to an abnormal sensitivity, and his claim should not be upheld. A particular off-shoot of this principle arises in cases where it is the plaintiff's business, rather than the plaintiff himself, that is affected by the alleged nuisance. How far does the law of private nuisance extend so as to protect business interests? The answer seems to be that the law will not protect such interests where the business conducted has the effect of making the premises themselves unduly sensitive to intrusions from neighbouring premises. The principal authority here is still *Robinson v Kilvert*,[2] where a tenant of ground floor premises used them for storing brown paper, while the owner retained control of the cellar and used that area for the manufacture of paper-boxes, a process requiring much hot and dry air. Unfortunately this affected the value of the paper stored above, but it was held that this did not amount to an actionable nuisance since it only affected the particular type of paper stored there and this was far too narrow and delicate an interest to be protected. This attitude seems to be the usual view the court takes in such cases,[3] unless perhaps the defendant knows of the potential nuisance and can easily and economically remedy it.[4]

1 (1908) 98 LT 718.
2 (1889) 41 ChD 88.
3 E g *Whycer v Urry* [1955] CLY 1939.
4 *Grandel v Mason* [1953] 3 DLR 65.

2.53 A contemporary problem in the law of nuisance is that some industrial activities which may otherwise be likely to be a source of nuisance actions are also important components in the national economy or providers of essential goods, or indeed major employers in the area surrounding the premises. In view of this type of factor, some defendants in nuisance actions have claimed that the utility of their conduct to society in general, including the plaintiff, should be amongst the factors borne in mind by the court in assessing liability. The courts, however, have not responded to this invitation; the individual's own proprietary right to the enjoyment of property has continued to prevail over what may be regarded as the interests of the community at large.[1] In *Miller v Jackson*,[2] a village cricket club was found liable in nuisance for cricket balls escaping from their ground notwithstanding the benefits conferred on the village by possessing the club, although it should be noted that no injunction was issued, and Lord Denning MR, dissenting, held that there was no nuisance, with strong regard paid in his judgment to the public benefit conferred by the game.[3] However, in *Kennaway v Thompson*,[4] it was specifically stated that the public interest should not necessarily override private rights and a limited injunction severely restricting the use of speedboats on the defendant's lake was awarded to the plaintiff in lieu of the damages awarded to her by the trial judge. A distinct question which may be considered briefly here is that of the malicious

intention of the defendant in causing the nuisance – does the law say that fumes
from a bonfire, for example, become any more intolerable if it is known that the
bonfire is being burnt deliberately to annoy the plaintiff? The law seems fairly
clear that the presence of malice is a relevant factor. The best-known illustration
of this is *Christie v Davey*[5] where the defendant wood engraver allegedly inter
alia hammered trays on the party wall with, and made wailing noises in the
general direction of, the plaintiffs' house; the defendant attempted to justify this
conduct on the basis that equally noisy music lessons were held in the plaintiffs'
house. It was held that such noises were made deliberately to annoy the plaintiffs and this rendered them unreasonable. It is significant that the defendant's
counter-claim that the music lessons amounted to a nuisance was rejected by
the court; malice is a factor in considering 'give and take' between neighbours.
This is confirmed by *Hollywood Silver Fox Farm Ltd v Emmett*[6] where the
defendant caused guns to be fired on his land adjacent to the plaintiff's farm
during the breeding season with the specific sole intention of alarming the
animals. Doubtless this may be capable of being regarded as an actionable nuisance irrespective of the presence of malice, but the case is important for its
rejection as irrelevant of the House of Lords' decision in *Bradford Corporation v
Pickles*,[7] where the defendant was held entitled to extract water from his land,
even though this was done with the intention of diverting water otherwise
destined for the plaintiffs' reservoir. This case was held to be of no applicability
to nuisance, and may be distinguished effectively on the basis that the plaintiffs
had not acquired a title to the water at that time and had no valid legal right to
protect – in such circumstances the presence of malice cannot create new legal
rights. However, in nuisance cases the plaintiff has a legal right to reasonably
quiet enjoyment and malice is a relevant factor in deciding whether a nuisance
is actionable.

1 E g *Bellew v Cement Ltd* [1948] IR 61.
2]1977] QB 966, [1977] 3 All ER 338.
3 See also *Adams v Ursell* [1913] 1 Ch 269.
4 [1981] QB 88, [1980] 3 All ER 329.
5 [1893] 1 Ch 316.
6 [1936] 2 KB 468, [1936] 1 All ER 825.
7 [1895] AC 587.

2.54 Thus, in assessing the standard of care to be adopted in a private nuisance
action, a wide range of factors must be considered, and the court will often have
to make a survey of a wide range of authorities and a large number of facts in
reaching a decision. A good example of this is *Halsey v Esso Petroleum Co Ltd*[1]
where the claim involved nuisance by noise, smell and noxious acid smuts from
an oil depot in Fulham and took twelve days to hear including a site visit; the
testimony of forty-one witnesses was heard, including twenty-four local residents and the judgment of Veale J amounts to some 8,000 words, though
equally this contains a most careful analysis of both legal and factual issues.
Most cases of course do not attain such lengths, but nonetheless complexities
always seem to abound – the legal principles overlap, the facts have to be determined precisely and an added complication is provided by the choice of remedies available. Damages may not be regarded as an appropriate remedy in many
cases since immediate and continuing harm may be taking place. There is also
some doubt as to whether nuisance claimants can recover damages for personal
injuries suffered – no clear authority exists either way though it might be seen as
unduly artificial to restrict the action thus.[2] Many plaintiffs will be seeking an
injunction to prevent the defendant occupier using his land as he has been doing

and some judges may refuse an injunction as being an excessive interference with the defendant's rights, while nonetheless holding that there has been an actionable nuisance and that an appropriate sum by way of damages be paid. Thus, in *Miller v Jackson*,[3] for example, while both Cumming-Bruce LJ and Geoffrey Lane LJ held that the escape of cricket balls from the defendants' ground was an actionable nuisance, the former refused to grant an injunction because of the wider issues in the case – the public interest in the continuation of the traditional cricket matches.

1 [1961] 2 All ER 145, [1961] 1 WLR 683.
2 *Street on Torts* (6th edn) p. 233.
3 [1977] QB 966, [1977] 3 All ER 338.

2.55 Consideration must now be given to the availability of defences to occupiers faced with actions in nuisance against them. It is clear that the plaintiff's consent to the nuisance will bar his claim,[1] as will his contributory negligence, and prescription is also a defence i e that the occupier has been creating the alleged nuisance for more than twenty years to the (actual or constructive) knowledge of the plaintiff,[2] thereby effectively creating an easement. It should be particularly noted that it must be the actual nuisance that continues for twenty years, not merely an activity which subsequently gives rise to complaints, as in *Sturges v Bridgman*[3] where the plaintiff, a doctor, built a consulting room at the end of his garden and after beginning to use it became aware, for the first time, of noise and vibration from the defendant's property which stemmed from his trade (confectioner) which he had carried on for many years. However, since the nuisance had only recently begun to cause annoyance and thus become actionable the defendant's claim of prescription failed.

1 *Pwllbach Colliery Co v Woodman* [1915] AC 634.
2 *Liverpool Corpn v H Coghill & Son* [1918] 1 Ch 307.
3 (1879) 11 ChD 852.

2.56 Other defences, however, though occasionally attempted, now seem to be unlikely to succeed. Occupiers have in the past endeavoured to evade liability on the perhaps simplistic ground that they were in possession and creating the alleged nuisance when the plaintiff moved into adjacent property; in other words, the plaintiffs came to the nuisance and therefore should not be allowed to sue. This contention is however not accepted by the courts; once again *Miller v Jackson*[1] is the most recent authority. The defendant cricket club contended, inter alia, that the plaintiffs had purchased their houses knowing of their proximity to the ground but the Court of Appeal (Lord Denning MR dissenting) held themselves bound by previous authority and ruled in favour of the plaintiffs on the issue. Similarly, notwithstanding dicta in *Nicholls v Ely Beet Sugar Factory*[2] which imply the contrary, it seems fairly clear that *jus tertii* (superior right to plaintiff's land vested in third party) is not a defence to actions in private nuisance, where mere possession is enough to ground a claim.[3]

1 [1977] QB 966, [1977] 3 All ER 338.
2 [1936] Ch 343.
3 *Winfield and Jolowicz on Tort* (11th edn) p. 386.

2.57 More complex is the position in relation to statutorily permitted activities. If an occupier is, say, a water authority accused of perpetrating a nuisance from their sewage works, is it open to the authority to defend the action by saying that they were working under clear statutory authority in dealing with the sewage? An attempt to clarify this problematic area of the law has recently been made in *Allen v Gulf Oil Refining Ltd*[1] where the House of Lords considered an action brought by a plaintiff complaining that the operation of the defendant's refinery amounted to a nuisance; the defendants raised as a total defence the statutory authority that had been granted for the construction of the plant. It was held that, on due consideration of the Gulf Oil Refining Act 1965, the permission to erect the plant carried with it implied permission to operate the refinery when completed and that the company would be immune from a nuisance action in respect of its normal operation. However if the nuisance from the plant and its operation exceeded the nuisance that might be anticipated from the operation of a typical refinery, then Parliament's intention to render the company immune would be defeated in the face of the unexpected and unintended nuisance in fact emanating. In truth, however, the decision in any case will depend on the wording of the statute in question. Typical clauses found in many statutes are known as 'nuisance clauses', preserving neighbours' common law rights or, alternatively, compensation clauses which establish neighbours' rights to reasonable compensation notwithstanding that their nuisance claims will be defeated by the defence of statutory authority. So, the position appears to be that statutory authority will be a defence to nuisance actions in respect of the kind of nuisances which Parliament might reasonably be taken to have envisaged as arising when passing the statute in question, at least in cases where the nuisance arises directly from the activity and is an inevitable consequence thereof. The significance of this defence therefore remains, but it is now limited and the nuisance action can still be brought at least in respect of nuisances beyond those reasonably expected to emanate from the new plant and, as such, this important decision enables the nuisance action to remain a valuable weapon against the occupiers of major industrial plants, especially insofar as nuisance may provide a remedy without proof of fault.[2]

1 [1981] 1 All ER 353, [1981] 2 WLR 188.
2 See para 2.58, below.

2.58 A final important factor to be considered as a possible defence for the occupier faced with a nuisance claim is his own lack of fault. A defendant may try and avoid liability by saying, for example, that his tree collapsed onto neighbouring premises because of some kind of insect activity which no-one could have foreseen, or that his chemical plant exploded due to a sudden freak thunderstorm, and in such cases a plaintiff will be in some difficulty in many cases in actually proving the presence of fault. Firstly, it may well be that the defendant's knowledge (or otherwise) of the state of affairs in question may be a relevant factor in considering whether it is reasonable to hold him liable i e whether the interference with the plaintiff's rights was unreasonable or not. Beyond this, however, the law is more complicated. In *The Wagon Mound (No 2)*[1] the Privy Council were faced with a case concerning a dockyard fire which spread unexpectedly to adjacent premises, with liability both in nuisance and negligence falling to be considered. Lord Reid[2] addressed himself to the relationship of these two concepts stating that negligence is not an essential element in nuisance – this, it is submitted, is correct given that a nuisance will very often arise from intentional acts where considerations of negligence are of little assistance. He then went on to say, however, that although negligence is not essential, 'fault of some kind is almost always necessary'. This opaque clause has given much difficulty, in two principal ways. Firstly, there is the problem of the nature of the difference, if any, between 'fault' and 'negligence'. This is capable of resolution on the basis that fault here is a broad term, implying a responsibility for what has occurred, even without blame attaching. This is well illustrated in a recent Commonwealth decision, *Clearlite Holdings Ltd v Auckland City Corporation*,[3] where the defendants were responsible for tunnelling work under the plaintiff's premises which were damaged as a result. The action was brought alleging both negligence and nuisance, but the claims of negligence were rejected. This, however, did not prevent the nuisance claims from succeeding since, it was stated,[4] the nuisance action did not depend on the presence of negligent conduct, but could succeed simply if the defendants had taken a risk[5] in the course of their work, which albeit unforeseeably had not paid off. This seems inconsistent with Lord Reid's further comment[6] that it may be 'justifiable not to take steps to eliminate a real risk if it is small and if the circumstances are such that a reasonable man, careful of the safety of his neighbour, would think it right to neglect it'. Lord Reid clearly only intended to impose liability in nuisance when the defendant is in some way culpable; the New Zealand court however endeavours to retain a vestige of truly strict liability, and perhaps the question of the extent to which negligence and nuisance interrelate is answered by asking which is the correct view given that neither is binding authority, though of course Lord Reid's dicta carry greater weight. If Lord Reid is correct, the defendant occupier is placed in a more favourable position, only being held liable when culpable, or, to put matters more precisely, when able to prevent the harm which has occurred. The wider liability proposed in the *Clearlite* case in some way perhaps goes too far in imposing such a burden on the defendant that there is nothing that he can do to avoid liability if unforeseen circumstances militate against him, and Mahon J did not consider *The Wagon Mound (No 2)*. It is therefore submitted that Lord Reid's view is to be preferred – fault for the purpose of the laws of nuisance is an unreasonable failure to consider a risk. The other difficulty with the comment that fault of some kind is almost always necessary simply arises from the equivocation therein; when is fault not at all necessary in nuisance cases? No answer has yet been provided; either Lord Reid was uncharacteristically departing from his usual precision of language or there is some residual kind of nuisance action where fault is not necessary; perhaps the *Clearlite* case could be defended on this ground, though it is difficult to see anything unique in its facts; perhaps also it is a reference to the special rules concerning highways.[7]

1 [1967] 1 AC 617, [1966] 2 All ER 709.
2 Ibid at 639 and 716 respectively.
3 [1976] 2 NZLR 729.
4 Ibid at 740.
5 Ibid at 741.
6 *The Wagon Mound (No 2)* [1967] 1 AC 617 at 642–643, [1966] 2 All ER 709 at 718.
7 See paras 2.62 ff, below.

2.59 The relationship of nuisance and negligence is thus of paramount importance and it might be concluded from the foregoing that nuisance has no real role of its own. This however would be an overstatement since private nuisance should be regarded as a stricter form of liability (fault-based rather than negligence-based) even if not now a form of strict liability, and therefore still has a distinct role in the law of tort. Additionally, it has been suggested by Denning LJ (as he then was), in *Southport Corporation v Esso Petroleum Co Ltd*,[1] a public nuisance action, that in such cases once a nuisance is proved to have emanated from the defendant, the burden of proof shifts and he has to justify the activities complained of, in order to show why the nuisance should not be actionable. This seems a somewhat isolated view, and may be better formulated on the view adopted by Singleton LJ and adopted as an alternative by Denning LJ in the same case (though overruled by the House of Lords[2] on the facts of the case) that the doctrine of *res ipsa loquitur* was applicable to nuisance cases. There could also possibly be a difference where an activity capable of being characterised as a nuisance causes pure economic loss, e g if fumes carelessly emitted from X's glue factory affect the trade of Y's adjacent restaurant. In such a case, the loss of profit would in the absence of any direct physical damage not be claimable in a negligence action,[3] but it could be argued that this principle has not yet been extended to nuisance cases and, indeed, since the nuisance action is specifically designed to protect enjoyment of land, this extension should not be permitted to take place.

1 [1954] 2 QB 182 at 197, [1954] 2 All ER 561 at 571.
2 [1956] AC 218, [1955] 3 All ER 864.
3 *SCM(UK) Ltd v W J Whittall & Son Ltd* [1971] 1 QB 337, [1970] 3 All ER 245.

2.60 Private nuisance and public nuisance are closely related – both hinge upon the interference by one with another's rights; both may well provide appropriate remedies in some fact situations, such as a major escape of fumes. Notwithstanding the foregoing, however, there are major differences, perhaps the most significant of which is that public nuisance is also a common law crime and a civil action may therefore only be brought in certain limited circumstances. As will be seen, though, public nuisance is capable of playing a not insignificant role amongst the prospective civil liabilities of the occupier of defective premises. The typical plaintiff will have to fall into one of two categories. To bring a civil claim under this heading, the prospective plaintiff has either to be one of a whole class of people affected by the activity complained of, or else will be the user of an adjoining highway. The justification for these restrictions appears to centre on the idea that the action is to be used in circumstances when it is unreasonable to expect one person to take legal action against an actual or prospective polluter, but where rather it is properly the responsibility of the community at large;[1] hence the criminal action, but also, where specific damage is shown to have resulted, the possibility of an aggrieved individual seizing on the fact that not only has a crime been committed, but that this has also caused him the specific damage complained of. Even then, however, the prospective plaintiff has to satisfy certain requirements. To bring his action he must establish that he has suffered loss and show that that loss is beyond that incurred by others affected by the alleged nuisance.[2] Any plaintiff may request the Attorney-General to apply for an injunction to prevent a public nuisance, where the usual criminal sanction is inadequate, by means of a relator action. It must also be established that the loss suffered is of sufficient magnitude to warrant legal protection.[3] Indeed, in this as in most other respects, a public nuisance claim will be dealt with in a similar fashion to a private nuisance claim – ultimate success will again depend on 'give and take' and general reasonableness as between the parties, irrespective of the fact that it is the plaintiff's more general rights that are being protected, not just his interest in land.[4] This is not to say, however, that the actions are identical. Quite apart from their use by different classes of plaintiffs, some differences may be discerned; in particular, there is no doubt that personal injuries are compensable in public nuisance actions,[5] while prescription is never a defence to a public nuisance claim.[6] It is also possible that the burden of proof is different in public nuisance cases.[7]

1 After Denning LJ in *A-G v PYA Quarries Ltd* [1957] 2 QB 169 at 191, [1957] 1 All ER 894 at 908.

2 *Rose v Miles* (1815) 4 M & S 101.
3 *Harper v G N Haden & Sons Ltd* [1933] Ch 298.
4 No such distinction was drawn in *The Wagon Mound (No 2)* [1967] 1 AC 617, [1966] 2 All ER 709.
5 E g *Mint v Good* [1951] 1 KB 517, [1950] 2 All ER 1159.
6 *Mott v Shoolbred* (1875) LR 20 Eq 22.
7 See para 2.60, above.

2.61 By far the most important problem in the law of public nuisance arises when it is being utilised by someone on a highway injured by a defect in premises adjoining the highway. The law is clear in its determination to protect the user of the highway from the sudden danger of falling masonry or branches and the problem is to maintain the balance between the highway user's right of passage and the occupier's interest in avoiding undue litigation. Thus, in *Noble v Harrison*,[1] part of the defendant's tree fell onto the adjacent highway, damaging the plaintiff's coach; it was held that though in general terms this was an appropriate case for a claim in public nuisance, in fact the defendant could not have known of the latent defect in the tree, and in the light of his lack of fault should not be held liable. Further, in *British Road Services Ltd v Slater*,[2] the occupier was held not liable when a road accident was caused indirectly by the over-hanging branch of an old tree, since the occupier could not be presumed to know of the slight danger posed by the branch, even after having occupied the premises for over twenty years. However, in other cases, all involving man-made structures rather than natural hazards, the courts have taken a harsher line. In *Tarry v Ashton*[3] a heavy lamp fell from the wall of the defendant's premises, injuring the plaintiff as she passed. It was held that the defendant had a duty to maintain the lamp so that it would not affect passing pedestrians and that delegation of its maintenance to a competent person would not amount to a defence. This case was followed by the Court of Appeal in *Wringe v Cohen*,[4] where the gable end of a house fell on to the plaintiff's shop in a storm. The defendant was held liable as landlord of the premises with responsibility to repair, irrespective of his lack of fault. Only the intervention of a trespasser or a latent defect will provide a defence, and then only in the absence of knowledge of the intervention or defect. The case is notable for a strong assertion of a strict form of liability,[5] though it may be queried whether the defences said to be available have the effect of considerably reducing the strictness. Its precise ambit is unclear; the report does not indicate whether it was a public or private nuisance; no mention is made of cases concerning similar natural hazards or why they were not regarded as relevant; the court's firm comments about nuisance to the highway are obiter. Though criticised, the case has not been overruled and it may therefore be said that the occupier of premises will owe a stricter duty to persons on adjacent highways, even if the effect of the exceptions permitted is to reduce the strictness of the liability in cases where the occupier cannot have known of the defect; however, following *Tarry v Ashton*,[6] the occupier will be strictly liable when the defaults of his independent contractor harm the user of the adjoining highway. He is responsible, if not at fault.

1 [1926] 2 KB 332.
2 [1964] 1 All ER 816, [1964] 1 WLR 498.
3 (1876) 1 QBD 314.
4 [1940] 1 KB 229, [1939] 4 All ER 241.
5 Ibid at 233 and 243 respectively.
6 (1876) 1 QBD 314.

2.62 Thus, the various aspects of the law of nuisance greatly affect the occupier. If the state of his premises is such as to cause interference to persons and property, liability in nuisance is likely to arise. Even though there are technicalities in the applicability and application of the tort, and notwithstanding the present situation where fault plays a dominant role, nuisance still has an independent role and is at once a valuable weapon in the plaintiff's armoury and a danger against which the occupier must guard in a wide range of cases, from disputes between neighbours about bonfires to major pollution incidents.

Occupiers' liability to trespassers

2.63 A final distinct set of common law rules governs the liabilities of the occupier of premises towards unlawful visitors on his land. Whether a visitor is or is not lawfully on the premises may in certain cases be unclear.[1] The legal relationship of occupier and trespasser has been greatly altered in recent years, and the law has moved far from its original stance that the occupier's right to his land, and the enjoyment of it, overrode any interest of the trespasser and the occupier could therefore often ignore the possible or actual presence of trespassers, as is well exemplified by *Robert Addie & Sons (Collieries) Ltd v Dumbreck*.[2] A child trespasser was playing on an unguarded item of machinery which was operated intermittently from another site; the child incurred fatal injuries when the machinery was suddenly activated, but the occupiers were held to be not liable, in the absence of any wilful intent to harm the child or recklessness as to his safety, and the law remained essentially unchanged, with emphasis instead placed on attempts to limit the category of trespassers, until 1972.

1 See paras 2.15–2.18, above.
2 [1929] AC 358.

2.64 In *British Railways Board v Herrington*,[1] the six-year-old plaintiff was injured while crossing an electrified railway line which bisected parkland owned by the National Trust. A footbridge was provided, but the plaintiff was by no means the first to cross the line through a well-defined, though unauthorised, track through the dilapidated fence and over the tracks themselves. There was evidence that the appellants knew of previous incidents when children had been seen on the lines near where the incident in question had occurred. The Court of Appeal held the appellants to have been in reckless disregard of the plaintiff's safety, and their appeal was ultimately unsuccessful since the House of Lords grasped the opportunity to reformulate entirely the law concerning the occupier's liabilities to trespassers on his premises, though since five separate judgments were given, the precise extent of the reformulation is somewhat unclear. Lord Reid held that occupiers were under a duty to be humane in their treatment of trespassers; they cannot remain callously indifferent to their presence, but in assessing whether they have done what they may reasonably be expected to do to safeguard trespassers regard should be had to a wide range of factors, including the expense of what needs to be done to protect trespassers, the resources available to the occupiers, their awareness (or otherwise) of the intrusion. Lord Morris of Borth-y-Gest made the crucial point, emphasising the change in the law, that the ownership of land was a ground of liability, not a cause for exemption from it, and that the occupier was under a duty to do what common humanity dictated – this would vary in each case with regard to the circumstances and the appellants should be held liable, given that there was a strong likelihood of trespass and the risk of grave injury if a trespass occurred. Lord Wilberforce stated that an occupier would owe a duty towards trespassers, for example, where the danger was near to a public place, or was a continuous peril, or one with likely grave consequences, or was one which might attract children; the nature and degree of the danger are considered, but always contrasted to the difficulty and expense of preventing the harm. Lord Pearson emphasised the appellants' failure to deter prospective trespassers, notwithstanding the regularity of the intrusion, while Lord Diplock held that, once it was known that trespassers were, or were likely to be, on an occupier's premises, a duty was owed to the trespassers by the occupier, with regard to such factors as the regularity with which danger occurred, the likely degree of attraction for children, and the expense of prevention and the availability of resources to the occupier. All five held the appellants liable, and what has come to be described as 'the duty of common humanity' was evolved.

1 [1972] AC 877, [1972] 1 All ER 749.

2.65 Fears that the different formulations would give rise to uncertainty have not (as yet) been fulfilled, and the range of factors to be considered is clear, and was well summarised by the Court of Appeal in *Pannett v McGuinness & Co Ltd*.[1] This case arose when the plaintiff, then aged five, entered a demolition site through an unguarded entrance, although he had previously been chased away on several occasions by the three men who had been detailed to guard the site (approximately 900 square metres in size). The plaintiff fell into a fire and was injured; his ensuing claim was upheld. Lord Denning MR outlined the relevant factors that could be distilled from *Herrington's* case.[2]

> (1) You must apply your commonsense. You must take into account the gravity and likelihood of the probable injury. Ultra-hazardous activities require a man to be ultra-cautious in carrying them out. The more dangerous the activity, the more he should take steps to see that no-one is injured by it. (2) You must take into account also the character of the intrusion by the trespasser. A wandering child or a straying adult stands in a different position from a poacher or burglar. You may expect a child when you may not expect a burglar. (3) You must also have regard to the nature of the place where the trespass occurs. An electrified railway line or a warehouse being demolished may require more precautions to be taken than a private house. (4) You must also take into account the knowledge which the defendant has, or ought to have, of the likelihood of trespassers being present. The more likely they are, the more precautions may have to be taken.

Applying these useful guidelines, the Court of Appeal held that there was such a risk of intrusion, especially in the late afternoon, which was when the incident took place, a better (i e even more expensive) guard should have been maintained by the occupiers. Further cases have shown the new principle to be functioning effectively; in *Harris v Birkenhead Corporation*,[3] the defendants were held liable for their failure to secure a derelict house in which a trespassing four-year-old girl was injured, while in *Southern Portland Cement Ltd v Cooper*[4] the Privy Council emphasised that where there was a serious danger from an allurement on premises (here a large soil heap close to a powerful live electric wire), the duty placed on the occupier would be a relatively onerous one, which the occupiers in the case had failed to fulfil, given that they knew that intrusions onto their premises often occurred. The other side of the coin is demonstrated by *Penny v Northampton Borough Council*,[5] where the infant plaintiff failed in his claim in respect of injuries incurred while trespassing on the defendants' rubbish tip. The Court of Appeal conceded that the regular trespasses of children were known to the defendants, but they could not be expected to foresee the actual incident which took place – the plaintiff was injured by an exploding aerosol can thrown onto a fire by another trespasser.

1 [1972] 2 QB 599, [1972] 3 All ER 137.
2 Ibid at 607 and 141.
3 [1976] 1 All ER 341, [1976] 1 WLR 279.
4 [1974] AC 623, [1974] 1 All ER 87.
5 (1974) 72 LGR 733, 118 Sol Jo 628.

2.66 One principal problem which does remain to be considered is the way in which the new principle will affect the adult trespasser. All the recent cases have involved young children, and much stress has been laid on the ignorance of children of the perils which may be encountered while trespassing, and the frequency with which they trespass i e the predictability of their trespassing. Clearly these factors are not so applicable in cases involving adults. Only one case has so far discussed the application of the new principles to adult trespassers viz the Court of Appeal decision in *Westwood v Post Office*.[1] (The case went on appeal to the House of Lords,[2] but they held, on a point of statutory construction, that the plaintiff was not a trespasser when the incident occurred.) Lawton LJ[3] held that the plaintiff was a trespasser on entering a lift motor room *en route* to a break from work, since this was not an authorised route. He stepped onto a trap-door in the room and fell through it, incurring fatal injuries, but since his employers had not foreseen the likelihood of the room being used as a short-cut, and had posted prohibitory notices on its door, Lawton LJ held that the admittedly unsafe condition of the floor did not render the defendants liable. It is submitted that this decision is correct – where there is no reason to anticipate a trespass, there is no reason to take any precautions against trespassers. However, the case does pose the question whether the adult trespasser will ever successfully sue the occupier. It is submitted that where an adult trespasser is injured by something the danger of which he can appreciate, e g an electrified railway line, or a deep pool which is the subject of clear warning notices, he will rarely be able to claim, unless his presence on the land is clearly predictable; this is in spite of the fact that a child may be able to sue in such a case, since the child is less able to appreciate the hazards and may not be able to read or to understand the significance of a warning notice. On the other hand, when there is a hidden hazard on the land which no one could reasonably be expected to anticipate, such as a deep mineshaft invisible in long grass, the adult and child should be treated alike, since neither can know of the danger.

1 [1973] QB 591, [1973] 1 All ER 283.
2 [1974] AC 1, [1973] 3 All ER 184.
3 *Westwood v Post Office* [1973] QB 591 at 608, [1973] 1 All ER 283 at 286.

2.67 One minor problem should also be briefly noted. The occupier may feel that he can protect himself against his potential liability to trespassers by exclusion clauses in the form of notices at the entrances to his premises, but, though permissible at common law, this may now fall foul of the Unfair Contract Terms Act 1977.[1] The controls on exclusion clauses and notices laid down by the Act apply to attempts to exclude liability for negligence and this is defined, inter alia, by section 1(1)(b) as including 'any common law duty to take reasonable care or exercise reasonable skill (but not any stricter duty)' – does this include the duty of common humanity? This duty is certainly a creature of the common law, but it is more difficult to assess whether it may be characterised as a duty 'to take reasonable care', which arguably creates an impression of the traditional negligence action. It is submitted, however, that the duty of common humanity does involve an obligation to take reasonable care in the situations where it arises, albeit perhaps at a lower level than in an ordinary negligence action. Therefore the occupier is not free even to erect notices warning trespassers of their lack of rights on entry; as has been seen, such notices will be of no effect in the event of the trespasser being killed or injured, will only take effect in the event of their being adjudged reasonable in the event of other damage being incurred, and may not even be used as evidence of the trespasser's consent to the risk of being on strange premises.[2]

1 See also paras 2.28–2.31, above.
2 Unfair Contract Terms Act 1977, s. 2.

2.68 The law on occupiers' liabilities towards trespassers is likely ultimately to be replaced by statutory provisions. The Law Commission[1] has proposed the replacement of the uncertainties of the common law with a statutory duty on occupiers to safeguard trespassers from death or personal injury if it is reasonable to expect such protection to be afforded. These proposals were the subject of the Occupiers Liability Bill 1978; however, this private member's measure failed to complete its passage through Parliament before the end of the session.

1 Law Commission Report No 75.

Statutory provisions

2.69 A recitation of these long-standing common law principles does not fully describe the occupier's liability for his defective premises. Increasingly, statutory intervention encroaches into the area and many occupiers will find themselves liable for breaches of statutory duty, civilly or criminally. Issues of criminal liability do not fall within the scope of this work, but the various instances of civil liability for breach of statutory duty must be considered.

2.70 The occupier of business premises is particularly affected by legislation, since the Health and Safety at Work etc. Act 1974[1] regulates the conditions of the workplace, insofar as they affect both employees and persons outside the workplace who may be affected by unhealthy or unsafe activities inside it. The Act lays down[2] various general duties ensuring that employers maintain their premises so as to facilitate the health and safety of employees, visitors and neighbours, covering both the premises themselves and machinery, etc., in them. However, no civil action is permitted where these general duties are breached,[3] but the common law of the employer's liability provides an analogous civil remedy in cases where an unsafe system of work is being operated.[4] Rather, there is another tier of rules, far more detailed in character, which stem from two sources, firstly the pre-existing legislation which has not been repealed, especially the Factories Act 1961 and the Offices Shops and Railway Premises Act 1963, and secondly regulations made under the 1974 Act, and in each case a civil action for breach of statutory duty is permitted,[5] though in the case of the pre-existing legislation to no greater extent. However, the regulations so far made under the 1974 Act have in general not been related to defects in the premises themselves, but rather towards various processes and practices often found in particular industries,[6] or purely administrative matters,[7] though more regulations are continually being put forward for consideration, discussion and eventual promulgation, and in due time more defective premises cases will be resolved through the medium of the 1974 Act. Meanwhile, however, we must stay with the pre-existing legislation and outline the salient features of civil liability thereunder insofar as they relate to defective premises.

1 For detailed treatment see, inter alia, Munkman *Employer's Liability* (9th edn) and Sweet and Maxwell (eds) *Encyclopaedia of Health and Safety at Work*.
2 Ss. 2–7.
3 S. 47(1)(a).
4 *Wilsons and Clyde Coal Co Ltd v English* [1938] AC 57, [1937] 3 All ER 628.
5 Health and Safety at Work etc Act 1974, ss. 47(1)(b) and 47(2).
6 E g Packaging and Labelling of Dangerous Substances Regulations 1978, SI 1978 No 209.
7 E g Health and Safety Inquiries (Procedure) Regulations 1975, SI 1975 No 335.

2.71 The Factories Act 1961 (and regulations made thereunder) applies to all workplaces where manufacture takes place, and by section 155 it is provided that the occupier of the factory will be responsible for any breaches of the duties laid down by the Act. The usual common law tests of occupation[1] presumably apply, but the occupier will still be liable in a civil action even though the actual offender has been convicted.[2] His duties are owed to anyone employed to work in the premises[3] and extend to cover ventilation of fresh air in the factory (i e attempting to remove the hazard of dust-related diseases),[4] and adequate lighting.[5] There are rigorous duties related to the fencing of dangerous machinery – moving parts of almost all machines must be fenced,[6] transmission machinery must be similarly guarded,[7] and any other part of machinery which may be regarded as dangerous must be fenced.[8] It is for the court to determine whether the machine or part in question is dangerous in normal use.[9] It should be noted that sections 12–14 create absolute duties, once the applicability of the sections has been decided. A similarly rigorous obligation exists[10] in relation to hoists and lifts in a factory – they must be of good mechanical construction, sound material and adequate strength, and shall be properly maintained with additional safety devices mandatory for passenger-carrying hoists and lifts,[11] and similar phrases are used in relation to other items. So, for example, chains, ropes and lifting tackle must be of sound material, adequate strength, good construction and free from patent defects,[12] as must lifting machines,[13] steam boilers[14] and steam receivers.[15] A requirement of proper maintenance[16] is also imposed in certain cases. An additional range of duties is provided at a different, lower, level e g section 28(1) which provides that a floor shall be kept in an efficient state (i e good repair) and shall be kept free from obstruction as far as is reasonably practicable, a duty akin, though not identical,[17] to the ordinary common law duty of care. A similar level of duty is laid down by section 29(1) in relation to means of access to the place of employment; here again the means of access must be made and maintained insofar as it is reasonably practicable to do so. Thus, in relation to factory premises, the occupier will find himself subject to many duties, of which the foregoing represents a mere sample, some of which will be analogous to common law duties, though still themselves important given the ready definition of the duty provided by the statute as opposed to the relative uncertainty of the common law. Other duties, however, will be seen to be of a stricter character, and it is obvious that the occupier should do all possible to fulfil these duties.

1 Paras 2.4 ff, above.
2 *Potts (or Riddell) v Reid* [1943] AC 1, [1942] 2 All ER 161.
3 *John Summers & Sons Ltd v Frost* [1955] AC 740, [1955] 1 All ER 870.
4 Factories Act 1961, s. 4.
5 Ibid, s. 5.
6 Ibid, s. 12.

7 Ibid, s. 13.
8 Ibid, s. 14.
9 *Cross v Midland and Low Moor Iron and Steel Co* [1965] AC 343, [1964] 3 All ER 752.
10 Factories Act 1961, s. 22.
11 Ibid, s. 23.
12 Ibid, s. 26.
13 Ibid, s. 27.
14 Ibid, s. 32(5).
15 Ibid, s. 35(4).
16 E g ibid, ss. 22, 27, 32(5) and 35(4).
17 See *Powley v Bristol Siddeley Engines Ltd* [1965] 3 All ER 612, [1966] 1 WLR 729.

2.72 If premises are not regarded as factory premises, they will in all probability fall within the ambit of the analogous legislation for non-manufacturing workplaces viz the Offices, Shops and Railway Premises Act 1963. Here again, various criminal penalties exist for contravention of the various duties laid down by the Act and associated regulations. Liability falls solely on the occupier of the premises, unless, additionally or alternatively, the Act renders anyone else liable. As far as civil liability is concerned, the extent of this in cases under the 1963 Act is a little unclear; since the Act was intended to provide a complementary range of remedies in non-manufacturing industries to those provided in other situations by the Factories Act, it is to be assumed that a civil action will lie in all cases where damage stems from a breach of the Act; this may perhaps be deduced from *Westwood v Post Office*[1] where the House of Lords considered the precise scope of the 1963 Act in finding the defendants liable for the death of the plaintiff while taking an unauthorised short-cut within their building; at no stage was there any doubt that a civil action based on section 16[2] of the Act was inappropriate. The Act lays down a similar range of duties to that provided by the Factories Act, including mandatory duties as to cleanliness,[3] overcrowding,[4] temperature[5] and ventilation.[6] By section 16 it is provided that floors, stairs and steps, passages and gangways are to be in a proper condition and free, so far as is reasonably practicable, from obstructions and objects or substances likely to cause persons to slip. Further provisions insist on the fencing of dangerous parts of machinery[7] and prohibit untrained[8] or young[9] workers from operating or cleaning many items of machinery.

1 [1974] AC 1, [1973] 3 All ER 184.
2 Below.
3 Offices, Shops and Railway Premises Act 1963, s. 4.
4 Ibid, s. 5.
5 Ibid, s. 6.
6 Ibid, s. 7.
7 Ibid, s. 17.
8 Ibid, s. 19.
9 Ibid, s. 18.

2.73 Mention should also be made of the Mines and Quarries Act 1954; this covers the state of one further category of business premises and, although not repealed as yet, it now operates as pre-existing legislation within the general framework of the Health and Safety at Work Act 1974. The owner of the mine is liable[1] but since he is defined as 'the person entitled for the time being to work'[2] the mine, this will effectively render the occupier liable for any infringement of the rules. The mineowner will be subject to a relatively onerous civil liability; section 159 establishes that a civil action for breach of statutory duty will lie though section 157 provides it is a defence to such an action to establish that 'it was impracticable to avoid or prevent the contravention'. The Act and its associated regulations lay down a veritable plethora of detailed controls to ensure the safety of those in extractive industries, especially coal mines, with respect to support,[3] shafts,[4] ventilation,[5] freedom from dust,[6] underground roadways,[7] etc. These are generally strict obligations, and have played a major role in encouraging safety in the extractive industries. It should be noted that in due course regulations will be introduced under the 1974 Act to replace the pre-existing legislation; equally it should be noted that this will be a long process and a dual pattern of legislation is likely to remain for some time.

1 Mines and Quarries Act 1954, s. 1.
2 Ibid, s. 181(1).
3 Ibid, s. 48(1).
4 Ibid, s. 30(1).
5 Ibid, s. 55(1).
6 Ibid, s. 74(1).
7 Ibid, ss. 34–41.

2.74 Other particular statutory duties imposed on certain occupiers may be dealt with more succinctly. If the occupier is occupying state school premises, any pupil injured thereon may bring a claim for breach of statutory duty; the duty in question is that under section 10(2) of the Education Act 1944[1] whereby a local education authority has to ensure that their school premises are maintained up to the prescribed standard, this being established by the Standards for School Premises Regulations 1972,[2] regulation 51 of which establishes liability in all cases where the design, construction and fire resistance of state school premises are not adequate to ensure the health and safety of their occupants i e a strict form of liability, more onerous than the duties of the normal occupier. Further categories of occupier subject to special duties beyond those laid down by the Occupiers' Liability Act are the inn-keeper and the hotelier. Their strict liability under the common law for loss of their guests' property was extended by the Hotel Proprietors Act 1956, section 1(2), to include a similar strict liability for damage to a guest's property. This duty (both as to loss and damage) only extends to cover overnight guests, and does not extend to vehicles.[3] Liability will be limited to £50 per article or £100 per guest if the innkeeper and his servants are not at fault in any way, unless the guest has expressly handed over the property into the innkeeper's custody for safekeeping, or has, due to the default of the innkeeper or his servant, been prevented from so doing,[4] so long as an appropriate notice to this effect[5] was posted and clearly displayed. Such notices are not affected by the Unfair Contract Terms Act 1977 since this expressly does not cover attempts to exclude liability in cases where that liability is stricter than in an ordinary negligence action.[6] It should also be noted that these duties both co-exist with the Occupier's Liability Act; neither acts as a bar to the other.

1 As amended by the Education (Miscellaneous Provisions) Act 1948, s. 7(2) and the Education Act 1968, s. 3(3).
2 SI 1972 No 2051.
3 Ibid, s. 2(2).
4 Ibid, s. 2(3).
5 Ibid, Sch 2.
6 Unfair Contract Terms Act 1977, s. 1(1)(b).

2.75 Statutory intervention has also occurred in areas formerly the preserve of the law of nuisance, or the action under the rule in *Rylands v Fletcher*. One major provision is the Control of Pollution Act 1974, bringing together a whole range of environmentally orientated measures, dealing with issues of waste disposal, water pollution, noise and atmospheric pollution. However, much of the Act is concerned only with licensing measures to criminal sanctions; additionally certain parts of the Act have not yet been brought into force. From the point of view of the occupier and his civil liability, the most important section is section 88, whereby any person suffering death or personal injury as a consequence of the deposit of poisonous, noxious or polluting waste on land may bring a civil action against the person who carried out the deposit, or allowed it to take place; the action can only be brought if the deposit in question is an offence under section 3(3) or section 18(2) of the Act (unlicensed disposal of potentially hazardous waste without cause).[1] It is however open to the occupier to plead in his defence that he took care to inform himself whether the deposit in question amounted to a contravention of the law, or took all reasonable steps to comply with the conditions of any disposal licence, as well as the plaintiff's default or assent to the risk of the plaintiff.

1 Control of Pollution Act 1974, s. 3(4).

2.76 However, this is not the only possibility of a civil action based on the Act, for the threat or existence of a criminal breach of the provisions of the Act and the many regulations made thereunder may irritate an individual so much that he will endeavour to have the activity complained of halted, by means of an injunction, as in *Hammersmith London Borough Council v Magnum Automated Forecourts Ltd*[1] where a taxi servicing centre open all day and night was developed on a petrol station site in a residential district of West London. Following complaints from neighbours, the local authority served a notice under section 58(1) of the 1974 Act, requiring the centre to close between 11 p.m. and 7 a.m.; when this was ignored, the authority sought and was granted an injunction under the power granted to the court by section 58(8), specifically allowing this course of action where it is felt that a prosecution for the offence would not be adequate in the case of any noise which amounts to a nuisance, notwithstanding that the local authority itself has suffered no nuisance. By section 59, the occupier of any premises affected by noise nuisance can bring summary proceedings, but more usually local authorities or water authorities are responsible for the administration of the rules. Therefore an aggrieved individual's right to bring an action seeking an injunction, while still of some importance, is to some extent overshadowed by the public bodies and the controls given to them by the Act; these may be the most effective method of preventing environmental hazards.

1 [1978] 1 All ER 401, [1978] 1 WLR 50.

2.77 There is an increasing number of statutes which deal with defects in premises and which not only impose duties on the occupier (and/or the owner and/or the landlord), but also, by reason of having their enforcement entrusted to local authorities, cause liabilities to be imposed on them, in addition. Because of the wide-ranging ambit of these duties, they are considered separately.[1] For the purposes of this discussion, particular note may be briefly made of the Public Health Act 1936, Part III[2] of which deems various nuisances to be 'statutory nuisances', including any premises prejudicial to health or amount ing to a nuisance,[3] or factory premises which are inadequately ventilated or are not free from noxious effluvia;[4] in all such cases, the local authority has the primary responsibility to deal with the nuisance by means of abatement notices (issued by themselves) and, if necessary, nuisance orders, issued by the magistrates.

1 See ch 8, below.
2 See paras 7.20 ff, below.
3 Public Health Act 1936, s. 92(1)(a).
4 Ibid, s. 93(1)(e).

2.78   Liability for the escape of water is no longer the preserve of the common law and is now also governed by statute. Under the Water Act 1981, section 6(1), statutory water undertakers will be held liable for any loss or damage arising from an escape of water, however caused, from their pipes or mains. By section 6(2) they will escape this liability only if the incident in question is the fault of the person suffering the loss, his servant, agent or contractor. By section 6(6) liability does not arise under the section if the undertaking is under a pre-existing contractual obligation to pay for the loss or damage in question. This is a major new example of strict liability.

2.79   Specific rules apply where the occupier creates a nuisance in the form of subsidence on other premises by dint of mining or similar extractive operations on his own land. The Coal Mining (Subsidence) Act 1957 places the National Coal Board under a duty to provide compensation in all cases where property damage is caused by subsidence in consequence of their mining operations, and extends to death or serious personal injury[1] in cases where no other civil remedy may be available; the law of nuisance does not normally provide for a right of support.[2]

1 Coal Mining (Subsidence) Act 1957, s. 12.
2 *Wyatt v Harrison* (1832) 3 B & Ad 871.

2.80   Other forms of energy and their manufacture also give rise to special rules beyond the ambit of the common law. Gas and electricity can amount to nuisances, or be the subject of an action under the rule in *Rylands v Fletcher*, though insofar as they are supplied under statutory authority, negligence seems to be essential before an action against the supplier can succeed.[1] However, the Gas Act 1965, by section 14, states that where gas in storage underground in the natural strata causes damage by escape or otherwise, 'the gas authority shall be absolutely liable in civil proceedings'.[2] An entirely separate set of rules has been devised, however, in cases involving nuclear installations. While, fortunately, there have been no major nuclear incidents in this country the possibility of an escape of radioactive matter, with great short – and long – term damage a possible consequence, has given rise to the realisation that the ordinary rules of civil liability would be entirely inadequate to deal with such a situation. The Nuclear Installations Act 1965 therefore sets out a specific control over the licensing of nuclear sites and, by section 7(1), makes it a duty of the licensee to ensure that no nuclear accidents occur, involving either the nuclear matter itself or its associated radiation, so as to affect other persons or their property; this is a strict duty – only the fact of damage need be proved to establish liability. By section 12 of the Act there is established a right to compensation in such cases, except where hostile action during war is responsible for the nuclear incident;[3] natural disasters, irrespective of their magnitude, do not affect the licensor's liability.[4] By section 13(6), the compensation may be adjusted to bring into account the fault of the plaintiff, but only if his share of the responsibility stems from an intentional or reckless act. The long-term hazards of radiation have given rise to special problems. The licensor is liable for up to ten years after the date of the nuclear incident.[5] For twenty years thereafter, the injured parties may still bring claims, but these are dealt with by the government from funds established for that purpose.[6] Additionally the licensor is only responsible for the first £5 million compensation (though he must insure or make other provision to cover this liability);[7] beyond this again, the government will foot the bill.

1 *Dunne v North Western Gas Board* [1964] 2 QB 806, [1963] 3 All ER 916.
2 Gas Act 1965, s. 14(1).
3 Nuclear Installations Act 1965, s. 13(4)(a).
4 Ibid, s. 13(4)(b).
5 Ibid, s. 16(5).
6 Ibid, s. 18 (see also Nuclear Installations Act 1969, s. 2(2)).
7 Ibid, s. 19.

2.81 The last set of special rules that fall to be considered is the extent of the occupier's liability for fires on his land. Under the Fires Prevention (Metropolis) Act 1774,[1] no occupier can be sued in respect of a fire which accidentally starts on his premises, whether in a metropolis or otherwise. The leading case of *Filliter v Phippard*,[2] however, interpreted this as only avoiding liability for fires started by purest chance – where there is no known cause, or no human cause. Therefore the occupier may still be liable in negligence[3] and/or nuisance[4] for damage caused by a fire or its spread, and under the rule in *Rylands v Fletcher* he will be liable where he is responsible either for the fire or for its spread, assuming in each case that all the other elements of the tort in question are satisfied, though in such cases outside the ambit of the Act the old common law defences remain, including act of third party (if not under the occupier's actual or notional control) or Act of God.[5] Special rules apply when the fire spreads in consequence of sparks emanating from railway engines; the statutory authority under which railways operate normally excuses the operator from liability unless he is negligent. However, in all cases, under the Railway Fires Acts 1905 and 1923 the railway operator is liable for damage to agricultural land or crops caused by fire from locomotives, up to a sum of £200 irrespective of the actual loss suffered.

1 Fires Prevention (Metropolis) Act 1774, s. 86.
2 (1847) 11 QB 347.
3 E g *Musgrove v Pandelis* [1919] 2 KB 43.
4 E g *Spicer v Smee* [1946] 1 All ER 489.
5 *Clerk and Lindsell on Torts* (14th edn) para 1511.

2.82 In conclusion, therefore, premises are a source of many and varied legal duties for their occupier. It may be said that while the law of property works to establish and protect interests in land, the common law increasingly, and with the assistance of Parliament, acts to limit the extent to which land can be enjoyed; duties are owed to visitors, trespassers and neighbours; particular duties are owed in respect of particular activities with much regard being had to the level of danger inherent in the activity before establishing the appropriate level of duty. On the other hand, the present state of the law is of great assistance to those coming onto land; irrespective of their status, they now receive substantial protection against deliberate and careless acts; all receive protection from a wide range of modern environmental hazards which an occupier may be minded to produce.

Chapter 3

The builder

3.1 This chapter deals with the liability of the builder, and additionally covers related liabilities stemming from building operations. The scope of the chapter, combined with its central position in a book on defective premises law, renders it essential to delineate clearly from the outset the actual coverage intended to be given by the chapter.

(1) The chapter covers liability not only of builders, but also, with regard to the complexity of most building operations, the liabilities of the range of sub-contractors and independent contractors who may also be employed to assist with the works. On the other hand, the chapter does not extend to cover the liabilities of professional men (architects, etc.) who assist at various stages of the building operation; a subsequent chapter deals with their liabilities.[1]

(2) The chapter also deals with the liability of developers, insofar as they exert some control over or carry some responsibility for the execution of works. Many modern developments follow a pattern whereby a developer, often a specific company set up for the purposes of the particular development in question, organises and prepares the operation, but leaves the execution of the construction work to a builder. This chapter will deal with their share of the responsibility for the building work, but insofar as they are liable *qua* vendors, the reader is referred to a subsequent chapter.[2]

(3) A further prospective party to an action concerning defective premises is the manufacturer of the materials used in the construction work by the builder or his contractor. It is particularly likely that the manufacturer of materials will find himself brought into a case as a result of the action initially being brought against the builder, and the builder endeavouring to shift the responsibility onto another.

(4) The chapter covers not only a wide range of different parties, but also involves a wide range of different legal remedies; no longer is the action for breach of the terms of the contract for building the sole remedy for a prospective plaintiff, as was the case for so many years. Now, additionally, he or she may be able to bring an action in negligence, or under various statutory provisions.

1 Ch 4, below.
2 Ch 6, below.

3.2 In the light of these various factors, this chapter will cover the following matters:

(1) the liability of the builder, etc., in contract, especially under the 1980 standard form JCT building contract;

(2) the additional liabilities of builders, etc., who are on the Register of the National House-Building Council;
(3) a note on the position of sub-contractors;
(4) the new tortious liabilities of builders at common law, and their liability under the Defective Premises Act 1972;
(5) civil liabilities of builders, etc., under the Building Regulations; and
(6) liability of manufacturers of materials.

Contractual liability of the builder

3.3 Notwithstanding the loss of its role as the sole remedy for the plaintiff aggrieved at the defective condition of premises, nonetheless the basic contractual action between the builder of a property and his employer (i e the person who has commissioned the work) still lies at the heart of any discussion of builders' prospective liabilities. It is, therefore, with consideration of liability under the usual building contracts for defects that we commence the substantive part of this chapter. It may be fairly said that building contracts have a reputation for complexity, and that this reputation is not unjustified. Arguably, their complexity stems from the need for such contracts to contain provision for a wide range of possible contingencies, such as weather delays, poor workmanship, issues of site access and inspection, etc., in the light of what are often the very large sums of money at stake. However, before the fear of this complexity grips the reader, it is important to make two basic points which assist the study of building contracts. Firstly, there is nothing legally distinct about contracts for building works; they are governed in all respects by the general law of contract (a knowledge of the basic elements of which is assumed for the purposes of this chapter). Secondly, the inherently complex nature of building contracts has led to the frequent use of various standard-form contracts.

3.4 Several different standard-form contracts are available, and their terms are frequently changed to reflect new problems and new legal developments. It is proposed to concentrate in this volume on the most widely used such form, namely that issued by the Joint Contracts Tribunal, an independent body composed of representatives from various interested parties, including the Royal Institute of British Architects, the Royal Institute of Chartered Surveyors, the National Federation of Building Trades Employers, and the various local authority associations. The most recent formulation of this contract, now generally known as the JCT form, was promulgated by the Tribunal in 1980, and it is to this most recent version that attention will be confined. Reference will be to the Private Edition of the form, with quantities, unless otherwise indicated. Of course, cases will for a few years yet still appear under previous forms of the contract, and it is not our intention to cover fully such provisions as are no longer part of the JCT form; on the other hand, most of the provisions concerning defects in the premises are substantially unchanged. It should also perhaps be re-emphasised that this book is concerned with the whole range of (civil) legal controls on defective premises and that in consequence some of the exhaustive detail will not be covered; many other works provide coverage of the standard-form contracts.[1] Some reference will also be made to provisions of the 'ICE Conditions of Contract', a separate set of standard-form terms promulgated by the Institution of Civil Engineers, the Association of Consulting Engineers and the Federation of Civil Engineering Contractors; these conditions are widely used in contracts for engineering works, as opposed to simple building works.

1 See, inter alia, Bickford-Smith and Freeth *Emden's Building Contracts and Practice* (8th edn) and Porter *Building Contract Conditions*.

3.5 The background against which the typical building contract functions needs to be noted briefly. The contract is normally made between the employer, i e the person commissioning the work, usually on land over which he has rights of occupation or ownership, and the contractor, the person who is to undertake the work, who will frequently have been selected by means of tender. The employer will in some cases be a development company, set up by the occupier to handle the building works. Similarly, on the other side, the contractor will generally be assisted by sub-contractors either of his own choice or nominated by the employer. The standard-form contracts provide for supervision of the contract at all stages by the architect.

3.6 It must be finally emphasised that this work is concerned with liabilities, for the present those contractually imposed, for defects in the premises; the many contractual terms which deal with other aspects of the building operation do not fall within the ambit of this volume, except insofar as they demonstrate the direction from which redress may be sought by those adversely affected by defects in the premises. Thus questions arising from delay in the work or the division of responsibility between builder and architect are not covered herein.

3.7 What then are the obligations of the contractor as far as the quality and safety of the premises he constructs are concerned, under a building contract? Most potential defects are within the ambit of the common law implied terms, laid down in various cases. The contracts with which we are here concerned are contracts for work to be done, or for work to be done with materials provided, and no statutory implied terms apply. Naturally it should be emphasised that as usual the implied terms apply only insofar as they are not overborne by specific terms in the actual contract documents.[1]

1 E g *Norta Wallpapers (Ireland) v Sisk & Sons (Dublin)* [1978] IR 114.

3.8 The first aspect of the implied terms normally regarded as present in building contracts is that the contractor impliedly promises to carry out the work in a proper and workmanlike manner. Emden[1] refers to this obligation as being an implied condition, and it is likely that any breach of this crucial implied term will have such serious consequences that this may be regarded as the correct view. Amongst the factors that may be taken into account in assessing the precise scope of the duty must be included the level of skill which the contractor purports to possess,[2] and it will also be relevant to consider, in a case where the work contracted for seems impossible to carry out, whether the contractor should have advised at the outset whether the work was capable of fulfilment instead of blandly contracting to carry out the work.[3]

1 *Emden's Building Contracts and Practice* (8th edn).
2 *Duncan v Blundell* (1820) 3 Stark 6.
3 Ibid; *Pearce v Tucker* (1862) 3 F & F 136.

3.9 A second aspect of the implied terms in building contracts covers any materials which the contractor supplies in connection with the work he is undertaking. It is impliedly warranted by the contractor that such materials will be fit for their intended purpose, and will be of good quality, in the absence of other more specific provisions.[1] Particular problems may arise, however. Does, for example, the fact that the defect in the materials is a purely latent one affect the contractor's liability, with regard to the fact that it may seem unreasonable to render him liable for a defect which he could not be reasonably expected to detect? The House of Lords have held that the contractor is still liable for defects in the quality of materials at least when it is still open to the contractor to obtain redress in turn from the manufacturer of the materials in question.[2] Where such redress is not so open to him, for example where the manufacturer of materials has protected his position with a valid exclusion clause known to both contractor and employer, then the contractor may not be held liable. A further problem arises where the employer specifies the materials; can the contractor still be held liable? Here the key issue seems to be whether there is still any reliance by the employer on the contractor's skill and judgment. If it is still open to the contractor to use his critical faculties and reject the specifications laid down he may be held liable;[3] if, however, no reliance whatsoever is placed on the contractor's skill then it is right to free him from liability for materials unfit for their purpose, since the employer is making that judgment. However, in other cases of defects in the quality of the materials, a somewhat different approach may be taken, as in *Gloucestershire County Council v Richardson*;[4] there a combination of very detailed specifications being laid down by the employer plus the fact that the contractor was obliged by his contract with the employer to purchase materials on terms which excluded certain of the manufacturer's normal liabilities was held sufficient to excuse the contractor from liability for latent defects in the materials in question. This does appear to be exceptional; normally the contractor will be readily held liable in most instances for defects in the materials which he supplies, even where they are not of his choosing; then he must either refuse to enter the contract, or at least object to the materials chosen at the earliest possible stage.[5]

1 *Young and Marten Ltd v McManus Childs Ltd* [1969] 1 AC 454, [1968] 2 All ER 1169.
2 Ibid.
3 *Cammell Laird & Co Ltd v Manganese, Bronze and Brass Co Ltd* [1934] AC 402.
4 [1969] 1 AC 480, [1968] 2 All ER 1181.
5 *Duncan v Blundell* (1820) 3 Stark 6.

3.10   The third aspect of the terms normally implied into building contracts concerns the suitability of the work for the purpose intended, in the case of dwelling-houses, the obligation is simply expressed as a requirement that the houses be fit for habitation. The extent to which this implied term will be held to apply will again vary with regard to, on the one hand, the degree of reliance placed by the employer on the contractor and, on the other hand, to the degree of specification laid down by the employer. Thus, in *Lynch v Thorne*,[1] detailed specifications had been laid down, and complied with by the contractor, and also he was in no respect in breach of any other implied terms e g as to workmanship. The Court of Appeal therefore held that although there was, prima facie, a duty to complete the house so as to be fit for habitation, this was negated where in effect extra work, beyond that stipulated by the contract, would be necessary to fulfil the implied duty. On the other hand, in *Greaves & Co (Contractors) Ltd v Baynham Meikle & Partners*,[2] the Court of Appeal held that consultant engineers were liable to indemnify a firm of contractors for defects stemming from faulty design work when, on the facts, they had impliedly warranted that their design would be adequate for the intended purposes. Overall, this implied term has been at least until now, perhaps of lesser importance in view of its irregular application; it is at its most important in the context of dwelling-houses, where an implication of fitness for habitation will be found[3] and is important protection for the house purchaser.

1 [1956] 1 All ER 744, [1956] 1 WLR 303.
2 [1975] 3 All ER 99, [1975] 1 WLR 1095. See also para 4.7, below.
3 *Hancock v B W Brazier (Anerley) Ltd* [1966] 2 All ER 901, [1966] 1 WLR 1317.

3.11 The recent House of Lords decision in *Independent Broadcasting Authority v EMI Ltd and BICC Ltd*[1] is a significant landmark in the development of implied terms in building contracts. The case concerned a large television mast, erected for the IBA to beam their programmes over a wide area of Northern England, the mast being of a new design. In bad, but not exceptional, weather conditions, viz high winds and freezing temperatures, the mast collapsed, after just over three years in service. The Court of Appeal[2] held that there was an implied term in the contract for construction of the mast that the mast should be fit for the intended purpose, i e that it should be able to withstand likely weather conditions in the area where it was built. The Court considered the contractual documents and found nothing to negate their view that the additional obligation, reasonable fitness for purpose, should, as usual, apply;[3] the contractors had promised to erect a mast, and it was implicit in that promise that the mast would achieve its desired object, insofar as it was within the power of the contractors to determine this. The House of Lords upheld this decision, holding that the main contractors were liable for breach of contract, taking responsibility for the materials and design provided by the nominated sub-contractor who had in fact carried out most of the work in question. Arguably, this case provides renewed support for the importation of an implied term as to fitness for purpose in building contracts, especially where the contractor undertakes to carry out work in such a way that the undertaking may be interpreted as a promise that the work will be done and will be suitable. In the words of Lord Fraser of Tullybelton,[4] 'in a building contract for work and materials a term is normally implied that the main contractor will accept responsibility to his employer for materials provided by nominated sub-contractor . . . The extent of the obligation is . . . a matter of construction of the contract. In the absence of a clear contractual indication to the contrary, I see no reason why one who is in the course of a business contract to design, supply and erect . . . is not under an obligation to ensure that it is reasonably fit for the purpose he knows it is intended to be used.' The implied term as to fitness for purpose will be especially important in 'package-deal' situations i e where the contractor provides a wide range of other services beyond the simple building work e g design and surveying. It has been held to apply in a case concerning the provision of a large development of 'overspill' dwellings where the Greater London Council's predecessor, the London County Council, carried out all the work necessary for the provision of a large estate in Andover; it was held that in consequence of their control over all aspects of the development, they were under a duty to make the houses fit for the intended purpose i e habitation.[5] However, it is fair to note that in the *IBA* case the contractor had had the opportunity to check the defective design, and was not bound by any stipulation by the employer. In the light of these points, it may be that the case is capable of being distinguished in the future.

1 (1980) 14 BLR 1. See also Stanton and Dugdale (1981) 131 NLJ 583.
2 (1978) 11 BLR 29.

3 Cf *Gloucestershire County Council v Richardson* [1969] 1 AC 480, [1968] 2 All ER 1181.
4 *IBA v EMI and BICC* (1980) 14 BLR 1 at 44–45.
5 *Test Valley Borough Council v Greater London Council* (1980) 13 BLR 75.

3.12 The JCT form approaches the problem of defective materials and work-manship in a different way. The contractor's principal obligation (by clause 2 of the 1980 JCT form) is to erect the building in such a way as to correspond with the Contract Drawings and descriptions in the Contract Bills, using materials and adopting standards of workmanship as are specified, subject to the approval of the supervisor of the works, normally the architect. Clause 8 expands these obligations; by clause 8.1 it is reiterated that materials used and workmanship must be as specified in the Contract Bills (or other specification in the 'without quantities' version of the JCT form), and by clause 8.2 the contractor may be called upon by the architect to vouch that this obligation has been complied with. A further sanction is provided by clause 8.3, whereby the architect can demand that completed work should be uncovered and inspected or that tests be carried out on the materials used in the works to assess their quality. If the work or materials are below the standard required by the contract then the contractor will have to pay for them; in other cases the cost is added to the contract price. In the event of default, further powers are granted to the architect; he can order removal of work or materials that fail to meet contractual specifications[1] and at any time he may reasonably order the dismissal of any person or firm employed on the site.[2] In the event of no standard being prescribed then compliance with the common law standards[3] may be assumed to be necessary. Where the standard laid down in the contract document is unattainable, clause 8.1 does not apply insofar as the standards are not 'procurable'; this term has been fre-quently criticised for its inherent uncertainty[4] and fairly criticised too; it implies, inter alia, that the contractor's own default might free him from the obligation in question. Keating[5] suggests that any contractor seeking to utilise this provision must notify the architect in advance before supplying materials or workmanship of a lower standard, but in the absence of judicial authority it must be said that this is speculative.

1 JCT form, cl 8.4.
2 Ibid, cl 8.5.
3 Paras 3.8 ff, above.
4 See e g Julian (1980) 130 NLJ 635.
5 Keating *Law and Practice of Building Contracts* (4th edn) p. 307.

3.13 The ICE Conditions of Contract lay down broadly similar provisions; by clause 36 materials and workmanship shall be as described in the contract and in accordance with the instructions of the supervising engineer; he has power to order appropriate tests to ascertain that this obligation is being fulfilled; again the contractor will have to meet the costs of the testing if he is held to be in default of his obligations. Again it is assumed that the common law implied terms may apply where there is no clear guidance in the contractual documents as to the appropriate standard of materials and workmanship.

3.14 The contractual liabilities of the builder ultimately depend of course on the actual contractual stipulations. However, he must now be increasingly mindful of a wide range of implied terms supporting the specific stipulations; he may be in danger of finding himself warranting not only his own work, but also that of his sub-contractors, not only patent defects in his work, but latent defects also, and not only the actual materials used but in addition the design work. Having ascertained some of the aspects of the builder's liability, the next question which must be raised is a more complex one – if there is a breach of the builder's contractual duties, what remedies are available to the employer against him?

3.15 Whereas perhaps it is fair to say that most breaches of contractual obligation occur and are subsequently discovered at a considerably later stage, e g the point of consumption of a defectively manufactured product or when an attempt to occupy a newly purchased house reveals the presence of a sitting tenant which unsatisfactory searches by the purchaser's solicitor have failed to reveal, in building contracts the position is often different, insofar as the employer has some continuing supervision over the progress of the contract through the presence of the architect with his array of predominantly supervisory functions and his powers of certification.[1] The question therefore arises as to the effect on the builder's contractual liability of any approval of the work done at any stage, even if it is in fact defective work, by the employer directly or via the architect. It should first be said that any specific clause subjecting the work to the approval of the employer will be construed strictly in the interest of protecting the builder,[2] though subject to that will be effective in securing a high standard of work. Once the employer has formally accepted the work under a clause of this kind or otherwise, however, then it is submitted that he is estopped from claiming against the builder, at least in respect of any patent defects which he had the opportunity to recognise and thus accept. More usually, however, it will not be the employer who accepts the work but the architect acting on his behalf who will assess the quality of the work and finally issue a certificate of completion, having meanwhile in all probability issued interim certificates concerning the completion of particular stages of the work. These are all essential stages in the JCT contract (see clause 30). These certificates, however, will not be issued until the architect has inspected the work done and in the case of the all-important final certificate this should not be issued until defects then existing have been rectified by the contractor – if the architect issues a final certificate notwithstanding the continuing visible presence of defects he may well be liable to the employer in negligence.[3] If defects are not detected by the architect due to fraudulent conduct on the part of the contractor, this conduct will vitiate the certificate in any case; this is specifically provided by clause 30.9 of the JCT form. Thus, the inspection, supervision and certification carried out by the architect on the employer's behalf may affect the builder's liability to some extent, but equally should it not prevent most defects from arising then at least it should ensure that they are remedied before completion.

1 See ch 4, below.
2 *Dallman v King* (1837) 7 LJCP 6.
3 See para 4.29, below.

3.16 The standard-form contracts contain certain provisions governing remedies for breach of the contractor's obligations. The JCT form, clause 17, establishes the appropriate procedures to be used where defects appear subsequent to the formal completion date of the works. Any defects, shrinkages or other faults which arise in consequence of an inadequate fulfilment of the contractor's obligations as to materials and workmanship, or due to frost damage during the progress of the works (but not after their completion) must be specified by the architect or other supervisory officer in a list given to the contractor within fourteen days of the end of the Defects Liability Period – this is normally a period of six months from the end of the actual workings. The contractor is then bound (by clause 17.2) to remedy all defects in the list, unless the architect directs otherwise. Additionally, prior to this stage, at any time during the Defects Liability Period, the architect may issue instructions requiring any defect to be made good within a reasonable time, under clause 17.3. All additional works are to be performed at the contractor's expense unless the architect has decided that the contractor may be excused from his normal obligations.

3.17 The first comment to make about clause 17 of the JCT form is that it provides the principal remedy for defective construction work. We will later be concerned with a wide range of remedies against the builder, in contract, in tort and under statutes, but it should be pointed out at this stage that many complaints about defective premises can be both unearthed and disposed of by means of the clause 17 procedures. The architect is under a duty to formulate a list of defects then existing and the contractor is usually obliged to remedy them; most defects will in practice have appeared at this stage – the long-term latent defect is the exception, not the rule. Having said that, some doubts do exist as to the precise ambit of clause 17. There is no indication as to whether the contractor will be held liable for all defects, or just those that are a result of his own endeavours. It is unclear, for example, whether the contractor will be obliged to repair work that is defective not because of defective execution but because of defective design. A further problem with clause 17 stems from the fact that the Defects Liability Period starts from the date the works are 'practically completed', an inherently vague term; for example, can the architect certify that there is practical completion when there are still defects? The answer seems to be that practical completion can be properly certified notwithstanding the presence of subsequently discovered latent defects.[1] However, the presence of even minor patent defects casts doubt on the architect's ability properly to certify practical completion – how can he so certify if obvious, remediable defects remain? If, on the other hand, trivial defects can be ignored for the purposes of practical completion, how trivial must those defects be? It is suggested that there must be some scope for trivial, easily remediable defects to be ignored for the purposes of practical completion; where this is the case, the architect could obtain a written promise from the contractor to make good the defects at a later stage[2] or, more arguably, could regard their continuing presence as a newly appearing defect and instigate the clause 17.3 procedure, thus obliging the contractor to remedy them.

1 *Westminster Corpn v J Jarvis & Sons Ltd* [1970] 1 All ER 943, [1970] 1 WLR 637.
2 Keating *Building Contracts* (4th edn) p. 325.

3.18 One or two analogous provisions may be noted here. Clause 18 of the JCT form governs cases where partial possession is taken by the employer; where this has occurred a separate Defects Liability Period arises in respect of that part of the workings. Under the ICE Conditions of Contract, clause 49 governs liability for defects. Under such contracts there is a 'period of maintenance', in many ways analogous to the Defects Liability Period; during this period, the contractor continues to carry some responsibility for the works and the supervisory engineer may within the period inspect the works and (within the period or fourteen days thereafter) order the contractor to repair or otherwise make good any defects then discovered.

3.19   It may well be that the execution of the works is of such a defective character that the employer will not wish to wait for completion of the works and then try and obtain redress for defects perhaps by then fully incorporated into the structure; rather he will seek to terminate the contract as soon as he discovers the defective character of the workmanship. This he is entitled to do by clause 27 of the JCT form, if the contractor has failed to conduct the works in a regular and diligent manner – this seems broad enough to encompass consistently poor work – and he is also entitled to determine the contractor's employment if the works are materially affected by a failure on the part of the contractor to remedy defective work or materials where the architect has issued appropriate instructions. The initial remedy for the employer is to issue via the architect a formal notice specifying the default in question; if the relevant default is continued for a period of a further fourteen days or if there is a subsequent repetition of the default, then determination of the contract can take place within a further period of ten days. Similar arrangements are provided in the ICE Conditions of Contract by clause 63, whereby the contractor's failure to remove rejected work or materials or his persistent or fundamental breach of his contractual obligations (if the subject of previous warnings) will entitle the supervising engineer to determine the contract and expel the contractor from the site with just seven days' notice.

3.20   Beyond these specific provisions there lies the general contractual doctrine of repudiation,[1] which indeed will form the sole remedy in this kind of situation if the specific clauses of the kind just discussed are not being used. An obvious and continuing failure by the builder to fulfil his contractual obligations will be readily construed as an implied repudiation of the contract on his part, if for example the continuing presence of the builder on the site represents such an obstruction as to render either further performance impossible or even replacement of the contractor and continuation of the work by another inadvisable. In the words of Devlin J (as he then was), 'A renunciation can be made either by words or conduct, providing it is clearly made . . . the party renunciating must "evince an intention" not to go on with the contract. The intention can be evinced either by words or conduct. The test of whether an intention is sufficiently evinced by conduct is whether the party renunciating has acted in such a way as to lead a reasonable person to the conclusion that he does not intend to fulfil his part of the contract.'[2] The repudiation must be accepted as such by the employer.

1 See, inter alia, *Chitty on Contracts* (24th edn) paras 1479 ff; Cheshire and Fifoot *Law of Contract* (9th edn) pp. 568 ff.
2 *Universal Cargo Carriers Corpn v Citati* [1957] 2 QB 401 at 436, [1957] 2 All ER 70 at 84.

3.21   The employer is free to decide not to accept the contract as repudiated and may instead insist on the contract being upheld and claim for damages in respect of any losses actually stemming from the breach of the builder's obligations. Equally he may wish to claim damages in respect of latent defects emerging after the Defects Liability Period. How then are damages assessed when a builder has performed part of his work defectively? Naturally the general rules governing the award of damages in contract cases apply here[1] and it is therefore especially important to establish that any damage in respect of which a claim is to be made is foreseeable damage. The House of Lords considered the issue of the proper measure of damages in building contract cases in *East Ham Corporation v Bernard Sunley & Sons Ltd*[2] and held that the proper measure in such a case was the cost of reinstatement of the works to the appropriate standard, with that cost being assessed at the time when the defects were actually discovered, even if the architect should have noticed them at an earlier stage (when the cost of reinstatement would have been appreciably less); it was within the contemplation of the parties at the time the contract was made that there was a serious possibility of defects which are missed in the inspection and examination procedures. It is submitted that the further formulation of the test of foreseeability in contract cases generally by the House of Lords in *Koufos v C Czarnikow Ltd*[3] does not affect the decision and comments in the *East Ham* case, which was not cited in the later case. Additionally, the more recent Court of Appeal decision in *H Parsons (Livestock) Ltd v Uttley Ingham & Co Ltd*[4] falls to be mentioned; in that case Lord Denning MR[5] formulated an alternative approach to the award of damages in breach of contract cases whereby differing tests are adopted in cases of actual property damage and cases where economic loss alone is incurred i e the building is worth less than anticipated; the suggestion is that in the former category of case the test for foreseeability is akin to that adopted in tort cases i e the slightest possibility of damage entitles the plaintiff to claim in full for his losses if it may be foreseen as possibly arising at the time of the breach. This would give the employer more generous damages in most cases, but it must be emphasised that the comments of the learned judge do not (yet) represent the law.

1 See paras 1.9 ff, above.
2 [1966] AC 406, [1965] 3 All ER 619. It should be noted that this case concerns repairs which had been carried out before the trial. For the correct approach in other cases, see paras 1.14 and 1.15, above.
3 [1969] 1 AC 350, [1967] 3 All ER 687.
4 [1978] QB 791, [1978] 1 All ER 525. See also para 1.19, above.
5 Ibid at 801–804 and 531–534.

3.22 In some cases the courts do not adopt the approach outlined whereby the cost of reinstatement of the work to the appropriate standard is awarded. Instead they may award a sum by way of damages to reflect the loss of value of the building in consequence of defective work. This may be done, it is suggested, where the cost of repair is unreasonable in the circumstances or where remedial work is impracticable in the particular circumstances of the case. In such instances, the diminution in value is to be assessed at the time when the defects are discovered.[1]

1 *Applegate v Moss* [1971] 1 QB 406, [1971] 1 All ER 747. See also para 1.43, above.

3.23 In all cases a range of additional matters may form the subject matter of a claim.[1] For example it may be possible to claim for loss of goodwill attendant on defective construction work by the builder[2] or for inconvenience and discomfort suffered during repair work and/or in consequence of the breach.[3] Lost profits arising from the inability to use a building because of the defects should on general principles be recoverable, as will be claims for alternative accommodation in the event of the premises being uninhabitable as a result of the defect. All claims will of course be subject to the requirement of reasonable foreseeability,[4] and the duty on the part of the plaintiff to mitigate his losses where reasonable.

1 See *Emden's Building Contracts and Practice* (8th edn) pp. 271–279 and Keating *Building Contracts* (4th edn) pp. 146–151 for more detailed coverage of this point.
2 *Anglo-Continental Holidays Ltd v Typaldos Lines (London) Ltd* [1967] 2 Lloyd's Rep 61.
3 *Cox v Philips Industries Ltd* [1976] 3 All ER 161, [1976] 1 WLR 638.
4 Paras 1.18 ff, above.

3.24 It is also open to the parties to a building contract to establish in advance the consequences of a breach of contract, including defective workmanship or the provision of inadequate materials, by stipulating fixed, liquidated damages as the remedy in the event of a breach. This is most frequently employed in cases of delay in completion, for whatever reason. However, before reliance can be placed on a liquidated damages clause, care must be taken to ensure that it does not fall foul of the rules concerning penalty clauses, as established in particular by *Dunlop Pneumatic Tyre Co Ltd v New Garage and Motor Co Ltd*,[1] where it was established that a clause where the fixed sum can in no way be taken as a genuine pre-estimate of the likely consequences of breach and is far in excess of the likely sum that may conceivably be lost, as foreseen at the time of the breach, will be struck down.

1 [1915] AC 79.

3.25 The claim for damages by the employer may not arise directly, but instead may manifest itself when the employer seeks to withhold some or all of the payment for the work on the grounds that its execution has been defective, or alternatively seeks to set off the cost of remedying the defects against the contract price or make such cost the subject of a counterclaim in the event of any litigation. As a general rule, the withholding of payment should not be undertaken lightly, in view of the legal consequences if the supposed ground for the withholding turns out to be legally invalid. Nonetheless, it is a common weapon in building contract disputes, particularly in circumstances of recession when cash-flow problems can on occasions be remedied by claims of defects to be set-off against the contractor's demands for payment. As between employer and contractor such disputes are handled in the usual way – arbitration in the case of a contract using the JCT form[1] or the courts. However, particular problems have arisen in recent years, doubtless in the light of the recession, concerning payments on interim certificates and associated sub-contractors' claims. Under building contracts, there is normally provision for interim payments to be made to the contractor as the work progresses, in view of the commitment he is continually under to continue to work, acquire materials, pay his workforce, etc. (in the case of contracts using the JCT form the relevant provisions are in clause 30.1). However, further clauses may entitle the sub-contractor to a due proportion of each payment as determined by the supervising architect (see JCT form, clause 35.12, 17–19 for the appropriate provisions in such contracts) and it has been held by the Court of Appeal in *Dawnays Ltd v F G Minter Ltd*[2] that on a proper interpretation of the (then) JCT documents, including those concerning sub-contracts (not appreciably changed in the 1980 version: now see form NSC 4, clause 23), the sub-contractor was entitled to full payment with no set-off possible for defects or any other claim for unliquidated damages.[3] In turn, however, this view has been the subject of criticism, obiter, by a majority of the House of Lords in *Gilbert-Ash (Northern) Ltd v Modern Engineering (Bristol) Ltd*[4] and this, combined with the exceptional nature of the bar on set-off in interim certificate cases as imposed in *Dawnays'* case,[5] leads to the submission that it is still possible to raise a set-off in a dispute concerning an interim certificate.[6]

1 See paras 3.29 ff, below.
2 [1971] 2 All ER 1389, [1971] 1 WLR 1205.
3 Cf *Algrey Contractors Ltd v Tenth Moat Housing Society Ltd* [1973] 1 Lloyd's Rep 369.
4 [1974] AC 689, [1973] 3 All ER 195.
5 [1971] 2 All ER 1389, [1971] 1 WLR 1205.
6 See *Emden's Building Contracts and Practice* (8th edn) pp. 93–98.

3.26 It is worth noting at this stage some particular points which may be construed as giving some advantage to the employer in disputes of the kind under discussion here. Firstly, it is normal for the employer to deduct a percentage from the interim payment he makes to the contractor, known as 'retention money', which he then duly retains, effectively as a form of insurance against defects arising in the work. By clause 30.2 of the JCT form a percentage (5 per cent unless agreed otherwise)[1] is deducted from the sum otherwise due under the interim certificate to the main contractor. A second point to note is that the employer will also be able to establish a lien over what is technically the property of the contractor in certain circumstances. For example, it may be specifically agreed by the parties that the employer will take a lien over the contractor's huts, materials, etc., on the site in the event of a determination of the contract (this is established for contracts using the JCT form by clause 27.4 thereof), while equally there may be an implied lien if there has been an advance paid to the contractor by the employer in respect of the purchase of materials which have not been installed in the construction at the time, thus providing some degree of security for the employer's advance.[2] Both these features may be of considerable assistance to the employer in assisting any claims he may have against the contractor.

1 JCT form, cl 30.4.1.
2 Keating *Building Contracts* (4th edn) p. 127.

3.27 Separate provisions will be applicable if a delay to the contract arises, as a result of defects in the work. Building contracts should always contain some provision as to what should happen in the event of any delay to the works in view of the wide range of extraneous factors – climatic, political, etc. The JCT form makes detailed provision for delay in clause 25. Liquidated damages are the remedy for the employer where work is delayed for whatever reason, at a predetermined rate. However, the date from which the contractor is obliged to pay these sums will be variable if he succeeds in obtaining an extension of time. In order to obtain this, the contractor must under clause 25 notify the architect of the likelihood of delay in writing, laying out the likely duration and the alleged causes for the delay; by clause 25.3 the architect must respond to this within twelve weeks, and if reasonably practicable, fix a new, more realistic completion date. An extension of time, delaying the time from which additional payments are to be made, will be granted only if the cause of the delay falls within the categories laid down by clause 25.4 whereby an extension of time will be granted if the delay is caused by external causes, e g Acts of God, exceptionally adverse weather conditions, civil unrest or government action affecting availability of labour or materials (including energy), or by the architect and/or employer prolonging the works, e g by insisting on tests where no fault on the part of the contractor is shown, by issuing late instructions or insisting on additional work being carried out, or by organisational causes, e g nominated subcontractors defaulting notwithstanding due supervision and encouragement, or the unavoidable inability to obtain labour or materials due to circumstances beyond the contractor's control. Thus if a defect causes a delay, it will be possible for the contractor to avoid liability (under the JCT form, in liquidated damages) if, and only if, he can establish that the defect arose as a consequence of the specified factors in clause 25.4. He will succeed in avoiding liability if the defects stem from weather conditions of an exceptionally adverse character – this may be regarded as particularly useful to the contractor faced with cracks or changed soil conditions, so long as the weather conditions were indeed unforeseeably unfavourable. He will also succeed if the defect stems from the so-called 'Clause 22 perils' – accidental damage caused by fire, and damage stemming from the bursting or overflowing of water tanks or other apparatus seem particularly likely causes of defects. The contractor also may succeed in avoiding liability if he can pass the buck on to nominated sub-contractors or suppliers causing the defects, but again he must show that the default did not stem from a failure on his own part to take steps to avoid or reduce the problem. In all cases other than these covered by clause 25.4, however, the contractor will be fully liable and, if no liquidated damages have been agreed, will be liable not only for the defect, but also for all consequential loss, if reasonably foreseeable.

3.28 A further possible consequence of work by the contractor not attaining the appropriate standard is that the contractor will endeavour to have the discrepancy between the standard contracted for and the standard actually attained treated as a formal variation of the contract. Because of the length of time over which a building contract operates, there will normally be provision for variation of its terms so as to take into account changing circumstances and new requirements by the employer without the need for the formulation of an entire new contract. The current JCT form embodies such a provision in the form of clause 13; this permits a wide range of variations to be made covering such matters as the alteration or modification of the design, quality and quantity of the works, the addition or omission of some of the works and variations in the standard and nature of materials and goods used in the contract. Such changes are normally made at the instigation of the employer via the architect, but it is possible for the contractor to vary without instruction, for example where his work is incapable of attaining the designated standard, and seek the subsequent written sanction of the architect. However as a method of dealing with defective work this is not particularly satisfactory; obviously the architect is in no way obliged to accept the variation, though equally the contract price is variable when variations are sanctioned. By clause 13.2, any formal variations do not vitiate the contract.

3.29 The complexity of the typical building contract means that disputes inevitably arise; if the contract (standard-form or otherwise) is badly drafted particularly intractable disputes may occur. There is therefore a clear need for a suitable method of handling disputes arising from building contracts and recourse to the courts does not necessarily provide such a suitable method; use of the traditional legal system embodies justified fears of excessive cost and prolonged delay in the resolution of disputes and may also involve the public disclosure in open court of matters which neither party would wish to have so aired. Expert adjudication of the often technical disputes in building cases is also not guaranteed in the courts. For all these reasons, it is normal for building contracts to embody a provision for arbitration of disputes arising therefrom. In general, arbitrations in building cases will be heard by an arbitrator named or nominated by an individual or organisation named in the contract who will exercise a quasi-judicial function in that he should be acting as an independent and impartial figure, albeit one usually in possession of some relevant skill or expertise – he is not however there to exercise his own judgment based on his skills or expertise, but rather is simply to use his skill to assess the evidence put by the disputing parties. If the arbitrator is indeed exercising a quasi-judicial function (as opposed to using his professional skills), he will be immune from liability for negligence.[1] The supervising architect may on occasions be appointed as the arbitrator; however if the matter of dispute is one in relation to which he may have some personal interest, the parties may, under the Arbitration Act 1950, section 24, seek to ask the court to revoke the arbitrator's authority on the grounds that he is not or may not be impartial.

1 *Sutcliffe v Thackrah* [1974] AC 727, [1974] 1 All ER 859; *Arenson v Casson, Beckman Rutley & Co* [1977] AC 405, [1975] 3 All ER 901.

3.30 The JCT form makes specific provision for arbitration of disputes arising from contracts which utilise the form. This is established by article 5 of the Articles of Agreement associated with the form, which are contractually binding as between the employer and the contractor. Any dispute may be referred to arbitration (with a few exceptions, none of which relate to defects in the premises); the arbitrator will be chosen by the President or Vice-President of the RIBA if the parties are unable to agree speedily (within fourteen days of the formal reference to arbitration) who should conduct the arbitration. However, it has been noted that the speed then seems to decrease; no power exists to ensure the speedy resolution of disputes by the arbitrator.[1] The ICE Conditions of Contract also provide for arbitration.[2]

1 Julian (1980) 130 NLJ 635.
2 Cl 66.

3.31 Controversy has recently arisen as to the impact of the Arbitration Act 1979, particularly section 1(2), whereby '... an appeal shall lie to the High Court on any question of law arising out of an award made on an arbitration agreement ...'. By section 1(3) this appeal takes place either with the consent of all the parties or alternatively with the leave of the court; in the latter instance it is laid down by section 1(4) that leave shall not be granted unless the legal issue in contention could substantially affect the rights of one or more of the parties. By section 1(5) the arbitrator whose decision is the subject of an appeal to the courts may be required to provide detailed reasons for his award if he has not already done so. The effect of these provisions together has been to raise fears that the flexible character of arbitration is endangered. Arbitrators may feel constrained to be more legalistic, with procedural rigidity setting in as a result of the requirement, effectively, that clear reasons be given; also, arbitrations may be seen merely as a prelude to more litigation as they are appealed to the High Court from where in turn of course further appeals are possible. The Court of Appeal has endeavoured to reduce such fears by attempting to restrict recourse to the courts. In *Pioneer Shipping Ltd v BTP Tioxide Ltd*,[1] a shipping contract case, it was held that cases should at the least not proceed beyond the stage of an appeal to a High Court judge (under section 1(4) the finality of the decision can be made a condition of the leave to appeal) and that leave should not be given in cases concerning clauses of no wider impact i e those not contained in any standard-form contract. However, these comments are difficult to enforce. There is thus a danger that arbitration in building contract disputes will in the future not represent the advantageous method of resolving the issue that it has been taken to represent until now; parties who wish to ensure that the arbitration is final should utilise the provisions of section 3(1) of the Arbitration Act 1979 whereby a clear agreement is made by the parties excluding the court's intervention and thus rendering the arbitrator's decision final.

1 [1980] QB 547, [1980] 3 All ER 117; affd [1981] 2 All ER 1030, [1981] 3 WLR 292. The House of Lords affirmed and developed the views of the Court of Appeal.

85

3.32 One important aspect of building contracts remains to be discussed viz the extent to which it is possible to exclude or restrict liability arising under the contract for defective work. Building contracts in general represent no exception to the common law principle that parties to contracts are free to exclude liability if they so wish. What is clear, however, is that in practice the contracts used to govern building cases do not as a rule contain exclusion clauses; the JCT form eschews any such clause, unless the provisions as to arbitration are to be regarded as exclusion clauses.[1] However, this does not mean that exclusion clauses are irrelevant; the particular circumstances of a case may cause an exclusion clause to be added to the contractual terms. Further, such clauses may well be found in some of the peripheral arrangements, e g there may be clauses restricting liability in estimates, or alternatively such clauses are often inserted into contracts made by specialist sub-contractors responsible for the provision and installation of technical plant such as lifts or escalators in a building. Thus we need to examine the extent of legal controls on such clauses.

1 See para 3.34, below.

3.33 The convoluted attempts of the common law itself to remedy the disadvantages of the doctrine of freedom of contract and the consequent over-ready use of comprehensive exclusion clauses need not now be considered. The House of Lords have recently confirmed in the case of *Photo Production Ltd v Securicor Transport Ltd*[1] that there is now no doctrine of fundamental breach as such, i e that there is no rule of law to the effect that a major breach of a contract destroys the entirety of that contract, including clauses purporting to exclude liabilities arising. Rather, the correct approach was to examine and construe the contractual terms, including the exclusion clause, and thereby determine whether the parties intended that the clause should apply in the event of the particular breach occurring. Thus, no general rule can be formulated; in building contracts as in other agreements the effect of a fundamental breach can only be assessed by a proper consideration of the relevant contractual terms, as evidence of the intention of the parties.

1 [1980] AC 827, [1980] 1 All ER 556.

3.34 Of far greater significance is the potential impact of the Unfair Contract Terms Act 1977. This major piece of legislation for the first time embodies something in the nature of a systematic overall package of controls on exclusion clauses, but its provisions as they affect attempts to exclude liability in building contracts are at once both complicated and (at times) unclear. The relevant provisions only apply to attempts to exclude liability by businesses,[1] but on the other hand not only clauses excluding all liabilities are governed by the legislation. The Act refers frequently to clauses 'excluding or restricting liability' and by section 13 this is defined broadly to encompass additionally the 'making the liability or its enforcement subject to restrictive or onerous conditions'[2] and the 'excluding or restricting of any right or remedy in respect of the liability, or subjecting a person to any prejudice in consequence of his pursuing any such remedy'[3] and the exclusion or restriction of any rules of procedure or evidence.[4] Thus, a wide range of clauses falls within the controls laid down in the Act e g an excessively high as well as a restrictively low liquidated damages clause or a provision establishing a stricter time limit for the bringing of a claim. Prima facie clauses which divert disputes from enforcement in the courts to determination by arbitration fall within the ambit of section 13(1)(b),[5] but this has been contradicted by section 13(2) whereby a written agreement to submit disputes to arbitration will not be treated as an exclusion or restriction of liability. Perhaps of greater significance is the need to distinguish a clause excluding or restricting liability from one which prevents liability arising in the first place, which latter category are not within section 13. The latter category includes clauses delaying the time when payment is due or a clause defining (restrictively) the obligations of the parties, though this second example is subject to section 13(1) whereby sections 2 and 5–7 of the 1977 Act only prevent attempts to exclude or restrict liability by restrictions of the relevant obligations. The significance of this partial coverage will become clear.

1 Unfair Contract Terms Act 1977, s. 1(3) See para 2.31, above.
2 Ibid, s. 13(1)(a).
3 Ibid, s. 13(1)(b).
4 Ibid, s. 13(1)(c).
5 Above.

3.35 What controls are then imposed by the 1977 Act? This question is answered differently, depending on which contractual obligations are purportedly being excluded by the offending term. An implied or express contractual obligation to take reasonable care or exercise reasonable skill in the performance of the contract is defined by section 1(1)(a) of the Act as within the term 'negligence'. Thus exclusion clauses purporting to control such liability are covered by the provisions of section 2 of the Act. Other contractual obligations are protected by the controls on exclusion clauses laid down by section 3 of the Act, but further complications are provided by the existence of separate, more onerous restrictions on the use of exclusion clauses in sale of goods contracts by section 6, which do not concern us for the moment, and analagous restrictions on exclusion clauses in contracts other than sale of goods contracts but under which nonetheless ownership or possession of goods passes, covered by section 7. This latter category embraces a wide range of agreements such as hiring or exchange but, most importantly includes contracts for work and materials, typical of many in building situations where the contractor provides materials and then installs them – these are outside the definition of contracts for the sale of goods which appear to contemplate transactions involving goods alone.[1]

1 Sale of Goods Act 1979, s. 2(1). See also *Robinson v Graves* [1935] 1 KB 579.

3.36 The controls on the use of contractual terms in building contracts purporting to exclude contractual obligations of care and skill[1] are most easily explained. By section 2(1) of the Unfair Contract Terms Act 1977, any such clause which purports to exclude liability for death or personal injury will be ineffective, while under section 2(2) liability for other loss or damage (and this will include all property damage and economic loss) can only be excluded if the exclusion clause satisfies the requirement of reasonableness, unhelpfully defined by section 11(1) as a requirement that the term 'shall have been a fair and reasonable one to be included having regard to the circumstances which were, or ought reasonably to have been known to or in contemplation of the parties when the contract was made'. It is almost impossible to suggest how this might be utilised in a building contract dispute. Perhaps the fact that the builder does not profess a professional skill militates in his favour; on the other hand, his continual presence at the works gives him a unique ability to know precisely what is going wrong (if anything), and this may persuade a court that he should not be able to exclude his liabilities; after all, the architect is only present in a supervisory role and is not to be regarded as a guarantor of the works.[2] More generally, it is suggested that such factors as the scope of the clause and the publicity attached to it are relevant in determining reasonableness. Specific assistance is given in cases where liability is restricted to a specified sum of money (thus including some liquidated damages clauses). In such instances, particular regard is to be paid to the resources which the person or firm responsible for the limitation clause would be able to utilise for meeting any relevant liabilities if they arose and the ease (or otherwise) of obtaining insurance cover to cope with the liabilities, under section 11(4) of the Act; these provisions are of obvious assistance to the small building contractor. By section 11(5) of the 1977 Act, it is for the contractor who seeks to rely on the reasonableness of a clause to establish that fact.

1 See para 3.8, above.
2 See ch 4, below.

3.37   As far as other contractual obligations are concerned, slightly less comprehensive but more complicated controls on exclusion clauses are established by section 3 of the 1977 Act. This states:

(1) This section applies as between contracting parties where one of them deals as consumer or on the other's written standard terms of business.
(2) As against that party, the other cannot by reference to any contract term—
  (a) when himself in breach of contract, exclude or restrict any liability of his in respect of the breach; or
  (b) claim to be entitled—
    (i) to render a contractual performance substantially different from that which was reasonably expected of him, or
    (ii) in respect of the whole or any part of his contractual obligation, to render no performance at all,
except in so far as (in any of the cases mentioned above in this sub-section) the contract term satisfies the requirement of reasonableness.

3.38   To establish the coverage of this section, it is important to distinguish several different situations. Firstly, where a business is contracting with another business (e g a building firm undertaking an operation for another company, such as the erection of a new factory or the demolition of internal office walls) section 3 has no application in most cases. However, it is necessary to distinguish a second situation where one business contracts with another 'on the other's written standard terms of business' – then section 3 will apply. The exact scope of this distinction will be discussed below.[1] Similarly exclusion clauses in a contract between a business and a consumer (defined by section 12 of the Act as, in effect, one who is not a business contracting with the other party who is in the course of a business) will attract the attention of section 3, thus covering a building firm taking on work for a householder. A fourth situation is where neither party is in business; this is outside the scope of the 1977 Act.[2] Thus section 3 only applies where a contractor is dealing either with a consumer or (on written standard terms of business) with another business.

1 See para 3.39, below.
2 Unfair Contract Terms Act 1977, s. 1(3). See para 2.31, above.

3.39   It is therefore crucial to explain what are and are not written standard terms of business, especially in the area of building contracts where standard-form contracts are available and widely used, but rarely in their entirety.[1] Unfortunately, the 1977 Act is sorely remiss in this respect, providing no definition whatsoever of this highly significant term. The Law Commission's bland assertion that no definition of the term was necessary since the courts could recognise without difficulty what were or were not written standard terms of business[2] seems to have been accepted by Parliament without demur. However, a few examples in the context of building contracts may suffice to illustrate the problems posed by the inherent vagueness of the phrase. One building firm may invariably do no more than adopt in its entirety the JCT or some other standard-form contract in dealing with other businesses and it is possible to argue that this is outside section 3 insofar as the firm is not using its own standard terms, but rather terms devised by someone else. It is suggested that this may be an over-restrictive interpretation, however, and that the better approach is simply to investigate whether the firm always uses the same terms, thus in this example adopting the JCT terms as their own. Another building firm might always base their contracts on the JCT or some other standard-form contract but depart from it to a limited extent, e g by adding an exclusion clause or varying the dates when payments are due. Can this be said to be use of written standard terms of business? It is suggested that such a case would fall within section 3 if the same adaptations were invariably used – this again would amount to that particular firm's written standard terms of business; however, if different variations to a basically similar contract were being employed greater difficulty arises. In the absence of any statutory guidance, it is submitted that a commonsense view would be that each case would have to be examined on its facts; for example, if the key terms of the contract are standardised or the variations do not affect the particular clause under discussion then it should still be regarded as a standard-form contract for the purposes of section 3.

1 See para 3.48, below.
2 Law Commission, Second Report on Exemption Clauses (Law Com No 69) para 157.

3.40 No apology is made for this somewhat inconclusive treatment of the scope of section 3. Such a treatment is inevitable when Parliament promulgates such sloppily drafted enactments. It does seem reasonably clear, however, that emphasis should be placed on an examination of the terms the particular contractor habitually uses, rather than on the contract in general and rather than the general standardisation or otherwise of the terms in question. It is to be hoped that brave contractors will undertake litigation to ascertain the meaning of the provision, but it is conceded that their legal advisers might be correct not to recommend such a course of action when faced with such uncertainty that no obvious result could confidently be predicted in many cases.

3.41 Once it is established that an exclusion clause has come within the scope of section 3, the difficulties are still not over. The effect of section 3(2) is to say that, for example in a case where a builder is seeking to rely on an exclusion clause in his contract, the builder can neither exclude his liability nor, alternatively, substantially change what he has promised to do with reference to the exclusion clause, unless that clause satisfies the requirement of reasonableness. The usual uncertainties as to what may be regarded as being reasonable apply here, just as with section 2(2).[1]

1 See para 3.36, above.

3.42 The third aspect of the Unfair Contract Terms Act to which attention needs to be drawn is section 7, which will cover work and materials contracts. It is clear from such cases as *Young and Marten Ltd v McManus Childs Ltd*[1] that implied terms generally similar to those laid down by legislation for sale of goods contracts apply in such contracts, and it is therefore unsurprising that the controls on exclusion clauses are similar in each instance. Again, there are several different sets of provisions in different contractual contexts. By section 7(2) a builder cannot exclude his liability against a private customer when the materials he installs (thereby passing ownership and/or possession from himself to the customer) are unfit for their purpose, do not correspond with description or sample or are of inadequate quality (this latter term seems somewhat vague – *quaere* whether there is such an implied term). In other cases encompassed by the section, i e for our purposes where a builder makes a contract for work and materials with another business, section 7(3) applies; this permits exclusion of liability in all cases but equally invariably will only permit such exclusion clauses to take effect if they satisfy the requirement of reasonableness.

1 [1969] 1 AC 454, [1968] 2 All ER 1169.

3.43 Once again the vague notion of reasonableness is explained to a limited extent by section 11, but in this instance some further assistance is given. By section 11(2) in cases where reasonableness falls to be determined under section 7(3), additional regard is to be paid to the matters referred to in Schedule 2 of the Act. These are as follows:

(a) the strength of the bargaining positions of the parties relative to each other, taking into account (among other things) alternative means by which the customer's requirements could have been met;

(b) whether the customer received an inducement to agree to the term, or in accepting it had an opportunity of entering into a similar contract with other persons, but without having to accept a similar term;

(c) whether the customer knew or ought reasonably to have known of the existence and extent of the term (having regard, among other things, to any custom of the trade and any previous course of dealing between the parties);

(d) where the term excludes or restricts any relevant liability if some condition is not complied with, whether it was reasonable at the time of the contract to expect that compliance with that condition would be practicable.

(e) whether the goods were manufactured, processed or adapted to the special order of the customer.

These additional criteria are of value in assisting the contractor and his advisers to determine whether an exemption clause is reasonable or not. The importation into English law of an attempt to assess the relative bargaining power of the parties is novel but realistic, while the examination of whether the offending clause is balanced by some appropriate inducement is a further example of the refreshingly realistic approach embodied by this part of the Act, at least. The final factor (whether the order is a special one or not) may be of particular significance in building contract cases; it is the specialist manufacturer of equipment who is particularly likely to adopt the 'work and materials' type of contract and, at least in the past, such a person has been particularly likely to use exemption clauses in his contracts. It is still fair to say that there are difficulties in assessing the reasonableness or otherwise of a clause under these provisions, but that the greater guidance offered in section 7 cases is welcome.

3.44 One further point should be noted concerning the applicability of the Unfair Contract Terms Act as regards builders who not only build premises but also then sell them, i e builder-vendors. At first sight, the 1977 Act does not apply to exclusion clauses inserted in builder-vendors' contracts but on closer examination Schedule 1, paragraph 1(b) only limits the scope of the applicability of sections 2–4 of the Act insofar as a contract relates to creation or transfer of an interest in land; in other words, it seems clear that any attempt by a builder-vendor to exclude liability for breach of the contract insofar as it is a breach of his obligations vis-à-vis construction will still be governed by the 1977 Act. In any event, the control of exemption clauses by section 7 of the Act is not restricted by Schedule 1 thereto.

3.45 Although exclusion clauses do not occupy a central role in the law relating to building contracts, they are still often to be found and therefore no apology is made for the full coverage of the Unfair Contract Terms Act's provisions (further justification may be found simply from the widespread fears of its potential for disruption held amongst many businessmen). Its effect may be summarised as the simultaneous creation of greater fairness in contractual dealings but also, as an unwelcome corollary, greater uncertainty. The Act will in most building contract cases have the effect of imposing the requirement of reasonableness on the wide range of exclusion clauses that fall within its ambit and it is this requirement which, as a result of the novelty of its presence in contractual situations and its unfortunate lack of definition or accompanying guidance, gives rise to the greatest difficulty of practical operation. It will be a brave adviser who would let his builder clients incur the expense of litigation over so uncertain and indefinable a concept as reasonableness, and ironically it is only such litigation that is ever likely to indicate a path through the uncertainty and lack of clear definition.

3.46 Special provision may be made in a building contract to ensure that the contractor is held liable to indemnify the employer against certain liabilities. Obviously the precise scope of such arrangements is a matter for agreement between the parties; however, the JCT form makes particular provision for such cases. By clause 20.1 the contractor must indemnify the employer for any liability for death or personal injury which is imposed on the employer in consequence of the execution of the works unless the contractor can himself establish that the liability was a result of an act or omission by the employer or someone for whom the employer is legally responsible – a difficult burden is thus placed on a contractor who seeks to avoid this indemnity liability. Similarly, by clause 20.2 of the JCT form the contractor is further liable to indemnify the employer against the latter's liability for losses other than those encompassed by clause 20.1, i e property damage, presumably including loss of value though this is not explicit; in this instance, however, it is for the employer to establish that the contractor or his sub-contractors, servants or agents are at fault. By clause 21, backing is given to the liabilities imposed on contractors (by clause 20) by an insistence that the contractor insures himself, and establishes that his sub-contractors are insured, against their liabilities, not only in relation to these indemnities, but generally in relation to any liability which may be imposed on them by third parties or in relation to the works undertaken. Cover must at least be provided until the end of the defects liability period. To ensure compliance with these provisions, by clause 21.1.3 the employer himself is entitled to take out insurance and deduct its cost from the sums payable under the contract if the contractor or sub-contractor are in breach of their obligations to insure.

3.47 Further arrangements apply in the case of certain other potential risks to premises. No insurance needs to be taken out against nuclear perils (by clause 21.3). More importantly, special provisions apply in the case of insurance against fire and other perils known as 'Clause 22 perils' which are defined in clause 1 and include storm damage, riot and burst water pipes, inter alia. Parties must decide which of three alternative clauses in the JCT form to employ. Clause 22A is appropriate where the contractor is to undertake the principal responsibility; he must then insure all the works (except his own plant and equipment and that of his sub-contractors) in the joint names of himself and the employer and this will cover any defects arising from 'Clause 22 perils' up to the end of the defects liability period. Clause 22B is appropriate where the employer agrees to accept the burden of insurance; in the event of any default the contractor may insure and charge for this. Clause 22C applies where work is undertaken in relation to a pre-existing building. Here, the employer will take the primary responsibility; however, any necessary remedial work within the ambit of clause 22 will usually be carried out by the contractor, but will be treated by him as a contractual fluctuation.

3.48 It is obvious that almost all major building work today is carried out under the aegis of a building contract and that in all but the most straightforward instances the parties will wholly or partly adopt an appropriate standard-form building contract. Any disputes which arise in relation to the works will normally arise between the parties to the contract and thus fall initially to be determined by reference to the building contract. How effective that determination will be will depend on the terms in question; the standard-form contract as exemplified by the JCT form is not without its problems – the drafting is not perfect in places[1] and not all the liabilities are delineated in a manner satisfactory to all interested parties, perhaps unsurprisingly. It is fair to say that the sections which cover defects liability are on the whole satisfactory. On the other hand, anyone who seeks to depart from the provisions of such forms must take care to ensure that their contract covers the detailed range of issues, and that their terms attain the kind of 'success-rate' which it is fair to attribute to the standard forms of building contracts. It is thus likely that, notwithstanding initial criticism, the 1980 version of the JCT form will gain recognition and will be utilised with at least the regularity of its predecessors and it is fair to state that in our view its provisions cover, and usually cover effectively, the relevant issues as regards defects in the premises.

1 See Julian (1980) 130 NLJ 635.

The NHBC scheme

3.49 Additional contractual liabilities are, in general terms, imposed upon the builder when he is a builder-vendor of a dwelling and is a member of the National House-Building Council's National Register of House-Builders and Developers. The significance of these additional liabilities may be gauged by two factors: firstly, figures produced by the National House-Building Council (hereinafter referred to as the NHBC) indicate that by early 1981 two million new houses were under the protection of the NHBC's scheme; secondly, the protection afforded through the liability created by section 1 of the Defective Premises Act 1972[1] does not apply in the case of houses within the ambit of the NHBC's protection. This is by virtue of section 2 of the 1972 Act, whereby the remedies under section 1 do not extend to the occupier of a dwelling-house where that occupier has had conferred on him rights in respect of defects in the state of the premises by virtue of 'an approved scheme', i e any scheme conferring such rights that has been formally approved by the Secretary of State; the NHBC's scheme of protection is the only scheme currently approved.[2]

1 See paras 3.104 ff, below.
2 The House-Building Standards (Approved Scheme, etc.) Order 1979 (SI 1979 No 381).

3.50 A brief word is in order concerning the status and background of the NHBC before considering the extent of the additional liabilities accepted by the Council's members. In essence, the scheme has its origin, just before World War II, as a method of self-regulation on the part of the building trade with the aim of raising the standard of house-building generally, and in particular combating the growing fears then developing concerning the problem of 'jerry-building'. Over the years the Council and its work received only limited, though always gradually increasing, support from builders of houses, but the major change in attitudes took place after the election of the Wilson Government in 1964, when a distinct possibility of considerable statutory control of the house-building industry emerged. At this juncture, the virtues of self-regulation became clearer to builders, and by 1973, over 20,000 builders (i e the vast majority) were registered with the Council.[1] As will be seen, the NHBC is now active in setting standards for building work and meeting and settling occupiers' claims, and it aims simultaneously to raise the standard of house-building in the United Kingdom, and to assist the occupier to obtain a remedy in those cases where the standard of building work remains at an unacceptable level.

1 Tapping and Rolfe *Guarantees for New Homes* p. 2.

3.51 As will be appreciated, a substantial majority of the country's building firms are now on the NHBC's register. The conditions for entry to the register are by no means simple, but in essence they are that the firm must be one engaged in some way in the provision of dwelling-houses for sale or letting to the public, thus embracing both builders and developers. The firm may anticipate that their application will be carefully examined by the NHBC with particular regard to technical standards of the past and present work undertaken by the firm, the firm's financial status and their links with other firms. If the application is accepted, this is as often as not subject to financial or other conditions, in which case the firm is particularly likely to be admitted to the register on a probationary basis only, at first.[1]

1 See Tapping and Rolfe *Guarantees for New Homes* ch 2 for further details.

3.52 Once admitted as a member, the builder[1] has imposed on him two related sets of obligations viz his duties towards the NHBC and the rights it in turn insists on the builder giving to his customers. As far as his relationship with the Council itself is concerned, little needs to be said in the context of this work; the NHBC imposes various requirements as to construction standards, as will be seen, and has considerable powers of inspection and certification to support them. The builder is also obliged by dint of his membership of the NHBC to offer the house-purchaser guarantees relating to the property. In the event of a breach of any of these obligations, the Council has extensive disciplinary powers, and may remove offending firms from its Register, give warnings invoking this threat, impose conditions only on compliance with which continued membership of the scheme will be allowed or insist on increased payments to the NHBC from the defaulting builder. These, then, are some of the mechanisms of self-regulation adopted by the building industry; it is fair to say that they in themselves provide sound support for the attempt to raise building standards, though it is also fair to say that the factor that militates even more in favour of compliance with the NHBC rules is that the building societies have recognised the higher standard of new houses constructed by NHBC members and have increasingly adopted a policy whereby they will not offer mortgage facilities in relation to new houses not constructed by NHBC members. Thus, any builder proposing to erect new dwelling-houses for which prospective purchasers will need mortgage facilities (i e virtually all houses, except flats, bungalows, etc. with retirement or similar use by established households in mind) will need to become NHBC members.

1 In this section this term may be taken as including developers; see paras 3.57 and 3.59, below.

3.53 Let us turn to the central issue – in what way is the NHBC member obliged to improve the quality of his work? Associated with this is the question of how his civil liabilities (and his customer's rights) are increased by reason of NHBC membership. The answers to these key questions lie in the three principal tenets of NHBC membership. Firstly, the member has to comply with quite detailed technical standards governing the quality of the building work; secondly, he must offer his customers the standard-form House-Purchaser's Agreement which confers on the purchaser additional rights; thirdly, the builder must also complete his work to a standard sufficient to obtain the Council's own Notice of Insurance Cover which in turn acts as an important additional safeguard for the customer.

3.54 As to the technical standards insisted on, it is clear that in some respects these go further than any statutory requirements, not least in the ever-increasing range of details which are covered. The technical requirements of the NHBC scheme list what are regarded as minimum standards for the erection of dwellings, covering both issues of general design and particular points for the guidance of the various trades engaged in house-building, and detailed specifications are also laid down, compliance with which will give clear compliance with the more general requirements. The issues covered by this dual pattern of standards range from such fundamentals as the materials used in the construction, the depth of the foundations and the strength of the structure through such details as minimum heights for ceilings to such minutiae as the number of electrical sockets in different rooms and the size and arrangement of kitchen fittings. This range of provisions is backed up by a considerable system of inspection of the premises during the construction work by the NHBC itself; the NHBC's policy is to visit any particular development on frequent (at least once a month) unannounced visits during the construction period, all the houses being visited at some stage of their construction.

3.55 If the house, during its period of construction, is found to be wanting insofar as it does not come up to the NHBC's technical standards, there are two courses of action open to the NHBC. Naturally, if some technical requirement has not been complied with, no certificate will be granted in relation to the premises, at least not until the defect has been remedied, within a specific period.

Alternatively, the Council may decide to take disciplinary action against the member concerned, this being particularly likely in the case of serious or recurrent breaches of the technical requirements, and this action may involve, after appropriate hearings and appeals, the ultimate sanction of expulsion from the register. On the other hand, if the NHBC is satisfied with the house in consequence of the random inspections, then it is bound to accept its issue of the Notice of Insurance Cover as binding, The Council is under a duty to issue this Notice if inspection has revealed no substantial breach of the requirements, this being one of the promises to its members under the rules, and once issued it is from the NHBC's standpoint conclusive, even if the actual defect was never discovered by the inspection. Similarly, the Council's Notice is effective if they issue the Notice while minor matters remain to be dealt with, unless specific factors cause the NHBC to endorse the Notice, such as where a purchaser insists on construction to less stringent standards.

3.56 From the standpoint of the house-purchaser, this provides only background assurance. It is of little avail if his house falls outside these general rules and he therefore needs to rely on the issue of the NHBC's Notice, showing the importance of the obligation imposed on the NHBC to issue the Notice even while matters still need to be dealt with, above, or on the promises made by the builder, in the House-builder's Agreement which builders who are members of the NHBC are obliged to offer to their purchasers at or before the time of sale. This is nominally a separate contract, for the benefits of which the purchaser has to provide separate consideration – a nominal ten pence. It is the rights conferred by this agreement that will form the primary remedy for the purchaser of a defective dwelling-house and so the contents of the Agreement must be examined, concentration being given solely to the current NHBC form, known as HB5 (1979), which took effect in relation to all new house construction after 1 April 1979.[1] No specific reference will be made to the analogous forms dealing with cases where a local authority is a vendor.

1 See Adams (1980) 130 NLJ 171 for a discussion of the new form with extensive quotation of its terms.

3.57 The current form initially establishes that the house-purchaser's rights under the Agreement are additional to any other rights conferred by the law, and the next three clauses of the Agreement go on to outline the builder's principal warranties. (The Agreement refers to the vendor's responsibilities, so bringing developers within the scope of the scheme, as well as builder-vendors; to be consistent with the rest of the chapter and to avoid confusion, references herein will be to builders, not vendors.) Clause 2 of the Agreement establishes a warranty by the builder that he is on the NHBC's register, and has applied to the Council for his premises to be inspected. Clause 3, sometimes referred to as the 'common-law rights' clause, provides a promise by the builder that 'the Dwelling has been or will be built in an effective and workmanlike manner and of proper materials and so as to be fit for habitation'. This clearly establishes the wide range of potential defects which fall within the ambit of the Agreement and, as will be seen, effectively extends the contractual rights of the purchaser to his successors in title. Clause 4 provides further that the builder will arrange for insurance cover by the NHBC[1] in relation to the dwelling. Further warranties describing the consequences of defective construction work are to be found in subsequent provisions of the Agreement. By clause 9, the builder is held liable to rectify any damage caused to a house caused by defects in adjoining or adjacent dwelling-houses where he has been involved in the construction thereof but, more importantly, it is clause 6 which establishes the builder's principal obligation in the event of his construction work proving defective. It states that the builder shall 'within a reasonable time and at his own expense remedy any defect in the Dwelling caused by a breach of the Council's requirements and any damage to the Dwelling caused by such defect'. Thus, subject to the various limitations on the remedy, discussed later, the NHBC scheme provides a specific obligation on the builder's part to return to the site and make good defects and their consequences. This may rightly be regarded as a considerable improvement on the position at common law, where, although damages are payable, no specific obligation on the builder to return exists.[2] The Agreement thus confers two related sets of obligation, the general warranties, particularly of sound construction, and the specific promise to put right any defects which may appear e g where the breach of obligation has led to a positive danger or loss of value of the premises.[3]

1 See paras 3.69 ff, below.
2 Adams (1980) 130 NLJ 171 at 173, *dubitante*.
3 Tapping and Rolfe *Guarantees for New Homes* pp. 94 ff.

3.58 Particular rules apply concerning the enforcement of the purchaser's rights under the Agreement, and clause 11 is the key to their discussion. Formerly, all issues arising from any alleged breaches of the Agreement had to be referred to arbitration, but, since 1974, a twofold system has applied. For any dispute concerning clause 3 of the Agreement, resort must be had to the courts. This may seem to be disadvantageous to the purchaser, putting him at a clear disadvantage vis-à-vis the builder, but it is fair to note that legal aid is not available in arbitrations, whereas in a court case at least some house-owners will have part of their costs defrayed by the Legal Aid Fund, the exact proportion obviously depending on the means of the individuals in question, with their capital resources being taken into account.[1] It is also pointed out that the courts are far more experienced in the assessment of general damages though this seems a rather self-perpetuating argument. It however seems reasonably clear that most claims by house-purchasers should be framed under other clauses of the Agreement, since clause 11 insists that any dispute other than one arising through the operation of clause 3 must be referred to arbitration, the actual arbitrator being selected by the Institute of Arbitrators, unless either party wishes to take both the dispute under the Agreement and a dispute under any other agreement (such as a contractual term imposing obligations beyond those imposed by the NHBC) to the courts. It may confidently be argued that the opportunity of a quicker and less formal arbitration by an experienced arbitrator represents one of the major advantages of the NHBC scheme over other available remedies.

1 Tapping and Rolfe *Guarantees for New Homes* p. 218.

3.59 The picture so far drawn of the advantageous rights and enforcement procedures given to the house-purchaser under the NHBC scheme is, it is fair to say, a somewhat one-sided one. In fact, the scheme operates subject to a considerable number of restrictions, albeit in many cases entirely sensible and justifiable ones. The Agreement defines most of the terms used therein but these definitions are drawn in a way that rarely hinders a purchaser's claim. For example the key concept of the 'Dwelling', the only premises covered by the scheme, is defined so as to cover not only the actual house, flat, etc., but also a wide range of associated works such as garages, so long as they are within the curtilage of the premises and are constructed simultaneously with the actual dwelling-house, except that lifts, fences and constructions of impermanent materials are specifically excluded.[1] The parties actually covered by the Agreement are also defined in clause 12; the 'Purchaser' includes not only the named first purchaser but also his successors in title and mortgagees in possession, thus enabling subsequent purchasers etc. to enjoy the benefits of both the 'common law rights clause' and the specific clause 6 obligations, while the builder or, in the terminology of the NHBC, the 'Developer', who is the other party to the Agreement, is defined exceptionally broadly as 'any person, partnership, company or organisation that arranges for the construction of dwellings or is concerned in or with such arrangements', thus embracing both builders and developers. Generally, the parameters of the scheme are, if not precisely, then at least broadly defined.

1 NHBC Agreement, cl 12.

3.60 More genuine restrictions are laid down through attempts to limit the time in which the purchaser is obliged to present his claim under the NHBC agreement. By clause 5, the builder is not liable for any breach of the warranty in clause 3,[1] if the defect or consequent damage does not appear until after the Initial Guarantee Period has expired, unless a wholly or partly unsuccessful claim has been made against the NHBC itself under its Insurance scheme.[2] Yet more significantly, the purchaser's rights under clause 6 are made subject to the requirement that the purchaser must report the defect to the builder within the Initial Guarantee Period, although if work undertaken fails to rectify the defect, the builder will continue to be liable even after the Initial Guarantee Period has expired. What then is the Initial Guarantee Period? The Agreement in essence defines the Period as one or two years from issue of the NHBC's own Notice of Insurance Cover,[3] which will generally occur, at the latest, at the time when contracts are exchanged. In exceptional circumstances, the period is varied; firstly, where the dwelling has been unoccupied for over twelve months from the issue of the NHBC's notice of insurance cover, in which case the Period runs from one year from the completion of the first purchase of the dwelling, and secondly, in relation to the Common Parts (i e parts of flats, etc., for which the purchaser is liable to share in repair costs, though not actually part of the property he owns) where the Initial Guarantee Period is two years from the issue of the (separate) insurance cover required for such parts, or, if later, a period of one year from the completion of purchase of the first flat in the building. In essence, then, the purchaser may usually only act against the builder within the first two years, except where the NHBC's Insurance Scheme has rejected a claim in whole or to some extent alleging a breach of the 'common law rights' clause. Even then, such an action will be subject to the usual contractual limitation period of six years from the accrual of the cause of action i e the date of the breach,[4] though the court's duty to extend the limitation period in cases of fraud[5] is widely interpreted in building cases. A good recent example is *Applegate v Moss*[6] where the defective foundations effectively concealed by the subsequent erection of the property were permitted to form the subject of an action ten years after the contract was made; the Court of Appeal held that notwithstanding the absence of any proven dishonesty, it was enough that it was inequitable for the defendant to be able to rely on a limitation point in view of the facts of the case i e the fact that concealment had inevitably taken place shortly after the defective foundations were constructed.

1 See para 3.57, above.

2 See paras 3.69 ff, below.
3 See paras 3.69 ff, below.
4 Limitation Act 1980, s. 2.
5 Ibid, s. 32.
6 [1971] 1 QB 406, [1971] 1 All ER 747. See also para 1.43, above.

3.61 Further restrictions are imposed by clause 7 of the NHBC agreement, which refers to five factors which will enable the builder to escape his liability under clause 6. Firstly, the purchaser, to safeguard his remedy, must give the builder written notice of any defects as soon as is practicable, although in some ways, this probably does not go as far as clause 6, where as has been seen the remedy is subject to the condition that the builder's liability only arises in relation to defects and damage notified to the builder in writing before the end of the Initial Guarantee Period. It has been suggested that these rules will be interpreted leniently,[1] and at least in the event of non-written notice being given, it will be open to the courts to state that the builder has waived this particular requirement, as in *Marchant v Caswell and Redgrave Ltd,*[2] where it was clear that the builder knew of the defects as a result of verbal complaints, so could not be permitted to complain of the lack of written notice subsequently. Secondly, clause 7 permits the builder to resist liability as against a subsequent purchaser if the previous purchaser has failed to notify the builder of any defects. Any potential injustice stemming from this rule can presumably be alleviated by specific enquiry before sale takes place; in any case, the rule does not apply as against a mortgagee in possession. Thirdly, it is stated that no liability under clause 6 will arise where the defect complained of is in relation to central heating boilers, electrical installations with moving parts or where damage is caused by such defects after the first twelve months of the Initial Guarantee Period. While it may be argued that it is right to exempt the builder from liability for defects that are in reality better laid at the door of the supplier who provides the equipment in question, it is unfortunate that a combination of privity of contract and the inability to sue in negligence unless both fault is proven and physical injury caused may leave the purchaser without a remedy for these equipment defects. Fourthly, and understandably, the builder is not liable for defects in and damage arising from anything built into the premises outside the principal building or sale agreement, while, fifthly, there is no liability for defective design, where the purchaser provided the relevant specifications.

1 Adams (1980) 130 NLJ 171.
2 (1976) 240 Estates Gazette 127.

3.62 Clause 8 also includes restrictions on the builder's liability; it states that no liability arises under the Agreement where defects or damage are caused by either wear and tear or gradual deterioration caused by neglect or by normal dampness, condensation or shrinkage. It may be argued that this clause raises certain difficulties. Of course its purpose is clear, and it represents a sensible recognition that all new houses will not retain their initial sparkle; it is conceded that a clause on the lines of clause 8 must be part of the Agreement in fairness to the builder. However, it is also submitted that the actual clause 8 has the potential to act against both parties' interests, since the concept of 'wear and tear', for example, is so inherently subjective that resolution of any dispute on the issue will not only be a long procedure, involving considerable factual analysis, but will ultimately also be an inherently unpredictable factor, making amicable settlement of disputes more difficult. Similarly, 'normal dampness' is capable of being a matter of considerable dispute, with scope for seriously conflicting arguments. In this particular instance, also, the terminology should be clearer in view of the considerable number of disputes that have arisen concerning modern houses and flats unduly suffering from dampness and/or condensation. Clearer guidelines, perhaps in corporating specific time-limits, would provide better guidance to both builders and purchasers in this respect.

3.63 One potential important defence to an action against the builder is the question of privity of contract. We have already seen[1] that, for the purposes of all parts of the Agreement, the 'Purchaser' is defined as including subsequent purchasers, as well as the initial purchaser, of a dwelling within the NHBC scheme. This, however, is not enough of itself to defeat an argument based on privity; it is clear that merely mentioning someone as a party to a contract does not of itself render them privy to that contract, able to enforce benefits or have liabilities imposed on them.[2] How, then, are builders prevented from raising issues of privity? The ideal method is of course for there to be an assignment to the subsequent purchaser of the benefit of the Agreement, under section 136, Law of Property Act 1925, with due formality, in particular with express notice in writing to the builder. This should normally take place, indeed for some years the NHBC provided a recommended form of express assignment, but still some failures to assign the benefit of the Agreement were taking place. Other methods, therefore, had to be considered, and the first reasonably successful attempt to control this problem was provided by the NHBC's rules of membership, which provide that a member shall not take any points in a dispute with a purchaser if they raise any lack of assignment; thus a member will face the risk of disciplinary proceedings in the event of a breach of the rule. Even this may not satisfy the purchaser, however, since it is possible to conceive of cases where the builder would opt for this course, e g where the alternative is for him to face a claim for the death and/or personal injury of a subsequent purchaser and his large family in a house fire caused by a defect.

1 See para 3.59, above.
2 See e g *Dunlop Pneumatic Tyre Co Ltd v Selfridge & Co Ltd* [1915] AC 847; *New Zealand Shipping Co Ltd v A M Satterthwaite & Co Ltd* [1975] AC 154, [1974] 1 All ER 1015.

3.64 The latest version of the NHBC Agreement has therefore attempted to cover this problem by clause 10, which states, 'This Agreement is made by the First Purchaser on behalf of himself and his successors in title and his and their mortgagees in possession. The Vendor undertakes that he shall not seek to deny liability under this Agreement on the ground that it has not been assigned.' This has the effect of providing a clear contractual undertaking by the builder not to use the lack of an assignment as a defence, but it is submitted that this of itself is no answer, since this admittedly clear obligation is still only owed to the first purchaser. The claim of the Agreement to be made on behalf of subsequent purchasers can only be sustained in law if it can be said that the subsequent purchasers are party to the Agreement and this still does not appear to be the case; the statement that the initial purchaser is acting 'on behalf of' his successors in title is one that will only have legal effect if it can be shown that the initial purchaser is acting as agent for the subsequent purchasers and this seems unlikely in the light of Lord Reid's statement in *Scruttons Ltd v Midland Silicones Ltd*[1] that the concept of agency can only be permitted to circumvent the doctrine of privity of contract in certain limited and closely circumscribed circumstances. In particular, Lord Reid noted that not only must the contractual document make it clear that the third party is intended to be protected, and the contract is expressly made on the third party's behalf (these factors are probably satisfied by clause 10), but also there must be authority from the third party, or at the very least (and then arguably) subsequent ratification and consideration must also move from the third party. These latter factors will be harder to establish against the builder; even if subsequent ratification is permissible, which is unclear, especially where there is no previous course of dealing,[2] it is difficult to discern any consideration moving from the subsequent purchaser at a time when they have no knowledge that a contract is being made or that there is a possibility that it will benefit them in any way. It does not seem possible to construct any argument based on any species of collateral contract either; again, the subsequent purchaser, a figure unknown at the time and possibly never materialising, is in no sense privy to any of the arrangements at the time of the initial sale; only the initial purchaser can sue in contract for the builder's failure to honour the 'no assignment' clause, and he has suffered no loss consequent on the breach, unless he is sued later by the subsequent purchaser as a result of his inability to obtain compensation from the builder due to lack of assignment, in which relatively unlikely situation,[3] the contract might be capable of use so as to provide the first purchaser with an indemnity.

1 [1962] AC 446 at 474, [1962] 1 All ER 1 at 10.
2 See *The Suleyman Stalskiy* [1976] 2 Lloyd's Rep 609.
3 See ch 6, below, for vendor's liability.

3.65 A further way in which the subsequent purchaser may be able to take the benefit of the Agreement might be if the NHBC Agreement falls within the ambit of section 78, Law of Property Act 1925. This states, by subsection (1): 'A covenant relating to the land of the covenantee shall be deemed to be made with the covenantee and his successors in title and the persons deriving title under him or them, and shall have effect as if such successors and other persons were expressed.' This was relied on in one of the rare reported cases in this area, *Marchant v Caswell and Redgrave Ltd*,[1] a decision of the Official Referee. It was stated[2] that the use in the NHBC Agreement of the words 'purchaser' and 'successors in title' made it clear that it was the intention of the parties to the agreement that the benefit of the contract should run with the land to operate as a covenant within the provisions of section 78 of the 1925 Act. The decision follows *Smith and Snipes Hall Farm Ltd v River Douglas Catchment Board*[3] and the general approach was recently endorsed in *Federated Homes Ltd v Mill Lodge Properties Ltd*[4] confirming that section 78 has the effect of annexing the benefit of the covenant to the convenantee's land. This seemingly straightforward *Marchant* decision is not without difficulty, however; indeed its approach has been described as 'more than dubious'.[5] What then are the objections to it? Firstly, although there is no statutory definition of the word 'covenant', it is normally regarded as connoting an agreement by deed,[6] being rarely used for less formal agreements, except occasionally in the context of leases.[7] This argument would not apply, needless to say, if the Agreement were to be incorporated into the terms of the contract and formally conveyed under seal. Indeed, a clause in the contract asserting that an assignment of the benefit of the NHBC Agreement will take place would give a purchaser protection. This major objection may be supplemented by the fact that for the benefit of any positive covenant to run, the covenantee must at that time, at common law, have a legal interest in the land benefited.[8] Since the NHBC Agreement is a separate contract made before the property is conveyed to the purchaser (thus becoming his), it would seem that it is incapable of being regarded as a covenant on this ground, too, in view of the lack of legal interest in the land on the part of the covenantee at the crucial time. It is unclear whether an equitable interest would suffice; it seems that this would represent an extension of the law, albeit perhaps a reasonable one in an area where common law and equitable principles have become intertwined.[9] In any event, at present it is clear that *Marchant v Caswell and Redgrave Ltd*[10] should not have too much reliance placed on it, and that section 78 should perhaps be regarded solely as governing the extension of the benefits of undoubted covenants to all the covenantee's successors in title, not just those with precisely the same legal estate in the land.

1 (1976) 240 Estates Gazette 127.
2 Ibid at 133.
3 [1949] 2 KB 500, [1949] 2 All ER 179.
4 [1980] 1 All ER 371, [1980] 1 WLR 594.
5 Adams (1980) 131 NLJ 171 at 173.
6 Megarry and Wade *The Law of Real Property* (4th edn) p. 720.
7 E g *Weg Motors Ltd v Hales* [1962] Ch 49, [1961] 3 All ER 181.
8 *Megarry and Wade* p. 720.
9 *Megarry and Wade* p. 761.
10 (1976) 240 Estates Gazette 127.

3.66 It may therefore be argued that in the absence of a proper assignment, no certain benefits of the NHBC Agreement will accrue to a subsequent purchaser, on the assumption that he will not benefit from any disciplinary proceedings instigated by the NHBC itself. From this it inevitably follows that, in the opinion of the authors, the first purchaser must formally assign the benefit of the Agreement, and the subsequent purchasers' solicitors should check that this has occurred. Indeed, it would seem not unreasonable to suggest that solicitors would be in danger of falling foul of their professional duties of care and skill for failure to check that assignment has taken place, were it not for the weight of opinion, especially that of the NHBC itself, contrary to that presently expressed.

3.67 Some further points fall to be made concerning the ambit of the NHBC Agreement. Firstly, it is doubtless clear that only defects and/or damage arising therefrom fall within the Agreement, thus excluding such key factors (to the purchaser) as the price paid for the premises. Such claims are left to be dealt with by the ordinary law of contract, and will generally not succeed, the *caveat emptor* principle still having great effect. Secondly, the Council refuses to accept any liability for claims from disgruntled purchasers who discover that their builder has falsely claimed to be an NHBC member; while of course justifiable from the Council's viewpoint, it is possible to draw faintly invidious comparisons with the broader responsibilities undertaken by insurance firms through the medium of the Motor Insurer's Bureau. This is perhaps an unfair criticism, however; in general terms, the degree of self-regulation imposed by the building industry is a sound advertisement for the principle itself. However, this is not the time for a general commentary on the NHBC and its work, since there has as yet been no discussion of the second aspect of the protection provided under the Council's aegis. A final shortcoming which needs to be noted is that the scheme only attempts to cover property damage; no claim may be made in respect of personal injuries. Recourse must be had to the law of negligence in respect of such injuries.

3.68 It is doubtless trite to point out that while there are many defects which may become patent at a very early stage in the history of a property, equally other defects may remain dormant for many years before becoming apparent; such latent defects may well include very serious matters such as structural defects in the foundations which in many cases have either not materialised for some years or have in their early stages been diagnosed as normal shrinkage or slight settlement. Obviously, such defects, once apparent, have a substantial effect on the value of the property and the NHBC has attempted to provide compensation for the house-purchaser affected by such types of defect, by providing insurance cover.

3.69 It will be recalled that the builder is obliged to obtain for the purchaser the NHBC's Notice of Insurance Cover, and that the builder makes a warranty to that effect by clause 4 of the Agreement. Further, by clause 5,[1] the builder will accept no claims in respect of defects arising after the Initial Guarantee Period unless a claim has been brought against the Council itself. All this emphasises the importance of the insurance provisions and a more detailed examination of its provisions is in order. The Notice has contractual effect as between the NHBC and the first purchaser, though is contingent on an NHBC Agreement being made in relation to the same property, and again subsequent purchasers are intended to take the benefits of the insurance scheme, since the NHBC Agreement includes the promises, just noted, by the builder to obtain insurance cover, and these promises are owed[2] to all subsequent purchasers. On the other hand, the authors' doubts as to the binding quality of the promises in question apply equally here.

1 See para 3.60, above.
2 See para 3.59, above.

3.70 The main thrust of the attack on the problem of the latent defect comes in Section III of the Council's insurance policy, which covers a period from the end of the Initial Guarantee Period,[1] normally two years after insurance cover commences, until ten years have elapsed from the day insurance cover commenced. In this period, it is the NHBC's own responsibility to meet the cost of major damage to the house, the specific provision being that they will compensate the purchaser for damage arising from defects 'requiring complete or partial rebuilding or extensive repair work'; this includes defects in the structure itself, as well as problems of subsidence, settlement, etc. There is no coverage during this period for minor defects, but this is obviously outweighed by the significance of the protection against latent defects. There are however some restrictions on the scope of the insurance cover. Section III of the policy will not compensate the householder where the cost of repairs necessary to remedy the defect is recoverable under other insurance at the time of the claim. Presumably where only part of the cost is claimable (e g the value of the house at the time of the discovery of the defect, per the Court of Appeal in the recent case of *Leppard v Excess Insurance Co Ltd*),[2] the NHBC will meet the extra sum required for full repair. Equally the Council would seemingly be able to pass the burden of compensation to either the householder's or the builder's insurers – the wording of the insurance policy is (deliberately?) ambiguous at this point. Further, conditions are attached to recovery under this section of the policy, mostly reflecting the conditions placed on recovery from the builder under the NHBC Agreement. Thus, no claim will succeed if the defect arose during the Initial Guarantee Period but was not notified appropriately at that stage, while defects caused by persons unconnected with the building operations or by design problems where the first purchaser was responsible also go uncompensated. Similarly, no claims will succeed in relation to defects where statutory compensation is payable, defects caused by later additions to the property, defects arising from lifts or swimming pools and, once again, defects arising from normal wear and tear, dampness, condensation and shrinkage.

1 NHBC Agreement, cl 12. See para 3.59, above.
2 [1979] 2 All ER 668, [1979] 1 WLR 512.

3.71 At this stage, it is convenient to note the further limitations, in the form of general exclusion, which apply to all claims under the NHBC insurance policy, not just Section III claims. Firstly, there are considerable restrictions on claims relating to consequential loss; the Council is not liable for professional fees, alternative accommodation, removal expenses, loss of enjoyment, inconvenience, distress or any other loss of a consequential character. This shows very clearly the concern of the NHBC to act purely as an insurer of the premises alone. Secondly, the Council is not liable for the common parts of flats, etc., beyond the purchaser's share. Thirdly, no liability is accepted for gradual deterioration caused by the neglect of the purchaser or purchasers, and, fourthly, the failure of a previous purchaser to notify the Council of defects will prevent a subsequent purchaser's claim from succeeding. Further, there are eleven conditions precedent to recovery in all claims, typical of the conditions on which most insurers rely – these cover various matters concerning procedures for claiming and assessment of compensation; perhaps the most important is the final condition viz that all disputes be referred to arbitration.

3.72 Additionally, there are several important financial constraints placed on the operation of the scheme. As far as Section III is concerned, these are as follows. Firstly, the insurance liability of the NHBC is limited to £10 million in relation to the houses constructed in any given year,[1] this being a total figure for liability under all sections of the insurance policy. This is an obvious way to establish a maximum possible liability which makes the NHBC's reinsurance arrangements easier to facilitate. Secondly, under Section III, a maximum is imposed in respect of the total amount of all claims concerning a particular dwelling. This figure is assessed by reference to the total initial purchase price of the dwelling (up to a maximum of whichever is the greater of £50,000 or twice the national average purchase price[2] of dwellings at that time as determined by the Building Societies Association) increased with reference to the housing cost index (or, if lower, by a formula involving the investment of the sum with a return of 15 per cent per annum compound interest). This complex formula ensures that a realistic amount is paid for all except the largest houses, with the overriding maximum effectively ensuring again that reinsurance will be a simple affair. A third restriction is designed to cushion the NHBC from the effects of any problems from massive errors by member firms; accordingly, under Section III, no more than £500,000 can be paid out in respect of any year's houses constructed by any member except that large firms constructing more than 2,500 houses per annum are assessed with reference to a different formula viz £200 multiplied by the number of new houses constructed by that builder for which NHBC protection is sought. Additionally, in the event of a run of claims seeming likely or actually materialising, the NHBC can reduce the maxima in the first and third categories to spread the consequences fairly of any shortfall in the funds available. Also, the maxima in the second and third categories relate to claims made under both Section III and Section II[3] of the NHBC insurance policy.

1 For the purposes of the scheme, the year runs from 1 April.
2 In October 1979, the average price was £24,693, per Adams (1980) 130 NLJ 195, 197.
3 See para 3.73, below.

3.73 Turning to Section II of the insurance policy, it may be seen that this is the method whereby the purchaser who would normally have rights against the builder under the NHBC Agreement, but is unable to enforce them, obtains protection from the Council itself. Adams[1] succinctly describes this section as 'the underwriting of the vendor's obligations under clause 6' of the NHBC Agreement, and this in turn shows the first of the various limitations placed on this underwriting, insofar as no protection is given by Section II against a failure to enforce any rights under clause 3 of that Agreement. Additionally, there are further requirements designed to establish that compensation will not be forthcoming from the builder. Either proceedings (via the courts or arbitration) must have been commenced within a year from the end of the Initial Guarantee Period but with the decision going unhonoured by the defendant or, alternatively, bankruptcy, liquidation or clear insufficiency of assets must have intervened so as to make the insistence on formal proceedings irrelevant. Claims under this section are subject to the same financial limits as claims under Section III,[2] but with an additional provision that only 90 per cent of a claim will be met by the NHBC, subject to the deduction not exceeding 2 per cent of the purchase price, again calculated so as to allow for inflation with reference to the housing cost under or, if lower, the notional return on an investment of that initial sum at 15 per cent per annum compound interest. The general exclusions and conditions relating to this and the other sections of the insurance policy have already been noted.

1 (1980) 130 NLJ 195.
2 See para 3.72, above.

3.74 Section I of the insurance policy deals with the liability of the NHBC at a yet earlier stage viz where the loss to the purchaser has occurred even before the Notice of Insurance Cover is issued, where the builder has failed to complete the construction. The classic case envisaged by the section is one where, between the contract for construction and sale being made and the notional time set for transfer of ownership to take place, the builder goes into liquidation, both preventing the prospective purchaser from recovering his money and leaving the house in a state of partial completion. Cover is however provided by the NHBC in a wide range of situations; so long as there is a contractual relationship in existence, whether a contract to acquire the freehold or a long lease or merely a contract of construction, in such cases cover will apply in the event of the building not being substantially completed – it is presumed that this latter phrase must be interpreted in a manner favourable to the purchaser if Section I is to fulfil its purpose – with the further condition that the builder must be prevented from completing the work by reason of bankruptcy, liquidation or fraud. The NHBC will either repay monies paid or authorise completion of the work up to the agreed purchase price. Additionally cover is provided after completion of the sale; not only is the purchaser indemnified against the consequences of a failure to complete the construction work up to its purchase price, he may also claim for compensation in respect of defects in the premises and for the full cost of completion of the work. Limitations are however imposed on this section of the policy too. Notice of the loss must be disclosed within a mere three months of the fraud becoming patent or the bankruptcy or liquidation taking place; non-compliance will result in failure of the claim. Additionally, full payment is not made; as in Section II, recovery is subject to a 10 per cent deduction, subject to this not exceeding 2 per cent of the initial purchase price (not index-linked in this instance) and an additional deduction will be made in respect of any reduction in the purchase price made in the light of bankruptcy, liquidation or fraud. The financial limits are also more stringent in their application to Section I; in respect of each dwelling, Section I claims may not exceed £5,000; in respect of each builder, the limit payable by the NHBC in respect of each year's newly con-structed houses is £125,000. The overall £10 million limitation of liability in respect to one year's houses applies equally here.

3.75 A further, but very different, point may be conveniently made here before discussion moves away from the liabilities of the NHBC itself. Simply put, since the NHBC carries out functions of inspection in relation to premises, can the new-found tortious liabilities of local authority inspectors under *Anns v Merton London Borough Council*[1] be translated so as to affect the NHBC if the inspectors fail to observe a defect during their inspection, assuming that this case extends beyond the liability of public bodies? Given the 'spot-check' system employed by the NHBC, the possibility of such an omission occurring is perhaps not insubstantial. On the other hand it may be argued that the fact that the inspection system is known and understood to be sporadic might be enough to make it unreasonable for the purchaser to act solely in the light of the inspec-tion, and in any case the Council cannot withdraw its insurance simply because a defect missed by inspection later becomes apparent. The Council have in any event now endeavoured to clarify the position in the present form of the Notice of Insurance Cover, which by clause 1(3) states specifically that only spot-check inspections are undertaken and that in consequence of this the Council and the Council's servants or agents will accept no liability whatsoever which may arise from the inspection. This is unaffected by the Unfair Contract Terms Act 1977 which, by Schedule 1, paragraph 1(a), does not in its controls on exclusion clauses affect provisions in contracts of insurance. It is therefore submitted that no negligence action against the NHBC in relation to its inspection functions is likely to succeed.

1 [1978] AC 728, [1977] 2 All ER 492.

3.76 The NHBC represents a major protection to the purchasers of new dwel-ling-houses. Quite apart from its attempts to raise the standards of construction, it provides two important routes to compensation for defective premises viz its sponsorship of the NHBC Agreement between the builder and the purchaser and subsequent purchaser of the property, and its own liability as the guarantor (in most respects) of the property, which in turn of course connects with the Council's role in raising standards. The subtlety of the overall scheme is evident. For failure to complete premises, the normal action against the builder in con-tract will provide the remedy, with a limited back-up provided by the NHBC insurance scheme. For the whole range of defects arising in the first two years (normally) of a house's life, the Agreement with the builder provides the prin-cipal remedy, with the NHBC acting once more as guarantor, though with fewer restrictions. After this period has elapsed, the builder fades from the picture in most cases; the NHBC itself accepts primary responsibility for compensating the disgruntled purchaser, but equally protects itself both from excessive litigation and excessive liability by confining its role to being an insurer against serious defects arising in the premises in question.

3.77 To represent the operation of the NHBC's various activities as flawless would doubtless be an overstatement. Objection has been made to the fact that the Council imposes limits in various ways on the amounts which can be claimed, and these may strike the individual purchaser as unfair and arbitrary, but in fairness it must be said that the limits are a good way of restraining the cost of the Council's insurance role, and further, that the limits were substantially increased in 1979 to compensate for previous failures to keep up with inflation the previous figure payable in respect of one dwelling had been £20,000 for the previous five-and-a-half years. Increased experience has improved the standard of drafting of most of the relevant documents; relatively few flaws can now be fairly discerned in this respect, perhaps the most potentially serious being the scope left by certain of the exclusionary provisions, for example, the exclusion of the builder's liability in respect of wear and tear, and normal dampness – dangerous imprecisions. It has to be conceded that what seems to be the most fundamental potential flaw, the problems of assignment, has given rise to gratifyingly few actual difficulties and exists, for the moment, as more of an academic hazard. Overall, then, few difficulties arise in the day-to-day operation of the NHBC.

3.78 Indeed, its achievements may rightly be chronicled. Since 1965, a sum of over £12 million has been paid out in respect of structural defects alone, inevitably in many cases providing a remedy where none would have been available in the light of the general legal rules then prevailing, and the role of the Council as guarantor; indeed, almost a further £4 million has been paid out in respect of bankruptcies of builders. On the other hand, these figures, when set against the numbers of private sector housing completions during the period,[1] perhaps provide evidence for an assertion that there has been an increase in the standard of house-building as a result of the Council's endeavours in this regard. More generally, the NHBC's work may be justly applauded as an excellent example of self-regulation by a large proportion of a traditionally fragmented industry, as an admirable model of risk distribution in an area of isolated, but occasionally spectacular, losses, and as a useful model showing the utility of arbitration systems, as opposed to compulsory recourse to the courts of law.

1 DoE Housing and Construction Statistics show that 148,800 new private houses were completed in Great Britain in 1978, the figure having gradually declined in recent years (e g 222,000 such completions in 1968).

3.79 Perhaps in due course, the benefits of the NHBC's arrangements will be made available in respect of a wider range of premises, such as commercially-owned residential properties, and in respect of a wider range of building operations, such as repairs and extensions (though it must not be forgotten that the Defective Premises Act 1972[1] may have a role in certain such situations). Similarly the Council's inspection work could be, perhaps, in future carried out more intensively and uniformly. In the meantime, it is sufficient to regard the NHBC's present schemes as representing useful protection and admirable value for the house purchaser, especially in its role as guarantor of the condition of premises.

1 See paras 3.104 ff, below.

The position of the sub-contractor

3.80 At this stage, additional comments need to be made about the special features of the position of the sub-contractor. Many matters will be dealt with by sub-contractors, especially where some distinct technical or design skill not possessed by the main contractor is required. Traditionally, the sub-contractor has been regarded as being in a contractual relationship with the main contractor alone. Thus, if the sub-contractor carried out defective work, his contractual obligations fell to be enforced by the main contractor with reference to the contract between them. This would usually once again be a complex and detailed standard-form contract in most cases, and the present version of greatest importance is the form NSC/4, or, in full, the JCT Nominated Sub-contract Conditions, used within the framework of the JCT contract to establish the contractor/sub-contractor relationship where the sub-contractor is nominated, i e chosen by the architect on behalf of the contractor. It should also be noted that there is an alternative approach to nomination under the 1980 JCT scheme but the equivalent conditions in form NSC/4a are not materially different for the purposes of this discussion.

3.81 Many matters are covered by the form NSC/4, including a number of the general issues covered as between employer and contractor by the main JCT form. For the purposes of this work, however, the principal clause is clause 14.3 whereby it is clearly established that defects in the work must be made good to the satisfaction of the contractor or his architect at the sub-contractor's expense. This liability will continue for the usual defects liability period of six months from the date of practical completion of the sub-contract work as determined by the architect. Also of importance is clause 29, which gives the contractor the right to determine the employment of a sub-contractor on various grounds, including the sub-contractor's failure to follow the agreed programme of work or a refusal after written notice to remedy defects or remove defective work. Thus the relationship between contractor and sub-contractor is governed by provisions analogous to those governing the employer/contractor relationship.

3.82 This is of only limited assistance to the employer; while it is true that he may hold the contractor responsible for defects in workmanship which although the fault of the sub-contractor have not been acted upon by the contractor, this is clearly not the normal situation. Often, the principal contractor will be able to validly claim for an extension of time while the defects in the sub-contractor's work are remedied. Further, the typical sub-contractor will be offering some special skills, perhaps as to design, which would not be covered by the employer/contractor contract unless specific provision were made. In the absence of such a provision, the employer might be without even an indirect remedy in such a case. So the advantages of establishing a direct contractual nexus between employer and sub-contractor have become increasingly clear in recent years and such a contract has now become part of the JCT contract arrangements in the case of nominated sub-contractors by forms NSC/2 and NSC/2a (the latter form again not differing in material particulars). These forms, if used, establish an obligation on the part of the sub-contractor, owed to the employer, to warrant the exercise of reasonable skill and care in the performance of his duties of design, selection of goods or materials or any specific obligation laid down. The employer in turn promises, inter alia, to pay the sub-contractor where the principal contractor fails to pay. Thus the employer now has a direct contractual remedy against the sub-contractor and has a useful additional weapon in his armoury.

3.83 In the case of a non-nominated sub-contractor, i e one chosen by the contractor though subject to the architect's written consent which may not be unreasonably withheld, and now referred to in the 1980 JCT form as a 'domestic sub-contractor', there continues to be no privity of contract, and from the date of practical completion, responsibility for the work passes to the principal contractor.

3.84 Important though the contractual remedies against builders are, it now has to be recognised that, increasingly, this form of action is gradually becoming subsumed in importance to the expanded role of tort liability. Why is this so? Many of the reasons stem from matters covered in the Introduction to this work. In particular, problems arose in respect of latent damage to buildings; this showed the contractual action in a poor light since, by the time such damage had been discovered, the contractual limitation period, running from the date of the defective workmanship, etc., which constituted the breach of contract, would often have expired. A tortious action, however, would not be time-barred since the limitation period in such cases only runs from the date when the damage occurs or, if later, could reasonably be expected to be discovered. It has been in just this type of case that the development of tortious actions against builders has principally occurred.

3.85 It is also right to note that another factor contributing to the relative decline in importance of contractual actions against builders has perhaps been the failure of the law of contract to provide any answer to what has been perceived as the problem of exclusion clauses. The traditional attitudes of *laissez-faire* that are generally regarded as forming the basis of the present law militated against any regular legal control of such clauses and more recent attempts by the judiciary to impose such controls have not met with resounding success as the saga of fundamental breach, for example, has well shown. It has been left to Parliament to impose suitable controls in recent years, chiefly in the form of the Unfair Contract Terms Act 1977, but by then those involved in building disputes had already become accustomed to looking outside the contractual framework for their remedy.

3.86 A final, more general, consideration to bear in mind is the relative rigidity of the law of contract. There are good reasons of business efficacy for a law of contract to be certain and clear, but the other side of this particular coin is that it is likely to stultify, to fail to reflect changing attitudes and to become over-thorough and over-meticulous in its approach. In the context of building contracts this may be clearly seen, with at least the traditional contractual remedies not able to cope with the increase in home-ownership and home transfer, and the contractual provisions becoming too complex for easy use; the inherently more flexible and more policy-orientated law of negligence has arisen to fill fairly and squarely these gaps in the legal protection of the householder, etc., and it is to the law of negligence as it affects the builder that we now turn.

Liability of the builder in negligence

3.87 For many years the builder of premises who owned the land upon which he constructed the premises was not liable in negligence for personal injury or damage to property occasioned by the defective state of those premises. Thus Scrutton LJ said in *Bottomley v Bannister*,[1] 'Now it is at present well-established English law that, in the absence of an express contract, a landlord of an unfurnished house is not liable to his tenant, or a vendor of real estate to his purchaser, for defects in the house or land rendering it dangerous or unfit for occupation, even if he has constructed the defects himself or is aware of their existence.' This decision was reached shortly before the judgment of the House of Lords in *Donoghue v Stevenson*,[2] and arguably as a result of that judgment the position had changed. However it was held by Atkinson J in *Otto v Bolton and Norris*[3] that the principle of *Donoghue v Stevenson* did not apply to the building of houses, and he ruled that a builder who builds a house for sale is under no duty either to a future purchaser or to persons who come to live in the house to take care that it is well constructed and safe.

1 [1932] 1 KB 458 at 468. See also *Cavalier v Pope* [1906] AC 428.
2 [1932] AC 562.
3 [1936] 2 KB 46, [1936] 1 All ER 960.

3.88 In 1961 the Court of Appeal of Northern Ireland had to decide whether *Donoghue v Stevenson* applied in a case where a builder who was neither vendor nor lessor was sued for negligence in repairing a floorboard. As a result of a plug of wood inserted by the builder in the floorboard giving way beneath the plaintiff's heel, she fell and was injured. It was held[1] that *Donoghue v Stevenson* was applicable, and this was followed by Nield J a couple of years later in *Sharpe v E T Sweeting & Son Ltd*.[2] In this case the defendant builders constructed a house for a local authority. The plaintiff's husband was the first tenant of the house. A reinforced concrete canopy fell on the plaintiff and caused her injury; the cause of the fall was the negligent reinforcement by the defendants of the concrete. In finding for the plaintiff, Nield J said,[3] 'the fact that the owner is also the builder does not remove the owner's immunity, but when the builder is not the owner he enjoys no such immunity'.

1 In *Gallagher v N McDowell Ltd* [1961] NI 26.
2 [1963] 2 All ER 455, [1963] 1 WLR 665.
3 Ibid at 463 and 675.

3.89 Thus, though the builder who was neither vendor nor lessor could be liable in negligence, the immunity of the builder/vendor and builder/lessor remained. However, this immunity was reconsidered, albeit obiter, by the Court of Appeal in *Dutton v Bognor Regis UDC*.[1] In deciding whether a local authority owed a duty of care to a subsequent purchaser of a house whose foundations the local authority's building inspector had failed adequately to inspect at the time they were constructed, the court was confronted by the argument that, if the builder were not liable (the plaintiff had settled her claim against the builder for a few hundred pounds on the basis of *Bottomley v Bannister*), then why should the person who merely inspected the builder's work be liable. Lord Denning MR and Sachs LJ met this argument with a denial that the principle of *Bottomley v Bannister* declaring the immunity in tort of a builder/vendor represented the law. Citing *Gallagher v N McDowell Ltd*[2] and *Sharpe v E T Sweeting & Son Ltd*[3] in which, as we have seen, the court restricted its judgment to those cases in which the builder was only a contractor and was not the owner of the house itself, Lord Denning said,[4] 'there is no sense in maintaining this distinction. It would mean that a contractor who builds a house on another's land is liable for negligence in constructing it, but that a speculative builder, who buys land and himself builds houses on it for sale, and is just as negligent as the contractor, is not liable. That cannot be right. Each must be under the same duty of care and to the same persons.' Sachs LJ stated that pre-*Donoghue v Stevenson* cases must be looked at in the light of the decision in that case, and *Otto v Bolton and Norris* was only a first instance decision. He therefore was quite happy to depart from the effect of the line of authority as represented by cases such as *Cavalier v Pope* and *Bottomley v Bannister* and agreed with Lord Denning.

1 [1972] 1 QB 373, [1972] 1 All ER 462.
2 [1961] NI 26.
3 [1963] 2 All ER 455, [1963] 1 WLR 665.
4 [1972] 1 QB 373 at 393–394, [1972] 1 All ER 462 at 472.

3.90   Five years later the House of Lords (though again obiter) considered the negligence liability of the builder and agreed with Lord Denning and Sachs LJ that a builder who was also the owner of a house was not immune from liability in negligence for defects in the building to a person who later acquired the building. The case in question, *Anns v London Borough of Merton*[1] again concerned the liability of a local authority for negligent or non-inspection of defective foundations by their building inspector, but it was considered, in the words of Lord Wilberforce,[2] 'unreasonable to impose liability in respect of defective foundations on the council, if the builder, whose primary fault it was, should be immune from liability'. He went on to say:[3]

> the same rules should apply to all careless acts of a builder whether he happens also to own the land or not. I agree generally with the views of Lord Denning MR on this point (*Dutton*'s case). In the alternative, since it is the duty of the builder (owner or not)' to comply with the byelaws, I would be of opinion that an action could be brought against him, in effect, for breach of statutory duty by any person for whose benefit or protection the byelaw was made. So I do not think that there is any basis here for arguing from a supposed immunity of the builder to immunity of the council.

1 [1978] AC 728, [1977] 2 All ER 492.
2 Ibid at 758 and 504.
3 Ibid at 759 and 504–505.

3.91   Though these remarks were obiter, it would have been a brave, indeed foolhardy man who did not assume that the days of the builder/vendor's immunity were numbered. Indeed the death-knell had already been sounded by Parliament in the form of the Defective Premises Act 1972, but the existence of legislation was seen as no ban to a demonstration of the vigour of the common law. Various matters still remained to be worked out, such as the nature of the duty incumbent upon the builder, the measure of damages to be imposed upon him and the time when the cause of action arises.

3.92   These matters arose for consideration by the Court of Appeal within a year of the decision in *Anns*, in *Batty v Metropolitan Property Realisations*.[1] A development company purchased land from a firm of builders, and the company and the firm agreed, having inspected the land, to assess its safety and suitability for housebuilding, that the builders would construct houses on the land and the company would finance the building and find purchasers.

After the houses had been built the plaintiffs took a 999 year lease of one of the houses and the adjoining garden. After the sale the company sold the reversion to the builders. Three years after the purchase of the house there was a severe slip of the natural strata of the hillside. This caused direct damage to part of the plaintiffs' back garden but did not directly or immediately damage their house or its foundations. However, the trial judge held that the house was doomed; no later than ten years from the trial the movement of the strata would cause the house's foundations to slide down the hill. They claimed damages from the development company for negligence and breach of contract and for negligence from the builder.[2] In dismissing the builder's appeal against the judge's decision that they were liable, the Court of Appeal held that the builder was under a duty to a potential occupier to act as a careful and competent builder would have acted in examining and investigating the land on which they proposed to build the house. The court did not accept the argument that the builder's duty extended only to defects in the site on which the house was to be built, and not to defects existing on neighbouring land.[3] Further, the court did not accept the argument that any duty owed by the builder must be limited to defects discoverable without subsoil investigation. A further argument, that no more extensive duty than that imposed upon a builder retained at arm's length by a contractor was owed by reason of the relationship between the first and second defendants and the part they played in inspecting and deciding to develop the site, was also rejected. This in sum imposes a heavy burden upon the builder. It would seem on general principles, that his standard of care is the standard of care exercised by the reasonable builder of his experience with his resources, with due regard being paid to the standard of construction laid down in the Building Regulations.

1 [1978] QB 554, [1978] 2 All ER 445. See Duncan Wallace (1978) 94 LQR 331.
2 A claim against the local authority for negligence and/or breach of statutory duty in respect of its duties with regard to inspection of the foundations failed at first instance.
3 [1978] QB 554 at 568–569, [1978] 2 All ER 445 at 455.

3.93 A difficult question concerned the kind of damage for which the builder was liable. The distinction between physical damage and economic loss and the application of that distinction in defective premises cases is discussed in detail elsewhere,[1] but clearly there was a strong argument in *Batty* that no physical damage had yet been caused to the house. Megaw LJ dealt with this point in two ways. The narrow reason for accepting the argument that the plaintiffs had suffered physical damage to their property was that, though the house and its foundations were undamaged, the garden had suffered physical damage. The wider reason on which Megaw LJ based this part of his judgment was founded on the test employed by Lord Wilberforce in *Anns v London Borough of Merton* in determining when the cause of action arose viz when the state of the building was such that there was present or imminent danger to the health or safety of persons occupying the house at the time when the action was brought. Megaw LJ said:[2]

> Was there not here imminent danger to the health or safety of persons occupying this house at the time when the action was brought? Indeed, Mrs Batty, one of the plaintiffs, has been awarded damages (of £250) for the consequences to her health and peace of mind of the foreseen disaster. Why should this not be treated as being a case of imminent danger to the safety and health of people occupying the house? No one knows, or can say with certainty, not even the greatest expert whether the foundations of the house will move and the house perhaps suddenly tumble tomorrow, or in a year's time, or in three years' time or in ten years' time. The law, in my judgment,

is not so foolish as to say that a cause of action against the builder does not arise in those circumstances because there is no *imminent* danger.

The fact that it was inevitable that at some time in the next ten years the house would be in ruins justifies this approach, although strictly the test adopted by Megaw LJ goes beyond the 'present and imminent' test suggested in *Anns v London Borough of Merton* insofar as that was designed to apply to the liability of the builder; but the matter would be more complex in cases where there was less certainty about the ultimate fate of the house.[3]

1 See paras 1.20 ff, above. See also Duncan Wallace (1978) 94 LQR 61, and Cane (1979) 95 LQR 117.
2 [1978] QB 554 at 571–572, [1978] 2 All ER 445 at 457–458.
3 See Cane, above, at 134–135.

3.94 The duty imposed by the Court of Appeal in *Batty* therefore renders the builder liable to persons occupying the premises for negligent work which causes the building to pose a threat to the health or safety of those occupying it. The measure of damages in such cases is clearly likely to be of importance. In *Batty* this was not an issue, as the parties had agreed damages of £13,000 subject to liability. It was clear that the house could not be economically repaired or restored, and therefore it may perhaps be assumed that the agreed sum in effect constituted a replacement measure of damages.[1] It is suggested that, where premises rendered defective as a result of a builder's negligence can be repaired or restored, the cost of repair will be the basis on which the damages will be assessed: where, as in *Batty*, they cannot be repaired, the replacement value will have to be awarded. The fact that liability is imposed for defects which cause a building to pose a threat to health or safety should mean that the effect of the repair or replacement basis is to compensate for the cost of averting that threat.[2] Such, at least, has the merit of consistency.

1 As Cane (1979) 95 LQR 117 at 127, n. 43, suggests, despite the absence of discussion in *Batty* of the basis of the damages awarded, replacement value seems to be the only rational basis consistent with the size of the award.
2 See Cane, above, at 126–128.

3.95 If it is accepted that the measure of damages in *Batty* is the replacement value, it may be asked whether the effect of an award of damages where the cost of repair is the appropriate basis is, *mutatis mutandis*, to have the similar effect of wiping the slate clean; in other words, should the plaintiff be compensated for any diminution in the value of the premises even after the work of repair has been carried out. For example, X builds a house, later occupied by Y. The foundations of the house are constructed negligently, and underpinning is found to be necessary. If it is discovered that, even after the underpinning, the market value of the house will be less than if no such work had been necessary, can Y sue X for the difference in value, in addition to the cost of repair? Support for the inclusion of an award for loss of value can be found in the decision of the New Zealand Court of Appeal in *Bowen v Paramount Builders (Hamilton) Ltd and McKay*.[1] The defendant builders constructed two flats with inadequate foundations on unstable land. The plaintiff was the second purchaser of the flats. Subsidence took place and the plaintiff sued the defendants in negligence. In effect the court anticipated the decision in *Batty* by holding that compensation could be awarded for the cost of repairing a defect before physical damage was caused by it, rather than waiting for the damage to take place and awarding damages to compensate for the greater loss that was then incurred. In addition, the court allowed a claim of $2,000 representing diminution in value of the premises after the repairs had been carried out. Richmond P said:[2]

> In one sense it can be described as economic loss, but it is economic loss directly and immediately connected with the structural damage to the building and as such is properly recoverable. The market value of the property prior to the subsidence occurring was the amount which an ordinary purchaser would pay for the property having regard to the condition in which the building appeared to be. It would be wrong to assess the market value before the subsidence on the basis of value to a purchaser who had actual knowledge of the latent defect.

As against this, Sachs LJ had earlier doubted that such a claim could be allowed, in *Dutton v Bognor Regis UDC*, essentially on the basis that the Public Health Act is not concerned with market values as such. It may be argued that the duty owed by the builder is not imposed in any way by the Public Health Act (though certainly the health and safety criterion is borrowed directly from the Act), but the further point of Sachs LJ, that the measure of damages for negligence is not the same as the measure of damages for breach of warranty must particularly be borne in mind. The measure of damages in tort and contract is considered in detail elsewhere; but there is no necessary reason why the *restitutio in integrum* measure of damages should not include diminution in value after repair work. The question is ultimately one of policy and is likely to remain unclear until the courts have the opportunity to give it detailed consideration. The important question of when damages are to be assessed is considered in the Introduction.[3]

1 [1977] 1 NZLR 394.
2 Ibid at 411.
3 See para 1.13, above.

3.96 As regards the question of the persons to whom the builder's duty is owed, Lord Wilberforce said[1] in *Anns v London Borough of Merton*:

> any weakness or inadequacy [in building foundations] will create a hidden defect which whoever acquires the building has no means of discovering: in legal parlance there is no opportunity for intermediate inspection . . . It must be in the reasonable contemplation not only of the builder but also of the local authority that failure to comply with the byelaws' requirement as to foundations may give rise to a hidden defect which in the future may cause damage to the building affecting the safety and health of owners and occupiers. And as the building is intended to last, the class of owners and occupiers likely to be affected cannot be limited to those who go in immediately after construction.

1 [1978] AC 728 at 753, [1977] 2 All ER 492 at 500.

3.97 Not surprisingly, counsel for the builders in *Batty* conceded that in general terms a builder could owe a duty of care to an occupier with whom he was not in privity of contract.[1] It seems clear that the builder's duty, like that of the local authority, is owed to owners and occupiers whose health or safety is threatened as a result of the builder's negligence. The New Zealand case of *Bowen v Paramount Builders (Hamilton) Ltd and McKay*[2] illustrates the operation of this, for in that case the builder was held to be liable to a subsequent purchaser. In responding to the argument that it would not be possible to control the class of purchasers to whom a duty of care was owed, Richmond P[3] emphasised the need for strict control by means of the principle of proximity: 'in other words, I take the view that the duty of the builder is *not* owed to anyone who purchases a building with actual knowledge of the defect or in circumstances where he ought to have used his opportunity of inspection in a way which would have given him warning of that defect'. Clearly therefore, unless the plaintiff has been informed of the existence of a defect, only some manifestation of the defect, such as to put him on guard, will prevent him from being able to claim. The courts are not likely to find against a plaintiff if he failed to employ a surveyor whose inspection would probably have revealed the defect.[4] If a surveyor were employed but, through negligence, he failed to discover the defect, then arguably the negligence would constitute a *novus actus interveniens* and the plaintiff would have no claim against the builder, but would be left to pursue a claim against the surveyor.

1 In this context it is interesting to note the case of *Sutherland v C R Maton & Son Ltd* (1976) 240 Estates Gazette 135, 3 BLR 87, in which counsel for the defendant builders conceded that a builder could be liable in negligence to a purchaser or subsequent purchaser. For comment see (1976) 3 BLR 88–89.
2 [1977] 1 NZLR 394. See para 3.95, above.
3 [1977] 1 NZLR 394 at 413.
4 See para 6.54, below.

3.98 Richmond P also[1] adverted to the difficult problem of the builder who negligently and in breach of contract creates a source of danger, so that he is sued in breach of contract by the building owner who, not having to wait for actual damage to occur nor being under an obligation to use the damages received to remedy the defective work, sells to a third party, who then claims against the builder in negligence. He suggested that a solution to this would be the liability of the vendor for failing to disclose to his purchaser a dangerous but latent defect of which he is aware;[2] thereby rendering the vendor and the builder joint tortfeasors. Alternatively it might be argued that the failure by the vendor to inform the purchaser of the defect would break the chain of causation between purchaser and builder,[3] but on policy grounds this might be deemed undesirable, as it would leave the purchaser without a remedy. In *Anns v London Borough of Merton* it was held[4] that the duty was owed only to an owner or occupier who was such when the damage occurred; i e when the state of the building was such that there was a present or imminent danger to the health or safety of such a person. This avoids the possibility of multiple recovery, but leaves the purchaser in an unenviable position.

1 [1977] 1 NZLR 394 at 414–415.
2 See paras 6.50 ff, below.
3 This, in effect, is the argument of Woodhouse J in *Bowen* at 418. See also the discussion of this point by Cooke J, ibid at 424 where it is indicated that if the damage suffered by the purchaser is the separate result of a second tort by the builders (which would not be the case in the example under consideration), the purchaser would have a claim against the builder.
4 [1978] AC 728 at 758, [1977] 2 All ER 492 at 504.

3.99 As we have seen,[1] it is still an open question whether a plaintiff might succeed in a claim for negligence against a builder where as a result of the builder's carelessness the premises, even after repair, are diminished in value, the main argument against success being that such diminution in value represents pure economic loss and as such is not compensable in the law of tort. Can it though be argued that where only 'questions of quality or amenity or commercial value'[2] are concerned, as opposed to threats to health or safety, as a result of negligent work by the builder, damages may be awarded? An argument can be made to suggest that the 'health and safety' criterion borrowed from the context of local authority liability under the Public Health Act is inappropriate to a builder, whose main concern is with profits, and the duty imposed upon him should mirror this concern and impose liability for defects of quality as well as dangerous defects.

1 Para 3.95, above.
2 Duncan Wallace (1978) 94 LQR 40 at 67.

3.100 Also, it may be argued that the words of Sachs LJ in *Dutton v Bognor Regis UDC*:[1] 'a builder who by his negligence creates a hidden defect is liable to anyone suffering damage from it just as a manufacturer is liable when a hidden defect in the goods he makes injures a workman using them and as a producer of consumable goods is liable when a hidden defect injures a consumer' impose a broader duty of care on the builder than the *Anns/Batty* formulation,[2] but it would seem that the words of Sachs LJ (which were preceded by 'It is obvious that') do no more than assert the builder's liability for damage causing personal injury as a result of his negligent work, which seems perfectly consistent with the 'health and safety' criterion.

1 [1972] 1 QB 373 at 402, [1972] 1 All ER 462 at 479.
2 See e g Green (1981) 131 NLJ 82.

3.101 As is discussed below,[1] it is very likely that the duty imposed upon (inter alios) the builder by section 1 of the Defective Premises Act 1972 is broad enough to include liability for defects of quality, and it might be inconsistent for liability under the Act to exist and yet be denied at common law.[2] Ultimately the matter is one of policy, which has received judicial expression on the one hand by Cooke J in *Bowen*,[3] who did not see 'any reason why the law of tort should necessarily stop short of recognising a duty not to put out carelessly a defective thing, nor any reason compelling the courts to withhold relief in tort from a plaintiff misled by the appearance of the thing into paying too much for it'; and on the other hand by Stamp LJ in *Dutton*,[4] who did not see

> any valid distinction between the case of a builder who carelessly builds a house which, though not a source of danger to person or property, nevertheless, owing to a concealed defect in its foundations, starts to settle and crack and becomes valueless, and the case of a manufacturer who carelessly manufactures an article which, though not a source of danger to a subsequent owner or to his other property, nevertheless owing to a hidden defect, quickly disintegrates. To hold that either the builder or the manufacturer was liable except in contract would be to open up a new field of liability the extent of which could not, I think, be logically controlled.

Some support for advocates of the view that a broader duty lies upon the builder can be found in the recent decision of Judge Edgar Fay QC, sitting as a deputy judge of the Queen's Bench Division, in *Hone v Benson*[5] where, on a preliminary point of law, he held a 'do-it-yourself' builder/vendor liable in negligence for damage resulting from negligent installation of a hot-water and central-heating system, caused to the purchaser. Such an act of negligence would not necessarily pose a threat to health or safety. Again the matter will remain unclear until it falls to be determined by a higher court, but it is suggested that ultimately liability of a builder in negligence for defects of quality is, despite the strong arguments of principle that can be made[6] unlikely to be imposed by such a court, essentially on the policy basis outlined in the quotation from Stamp LJ above, and the criterion of a threat to health or safety will continue to be employed.

1 See paras 3.104 ff, below.
2 See Gravells [1979] Conv 97 at 110–111, where, in addition, the recommendations of the Law
   Commission (Law Com No 40) are prayed in aid to support the argument for liability for defects
   of quality.
3 [1977] 1 NZLR 394 at 423. See also Bailey (1981) 131 NLJ 671.

4 [1972] 1 QB 373 at 414, [1972] 1 All ER 462 at 489–490.
5 (1978) 248 Estates Gazette 1013. See also para 6.46, below.
6 See e g Gravells [1979] Conv 97 at 108–111; Bailey (1981) 131 NLJ 671.

3.102   In *Batty*, Megaw LJ[1] quoted Lord Wilberforce in *Anns*, who, in deciding when the cause of action arose, held that it arose when the state of the building was such that there was present or imminent danger to the health or safety of persons occupying it, and applied this to the facts of *Batty*, thereby effectively approving the application of this test to the builder in determining the time from which the six years' limitation period was deemed to run. It has been suggested elsewhere[2] that this test should be read in the light of the formula proposed in *Sparham-Souter v Town and Country Developments (Essex) Ltd*,[3] to the effect that time should not begin to run until the owner discovered, or with reasonable diligence ought to have discovered, the defective state of the premises, and this seems equally applicable to a claim in negligence against the builder. Clearly there may be difficulties concerning the time when danger becomes imminent, though, as we have seen, Megaw LJ took a broad view of this.[4] In another recent decision of Judge Fay QC,[5] the learned judge was of the view that the date when time begins to run with defective buildings is whichever is the later of two events; either when the plaintiff first acquires his interest in the property or when he first learns of the damage caused by the negligent construction; and knowledge of the damage has to be not merely awareness of the symptoms, such as cracking in walls, but knowledge of the disease, i e the cause of the cracking. This seems perfectly consistent with the way in which the negligence liability of the builder has developed.

1 [1978] QB 554 at 571, [1977] 2 All ER 445 at 457.
2 See para 1.39, above.
3 [1976] QB 858, [1976] 2 All ER 65.
4 See para 3.93, above.
5 *Eames London Estates Ltd v North Hertfordshire District Council* (1980) 259 Estates Gazette 491.

3.103   All in all, the last decade has seen a considerable extension in the liability of the builder for defective work in the form of a negligence action. The existence of contractual duties owed by the builder will prevent neither his co-contractor nor a third party (provided the third party is an owner or occupier whose health or safety is presently or imminently threatened as a result of the defective work), from claiming damages in negligence. The employment of this criterion of a threat to health or safety in determining the time from which the limitation period begins to run means that there will be no time when the builder can feel altogether free from potential liability for premises which he has constructed.

3.104   At the same time, statutory intervention in this area has taken place in the form of the Defective Premises Act, and the nature and scope of this now falls to be considered. The Defective Premises Act 1972, prompted by a Law Commission Report,[1] came into force on 1 January 1974. Section 1, based upon the common law contractual duties of the builder,[2] imposes on 'a person taking on work for or in connection with the provision of a dwelling[3] (whether the dwelling is provided by the erection or by the conversion or enlargement of a building)' a duty 'to see that the work which he takes on is done in a workmanlike or, as the case may be, professional manner, with proper materials and so that as regards that work the dwelling will be fit for habitation when completed'.[4] The duty is owed to any person to whose order the dwelling is provided and also to every person who acquires a legal or equitable interest in the dwelling.[5]

1 Law Com No 40.
2 See paras 3.81–3.19, above.
3 The premises to which the Act applies are therefore limited so as to exclude, for example, industrial and commercial premises which will, however, be covered by the common law.
4 S. 1(1). See generally North (1973) 36 MLR 628; Spencer [1974] CLJ 307, [1975] CLJ 48; and more specifically in the context of builders' liability, Gravells [1979] Conv 97 at 99–100.
5 S. 1(1).

3.105 Although the position is far from clear[1] it seems safest to assume that section 1(1) incorporates liability for pure economic loss within its ambit. This follows from the intention of the Law Commission to provide greater protection to the purchaser of a dwelling in respect of defects of quality.[2] The duty under section 1(1) would appear to be a strict one, rather than a duty of care, and the threefold duties of the builder must all be satisfied;[3] thus a dwelling may be fit for habitation, but if it was not constructed with proper materials, there will be a breach of the section. The duty therefore has elements of both contract and tort; defects of quality have long been regarded as compensable only in the law of contract; on the other hand, the duty is owed not only to the original purchaser, but to later purchasers also, provided they do not fall foul of the limitation period. Section 1(5) provides that any cause of action in respect of breach of the duty imposed by section 1 is deemed to have accrued at the time when the dwelling was completed,[4] despite the fact that the defect may not have manifested itself during the six year limitation period and may indeed remain hidden during the whole time that the period is running. A positive feature of the Act is the outlawing, in section 6(3), of any term of an agreement which purports to exclude or restrict the provisions of the Act.

1 See Spencer [1974] CLJ 307 at 319–320.
2 Law Com No 40, para 34.
3 For detailed discussion of those duties at common law see paras 3.8 ff, above.
4 The notion of 'completion' is far from precise: see North (1973) 36 MLR 628 at 630.

3.106 A major restriction on the operation of the Act is contained in section 2. This in effect provides that where a dwelling is built in accordance with an 'approved scheme', the duty owed under section 1 in inapplicable. The main scheme in existence is the NHBC scheme[1] and so widespread is its use that effectively the duty owed by the builder under section 1 is confined to conversions and alterations, to which the NHBC scheme does not apply, although of course a builder outside the NHBC or any other approved scheme will owe a duty under section 1.

1 For detailed discussion of the NHBC scheme see paras 3.49 ff, above.

3.107 Section 3 of the Act provides that:

> where work of construction, repair, maintenance or demolition or any other work is done on or in relation to premises,[1] any duty of care owed, because of the doing of the work, to persons who might reasonably be expected to be affected by the defects in the state of the premises created by the doing of the work shall not be abated by the subsequent disposal of the premises by the person who owed the duty.

This would appear to be entirely redundant in view of the developments of the common law in the last ten years, and, insofar as it may be regarded as creating liability at all, it creates probably a narrower liability than the common law has done.[2]

1 Broader, therefore, than s. 1.
2 See Spencer [1975] CLJ 48 at 56–58; for a better view, see North (1973) 36 MLR 628 at 633–634.

3.108 In sum therefore, the Defective Premises Act contributes little to the increasing burden of liability on the builder. The potential advantages to a plaintiff of a strict duty owed by the builder for, inter alia, defects of quality, are subtly eroded by a restricted (in comparison with the common law) limitation period and the decision by Parliament to treat the NHBC scheme as a replacement for rather than an alternative to liability under the Act.

3.109 As we have seen, the provisions of the Defective Premises Act 1972 cannot be excluded or restricted by any agreement. It is theoretically feasible for the builder to exclude or restrict his tortious duties, but this is subject to a number of restraints. As noted above[1] the Unfair Contract Terms Act 1977 outlaws exclusions or restrictions, whether by means of a contract term or a notice given to persons generally, of business liability for death or personal injury resulting from negligence.[2] Liability for other loss or damage can only be successfully restricted insofar as the contract term or notice satisfies the requirement of reasonableness. If the purported exclusion is contained in a contract term, for example as between builder/vendor and purchaser, its reasonableness will be determined in the light of section 11(1) of the Act, which requires that 'the term shall have been a fair and reasonable one to be included having regard to the circumstances which were, or ought reasonably to have been, known to or in the contemplation of the parties when the contract was made'. If the purported exclusion is contained in a notice which is not of contractual effect, the test under section 11(3) is 'that it should be fair and reasonable to allow reliance on it, having regard to all the circumstances obtaining when the liability arose or (but for the notice) would have arisen'. The uncertainty generated by this piece of legislation noted above[3] in the context of liability for breach of contract is equally a problem as regards negligence liability, and the comments made above are equally applicable here.[4]

1 See paras 3.34–3.45, above.
2 Unfair Contract Terms Act 1977, s. 2(1).
3 See paras 3.34–3.45, above.
4 See also paras 1.53 ff on exclusion of liability generally.

The Building Regulations

3.110 Beyond all the possible contractual liabilities of a builder, beyond all his tortious liabilities and his liability under the Defective Premises Act, and beyond such self-imposed liabilities as those incurred by members of the NHBC, there exists one further potential civil liability for the builder who constructs defective premises. The liability in question is that imposed by section 71(1) of the Health and Safety at Work Act 1974, whereby, inter alia, it is provided that 'breach of a duty imposed by building regulations shall, so far as it causes damage be actionable except insofar as the regulations provide otherwise'. By section 71(4) 'damage' is defined for the purposes of section 71 as including 'the death of, or injury to, any person (including any disease and any impairment of a person's physical or mental condition' – a singularly unhelpful partial definition which begs such key issues as to the extent of liability imposed in respect of, for example, property damage and economic loss. By section 71(3) this action for breach of the statutory duties imposed by the regulations exists without prejudice to other liabilities at common law. However, the action will not succeed if the regulations themselves constitute a defence,[1] nor will an action be successful if the building in question was constructed before section 71(1) takes effect, except where the regulation is imposed by virtue of section 65(2) of the 1974 Act (continuing requirements) or section 62 of the Public Health Act 1936 (governing application of byelaws to pre-existing buildings).

1 Health and Safety at Work Act 1974, s. 71(1).

3.111 There is, however, one far greater obstacle to bringing an action for breach of statutory duty by virtue of section 71 of the 1974 Act. This obstacle is simply but critically that the section is not yet in force, other than for the purpose of making regulations to be made in respect of it;[1] no indication has been given by the present government that section 71, along with other parts of the Act which are not yet in force, will be brought into effect in the near future. We are thus left in the extraordinary position of having been provided by Parliament with a highly significant method of redress in respect of defective premises, one indeed which may well be the easiest and most comprehensive method of redress in many cases since there is no need to prove the existence of a duty,[2] but which is not in force and shows no sign of so becoming.[3] This liability thus 'waits in the wings' as far as the position today is concerned.

1 The Health and Safety at Work etc. Act 1974 (Commencement No 4) Order 1977 (SI 1977 No 294).
2 See paras 3.119 ff, below.
3 See Spencer (1981) 131 NLJ 644.

3.112 This also of course poses a quandary for authors of works such as this. It is however proposed to give a resume of the key features of the statutory duties imposed by the Building Regulations in respect of defective premises as a guide to this major method of control on building operations (albeit at present with no direct civil remedy) and as an indication of the scope of civil liability that will be imposed when (or if) section 71 of the Health and Safety at Work Act is given effect.

3.113 The Building Regulations may be seen as a classic example of the increase in governmental control over day-to-day living where a small initial degree of intervention has burgeoned into a comprehensive panoply of what may, depending on one's political viewpoint, be regarded as useful controls or excessive interference. They also illustrate the ever-increasing tendency to place the responsibility for state intervention in the hands of central, rather than local government. The history of the Regulations is in essence a gradual realisation during the nineteenth century that Britain's housing conditions were often intolerable – inadequately constructed houses surrounded by squalor in unhygienic surroundings were the norm for many in newly industrialised towns and cities. Slowly the convenient *laissez-faire* ideals were eroded by the extent and increased awareness of the problem and legal controls came on two fronts, with the passing of the Public Health Acts of 1848 and 1875 and the increasing use of byelaws by local authorities to regulate housing conditions.

3.114 In more modern times the Public Health Act 1961 is the keynote in the move towards central control and supervision over the Building Regulations establishing by section 4 mechanisms for the preparation of uniform Building Regulations which eventually took effect in 1966. The present position is that the current Building Regulations date from 1976[1] and came into force on 31 January 1977.[2] Previous sets of Regulations (from 1965 and 1972) apply as from time to time amended to buildings the plans of which were deposited before this date even if the work was carried out later; here we will confine our attention only to the most recent set of Regulations, though in most respects there are few significant differences.[3] These Regulations at present apply throughout England and Wales, except in the twelve Inner London Boroughs and the City of London. These latter areas have their own regime of building controls under the London Building Acts 1930 to 1978, as the original 1930 Act and its various subsequent amendments are now to be known.[4] A comment on these provisions and the extent of civil liability in respect of them will appear later.[5]

1 Building Regulations 1976 (SI 1976 No 1676).
2 Ibid, reg A2.
3 For a convenient summary of the principal changes between the 1972 and 1976 Regulations see Cutmore *Shaw's Commentary on the Building Regulations 1976* p. 3.
4 Greater London Council (General Powers) (No 2) Act 1978, s. 7(5).
5 See paras 3.122 ff, below.

3.115 Changes in the structure of these controls may occur in consequence of the Health and Safety at Work Act 1974. By section 70, the power to make Building Regulations (though not previous Regulations themselves) now extends to Inner London. However, although this section is in force, no use has yet been made of its provisions. If such use is made in the future, however, it will of course presage the gradual diminution in importance of the distinction between Inner London and the rest of England and Wales. Once again, however, no indication has been given that extensive use of this power is in mind at present.

3.116 What then falls within the ambit of the present set of Building Regulations? Almost all construction work is within their scope, with the exception of certain exempted buildings e g most schools, other buildings constructed by local authorities under the legislation relating to allotments and buildings belonging to a statutory undertaking or authority,[1] also many mine buildings or moveable dwellings, etc.[2] Additionally, certain premises are partly exempted from the operation of the Regulations; these are predominantly single storey buildings such as separate outhouses, contractors' and other huts erected in connection with building or related work, detached garages or any building used purely for storage of materials or the keeping of plant or the housing of livestock and in these instances, most of the Building Regulations do not apply.[3] However, the Regulations generally apply during the erection of buildings as well as in relation to those newly completed.

1 Public Health Act 1936, s. 71.
2 Building Regulations 1976, above, para A5(1).
3 Ibid, para A5(2), Sch 2.

3.117 Within these parameters, the Regulations provide a highly comprehensive set of rules, establishing standards to be attained at all stages of construction work. Materials used in building work must be of an appropriate quality and character, buildings must be erected on adequately prepared sites and must in this and other respects offer adequate resistance to moisture; detailed provisions establish the structural stability which buildings must attain. Further, extensive regulations exists concerning fire resistance and, presumably in the event of this not being adequate, suitable means of escape from fire must be available. Other sections of the Regulations mandate the provision of adequate heat and sound insulation, while safety regulations are imposed on stairways, ramps, etc. Provisions also cover hygiene-related matters such as refuse disposal, drains and sewers, while the health and safety of occupiers and neighbours are aided by the provisions as to chimneys, flues, heat-producing appliances and incinerators. Regulations also further the quality of the occupiers' environment by laying down rules as to adequate light and ventilation.

3.118   It would be wrong, however, for the assumption to be made from the foregoing paragraph that the Regulations lay down general guidelines only. In fact they are hallmarked by the very extensive detail with which they usually establish their standards. One or two examples may suffice: the rules as to safety on stairways do not merely insist that their users be reasonably safe but instead certain objective requirements are laid down, including, inter alia, that there shall be a level, unobstructed landing at the top and bottom of a stairway, that there shall be headroom of over two metres above the entire staircase and that no door may be placed across a staircase.[1] In the realm of the rules ensuring adequate light, likewise specific requirements exist as to the precise shape of the shaft through which light must be able to penetrate to the windows.[2]

1   Building Regulations 1976, above, para H2.
2   Ibid, para K1.

3.119   Perhaps the easiest way to indicate the potential impact of the Building Regulations, were it possible for civil actions against builders to be based on a breach thereof, is first to indicate the general advantages which such an action, if available, would confer, then proceed to discuss in some detail how typical cases may come within the detail of the Regulations. As to the advantages of an action framed under section 71 of the Health and Safety at Work Act 1974, the usual main advantage of an action for breach of statutory duty as opposed to an action in negligence is apparent viz the fact that there is no need for the duty in question to be established by the plaintiff, since the statute spells this out clearly for all to see. In this instance, however, a further advantage lies with the action for breach of statutory duty because the clear and precise way in which most of the obligations imposed by the Building Regulations are laid down enables the parties to see at once whether a breach of duty has occurred. Whereas in negligence an assessment, inherently vague and unpredictable, has to be made as to the reasonableness of the parties' conduct in assessing whether a breach has occurred or not, in the statute-based action, it is a simple matter to measure or calculate whether the particular mandatory obligation imposed by the Regulations has been complied with or not.

3.120   How, then, might the occupier of defective premises utilise this action for breach of statutory duty? Many cases have arisen where premises have been constructed on an inadequately surveyed and prepared site. If the site has been improperly or inadequately cleared or where it has been necessary to drain a site before construction to protect the building against moisture and this has not been adequately done, there will be a clear breach of the Building Regulations,[1] while similarly the builder must construct the floors of the building next to the ground against moisture rising from the ground,[2] and walls must also be protected to prevent moisture damaging materials used in the building or from entering the interior of the building.[3] In more serious cases where the foundations turn out to be inadequate, the occupier may wish to have recourse to paragraph D3 of the Regulations whereby the foundations shall safely support the building so as not to cause settlement or other movement which would impair the stability of the building, and be of sufficient depth to protect the building from damage as a consequence of swelling or shrinking of the subsoil. The Building Regulations could also form the basis of a useful remedy where premises catch fire in consequence of defective construction; here it may be that a tortious action might be difficult to bring since if the damage has been extensive, proof of fault might be difficult; in any action for breach of statutory duty, however, Part E of the Building Regulations lays down extensive rules as to, for example, fire resistance of various structural elements e g any separating wall (i e between two adjacent buildings) shall not have a fire resistance of less than one hour,[4] and breach of this type of objective requirement, typical of the Regulations relating to fire protection, should be easier to establish. It is even arguable that the occupier faced with nuisance by noise from an adjoining property could act against the builder alleging a breach of his obligations in respect of insulation against sound[5] instead of relying on the vagaries of the law of nuisance in an action against the neighbour.

1 Building Regulations 1976, above, para C2.
2 Ibid, para C3.
3 Ibid, para C6.
4 Ibid, para E5(2)(a).
5 Ibid, para G1.

3.121   It is clear that the civil action created by section 71 of the Health and Safety at Work Act 1974 has a wide significance; in particular all that need be done to assess its potential impact is to consider how many of the leading cases on builders' liability in negligence could equally well be framed as a civil action based on a breach of the duties imposed by the present Building Regulations, with no argument about the existence or otherwise of a duty, and as to its scope, being heard. It is therefore to be hoped, although perhaps in the present political climate not to be anticipated, that action will soon be taken to bring section 71 fully into force; this will greatly benefit the victims of poor construction work but, it is suggested, would not unduly prejudice the builder who after all should be complying with the Regulations in any event.[1]

1 However see *Anns v London Borough of Merton* [1978] AC 728 at 759, [1977] 2 All ER 492 at 504–505, per Lord Wilberforce, for the view that such civil liability already may exist, irrespective of s. 71. See also para 5.21, below.

3.122   It has been noted already[1] that a separate regime of regulation of building regulation at present applies in relation to the twelve Inner London Boroughs and the City of London. A word is in order as to its effect, given the amount of building work in this densely populated and commercially active area. In this area, building work is governed by the London Building Acts 1930 to 1978 and byelaws made by the Greater London Council (GLC) thereunder. The GLC employs district surveyors to ensure compliance with this collection of rules. The general range of matters covered is not dissimilar to the national Building Regulations; by the London Building Act 1930 there are rules establishing clear, if basic, standards for space, light and ventilation in and around buildings; the London Building Acts (Amendment) Act provides considerable powers in relation to building construction, including questions involving party walls, fire precautions, separation of buildings, etc.

1 See para 3.112, above.

3.123   What is not clear, however, is whether an action for breach of statutory duty can be brought against a builder who is in default of his obligations under these rules. Formerly it could perhaps have been submitted that the intention of Parliament, which has in some mystical fashion to be divined in discussions such as this concerning the availability of breach of statutory duty actions, was that a clear indication of the existence of such a duty was required, the evidence for this proposition being the recent promulgation of the specific right to civil action by way of section 71 of the Health and Safety at Work Act 1974; thus in the absence of any parallel provision giving a right to civil action in respect of the London legislation, no such right existed. This argument may still be put forward, but with some diffidence, given the decision in *Marsh v Betstyle Construction Co and the Greater London Council.*[1] In this case the salient feature for our present purpose was that the GLC's district surveyor was negligent in the exercise of his functions under section 82 of the London Building Acts (Amendment) Act 1939, which entrust him with the supervision of building and building works. It was held in a briefly reported case, by Judge Lewis Hawser QC, that the GLC were liable vicariously for their servant's breach of statutory duty. The significance of the case is that section 82 gives no particular indication that it will provide the basis of a civil action. It is however submitted that the case may nonetheless be distinguished as a decision on that specific section alone on the ground that the section imposes a duty on the local authority itself, and not on the builder, and on the more general point that care should be taken not to transfer the right of civil action in respect of one statutory duty to other statutory provisions – each duty should be considered in isolation.

1 [1979] CLY 1875.

3.124   Overall, therefore, considerable doubt must be expressed as to whether any civil action can be brought in connection with the statutory duties imposed by the London Building Acts 1930 to 1978; if the authors' submission that no such right exists is correct, this would at least have the virtue of placing Inner London in line with the rest of the country. It is also suggested, however, that this is an equality of misery, and that many of the problems of actions against builders could be solved if actions for breach of the statutory duties imposed by the Building Regulations and the London Building Acts were available.

3.125   The future of these building controls is a matter for discussion at present. The government has recently produced a White Paper on the Future of Building Control,[1] in which it proposes to recast the Building Regulations so that they remain as a detailed set of standards for domestic buildings, while for other premises a minimal set of Regulations will be accompanied by a wide range of different standards and codes. There is proposed a greater degree of exemption from the Regulations' requirements e g for minor works. Also, it is proposed to align standards in Inner London more closely with those in England and Wales. Work is already in progress on recasting the Regulations.

1 Cmnd 8179 (1981).

Liability of the supplier of the materials

3.126   Not all defects arising from building operations are either in fact or in law of necessity the responsibility of the builder. The builder may carry out his own functions entirely properly, but the premises may nevertheless be defective because the materials used in the work are not up to standard. It should of course be stated that the builder is not without responsibility in this regard, and will be in breach of both his contractual obligations and his general duties of care if he uses materials that are obviously defective; indeed his contractual liability will be stricter, involving warranties as to the quality of the materials.[1] However, should the cause of the defect lie with the manufacturer of the materials, the builder will, if he has been held contractually liable, seek an indemnity from the supplier and/or manufacturer of the materials used. Thus, in considering liability in respect of materials used, it will be necessary to consider both contract and tort actions for defective products; the contractual action will lie where there is privity e g between the supplier of goods and the builder who purchases them directly from him, while in other cases, e g actions against manufacturers of materials where the sale has been through an intermediate supplier, tortious remedies must be used.

1 See para 3.9, above.

3.127   As far as contractual liability is concerned, the first question to be asked is whether the supply of goods for use in the construction process is under a contract purely for the sale of those goods or, alternatively, under a contract for work and materials. In the latter event, the relevant terms and the extent to which exemption clauses are used are effectively the same as under the general rules relating to building contracts.[1] However, in the case where the contract is purely a contract for sale of goods, a separate legal regime applies.

1 See paras 3.42 and 3.43, above.

3.128   Under the Sale of Goods Act 1979[1] (consolidating previous enactments) a seller of goods promises the purchaser that the goods in question will accord with their description,[2] be of merchantable quality[3] and also be fit for the purpose[4] for which they are required. These are strict obligations in the sense that the conduct and knowledge of the seller are irrelevant. They are, for the most part also, onerous obligations, in the sense that even a slight deviation may be regarded as a breach,[5] and also in the sense that they are stated to be conditions of the contract i e when there is a breach the purchaser is entitled to regard the contract as being at an end. It is however fair to say that the implied condition of merchantability is regarded less strictly by the courts at times[6] and that the purchaser must make clear his purposes in effecting the transaction if they are other than the obvious and usual purposes if he wishes to rely on the implied term as to fitness for purpose.[7] Neither of these section 14 implied terms apply in relation to sales other than in the course of a business.[8] However, the Sale of Goods Act has for long provided a key remedy against suppliers of defective building materials, and will doubtless continue so to do, in view of its ready availability and its ease of use in a wide range of situations.

1 For detailed discussion see inter alia Atiyah *Sale of Goods* (6th edn).
2 Sale of Goods Act 1979, s. 13.
3 Ibid, s. 14(2).
4 Ibid, s. 14(3).
5 *Arcos Ltd v E A Ronaasen & Son* [1933] AC 470.
6 *Cehave NV v Bremer Handelsgesellschaft GmbH, The Hansa Nord* [1976] QB 44, [1975] 3 All ER 739.
7 Sale of Goods Act 1979, s. 14(3).
8 Ibid, ss. 14(2), 14(3).

3.129   Thus, a supplier of cement which he describes in the contract as having a low alumina content will be contractually liable if in fact it turns out to be of high alumina content,[1] irrespective of any liability for misrepresentation. Similarly the legislation will cover the case where a specific material, e g specially treated timber, is bought at a high price for a particular purpose, such as decorative facing on an exposed site, but turns out to be in fact ordinary timber which weathers quickly – this would be a breach of the implied term as to merchantability.[2] Equally, had the purchaser placed specific reliance on the expertise of the seller in selecting appropriate timber for a stated purpose, an action under section 14(3) would be appropriate. In all cases, not only is the innocent purchaser entitled to treat the contract as at an end, he is also able to claim damages in respect of specific losses suffered as a consequence of the breach, in accordance with the usual contractual rules as to foreseeability.[3] The action is not restricted in terms of the types of losses in respect of which claims may be brought; rather it is the doctrine of privity of contract which limits its availability.

1 Sale of Goods Act 1979, s. 13.
2 *H Beecham & Co Pty Ltd v Francis Howard & Co Pty Ltd* [1921] VLR 428.
3 See paras 1.18 ff, above.

3.130 On the other hand, the reverse is true in respect of the tortious actions in respect of defective products; the duties owed by the manufacturer and (to a lesser extent) the supplier are general duties which may be enforced by anyone affected by a breach thereof but claims may not be brought in respect of all losses suffered. The negligent manufacturer of goods falls within the so-called 'narrow *ratio*' in *Donoghue v Stevenson*.[1] This case, in addition to its general importance on the law of negligence, also established that the manufacturer of a product would be liable to anyone who was injured by it, so long as they intended the product to reach its ultimate consumer or user in the form in which it was manufactured i e without the likelihood of an intermediate inspection which might reveal the existence of any defect, and on the assumption that damage was a foreseeable consequence of the absence of care in the manufacturing process.[2] The significance of the decision has been enhanced in many subsequent cases by extension of its principles to cover persons other than manufacturers. Thus, erectors or assemblers of plant also now fall within the same principles as govern the liability of manufacturers.[3]

1 [1932] AC 562.
2 Ibid at 599, per Lord Atkin.
3 *Brown v Cotterill* (1934) 51 TLR 21; *Howard v Furness Holder Argentine Lines and A and R Brown Ltd* [1936] 2 All ER 781.

3.131 However, the negligence action is not, and is never likely to be, the answer to all problems of defective materials. As in all types of negligence action, the plaintiff injured by defective materials has to make the running; it is for him to prove the case by showing that the manufacturer of the materials is at fault in some way, and problems of lack of evidence, or lack of access to it, or lack of resources to gain access to it, may all present major obstacles to the prospective plaintiff. It is indeed these general obstacles that have led to calls for strict liability to be imposed on the manufacturer of defective products. This has been recommended by the Pearson Commission[1] and is the subject of an EEC Draft Directive on Products Liability, but as yet no clear date for its introduction can safely be predicted.

1 Cmnd 7054 (1978). See also Law Com No 82.

3.132   The restrictions on the scope of the manufacturer's liability embodied in Lord Atkin's speech[1] also take on a particular significance in cases concerning defective building materials. On the normal assumption that building works are carried out by an experienced builder, under the supervision of a qualified architect (and it should be borne in mind that he too may be liable in negligence),[2] it is likely that there will be an intermediate inspection of the materials, and one which, given the experience and qualifications of those involved in the building work, would be very likely to reveal most defects. Only the most undetectable and/or unknown of latent defects, or very technical defects, such as in, say, lift machinery, may be likely to pass unnoticed, and only in respect of such defects may the manufacturer of building materials be held liable. Indeed, the mere fact that the materials do not pass directly into the premises but are subjected to the processes of installation may provide the manufacturer with the defence that the materials may have been rendered defective by their installation rather than by their manufacture.[3]

1 See para 3.130, above.
2 See ch 4, below.
3 *Evans v Triplex Safety Glass Co Ltd* [1936] 1 All ER 283.

3.133   Perhaps the biggest limitation placed on the efficacy of the negligence action stems from the insistence that damage be caused before an action may be brought. The common law insists that such damage be within the boundaries of remoteness[1] – a normal and fair restriction – but also appears to lay down a principle that no purely economic losses are compensable through the mechanisms of the law of negligence.[2] This has serious implications for the owner or occupier of premises wishing to act against the manufacturer of defective building materials. Happily, most defects in building materials do not result either in personal injury or even, in many cases, physical damage to the fabric of the building. Of course when this is the case a claim may be brought by persons affected in respect both of the physical harm, and any directly consequent economic loss.[3] However, in the absence of any type of physical damage, such as cases simply where the building cannot be used for profitable activities e g a roller-skating rink that turns out to be unable to stand the weight of crowds of users, or where the building falls in value as a consequence of the defects in the materials directly, or indirectly, perhaps through a shortened life expectancy of the structure, the prospective plaintiff will find himself in legal difficulties.

1 *The Wagon Mound* [1961] AC 388, [1961] 1 All ER 404.
2 *SCM (UK) Ltd v W J Whittall & Son Ltd* [1971] 1 QB 337, [1970] 3 All ER 245.
3 Ibid.

3.134   It is possible for various arguments to be made on behalf of a plaintiff who suffers pure economic loss stemming from defective building materials, even where there is no physical damage whatsoever.[1] In a situation where the economic loss is a clearly and obviously foreseeable consequence of the manufacturer's breach of his duty of care, this alone might be enough to allow recovery,[2] while reliance could also be placed on the significant Commonwealth decisions of *Rivtow Marine Ltd v Washington Iron Works*[3] and *Caltex Oil (Australia) Pty Ltd v The Dredge 'Willemstad'*,[4] both of which appear to offer a more flexible view of claims for purely economic loss. Most importantly in respect of liability for building materials, it may also be appropriate to refer to *Anns v London Borough of Merton*[5] where, as we have seen,[6] the rule in negligence claims stemming from defective construction work is that once there is a present or imminent threat to the health and safety of its occupants, then a claim may be brought for the necessary repair or replacement costs even though no physical harm has occurred at that time. It seems but a short step to apply this not only to those who negligently construct premises but also to those who negligently manufacture and supply materials for use in the construction. Thus, in a typical case where premises are unable to be used for their intended (profitable) purpose e g where a new cinema has to be closed because fittings have been negligently manufactured and do not satisfy fire regulations, or where premises decline in value because of defective building materials, such as properties constructed with high alumina cement, the owner or occupier now at least has a respectable argument in his favour that he should be compensated for his economic loss, and one which the courts, if they follow the lead of their Commonwealth brethren, will uphold.

1 See also paras 1.20 ff, above.
2 *Ross v Caunters* [1980] Ch 297 at 321, [1979] 3 All ER 580 at 598.
3 (1973) 40 DLR (3d) 530.
4 (1976) 136 CLR 529.
5 [1978] AC 728, [1977] 2 All ER 492.
6 See para 3.93, above.

3.135   The tortious remedy thus has ample potential for use; the existence of a notional duty is well-established and the range of compensable damage is increasing. Its advantages in respect of its freedom from the constraints of the doctrine of privity and its longer limitation period are well-known, as compared with the traditional contractual action. The picture with regard to the controls placed on exclusion clauses is less clear; in most tortious cases no question of contractual exclusion clauses will arise in view of the lack of privity, and it is difficult to envisage situations where non-contractual notices might occur, though if they do section 2 of the Unfair Contract Terms Act 1977 will apply to curtail their effect totally (where death or physical injury ensues), or partially (by imposing a requirement of reasonableness) in other cases. In contract cases, the exclusion clauses will be firmly controlled; in a Sale of Goods contract, section 6(2) of the Unfair Contract Terms Act 1977 prevents any purported exclusion of the statutory implied term in the course of business from taking effect as against a consumer while of greater relevance to the kind of case we are considering is section 6(3), which states that these implied terms may not be excluded or restricted as against a non-consumer except insofar as the exclusion is able to satisfy the requirement of reasonableness. In assessing the question of reasonableness here, specific regard is to be paid to factors listed in Schedule 2 of the Act, whereby the court is directed to consider as relevant the relative strength or otherwise of the parties' bargaining positions, the presence of any inducement (e g as to price) leading to acceptance of an exclusion clause, the state of the customer's knowledge as to the presence of the term, the reasonableness of any contingencies which bring the clause into play and the question of whether the contract is a 'one-off' special order or not. Clearly the effect of these criteria is to aid the customer who may be regarded as the 'victim' of an onerous standard-form contract, but it is questionable whether the typical businessman or company contracting with a supplier of building materials falls easily within this stereotype. Contracts for work and materials can only exclude liability under the analogous provisions of section 7 of the Unfair Contract Terms Act 1977, discussed above.[1]

1 See paras 3.42 and 3.43, above.

3.136 So far, the discussion of the position of the supplier of building materials has proceeded on the basis of the general law. However, in many cases, the supplier of building materials is further protected by becoming involved in the mesh of standard-form building contract provisions, and particular consideration needs to be given to this aspect of his prospective liability. Clause 36 of the 1980 edition of the JCT form governs the contractual position of the so-called 'nominated supplier' (as opposed to the unnominated supplier whose position is solely governed by the general law, discussed already) vis-à-vis the contractor. A nominated supplier is either one named in the contract bills or subsequently named in an architect's instruction, or alternatively a sole supplier (i e one who has by contract to be chosen or is the only available supplier), in each case if the payment to the supplier is made via a prime cost sum created by the expenditure of a provisional sum or in a variation. It is likely that the normal method of nomination will be via a new form issued under the aegis of the JCT, viz a 'Standard Form Tender for Nominated Suppliers'. This is sent to the supplier who, if he accepts, completes and returns it, is then a nominated supplier, and will promise the main contractor to supply the goods in question with an associated warranty that he will exercise reasonable skill in relation to the materials, including their selection and design, and he additionally makes promises concerning the provision of information and the punctuality of supply.

3.137 In addition to these terms, there are further obligations placed on the nominated supplier by clause 36 itself, which creates the actual conditions of sale. The supplier promises to the contractor that he will supply materials of the quality and standard specified, a typically strict contractual obligation. If the goods turn out to be defective, then replacement (and associated expenses) may be demanded by the contractor until the end of the Defects Liability Period.[1] However, this is not the case if the materials have defects which should have been revealed before or during their use, or if the defects can be shown by the supplier to be the fault of another e g through the contractor's neglect, misuse or poor storage. Further conditions imposed include provisions as to full payment, punctual delivery, and as to ownership of the materials – in all cases this passes on delivery of the goods, irrespective of issues of payment. Arbitration is the forum for resolution of disputes in these cases only if the subject of the dispute is similar to a dispute under the main contract already referred to arbitration. It is of particular importance to note that the foregoing conditions are prerequisites of the status of nominated supplier; any departure therefrom will render clause 36 entirely inapplicable, and the supplier will only have an unnominated status. Clause 36 does not permit any change in the conditions for nomination, even by the supplier – they must all be present for clause 36 to operate.

1 See para 3.16, above.

3.138 If the supplier wishes to insert an additional exclusion clause, over and above the clause 36 conditions, this is permissible, but two consequences immediately follow. The first is, of course, the intervention of the Unfair Contract Terms Act 1977. The supplier's attempts to exclude his liability in respect of the contract terms as to quality statutorily implied by the Sale of Goods Act 1979 will fail as against a consumer, per section 6(2), while the terms will only survive as against a person dealing otherwise than as a consumer if they satisfy the requirement of reasonableness, per section 6(3).[1] Attempts to exclude other specific contractual liabilities will be in danger of falling foul of section 3 of the 1977 Act.[2] The supplier is not free to exclude his liability as against a consumer (i e a person dealing other than in the course of a business) or against another businessman where one party deals on another's written standard terms of business – whether terms amount to written standard terms of business is in essence a factual one. The supplier must in these circumstances ensure that his exclusion clause, if he seeks to rely on it to permit a different performance of the contractual obligation from that intended or to render no performance at all, satisfies the requirement of reasonableness imposed by section 3(2) of the Act, this to be assessed under section 11(1) of the 1977 Act with regard to the circumstances prevailing at the time the contract was made.

1 See also Unfair Contract Terms Act 1977, Sch 2 discussed above, para 3.43.
2 See paras 3.37–3.41, above.

3.139 Secondly, any such exclusion clause adding to the provisions of clause 36 must be approved by the architect in writing prior to the finalisation of the contractual arrangements; when this is done, the contractor's liability to the employer will be limited in precisely the same way as the supplier's liability to the contractor. It may be argued, however, that the reasonableness or otherwise of the exclusion clause in question may fall to be assessed differently in the two contracts in the light of the possibly differing states of knowledge of the contractor and employer at the relevant time. Overall, then, the position of the nominated supplier of building materials is an important one; he will clearly be involved in many disputes and it is to be hoped that the new arrangements in the 1980 edition of the JCT form will prove to be a satisfactory base for their resolution.

Conclusion

3.140 Such are the many and varied prospective liabilities of the builder in respect of defective premises that it is necessary to draw the respective strands together. The traditional contractual remedies of the employer against his contractor continue to be of great significance; the rise of alternative remedies ought not to be allowed to mask the fact that the contractual form of action will be the major remedy against the builder in respect of defects in building work which are immediate and patent. Indeed, the employer is entitled to insist that major defects be remedied before the building is fully accepted. No version of the JCT form, or the other standard-form contracts used in respect of building and engineering works, has escaped criticism, and this will doubtless also be the case with the 1980 edition of the JCT form, but the fact that such contracts may be (justly) criticised at times must, in fairness, be coupled with a recognition of the tremendous value of their role in rendering the formation of building contracts a far easier task than might otherwise be the case. Whether the precise form is adopted or not, it at least provides a good basis for negotiation at the pre-contractual stage. It is perhaps churlish to pass adverse comment on the great complexity of the provisions of the standard-form contracts; it may be argued that this is an inevitable consequence of the complex, multipartite nature of contracts for major building works, and it may additionally be suggested that the importance of such work, and the amounts of money involved, render the involvement of legal and other professional assistance inevitable.

3.141 The additional contractual arrangements under the aegis of the NHBC may sometimes be regarded as a very limited gloss on the general contractual provisions, but it is suggested that this is unfair. While it is true to characterise the protection afforded to house-purchasers, especially after the first two years after completion have elapsed, as being of a basic character, this is to underplay the importance of the guaranteed nature of the remedy, with the NHBC itself providing what must be regarded as a crucial back-up role, given the invariable exigencies and uncertainties of the building trade. It is also of importance to bear in mind the extension of the utility of this remedy beyond purely contractual frontiers by assignment of its benefit; whatever the precise legal niceties of the apparent obligation to assign are, the happy fact is that assignment to subsequent purchasers of the benefit of the NHBC agreement does normally take place, greatly extending the range of persons covered by the scheme. Within its admittedly limited ambit, the scheme is of not inconsiderable importance.

3.142 The recent rise in importance of tortious remedies against builders is now capable of being seen, perhaps with some benefit of hindsight, as an inevitable and logical development or extension of the principles of negligence. It is now easy for us to say that there should never have been any rigid distinction between negligence actions in respect of defective chattels and in respect of realty, although the law was slow to recognise this. It is easy for us to say today that the use of the law of negligence to protect the house-purchaser against the builder is just another facet of the activities of the law of tort as a vehicle of consumer protection. After all, the family home stands out, even beyond the family car, as the largest item of consumer expenditure incurred by owner-occupiers, at least. Again, however, the law has taken almost half a century to come to this conclusion, and in eventually permitting tortious actions against builders in respect of realty has created its own problems.

3.143 From the consumer viewpoint, the expansion of the role of negligence in defective premises cases has been a continuing story of success – an ever-widening range of parties have fallen within its ambit; the amount recoverable has expanded to cover claims for what to a traditional lawyer now look like claims for pure economic loss. From the builder's viewpoint, and that of his insurer, this presents a very different picture, however; the proverbial floodgates seem to have just burst. It therefore must be asked whether the consumer's most optimistic expectations (and the builder's worst fears) will come to fruition or not. It is submitted that at least for the time being the liability of the builder in negligence will remain a crucial plank in the edifice of actions available in respect of defective premises; the liability has already become a clear and reasonably well-defined one and, it is thought, is in tune with the current vogue for consumer protection. Few obvious loop-holes exist. Given that the problems with economic loss are the creation of the House of Lords, it is unlikely to expect that body to turn around and overrule its recent decisions; rather, a slower process of explanation and resolution by the courts seems more likely.

3.144 Both the contractual and tortious actions against builders in respect of defective workmanship seem likely to continue to operate in parallel, for each has its own distinct role. Contract claims are the obvious initial remedy of the employer, but the tortious action has a far wider scope, reaching parties the contractual action can never hope to reach, by reason of its freedom from the privity rules, and stepping forward into times which the contractual action cannot go by reason of issues of limitation. The existence of these two actions, not to mention the plethora of other actions, especially those created by statute, will mean that the builder will continue to be in the forefront of claims in respect of defective premises, though the extent to which he has to share that limelight with other prospective defendants is the issue at the core of what follows in subsequent chapters.

Chapter 4

The professional man

4.1 This chapter describes and analyses the civil liability of professional men for defective premises. The categories of professional men who may incur such liability are twofold. First there are those who are concerned with the design of premises and the supervision of their construction. This category comprises architects and engineers. Secondly there are those who, as a part of their professional duties, give advice concerning premises, and who incur liability to another as a result of a negligent exercise of those duties. This category includes surveyors, valuers, estate agents and solicitors. In each case the fact that the duty owed by the professional man is exercised carelessly may render him liable in a civil action for damages suffered by the person or persons to whom the duty is owed. First, duties in contract owed by these professional men will be discussed, then their duties in tort, with emphasis on the recent expansion of tort liability in the area of professional negligence. Duties may also be owed by professional men under the Defective Premises Act 1972, and these will be considered; and exclusion and limitation of liability, and the role of the Unfair Contract Terms Act 1977, will be discussed.

Liability in contract

A ARCHITECTS AND ENGINEERS

1 DEFINITION
4.2 There is no statutory definition of either of these professions. Their various duties are described in detail below but a brief working definition of each will be in order.

i *Architect*
4.3 An architect was defined by the Architects' Registration Tribunal[1] (definition cited by the Divisional Court in *R v Architects' Registration Tribunal, ex parte Jagger*)[2] as 'one who possesses with due regard to aesthetic as well as practical considerations, adequate skill and knowledge to enable him (i) to originate, (ii) to design and plan, (iii) to arrange for and supervise the erection of such buildings or other works calling for skill in design and planning as he might in the course of his business reasonably be asked to carry out or in respect of which he offers his services as a specialist'. By section 1(1) of the Architects Registration Act 1938, no-one may practice or carry on business under any name, style or title containing the word architect unless he is a person registered by the

Architects' Registration Council, and hence the above definition is as close as one is likely to get to a formal definition.

1 A tribunal set up under the Architects Registration Act 1938 empowered to hear appeals against refusals by the Architects' Registration Council to register individuals as architects.
2 [1945] 2 All ER 131 at 134.

ii *Engineer*
4.4 The title 'engineer' covers a wide variety of activities. For our purposes an engineer can be defined, in Keating's words, as 'one who, in relation to engineering or constructional works, carries out duties analogous to those carried out by an architect in a building contract'.[1] Anyone may call himself an engineer, but in practice an engineer will usually be a member of a professional body, such as the Institution of Civil Engineers. As we shall see, there are at times differences between the powers and duties of engineers and architects, but it can be assumed that, unless differences are clearly spelled out, their powers and duties are the same, and references to 'architect' can be taken to include 'engineer'.

1 *Keating Building Contracts* (4th edn) p. 199. *Hudson's Building and Engineering Contracts* (10th edn) and *Emden's Building Contracts and Practice* (8th edn) are the leading works on the powers and duties of architects and engineers as well as on building law generally.

2 DUTIES OWED IN CONTRACT BY THE ARCHITECT AND THE ENGINEER
4.5 The primary function of the architect or engineer is to carry out the duties that he owes in contract to his employer. In any case the particular duties owed will depend upon the facts of the case and the terms of the contract, though in general terms it has been clear for centuries that a person who practises a profession involving the need for special skill is under a duty to observe the standard of skill and competence that is exercised by a reasonably competent practitioner at that profession.

4.6 Although it is conceivable that the architect or engineer may already be employed by the employer who commissions him, usually the two will be strangers, and will enter into a contractual relationship either as the result of a competition or an individual agreement. The contract need not be, and often is not, in writing. Where the contract is written, the most common form is the RIBA Conditions of Engagement. These conditions fix fees based on a percentage of the estimated final cost of the works and also set out certain of the conditions of employment which may be made applicable if the RIBA scales of fees are adopted. The general duties owed by the architect to his employer, as suggested by Hudson, with the amendments and developments of later editions, are listed below.

(1) To advise and consult with the employer (not as a lawyer) as to any limitation which may exist as to the use of the land to be built on, either (inter alia) by planning legislation, restrictive covenants or the rights of adjoining owners or the public over the land, or by statutes and byelaws affecting the works to be executed.
(2) To examine the site, subsoil, and surroundings, or to make arrangements for such an examination, including advising on the need for the employment of specialists or consultants.
(3) To consult with and advise the employer as to the proposed work.
(4) To prepare sketch plans and a specification, having regard to all the

133

conditions known to exist, and to submit them to the employer for approval, with an estimate of the probable cost, if requested.

(5) To elaborate and, if necessary, modify or amend the sketch plans, and then, if so instructed, to prepare drawings and a specification of the work to be carried out as a first step in the preparation of contract documents, including advising on the need for the employment of any specialists or consultants.

(6) To consult with and advise the employer as to the form of contract to be used (including whether or not to use bills of quantities) and as to the necessity or otherwise of employing a quantity surveyor (engineers usually do not employ an independent quantity surveyor) to prepare bills and carry out the usual valuation services during the currency of the contract.

(7) To bring the contract documents to their final state before inviting tenders, with or without the assistance of quantity surveyors and structural engineers, including the obtaining of detailed quotations from and arrangement of delivery dates with any nominated sub-contractors or suppliers whose work may have to be ready or available at an early stage of the main contractor's work.

(8) To advise the employer as to tenders received and the selection of the main contractor, and to arrange starting dates and the contract period if this has not already been done.

(9) After work has started, to supply the builder with copies of the contract drawings and specification, and any further drawings, details or instructions which may be necessary for the work, including work to be done by nominated sub-contractors, to make any further nominations which may be necessary, and to advise the employer if any variation of the work becomes necessary or desirable.

(10) To supervise the work, making sure in the employer's interest that the contract is complied with in every respect, to value, with or without the assistance of a quantity surveyor, the work both for purposes of interim payment and final payment, and generally to administer the contract so that full effect is given to all its provisions.

(11) To act as certifier on such matters as the terms of the contract may require, up to and including the final certificate – for instance, on questions of extension of time, on practical completion, on payment direct of sub-contractors, and on various claims for additional expense which the contractor may be entitled to make under the terms of the contract.

For our purposes, only those duties which entail potential civil liability for defective premises will be discussed in detail, all of which can normally be assumed to exist from the fact of employment, subject to any express terms to the contrary.

Design[1]
4.7 The standard of the duty owed by the architect or engineer as regards design will generally be that of reasonable care. 'As architect, he is in the same position as any other professional or skilled person, and whether it be in the preparation of plans and specifications, or the doing of any other professional work for reward, is responsible if he omits to do it with an ordinary and reasonable degree of care and skill.'[2] However, it is always possible for the architect to take on further duties, either expressly or by implication. Thus, in *Greaves & Co*

(Contractors) Ltd v Baynham Meikle & Partners[3] the defendants were consultant structural engineers who were engaged by contractors under a package deal[4] with building owners to design a warehouse. They were told that the warehouse was to be used for storing and moving oil drums loaded on to fork-lift trucks on and around the first floor. After a few months cracks appeared on the first floor, attempts to remedy the problem failed, and as a result the warehouse was of very limited use. The contractors, being absolutely liable to the building owners to repair the damage and prevent further deterioration, claimed a declaration of liability against the defendants. It was held that the defendants were in breach of an implied warranty that the floor would be fit for the purpose for which they knew it was required. This decision depended upon the particular facts and circumstances of the case, and was not intended to establish any general principle as to the obligations and liability of professional men. If, on the facts of the case, the court had found that there was no implied warranty, and that the design, despite its failure, was one that a reasonably competent structural engineer would have employed, there would of course have been no liability. However, concern is likely to be aroused as a result of certain dicta by Lord Scarman in the recent House of Lords decision in *Independent Broadcasting Authority v EMI Ltd and BICC Ltd*,[5] a case involving the liability of a main contractor for defects in construction work, the design of which was undertaken by a nominated sub-contractor, whose liability was also in question. Lord Scarman argued that the design responsibility extended to ensuring that the design was reasonably fit for the purpose made known to the designer, rather than involving simply a duty to exercise the care and skill of the ordinary competent member of the designer's profession. Although Lord Scarman stated that the design duty of a person supplying an article could not be equated with the obligation of a professional man in the practice of his profession, he stated in his conclusion: 'In the absence of any terms (express or to be implied) negativing the obligation, one who contracts to design an article for a purpose made known to him undertakes that the design is reasonably fit for the purpose.' The implications for the architect or consultant engineer are potentially serious.

1 See *Emden's Building Contracts and Practice* (8th edn) p. 463.
2 Per Osler JA in the Canadian case of *Badgley v Dickson* (1886) 13 AR 494 at 500. See also *Worboys v Acme Investment Ltd* (1969) 210 Estates Gazette 335 where it was held that the failure of an architect to include downstairs lavatories in homes constructed to his design was, in the absence of professional evidence that he had failed to exercise due care, not negligence.
3 [1975] 3 All ER 99, [1975] 1 WLR 1095.
4 A 'package deal' is another name for the design and build contract whereby, in addition to carrying out the building work, the contractor offers to perform the architect's duties as well.
5 (1980) 14 BLR 1 at 48. See para 3.11, above. See also Stanton and Dugdale (1981) 131 NLJ 583 at 584–585.

4.8 A further point on the potential liability of an architect for defective design is that he will not be liable where, as in *Turner v Garland and Christopher*[1] he is employed to design buildings with instructions to put in some new invention of which he has no knowledge and professes none. In this case, Erle J charged the jury that if out of the ordinary course an architect was employed on some new matter (here new patent concrete roofing) in which he had no experience and which had not had the test of experience, failure could be consistent with skill. This is, however, subject to the architect's duty to warn the employer of risks, which may arise where, for example, new techniques of construction in novel materials are to be used.

1 (1853) Hudson's BC, 4th edn, vol 2, p. 1.

4.9 Problems of liability for defective design are particularly acute for the innovative architect, and he will have to take especial care to obtain the best possible advice when contemplating a break from tradition in the design. Although he is clearly under a duty to advise his employer of any potential risks in employing the novel design, he will not normally be able to escape liability simply by securing the employer's approval of the design, particularly if the design defect which later causes contention is one concerning construction techniques.[1] In the Canadian case of *City of Brantford v Kemp and Wallace-Carruthers & Associates Ltd*[2] an architect appointed to design a police station and firehall engaged a professional engineering firm to prepare a structural design for the foundation of the two buildings. The site required particular consideration because it was a garbage dump over a canal. The firm did not carry out adequate examination of the soil conditions and recommended a plan which contained an element of risk, when there was an alternative which was foolproof. The employer (or the architect, as the employer's agent) ought to have been informed of the risk, so that he could decide whether to take it, or to play safe and rely on the foolproof design. The failure to inform and the inadequate examination constituted breaches of duty by the defendant firm.

1 If however the employer gives express approval of the aesthetics of a design, the architect will normally not be liable.
2 (1960) 23 DLR (2d) 640. See also *Surrey District v Church* (1977) 76 DLR (3d) 721 (discussed at para 4.81, below).

4.10 An architect may not delegate his duty to design, or, indeed, any of his duties, without the consent of his employer, as his employment is a personal contract. Thus, in *Moresk Cleaners Ltd v Hicks*[1] the defendant architect was employed to draw up plans, specifications and contracts for the building of an extension to the plaintiffs' laundry. The defendant invited a contractor whose partners were qualified engineers to design the building, which involved the design of a reinforced concrete structure on a sloping site, and then submit a price for the work that was to be done. The architect approved the drawings and the contractor was invited to build the structure. Within two years after completion defects became apparent in the building, because of negligent design, in that firstly the purlins were not strong enough to support the roof, and secondly the portal frames should have been tied together. The architect claimed in the alternative that it was an implied term of his employment that he could delegate specialised design tasks to qualified sub-contractors, and he had done so; or that he had implied authority to act as the employers' agent to employ the contractors to design the building. Both arguments were rejected by the court.

> In my opinion he [the architect] had no implied authority to employ the contractor to design the building. If he wished to take that course, it was essential that he should obtain the permission of the building owner before that was done . . . If the defendant was not able, because this form of reinforced concrete was a comparatively new form of construction, to design it himself, he had three courses open to him. One was to say 'this is not my field'. The second was to go to the client, the building owner, and say: 'this reinforced concrete is out of my line. I would like you to employ a structural engineer to deal with this aspect of the matter.' Or he can, while retaining responsibility for the design, himself seek the advice and assistance of a structural engineer, paying for his service out of his own pocket but having at any rate the satisfaction of knowing that if he acts upon that advice and it turns out to be wrong the person whom he employed to give the advice will owe the same duty to him as he, the architect, owes to the building owner.[2]

1 [1966] 2 Lloyd's Rep 338.
2 Ibid at 342, 343, per Sir Walker Carter QC, Official Referee.

4.11   Clearly, recourse must be had to the terms of the architect's employment in order to discover to what extent, if any, the employer has expressly or impliedly agreed that the architect's duties are any different from those which he is ordinarily obliged to discharge. The traditional arrangement whereby the architect designs the work and the contractor brings it to completion is often inappropriate nowadays, given the increase in specialisation and the complexities of modern buildings. Often an architect will not be qualified to carry out particular aspects of design, and therefore he will need to employ specialists. If he envisages such a need, he will have to ensure that the power to nominate specialist sub-contractors is included in his contract of employment, and he will have to consider whether he or they are to have ultimate responsibility for their design. By clause 1.22 of the RIBA Conditions of Engagement it is provided that 'the architect will advise on the need for independent consultants and will be responsible for the direction and integration of their work but not for the detailed design, inspection and performance of the work entrusted to them'. Clause 1.40 provides that 'the architect may recommend that specialist sub-contractors and suppliers should design and execute any part of the work. He will be responsible for the direction and integration of their design, and for general inspection of their work in accordance with stage H of the normal services,[1] but not for the detailed design or performance of the work entrusted to them.' If the current JCT form of contract is used, a nominated sub-contractor for design purposes warrants the exercise of all reasonable skill and care in the design, so the employer is protected. Arguably[2] failure by an architect to recommend the securing of such a warranty to his employer would constitute a breach of duty by the architect if the architect would otherwise be able to escape liability by means of clause 1.40. If the architect does not employ clause 1.22, clause 1.40 or equivalent provisions in his contract of employment, he will remain liable for defective design, even if it is otherwise clear that a concurrent liability for defective design, arises against the sub-contractor and/or the main contractor as a result of some acceptance by them of express responsibility for design. However, he will normally be able to recover from an independent consultant whom he employs, less often against a specialist sub-contractor unless he is able to bring a claim under *Hedley Byrne & Co Ltd v Heller & Partners Ltd*.[3] If clause 1.22 or 1.40 is employed, it must be considered whether the Unfair Contract Terms Act applies. It may be argued that since these two clauses delineate areas of responsibility rather than purporting to exclude liability, the Act does not apply. Treitel[4] suggests a test for determining whether a clause defines or excludes liability: viz whether the events in which a clause operates are beyond the control of the party who is exonerated: if they are, the clause is likely to be regarded as defining the duty of that party rather than exempting him from liability. If this is a valid test, it would support the argument that clauses 1.22 and 1.40 define rather than exempt, as they will be employed in cases where the architect has to call on specialists because the design required is not one that he is qualified to make.

1 See RIBA Conditions of Engagement, Part 2:1.
2 Keating *Building Contracts* (4th edn) p. 212. See para 4.19, below.
3 [1964] AC 465, [1963] 2 All ER 575. See para 4.70, below.
4 *The Law of Contract* (5th edn) p. 172.

4.12   Where the architect does employ consultants or sub-contractors it will not be enough for him to establish that he selected a reputable and well-qualified person for the task, and was therefore not careless in his choice. It would seem that he is in the position of guaranteeing the professional competence of those to whom he chooses to delegate his function, in that he undertakes that the building will be properly designed with all due care and skill.

4.13 Finally it should be noted that, in the words of Sachs LJ in *Brickfield Properties Ltd v Newton*,[1] 'the architect is under a continuing duty to check that his design will work in practice and to correct any errors which may emerge'. Thus the design duty does not come to an end when work begins, and this is significant not only concerning liability but also the time from which the limitation period will begin to run.

1 [1971] 3 All ER 328 at 336, [1971] 1 WLR 862 at 873.

Examination of site

4.14 The architect is under a duty to examine the site to determine its suitability for the envisaged work. This does not have to be a personal examination[1], but the architect runs the risk of liability if he accepts the inaccurate report of a third person. In *Moneypenny v Hartland*[2] the defendants employed the plaintiff as architect and engineer for the building of a bridge. A third party, previously employed by the defendants to ascertain by boring the nature of the soil, was asked by them to inform the plaintiff of the results of this, which he did. The plaintiff did not examine the soil himself, but laid the foundations of the bridge, which later gave way. It was held that he was not entitled to recover his remuneration.

1 See *Columbus Co v Clowes* [1903] 1 KB 244.
2 (1826) 2 C & P 378.

4.15 In *Columbus Co v Clowes*[1] an architect was employed to make plans of a building to be erected on a site of which the plaintiffs were the lessees. The architect accepted the word of a third person that the site was of certain dimensions, and drew up his plans accordingly and had quantities taken out. The site was in fact larger than he had been told. However, the plaintiffs, having paid the architect £200 for his services, were never able to raise funds to build on the site, so they parted with the lease. Later they discovered the architect's error and sued for the £200 on the grounds of a total failure of consideration or, alternatively, on the grounds of negligence. It was held that there had not been a total failure of consideration, but that the plaintiffs were entitled to damages on account of the architect's negligence. However, the plaintiffs had suffered no loss from the negligence, and therefore were entitled to nominal damages only (£2) for that, though they were awarded a further £40, being the cost of adapting the quantities that had been taken out to a correct plan.

1 [1903] 1 KB 244.

4.16 The examination should be such as to enable determination of whether the land is sufficiently extensive to incorporate the proposed building(s) and also should involve examination of the subsoil so as to determine the correct design for foundations. Further examination may be necessary, particularly in the case where a house is being built, while the foundations are being constructed, especially after excavation has been completed and before the foundation concrete has been poured. Further, the architect should examine the condition of any structures on the land,[1] and he should also consider whether there are rights of way or light or air or other easements affecting the land, for he may be liable to his employer for any loss suffered as a result of defects in his plans caused by a failure to take account of such matters.[2]

1 See *Clay v A J Crump & Sons Ltd* [1964] 1 QB 533, [1963] 3 All ER 687 on the duty owed in such circumstances to third parties. See para 4.87, below.
2 See e g *Armitage v Palmer* (1960) 175 Estates Gazette 315.

4.17 In a case where examination of the site involves the need for specialist consideration, for example in relation to soil conditions, the same factors as discussed in the section on design will apply concerning the delegation of the architect's duties, and again it will probably be in the interests of both building owner and architect if such third parties are employed directly by the building owner.

4.18 Again the architect is not guaranteeing the works (unless there exists a contractual provision to the contrary), merely operating under a duty to exercise reasonable professional skill. This does not mean, of course, that he can simply adopt the findings of the building inspector or district surveyor, just because they may in certain cases be better equipped than he to pass judgment on foundations, but if he has done his work and reached the same conclusion as a well-qualified and experienced building inspector, it will be difficult, as Hudson[1] suggests, to establish liability if the foundations prove ultimately to be defective.

1 *Hudson's Building and Engineering Contracts* (10th edn) p. 134.

Duties concerning nominations
4.19 A more questionable area of potential liability, but one certainly meriting consideration, concerns the duty of the architect to obtain from nominated subcontractors formal undertakings and warranties as to the suitability of work or goods, by way of collateral contract with the employer (with identical warranties being written into the main contract) and to ensure that there are no exemption clauses. Hudson[1] suggests, though tentatively, that the courts might not regard this as placing too high a standard of care on the architect. Certainly in the absence of such undertakings or warranties the potential loss to the employer, in the likely absence of a successful action for negligence, is very high. This is no doubt in part an effect of the problem of nomination.[2] It remains to be seen whether the courts would impose a duty in such circumstances on the architect, though presumably the likelihood would be greater in a case where he made no attempt to balance the absence of undertakings and warranties or the presence of exemption clauses with the reputation and price of the sub-contractor than in a case where he made such a balance.

1 *Hudson's Building and Engineering Contracts* (10th edn) pp. 141–142.
2 See *Gloucestershire County Council v Richardson* [1969] 1 AC 480, [1968] 2 All ER 1181; *North West Metropolitan Regional Hospital Board v T A Bickerton & Son Ltd* [1970] 1 All ER 1039, [1970] 1 WLR 607. A particular example of such problems is the case where a sub-contractor whose techniques are highly specialised is nominated, and the architect is, on account of their specialist nature, unable to ascertain their suitability for their purpose either before the building work takes place or thereafter. See *Hudson* p. 141 and the *Gloucestershire County Council* case.

Recommending builders
4.20 An architect does not guarantee the solvency or capability of a builder or contractor (unless specifically in his contract of employment) but, by analogy with the law governing estate agents letting houses,[1] it would seem that he may be in breach of duty if he fails to make inquiries concerning such solvency or

capability, if it is he rather than the employer who is responsible for choosing the builder, particularly if he has knowledge of local builders or ready access to such knowledge.

1 See *Heys v Tindall* (1861) 1 B & S 296.

Liability for materials

4.21 An architect may incur liability to his employer if he fails to make proper inquiries concerning the suitability of materials and simply accepts the recommendation of a supplier. In *Sealand of the Pacific v Robert C McHaffie Ltd*[1] the defendants, who were naval architects, were retained by the plaintiffs to carry out alterations to an underwater aquarium. A supplier of concrete products recommended a certain product to the plaintiffs and later to the defendants. The use of this product for the recommended purpose was unusual and it ultimately proved to be unsuitable. The plaintiffs claimed against, inter alios, the architects, and it was held that a contractual duty was owed by the architects to make further inquiries and not simply to rely on the recommendation of the supplier. Further inquiries would have revealed the unsuitability of the product for its proposed use. In this case it was admitted that it was part of the architect's duty to consider the suitability of the product. Any suggestion that this can be said to be a universal duty on an architect must be made with hesitation, given the absence of other case law, but it is suggested that to impose such a duty more widely than on specialist architects, or general architects in cases where a basic inquiry would reveal unsuitability of a product, would be unduly harsh.

1 (1975) 51 DLR (3d) 702. It was held by the British Columbia Court of Appeal that the individual employee of the defendant architects who had in effect endorsed the supplier's recommendation of the product to the plaintiffs was not liable as, in his individual capacity, he was in breach of no duty owed to the plaintiffs.

Duty to ensure compliance with the law

4.22 It is part of an architect's duty to ensure that the building work complies with the requirements of the statutes and byelaws[1] and building regulations which regulate building works in the area. This may involve, for example, the need to serve notices on local or other authorities and the need to submit plans for planning approval or byelaw consent.[2] Thus, for example, a failure by the architect to ensure that the Fire Prevention Officer inspects and certifies the building, or a failure to secure inspection and certification by the local authority that the building satisfies the Building Regulations, will constitute a breach of his duties to his client; for, quite apart from the sanctions that a failure to observe the legal requirements[3] would entail, the building may as a consequence be seriously defective. This does not mean that an architect is expected to be a lawyer, but he will have to have a good working knowledge of the law as it affects his professional activities.[4]

1 See *Townsends (Builders) Ltd v Cinema News and Property Management Ltd* [1959] 1 All ER 7, [1959] 1 WLR 119; *Strongman (1945) Ltd v Sincock* [1955] 2 QB 525, [1955] 3 All ER 90.
2 See *Hudson's Building and Engineering Contracts* (10th edn) p. 142.
3 See e g *Hopkins v Smethwick Local Board of Health* (1890) 24 QBD 712.
4 See e g *Jenkins v Betham* (1855) 15 CB 168 (surveyor and valuer).

Supervision

4.23 An important aspect of the architect's duties to the building owner is the duty to supervise the building works. This does not require him to be constantly on site, but he must give such reasonable supervision as will enable him to give

an honest certificate that the work has been carried out according to the contract. Thus in *Jameson v Simon*[1] an architect was employed to plan and supervise the building of a house. He made weekly visits to the site, but failed to
inspect the bottoming of the floor before the cement was laid down. In fact the
bottoming had not been done according to contract, and soon after the plaintiff
occupied the house, he discovered dry rot. It was held that the architect had
broken his duty to give reasonable supervision, and that he was liable in
damages to the employer. This is by no means an absolute duty, particularly if,
as in *Cotton v Wallis*,[2] the building contract requires the work to be completed
to the architect's reasonable satisfaction. In that case a house was constructed
for the defendant, the plaintiff being employed as architect. At the end of the
defects liability period (six months) the plaintiff issued a final certificate. A
couple of years after the completion of the house the plaintiff sued the defendant for his fees and expenses. The defendant counterclaimed for damages for
failure to exercise professional skill in supervision of the contract work. The
court found that there was a certain amount of inferior material and scamped
workmanship. Nevertheless, since the house was being built down to a price, it
was held that a certain tolerance was to be expected, and that there had been no
breach of duty by the architect.

1 1899 1 F (Ct of Sess) 1211.
2 [1955] 3 All ER 373, [1955] 1 WLR 1168.

4.24   The architect will normally (depending on a variety of factors) visit the
site about once a week. Presumably if he has reason to doubt the competence of
the contractor, is not excessively busy, and does not have to travel too far, he
might be in breach of duty if he failed to visit more frequently (though only
nominal damages would be likely unless it could reasonably be shown that his
failure to attend led to a failure to realise that work was done incorrectly, or not
at all, and that this led to loss). However, supervision of any contract of substance will not usually be carried out by the architect alone. An assistant architect from his firm may attend instead for some of the period of supervision, or a
clerk of works or an engineer be appointed. A clerk of works, who will be experienced in the building trade, perhaps to the level of foreman, is likely to be
employed under any contract where constant supervision is required, to be present continuously upon the site with the purpose of ensuring that the quality of
materials and workmanship comply with the contract requirements. He will
almost always be employed and paid for by the building owner. A resident engineer will usually also be employed and paid by the employer. When this is so, he
will be a servant, not an independent contractor.[1] His presence will be made
necessary by the size, and sometimes also the locality, of the particular project.
His position and functions vary greatly. He may be a fully qualified engineer, in
constant residence on the site with full powers, and in some cases with an independent rather than employee status;[2] or he may be the equivalent of a clerk of
works with no greater powers than those of a negative character – to disapprove
unsatisfactory materials or workmanship, subordinate to the architect.

1 *Morren v Swinton and Pendlebury Borough Council* [1965] 2 All ER 349, [1965] 1 WLR 576.
2 See e g *Re an Arbitration between Rio de Janeiro Flour Mills and Granaries and De Morgan,
Snell & Co* (1891) 8 TLR 108; affd (1892) 8 TLR 292.

4.25   Thus the architect's supervision will be supplemented by others. The
general rule is that the architect will be liable for the people whom he employs,
but not for people employed by the building owner, unless he gives wrong

instructions or delegates a matter which is his own responsibility. It is not expected that an architect should carry out personally all the acts that go together to constitute the duty of supervision, but he cannot evade responsibility for the negligent discharge or non-discharge of those acts. Thus in *Leicester Guardians v Trollope*[1] the plaintiffs employed the defendant firm of architects in connection with the building of an extension to an infirmary. It was a term of the agreement that a clerk of works should be engaged. Four years after the work was completed, dry rot in the floor was discovered. It transpired that there had been a departure from the design, which was intended to prevent dry rot occurring. The architect argued that the dry rot was the fault of the clerk of works. It was held that the architect, who admitted that he had taken no steps to see whether the design had been carried out in relation to the floor, was liable to the employer, for this was not a matter of detail which could be left to the clerk of works. Again, in *Lee v Lord Bateman*[2] an architect was employed to supervise the rebuilding of premises after a fire. The clerk of works appointed by the employer was of the view that certain beams need not be replaced, and the architect adopted this view without inspecting the beams. The beams later proved to be inadequate. Cave J charged the jury that the question whether new beams were required was one for the architect, not the clerk of works, and therefore the responsibility was on the architect if he adopted the clerk of works' view without inspecting the beams. It will of course always be necessary to examine the terms of the architect's contract of employment to see precisely what the extent of his duty of supervision, if any, is. Subject to this, the architect, unless he is his employer, will by no means be liable for all the defaults of the clerk of works. Unless the architect could reasonably be expected to have observed on his regular visits (assuming these to be reasonably often) those acts or omissions which cause or fail to prevent defects to the premises, he will not be liable.

1 (1911) 75 JP 197. See also *Saunders v Broadstairs Local Board* (1890) Hudson's BC (4th edn) vol 2, p. 164.
2 (1893) Times, 31 October.

4.26   Where the architect fails to discover at the time when the work is done that the quality of the work or the materials used were not up to the standard provided for in the contract, this may involve loss to the employer where there is a defects liability period[1] which has expired by the time the lack of quality is discovered. The architect's liability to the employer for this negligence (assuming a breach of duty can be established) is likely to be the difference between the amount for which the builder is liable and the total cost of the repairs, or the whole cost of rectifying the defects.[2]

1 See para 3.16, above.
2 *Emden's Building Contracts and Practice* (8th edn) p. 469.

4.27   The duty to supervise should not usually mean that the architect will be liable beyond a standard of reasonable care, unless he has bound himself by contract to some stricter duty. This begs the question of what is meant by reasonable care and, as the following case indicates, the determination of this question may sometimes lead to controversial results. In *Florida Hotels Pty v Mayo*[1] an architect was retained to give the necessary periodical supervision and inspection to ensure the execution of certain works generally: though constant supervision was said in the contract not to form part of the duties undertaken by him. The building owner did not employ a main contractor, but used his own employees in conjunction with the architect to supervise the work, which included a concrete swimming pool. The architect visited twice a week, including one particular day when the reinforcement for the concrete aprons of the pool was not yet fixed. The reinforcing mesh was improperly laid by the building owners' employees, such that the mesh's reinforcing strength was greatly reduced, and the concrete was poured before the architect's next visit. Later, when the framework was prematurely removed on the instructions of the building owner, the concrete collapsed and injured a workman. When sued, the building owner joined the architect as a third party. It was held that the architect was in breach of his duty to the building owner to supervise the work with due care and skill. He was under a duty to inspect formwork and reinforcement before pouring and not to assume that the foreman would postpone pouring of concrete until the next inspection. He should have clearly and expressly instructed the foreman not to pour the concrete until the architect had been notified, and had carried out an inspection. This arguably takes the liability of the architect further than the English courts would be prepared to go, except that, unlike the Australian courts in this case, they might be prepared to accept that particular care would be required from the architect in such a set of circumstances given the fact that the building owner was the direct employer of the men on the site.

1 (1965) 113 CLR 588. The controversial (to English eyes) scope of the duty imposed in this case merits a detailed description of the facts of the case. See also *City of Prince Albert v Underwood, McLellan & Associates Ltd* (1969) 3 DLR (3d) 385.

4.28 The RIBA Conditions of Engagement contain a number of provisions concerning the architect's duty to supervise. Clause 1.33 provides that 'the architect . . . shall make such periodic visits to the site as he considers necessary to inspect generally the progress and quality of the work and to determine in general if the work is proceeding in accordance with the contract documents'. Clause 1.60 provides that 'during his on-site inspections made in accordance with clause 1.33 the architect shall endeavour to guard the client against defects and deficiencies in the work of the contractor, but shall not be required to make exhaustive or continuous inspections to check the quality or quantity of the work', and clause 1.34 provides that 'the architect shall not be responsible . . . for any failure by the contractor to carry out and complete the work in accordance with the terms of the building contract between the client and the contractor'. This therefore incorporates the general principle that not only does the architect not exercise the function of intervening in or controlling the day-to-day operations of the contractor, but indeed the contractor has the right, in the absence of express provisions to the contrary, to carry out the work in the manner he chooses. Clause 1.61 provides for the employment of a clerk of works 'where frequent or constant inspection is required', and clause 1.62 for the appointment of a resident architect 'where the need for frequent or constant on site inspection by the architect is agreed to be necessary'.

Certificates
4.29 Prior to 1974 it was thought, on the authority of *Chambers v Goldthorpe*[1] that the architect acted as a quasi-arbitrator in certifying for amounts due to a contractor under a building contract, and consequently was not liable to the building owner for negligence in so acting. However this decision was overruled by the House of Lords in *Sutcliffe v Thackrah*.[2] The defendant architect issued interim certificates to builders during the carrying out of

building works. Before the work was completed the building owner dismissed the builders, and another firm completed the work. Later, the original builders went into liquidation. Subsequently it was discovered that the interim certificates covered a good deal of defective work. The insolvency of the original builders effectively precluded an action against them, so the employer claimed damages from the architect for the loss that he had suffered due to the negligent certification. The House of Lords held that the architect in issuing interim[3] certificates did not act as a quasi-arbitrator; he was under a duty to act fairly, and was liable to the building owner in negligence. Though, as the House of Lords emphasised,[4] it will frequently be difficult to prove negligence for over-certification against an architect, the need for care on the part of the architect in this, as in all aspects of his work, cannot be over-emphasised.[5]

1 [1901] 1 KB 624.
2 [1974] AC 727, [1974] 1 All ER 859. Further, the quantity surveyor, whose basic function is that of 'taking out in detail the measurements and quantities from plans prepared by an architect for the purpose of enabling builders to calculate the amounts for which they would execute the plans' (per Morris J in *Taylor v Hall* (1870) IR 4 CL 467 at 476) may also be employed (he is normally employed by the building owner) to prepare detailed recommendations to the architect of the value of work done by the contractor for the purpose of interim certificates, and preparing the final account. Insofar as he negligently over-values defective work of the contractor he may be liable to the employer for negligent discharge of his duties.
3 This would apply to final certificates also.
4 [1974] AC 727 at 760, [1974] 1 All ER 859 at 883.
5 Prior to 1976 it was arguable that where the JCT standard form of building contract was employed, a particularly high standard of care in exercising his function of supervision was incumbent on the architect. Clause 30(7) provided that the employer lost all further right to complain of work done in breach of contract upon the issue of the final certificate, unless before then he had issued notice of arbitration. The only exception of importance to this concerned defects which would not have been disclosed by reasonable inspection on examination at any reasonable time during the carrying out of the works or before the issue of the certificate. It was suggested (*Hudson's Building and Engineering Contracts* (10th edn) pp. 126, 152) that the supervision usually provided by the architect was totally inadequate to afford reasonable protection to the employer's interests, and arguably an architect who recommended a contract in that form was impliedly undertaking a degree of supervision such as to compensate the employer to some extent for the loss of his right to complain about defects. This would have placed a heavy burden on the architect. However, the 1976 revision of the JCT form (retained in the 1980 form) provides that the final certificate's conclusive effect as regards quality of materials or workmanship applies only where those matters are to be to the reasonable satisfaction of the architect. Duncan Wallace comments (*Hudson* (10th edn, 1st supplement) p. 491): 'Since little if any work is likely to be described in modern contracts in this way, and since, even when this is so, the satisfaction may not in any case be binding on the employer, for practical purposes the certificate is no longer likely to prove a serious obstacle to an employer alleging defective work.' The effect of this as concerns the architect is that an obligation of detailed, strict supervision may no longer need to be implied where the JCT form of contract is recommended.

Collateral contract
4.30 It has seemed to us to be more appropriate to deal with the liability of a professional man on a collateral contract together with his liability for misrepresentation, given the close links between those two forms of liability, and readers are consequently referred to the appropriate sections below for discussion of this topic.

B SURVEYORS AND VALUERS[1]

4.31 In this section we consider the contractual liability of the surveyor/valuer where it is claimed that his survey or valuation failed to reveal defects in the property under consideration. He may be a chartered surveyor, a valuer, an estate agent, indeed even an architect.[2] The criterion is that he is a person holding himself out[3] as having professional expertise in surveying and/or valuing.[4] Here we are not concerned with liability for creation of the defective state of the premises; the surveyor did not design the building or supervise its construction; but he is liable for his failure to act as a reasonable surveyor would, in discovering and reporting on those defects in the premises that it would be reasonable to expect a reasonably competent surveyor to discover and report on. He is liable therefore for breach of duties relating to the inspection of the premises, rather than being responsible for the state of the premises.

1 See generally M Brazier [1981] Conv 96 J Murdoch (1981) 257 Estates Gazette 893–899, 1012–1016, 1129–1132.
2 See e g *Moss v Heckingbottom* (1958) 172 Estates Gazette 207.
3 See e g *Freeman v Marshall & Co* (1966) 200 Estates Gazette 777.
4 For the purposes of brevity he will be referred to henceforth as the surveyor.

4.32 The first, and most important question to be considered is: what are the terms of the contract between the surveyor and his client? Failure to discover a particular defect may or may not constitute a breach of contract depending on the terms of the contract. For example, defects that ought to be revealed by a structural survey would not necessarily be revealed by a valuation survey without the surveyor in the latter case being liable for breach of contract. From the surveyor's point of view it is important that the agreement with the client makes it quite clear what his duties are. For example, if a client asks a surveyor to value premises which he is contemplating buying, the figure eventually provided may well be based on the fact that certain defects in the premises render them less valuable than they would otherwise be. Is the surveyor to be liable to the client for failure to inform him of the basis on which he arrived at his valuation, if the client later purchases and discovers the defects, which turn out perhaps to be more serious than the surveyor had anticipated (though his valuation was made with reasonable care)? Such potential difficulties can at least be mitigated if care is used in establishing precisely what the surveyor is called upon to do.[1]

1 This is particularly necessary given the potentially limited scope of exclusion and limitation clauses as a result of the Unfair Contract Terms Act 1977. See para 4.104, below.

4.33 Breach of the duties of a surveyor can clearly take many forms, depending on the particular task undertaken, and the conditions or circumstances operating at the time of the inspection. In *Grove v Jackman and Masters*[1] the plaintiff purchased a brick bungalow following a survey by the defendants, auctioneers and surveyors, who described it as 'soundly constructed on good modern principles of building'. It was later discovered that certain wooden floors and joists were in an advanced state of dry-rot, the damp course was not of good quality, the air brick ventilators were useless, the roof was badly constructed and the general condition of the bungalow was poor. The defendants argued that they could only have discovered the rot by lifting floorboards, and this they could not do as at the time of their inspection the prospective vendor was still in occupation. It was held that there were indications in the house warning a competent and careful surveyor of the possible presence of dry-rot. The defendants should have arranged or advised the plaintiff to arrange for the floorboards to be taken up, and more thorough investigations made, and hence they were held to be liable to the plaintiff. In *Wooldridge v Stanley Hicks & Son*[2] a firm of surveyors and valuers was employed by a bank to survey premises which the plaintiff, who had applied to the bank for an advance on mortgage, wished to purchase. The survey failed to disclose the presence of dry-rot. In a letter from the bank to the defendants there was a postscript which contained an express request from the plaintiff to pay particular attention to the presence of dry-rot and woodworm. It was held that for the purpose of examining the premises for dry-rot, the plaintiff was employing the defendants. All the rooms in the premises (a guest house) had been occupied and furnished at the time of the defendants' inspection, and the vendor did not want her guests to know that she was selling, so the defendants had not been able to make a detailed examination. Nevertheless the court accepted the view of an expert witness that it was highly probable that signs of dry-rot were present at the time when the survey was carried out, and hence the defendants were liable to the plaintiff.

1 (1950) 155 Estates Gazette 182.
2 (1953) 162 Estates Gazette 513.

4.34 The decision in this case may be contrasted with *Thorne v Harris & Co*[1] where the plaintiff employed the defendants, a firm of surveyors and valuers, to survey a bungalow. The survey failed to disclose the presence of wet-rot and dry-rot. At the time of the survey it was not possible for the defendants to pull up the floorboards and make a complete survey which would have disclosed the rot, as the bungalow was furnished. The court did not find that there were other factors present which should have led the defendants to suspect the presence of rot, and consequently found in their favour.

1 (1954) 163 Estates Gazette 324.

4.35 Problems of damp and rot are by no means the only ones that may involve the surveyor in liability. In *Daisley v B S Hall & Co*[1] the defendants, a firm of chartered surveyors, were employed by the plaintiff to carry out a full structural survey on an eight-year-old house that he was planning to buy. In a lengthy report the defendants said that there was very little evidence of the typical shrinkage and settlement cracks often found in main walls and beneath windows, although they did draw the plaintiff's attention to a slight crack under a bedroom window, and recommended that this be carefully watched for evidence of further movement if future cracks occurred. There was no mention in the report of the nature of the subsoil (shrinkable clay with flints in it on chalk) or the presence of poplar trees (of which there was a row on the land, with gaps where two had been felled), which on that kind of subsoil are notorious in the building trade for drying out the clay around their root systems and causing it to shrink. The surveyor did not realise that the trees were poplars. Later settlement was found to have taken place, allegedly due to the shrinkage of the clay. In an action for damages against the surveyors, the court held that a reasonably competent surveyor was under a duty: (1) in the case of a house under ten years old as close to a row of poplars as this, where two had been felled for no apparent reason other than to reduce the risk of root damage, to ascertain by effective means the nature of the subsoil; (2) if he found the subsoil to be shrinkable clay, to consider whether damage which might be due to this cause had already taken place, and to tell his client of the nature of the risk and advise him concerning purchase of the property accordingly. Here the surveyor had been alive to the importance of the subsoil, but had not realised that the trees were poplars. He should have done, and was accordingly liable.

1 (1972) 225 Estates Gazette 1553.

4.36 Again, in *Morgan v Perry*[1] the plaintiff purchased a house following a survey by the defendant, a chartered surveyor. The report mentioned only minor hair-line plaster cracks as defects. Later a serious settlement took place; the top weathered soil on the site to a depth of about eleven feet was slipping on the consolidated clay beneath. The house was worthless, and demolition was recommended. The court held that various factors should have put the defendant on guard; repointing had taken place, though the house was only four years old; the shape and extent of a crack over the kitchen door; over-papering; the fact that the house was built on a steep slope; a slope in the floors; repairs to the roadway outside. The defendant was thus liable.

1 (1973) 229 Estates Gazette 1737. See also *Lees v English & Partners* (1977) 242 Estates Gazette 293, where the defendants, surveyors, failed to draw the plaintiff employer's attention to a very bad tie between some new and old brickwork and to the risk of movement and cracks, which subsequently occurred. They were held liable.

4.37 In the earlier cases on surveyors' liability for negligent surveys, the courts were content to award damages (where the surveyor was found to be negligent) on the basis of the cost of repairs. Thus, in the *Grove*[1] case damages were awarded to cover the cost of the necessary repairs (plus a sum for the period during which the repairs were being effected, during which time the plaintiff had to live in a hotel,[2] and a further sum in respect of furniture removal and storage). Again, in the *Wooldridge*[3] case the measure of damages was said to be the cost of making good the defects caused by the presence of the dry-rot.

1 See para 4.33, above. See also *Last v Post* (1952) 159 Estates Gazette 240, where the plaintiff was awarded £250 damages, being the cost of repairing a roof whose defective state the defendant's survey had failed to reveal.
2 See also *Hood v Shaw* (1960) 176 Estates Gazette 1291.
3 See para 4.33, above.

4.38 However, an alternative basis for the measure of damages in such cases was stipulated in the decision of the Court of Appeal in *Philips v Ward*.[1] In this case the plaintiff purchased a property for £25,000, following a favourable report by the defendant surveyor, who had negligently failed to detect the presence of death watch beetle and worm in much of the timber in the house. The cost of effecting the necessary repairs in 1952 (when the survey had been made) was £7,000; by the time the case was heard in 1956, this cost had substantially increased. The court found that, having regard to the bad condition of the timber, the 1952 value of the house was £21,000, so in other words there was a £3,000 difference between the cost of repair and the diminished value of the house at 1952 prices. It was held that the proper measure of damages was the difference between the value of the property in the condition described by the defendant and its value as it should have been described; and that damages were to be assessed at the time when the damage occurred, i e 1952. Cases since 1956 have followed *Philips*, awarding damages on the basis of the difference in value e g *Moss v Heckingbottom*[2] where in addition £250 was awarded for physical inconvenience suffered by reason of the presence of the defects in the premises. Such consequential losses should be borne in mind when considering the likely damages. Clearly their existence and extent will depend upon the facts of each particular case; thus, in *Freeman v Marshall*[3] where a survey was negligently made on premises which the plaintiff wished to purchase and rent out as flatlets, the damages for the difference in value had added to them a sum of £147 for loss of rent. Again, in *Morgan v Perry*[4] (where in addition it was held that *Philips v Ward* applied just as much to a house whose value was reduced as to a house whose value had been erased completely), damages for consequential loss were awarded to cover the reasonable cost of discovering the true loss suffered by the plaintiff. In *Daisley v B S Hall & Co*[5] the value of the house without the tree root hazard at the time of the breach of contract was £13,250; its real market value with the root hazard was £11,500. However, the risk of underpinning becoming necessary had greatly receded between then and the date of the trial, and the defendants argued that the court should not ignore this fact in assessing the damages. It was held that the proper time to look at the assessment of the loss was at the time of the breach: 'What is sauce for the goose is sauce for the gander; and if Mr Daisley would never be entitled to recover more than £1,750 as *Philips v Ward* appears to me clearly to establish, it must follow that he will never be entitled to recover less.'[6]

1 [1956] 1 All ER 874, [1956] 1 WLR 471. As McGregor notes, the measure of damages in cases such as *Philips v Ward* is more accurately described as the difference between the purchase price paid and the value properly described. See *McGregor on Damages* (14th edn) para 979.
2 (1958) 172 Estates Gazette 207. See also *Lees v English & Partners*, para 4.36, n. 1, above.
3 (1966) 200 Estates Gazette 777.
4 See para 4.36, above.
5 See para 4.35, above.
6 (1972) 225 Estates Gazette 1553 at 1557, per Bristow J.

C SOLICITORS[1]

4.39 As a professional man, a solicitor is under a duty to exercise his various functions with the reasonable care to be expected from a reasonably competent member of his profession. Liability for failure to satisfy this requirement may arise with regard to defective premises, though only in limited circumstances. In *Collard v Saunders*[2] a solicitor advised his client to employ a person who was an unqualified surveyor to survey a house which the client subsequently purchased. The survey was carried out negligently, and the client sued the solicitor, who admitted liability. The defects in the house which the survey failed to reveal reduced the value of the house by £250, and this, following *Philips v Ward*,[3] was held to be the proper basis on which the damages payable by the solicitor were assessed, rather than employing a cost of repair basis. In addition the client was awarded damages for personal inconvenience, the cost of alternative accommodation and injury to his health caused by anxiety, and he received judgment for £900.

1 See *Charlesworth on Negligence* (6th edn) paras 1004–1020.
2 (1971) 221 Estates Gazette 795.
3 [1956] 1 All ER 874, [1956] 1 WLR 471.

4.40 It is very unlikely that a general duty lies on a solicitor to recommend to his client the advisability of commissioning an independent survey of premises whose purchase he is contemplating, though of course it is highly desirable that such advice be tendered. In particular circumstances though a solicitor might be liable to his client for failure to advise the commission of a survey. If, for example, a solicitor is aware that particular premises are, or are highly likely to be structurally unsound, perhaps because he has had dealings with those premises previously, or is aware that the area in which they are located is prone to subsidence, it is arguable that he would be in breach of his duty to the client if, at least, he failed to advise him of this knowledge, thus putting him on guard so that he would be likely to employ a surveyor, and it may be that his duty would extend further to actually advising the client to employ a surveyor. Failure to provide such advice would, it is suggested, represent a failure to attain the standard of the ordinarily competent solicitor, but in the absence of authority liability in such a case must remain speculative.

Liability in tort

4.41 Before discussing in detail the duties owed and the circumstances in which liability can arise, it is proposed to examine the recent expansion of tort liability into the area of professional negligence. As will be seen, this development has particular significance for the professions under discussion, given the assumption, held until very recently, that where a practitioner of the profession in question had a contractual relationship with a person alleging negligence against him, any claim had to be a claim for breach of contract only; the contract defined the duty and there could be no liability in the tort of negligence.

4.42 In general a person who practises a profession is bound to observe the standard of competence and skill that could reasonably be expected to be exercised by a reasonably competent practitioner of that profession.[1] This does not provide a guarantee of success, nor of the highest possible standard of skill, but if the defendant either does not possess the requisite degree of skill, or possesses it but fails to exercise it, then an action in negligence will lie. The fact that the professional man is guilty of 'only' an error of judgment will by no means necessarily exculpate him; some errors of judgment will be consistent with the due exercise of professional skill, others will not; all will depend upon whether he has measured up to the standard of the ordinary skilled practitioner of his profession.[2]

1 *Brown v Boorman* (1844) 11 Cl & Fin 1, 65 R & R 1; *Lanphier v Phipos* (1838) 8 C & P 475.
2 *Whitehouse v Jordan* [1981] 1 All ER 267, [1981] 1 WLR 246.

4.43 It is only very recently that it has been suggested that, for example, the action of the building owner against his architect or that of the client against his solicitor might be an action in the tort of negligence and not simply an action for breach of contract. We shall examine briefly the way in which the law in this area has developed. In *Columbus Co v Clowes*[1] an architect was employed by the plaintiffs to make plans of a building to be erected on a site leased by the plaintiffs. The architect accepted the word of a third person that the site was of certain dimensions, and made his plans on that basis (which turned out to be erroneous) without ever measuring or surveying the site. The plaintiffs paid him for the plans, but ultimately failed to raise funds to build on the site and parted with the lease. They later discovered the error in the plans and sued for the return of the money. It was held that there had been no total failure of consideration, but that nominal damages could be awarded for the architect's negligence. Wright J said,[2] 'Whether the action be one of contract or of tort, it is clearly one which is rightly brought in the High Court.' However, later the same year in *Steljes v Ingram*[3] it was held that an action against an architect to recover damages for not using due care and skill in supervising the erection of a house, which he had undertaken to supervise, was an action 'founded on contract' within the meaning of section 116 of the County Courts Act 1888, and the plaintiff was only entitled to county court costs.

1 [1903] 1 KB 244.
2 Ibid at 248.
3 (1903) 19 TLR 534.

4.44 Both these cases were concerned with redundant rules as to costs (though this was not specifically adverted to in the judgment in *Columbus*). This, according to Oliver J in *Midland Bank Trust Co Ltd v Hett, Stubbs and Kemp*,[1] does not make them authority for the proposition that the professional man's liability to his client is contractual only. Oliver J quoted A L Smith LJ in *Turner v Stallibrass*:[2] 'the rule of law on the subject, as I understand it, is that if in order to make out a cause of action it is not necessary for the plaintiff to rely on a contract, the action is one founded on tort; but, on the other hand, if, in order successfully to maintain his action, it is necessary for him to rely upon and prove a contract, the action is one founded upon contract'. For the purposes of section 116 of the County Courts Act 1888 the question whether an action was one 'founded on a contract' or 'founded on a tort' depended on the substance of the matter, even though there might be alternative liabilities.[3]

1 [1979] Ch 384 at 410, [1978] 3 All ER 571 at 590, *mutatis mutandis* (Oliver J was discussing *Jarvis v Moy, Davies, Smith, Vandervell & Co* [1936] 1 KB 399, a case concerning the liability of stockbrokers).
2 [1898] 1 QB 56 at 58.
3 See *Sachs v Henderson* [1902] 1 KB 612; *Edwards v Mallan* [1908] 1 KB 1002.

4.45 Quite apart from the question of costs, however, the court in *Steljes v Ingram* was not prepared to find that an architect owed a duty in tort to his client. Thus, Phillimore J said:[1] 'it seems to me scientifically incorrect to say that the cases of claims for breach of duty arising out of . . . the employment of a professional man are claims in tort and not claims in contract'. This approach received support in *Groom v Crocker*,[2] a case involving a claim against a firm of solicitors for damages for injured feelings and reputation. It was held that the claim had to be in contract, not in tort. Scott LJ said,[3] 'A solicitor, as a professional man, is employed by a client just as much as is a doctor, or an architect, or a stockbroker, and the mutual rights and duties of the two are regulated entirely by the contract of employment.'

1 (1903) 19 TLR 534 at 535.
2 [1939] 1 KB 194, [1938] 2 All ER 394. See *Davies v Lock* (1844) 3 LTOS 100 at 125; *Bean v Wade* (1885) 2 TLR 157.
3 [1939] 1 KB 194 at 222, [1938] 2 All ER 394 at 413.

4.46 The important decision in *Hedley Byrne & Co v Heller & Partners Ltd*[1] which established that, in the words of Lord Morris,[2] 'if someone possessed of a special skill undertakes, quite irrespective of contract, to apply that skill for the assistance of another person who relies on such skill, a duty of care will arise', might have been thought to have important implications for the potential liability in tort of a professional man to his client. However, in *Clark v Kirby-Smith*,[3] where a solicitor who had been expressly instructed to give a notice under the Landlord and Tenant Act 1954 failed to do so, with the result that his client lost his right of renewal, Plowman J followed *Groom v Crocker* and rejected the argument that *Hedley Byrne* imposed liability on a solicitor in negligence to his client.

1 [1964] AC 465, [1963] 2 All ER 575.
2 Ibid at 502–503 and 594.
3 [1964] Ch 506, [1964] 2 All ER 835.

4.47 This was followed in *Bagot v Stevens Scanlan & Co Ltd*.[1] The defendant architects agreed to supervise the laying of a drainage system on the plaintiff's land. The plaintiff claimed that, as the result of failure by the defendants to exercise reasonable care and skill in carrying out their duties under the contract, several pipes in the drainage system broke and water escaped and caused damage. The issue before the court was one of limitation, for the writ was issued more than six years after the performance of the defendant's contractual duties.[2] It was held that the duty was contractual only; hence the action was statute barred. Diplock LJ (sitting as an additional judge of the Queen's Bench Division) accepted the argument that it was by virtue of the contractual relationship that the duty arose, and it had no existence apart from that relationship. The court regarded those cases where there was concurrent liability in contract and tort as limited to 'cases where the law in the old days recognised either something in the nature of a status like a public calling (such as common carrier, common inkeeper, or a bailor and bailee) or the status of master and servant'.[3]

1 [1966] 1 QB 197, [1964] 3 All ER 577.
2 For discussion of limitation periods, see paras 1.35–1.45, above and paras 4.54–4.59, below.
3 [1966] 1 QB 197 at 204–205, [1964] 3 All ER 577 at 580.

4.48 Thus, the basis of *Clark* and *Bagot* would appear to be that, in the words of Oliver J in the *Midland Bank* case[1] 'the duty of care which would otherwise arise from a relationship of the sort described in *Hedley Byrne* has no existence where that relationship is a contractual one'. Although the basis of this might depend to a large extent on cases decided within the context of costs recoverable under the County Courts Act 1888 and its descendants, nevertheless the rule seemed firmly entrenched.

1 [1979] Ch 384 at 422, [1978] 3 All ER 571 at 600.

4.49 However, these cases had been decided in the very early days of the *Hedley Byrne* principle, and their relationship with that principle fell to be assessed in 1976 in the case of *Esso Petroleum Co Ltd v Mardon*.[1] Here the defendant entered into negotiations with the plaintiffs with a view to becoming tenant of a garage. During the negotiations the plaintiffs made estimates of annual throughput which were prepared negligently. In reliance on the estimates, the defendant entered into a contract with the plaintiffs and suffered loss for which he counterclaimed when sued by them for the price of petrol supplied. The Court of Appeal found the plaintiffs liable both in contract and under *Hedley Byrne*, despite the fact that the facts giving rise to the contractual duty gave rise also to the tortious duty. Lord Denning MR expressly disapproved *Groom, Clark* and *Bagot* and said,[2] 'in the case of a professional man, the duty to use reasonable care arises not only in contract, but is also imposed by the law apart from contract, and is therefore actionable in tort'.

1 [1976] QB 801, [1976] 2 All ER 5.
2 Ibid at 819 and 15.

4.50 This decision was not altogether free from criticism.[1] Nevertheless it found support in the later decision in *Midland Bank Trust Co Ltd v Hett Stubbs and Kemp*.[2] Here a solicitor negligently failed to register an option as an estate contract, and, when the grantor of the option later sold the land in question to a third party and defeated the option, the grantee sued the solicitor for negligence. The solicitor argued that the cause of action lay in contract only and hence fell outside the limitation period. Oliver J held that there was no rule of law which precluded a claim in tort for breach of a duty to use reasonable care and skill if there was a parallel contractual duty of care. He therefore preferred the decision in *Esso* to those in *Groom* and *Bagot* and held the solicitors liable in tort.

1 See e g Parris (1977) 127 NLJ 108.
2 [1979] Ch 384, [1978] 3 All ER 571.

4.51 More recently in *Ross v Caunters*[1] Megarry VC agreed with the decision in *Midland Bank*. A firm of solicitors was appointed to advise a testator on the drafting and execution of his will, under which the plaintiff was named as a beneficiary. The solicitors failed to warn the testator that under section 13 of the Wills Act 1837 attestation of the will by a beneficiary's spouse would invalidate a gift to the beneficiary. The plaintiff's husband attested the will, which was then returned to the solicitors, who failed to notice that he had attested it. The plaintiff claimed damages in negligence for the loss of the gifts to her under the will, which were, of course, void because of her husband's attestation. It was held that it was not inconsistent with the solicitor's liability to his client for him to be held liable in tort to a third party, having regard to the fact that the solicitor could be liable to his client in negligence both in contract and in tort. Again, therefore, *Groom* was not followed.

1 [1980] Ch 297, [1979] 3 All ER 580.

4.52 The effect of these recent decisions, it is suggested, particularly in the light of the lucid reasoning and analysis by Oliver J and Megarry VC, is clearly to establish that the professional man today may face concurrent liability in tort and in contract. The fact that he owes contractual duties to his client does not preclude the existence of tortious duties which may be owed to the client and in addition to third parties. We shall now consider the tortious duties owed by the professional man, in the course of which the particular implications of this expanded liability with regard to questions of, for example, limitation and measure of damages will fall to be considered.

A LIABILITY TO THE EMPLOYER

1 NEGLIGENCE
4.53 As we have just noted, the professional man owes tortious duties to his client in addition to his contractual duties. Whichever cause of action is adopted by the client, it will be on the basis of a failure by the professional man to reach the standard of proficiency that may reasonably be expected of the reasonable practitioner of his particular profession. Hence negligence by the professional man will constitute a breach of both his contractual and his tortious duties to the client, and to that extent it is irrelevant whether the client chooses to sue him in contract or tort. The main importance of the availability to the client of alternative actions lies in the different rules applicable to tort claims on the one hand and actions for breach of contract on the other concerning such matters as limitation periods, measure of damages, remoteness of damage, and exclusion and limitation clauses. In so far as these differences have particular implications for the potential liability of the professional man, they are considered below, but reference should also be made to the general discussion of remoteness, limitation etc. in chapter 1,[1] and also to the examination there[2] of the general expansion of civil liability for defective premises whose particular implications for the professional man are reflected in the discussion below.

1 See paras 1.9 ff, above.
2 See paras 1.30–1.34, above.

Limitation periods

4.54 As we have seen[1] section 2 of the Limitation Act 1939 provides that actions founded on simple contract or tort shall not be brought after the expiration of six years from the date on which the cause of action accrued; in cases of breach of contract the cause of action accrues when the breach occurs, in cases involving the tort of negligence the cause of action accrues when there has been a breach of duty and damage to the defendant. We have examined the ways in which 'damage' in tort cases has been interpreted, and noted the test proposed in the *Sparham-Souter v Town and Country Developments (Essex) Ltd*[2] case, that the limitation period does not begin to run in tort cases until the owner could reasonably have discovered the defective state of the property, and suggested that the formula proposed by the House of Lords in *Anns v London Borough of Merton*[3] that the limitation period begins to run when the state of the building is such that there is present or imminent danger to the health or safety of persons occupying it, is to be read in the light of the *Sparham-Souter* test. The particular implications of this for the professional man whose client is contemplating suing him for negligence in the performance of his professional duties now fall to be considered.

1 See paras 1.35–1.36, above.
2 [1976] QB 858, [1976] 2 All ER 65.
3 [1978] AC 728, [1977] 2 All ER 492.

4.55 It seems likely that the limitation period in a tort action brought by a building owner against, for example, his architect, will be more to his advantage than the limitation period for a breach of contract action. As noted above, time in a breach of contract action runs from the breach of duty.[1] *Brickfield Properties Ltd v Newton*[2] makes it clear that the architect is under a continuing obligation to check that his design will work in practice and to correct any errors that may emerge, though this obligation will continue only until the completion of the works. If the more restrictive *Anns* formula of threat to health or safety were to be employed in isolation, this might mean that, in a case where a building was designed negligently, so that it presented a threat to health and safety from the date of construction, there would effectively be no difference between the contractual and tortious limitation periods as against the architect. If the building only began to present such a threat at a later date, or (as we have suggested is the true rule), if the *Sparham-Souter* formula were applied (assuming the damage were not patent) then the limitation period in tort would be more beneficial to the building owner.

1 See e g *Bagot v Stevens Scanlan & Co Ltd* [1966] 1 QB 197, [1964] 3 All ER 577.
2 [1971] 3 All ER 328, [1971] 1 WLR 862.

4.56 Recently in *Eames London Estates Ltd v North Hertfordshire District Council*[1] it was held by the Official Referee, Judge Fay QC, in an action against (inter alios) an architect, that with defective buildings the date when time begins to run in tort is whichever is the later of two events: either when the plaintiff first acquires his interest in the property or when he first learns of the damage caused by the negligent construction. It was also held that for the limitation period in tort to begin to run, knowledge of the damage has to be not merely knowledge of the symptoms, for example cracks in walls, but must be knowledge of the actual malady, for example, as in the *Eames* case itself, differential subsidence of the foundations, the cause of the cracks. This seems entirely consistent with the linking of the *Anns* and *Sparham-Souter* tests that we have suggested above.

1 (1980) 259 Estates Gazette 491. For discussion of other aspects of this decision see para 4.83, below.

4.57 The implications of this for other professional men have yet to be worked out. Consider the case of a surveyor who negligently fails to detect the presence of dry-rot in the roof timbers of a house that he is commissioned to survey. It might be argued that, assuming the dry-rot to constitute a present or imminent threat to health or safety, the limitation period in contract and tort would be the same. This might seem rather harsh on the occupier, who realistically has no practical means of knowing that there is dry-rot present, and indeed is likely to assume that it is not present in the light of the surveyor's report. It seems quite consistent with the tenor of *Dutton* and *Anns* to assimilate the surveyor to the architect, local authority and builder. On this basis, assuming that *Anns* must be read in the light of *Sparham-Souter* as regards limitation, the limitation period in tort will not begin to run until the occupier could reasonably have realised that the state of the building presented an existing or imminent threat to health and safety.

4.58 As a further example of the kind of case which this extension of the law would cover is the situation where a surveyor negligently states that certain open beams in a room are free from woodworm or beetle. The client purchases the house and causes the beams, for purely aesthetic reasons, to be plastered over. This effectively conceals the gradual deterioration of the beams due to the ravages of the beetle and the worm for a period of ten years, when the beams collapse and structural damage to the property ensues. Assuming the contract with the surveyor is not under seal, it is suggested that in such a case, the earlier case law as exemplified by *Bagot v Stevens Scanlan & Co Ltd*[1] would preclude recovery; the more recent case law, effectively overruling *Bagot*, would allow recovery in tort.

1 [1966] 1 QB 197, [1964] 3 All ER 577.

4.59 More problematical is the case of the solicitor who, as we have seen, may be liable in limited circumstances for breach of his contractual duties, in respect of advice (or failure to advise) concerning premises. Despite the fact that he is one stage removed from the surveyor, it is arguable that the limitation period in tort against him should not begin to run until awareness of the present or imminent threat posed by the defect could reasonably be expected of the occupier. It might appear somewhat inconsistent to accept the argument that the time of the breach of duty was the time when the damage was incurred in the case of the solicitor while rejecting that argument in the case of the architect, surveyor, builder and local authority.

Measure of damages
4.60 The object of the award of damages for breach of contract is, as we have seen,[1] to put the plaintiff in the position he would have been in if the contract had been carried out. The purpose of the award of damages in tort cases is to put the plaintiff into the position he would have occupied had the tort not been committed. This distinction may be of significance where the client of a professional man is faced with a choice of causes of action, and,

depending on the circumstances, an action for breach of contract may secure a larger award of damages, or it may be the tort action that will secure a greater award, or there may be no difference between the two. The implications of this distinction for professional men merits consideration.

1 See para 1.9, above.

4.61 Since 1956 cases concerning the liability of surveyors for defective surveys have all involved application of the basic principle, as enunciated by the Court of Appeal in *Philips v Ward*,[1] that the measure of damages is the difference in value between the property if it had been in the reported condition and its value had the true condition been known. In *Philips* this was contrasted with the cost of repair but the court held that the cost of repair could not be recovered. This of course was an action in breach of contract. Would the position be any different now that the surveyor could alternatively be sued in tort? The fact that what is complained of in an action against a surveyor by his client, whether in contract or tort, is that, by overstating the value of the property the surveyor has caused the client to pay too much, is, it is suggested, likely to mean that even if the claim is brought in tort, the measure of damages will be based on the difference in value. However, unlike *Philips v Ward*, a court might now assess damages as at the date of the trial, rather than when the damage occurred, following *Dodd Properties (Kent) Ltd v Canterbury City Council*.[2]

1 [1956] 1 All ER 874, [1956] 1 WLR 471.
2 [1980] 1 All ER 928, [1980] 1 WLR 433. See para 1.17, above.

4.62 Nevertheless, the possibility that a court might be prepared to award damages in tort against a surveyor on the basis of cost of repair should not perhaps be entirely discounted, and certainly this would be an attractive option where the cost of repair was greater than the difference in value. Even if this option did exist, the cost of repair will certainly not necessarily always be greater than the difference in value,[1] and consequently the fact that difference in value is likely to be the appropriate measure whether the claim is in breach of contract or tort will not necessarily operate to the disadvantage of the plaintiff.

1 See e g *Upstone v G D W Carnegie & Co* 1978 SLT (Sh Ct) 4, (1978) 122 Sol Jo 285.

4.63 As regards architects and engineers, the question of measure of damages was given detailed consideration by the New Zealand Court of Appeal in *Bevan Investments Ltd v Blackhall and Struthers (No 2)*.[1] In this case the plaintiff employed the first defendant (B) to design a recreation centre. B employed the second defendant (S), a structural engineer, to assist in the design of the building. Construction began in early 1969, but was abandoned in September 1969 because of structural defects in design. In the Supreme Court[2] it was held that the contract between the plaintiff and B included an implied term that reasonable care and skill would be used in the design and supervision of the construction of the building and, though there was no direct contractual relationship between S and the plaintiff, it was held that S, in the terms of his employment by B, was liable to indemnify B on the basis of a similar implied term to use reasonable care and skill. S appealed to the Court of Appeal against the assessment of damages, which was based on the cost of reasonable and necessary work to make the building conform to the contract[3] (together with consequential losses)[4] to be assessed as at the date of the trial.

1 [1978] 2 NZLR 97.

2 [1973] 2 NZLR 45.
3 See *Bellgrove v Eldridge* [1954] ALR 928, 28 ALJ 319.
4 Essentially loss of profit during the period of delay.

4.64 S argued that a contract to exercise proper professional skill was very different from a contract to produce a result.[1] A professional man designing a building could only be liable to pay damages for the consequences of his failure to provide a correct design; he could not be called upon to give the client the structure designed.[2] Although in many cases involving professional negligence by engineers the measure of damages was the cost of making good the defective work,[3] this was because in those cases that was the best way to mitigate the loss. In this case, it was argued, where the negligent design had caused the erection of a useless structure, the appropriate measure of damages was the cost of demolition of the building and the restoration of the site to its original state, less the salvage value of the usable part of the work done by the contractors.

1 See *Auburn Municipal Council v ARC Engineering Pty Ltd* [1973] 1 NSWLR 513, especially per Hutley JA at 531.
2 But see *Independent Broadcasting Authority v EMI Ltd and BICC Ltd* (1980) 14 BLR 1.
3 For example: 'thus, if the results of the careless failure to specify a beam of a certain strength can be rectified by the insertion of a replacement beam, those costs are the measure of damages that it is in the contemplation of the parties to the contract that the consequences of breach of contract will within reason be made good': per Hutley JA in *Auburn Municipal Council v ARC Engineering Pty Ltd* [1973] 1 NSWLR 513 at 531.

4.65 This argument was not accepted by the Court of Appeal. Richmond P,[1] in the course of a masterly judgment, did not accept the assumption upon which the argument was based: 'that the only possible measure of damages, in a case involving a completely useless building, was to be fixed by such an amount as would put the owner of the building back into the position he was at the time when he was induced by the negligence of the engineer to embark upon a futile enterprise'. This effectively was to employ the tortious basis of *restitutio in integrum* and there was no reason why this rather than the general rule of putting the plaintiff into the position he would have been in if the contract had been performed should not be the starting point in an action against an engineer for breach of his professional duties.[2]

1 [1978] 2 NZLR 97 at 108.
2 See also [1978] 2 NZLR 97 at 129, per Casey J.

4.66 However, as Richmond P emphasised later, there is an important difference between, for example, an action for breach of contract against a builder and a breach of contract action against an engineer. As against the builder, a plaintiff is entitled to be put into the position he would have been in if the builder had completed the building in accordance with the contract. 'A plaintiff who is suing an engineer, on the other hand, must establish what his position would have been if the engineer had in fact exercised proper care and skill.'[1] If the contract price for the building, based on a properly prepared design, would have been higher than that where the design was defective, it would have to be established, on the balance of probabilities, by the plaintiff employer, that if due care and skill were used by the engineer (or architect) he would have proceeded with the erection of the building in accordance with the plans. If this could be established, the damages would be assessed in accordance with the correct principles applicable to a breach of contract action, i e the reinstatement cost. However, if proper care and skill by the engineer would have resulted in a situation where the employer would have abandoned the idea of building, then the approach suggested by Hutley JA in the *Auburn* case would be correct (i e the total destruction of the building and the restoration of the site to its original state). In the instant case the court believed that the plaintiff would have gone ahead with a building which, it was found, if properly designed would have exceeded the cost of the building actually designed by the defendants by $8,000.[2]

1 [1978] 2 NZLR 97 at 108.
2 Ibid at 111.

4.67 This, it is suggested, is the correct approach in cases where defective design or careless supervision is pleaded by a plaintiff in a breach of contract action, though in a case where negligent supervision has failed to detect work or materials whose quality is not as good as that provided for in the contract an alternative basis would be the difference between the amount for which the builder is actually liable and the total cost of the repairs.

4.68 As regards the tort liability of the architect or engineer to his employer, it is suggested that, no less than the builder or local authority, the architect or engineer is concerned with the production of buildings or structures[1] and consequently will be liable, on the same basis as the builder or local authority, where as a result of his negligence a building presents a present or imminent threat to health or safety, to compensate the person owed a duty enabling him to restore the building to a state where it is no longer a threat to health or safety.[2] The duty is owed to the person who is owner or occupier when the damage occurs,[3] be that person the building owner with whom the architect contracted to do the work, or a third party, perhaps a purchaser from the architect's employer. Consequently, if the employer chooses to claim against his architect in tort, the measure of damages will be such a sum as will restore the building to a state where it no longer constitutes a threat to health or safety. This, depending on the circumstances, will be the cost of repair or the cost of replacement and, it is suggested, is likely prima facie to be the same as in a breach of contract claim, at least in circumstances similar to those in *Bevan*.[4]

1 See paras 1.30–1.34, above.
2 *Anns v Merton London Borough Council* [1978] AC 728, [1977] 2 All ER 492. Cane (1979) 95 LQR 117 at 127–128.
3 *Anns v Merton London Borough Council* [1978] AC 728 at 758, [1977] 2 All ER 492 at 504.
4 The question of the date at which damages are assessed is considered at paras 1.13–1.17, above.

Remoteness of damage
4.69 As we have seen,[1] the classic distinction between contract and tort as concerns remoteness of damage is that for damages in contract to be recoverable they must be such that the parties at the time of making the contract would reasonably contemplate them as being a serious possibility; in tort they must be of such a kind that a reasonable man at the time when the tort was committed would foresee them (as being of a rather lower degree of probability). In many cases of professional negligence, the words of Beattie J in *Bevan Investments Ltd v Blackhall and Struthers (No 2)* may well be apposite. He said,[2] 'In the present case, however, I am not persuaded that the scope of damages sustained by the plaintiff for which liability is sought to be placed on either or both of the defendants is greater or less whether viewed from the point of view of contract or from tort. In either case the damages were in my opinion reasonably

foreseeable as the natural and probable consequence of defective design.' Clearly much will depend upon the particular circumstances of the case, but it is possible to imagine instances where it may be more advantageous to a plaintiff to rely upon a claim in tort, where the damages foreseeable at the time of the breach may be recovered, rather than in contract, where recovery is restricted to those losses foreseeable at the time of the contract, quite apart from the fact that a lower degree of probability is required to satisfy the remoteness test in tort than in contract. If, for example, it is within the parties' contemplation in an architect/owner contract, at the time of making the contract, that defective design by the defendant will, given the cost of materials at that time, require £X to reinstate the defective building (on the assumption that losses resulting from increases in costs of materials do not fall outside the remoteness rules) it may be that if the price of the materials necessary for reinstatement has risen between the time of contract and the time of breach, such an increase could be taken into account in assessing the damages available in a tort claim.[3] On the other hand damages may have been contemplated by the parties at the time of making the contract which would not have been foreseen by a reasonable man at the time of the breach. Again questions of 'cause of action shopping' arise, but in principle it is suggested that a plaintiff with alternative claims in contract and tort should be allowed to frame his claim in the cause of action that will be most beneficial to him.

1 See paras 1.18–1.19, above.
2 [1973] 2 NZLR 45 at 69.
3 See Feldman (1980) 43 MLR 708 at 711–712, discussing the decision of the New Zealand Court of Appeal in *Inder Lynch Devoy & Co v Subritzky* [1979] 1 NZLR 87.

2 NEGLIGENT MISREPRESENTATION
4.70   Liability in tort to the employer may arise from a negligent pre-contract statement, under the principle of *Hedley Byrne & Co Ltd v Heller and Partners Ltd,*[1] where it was held that a duty of care was owed by one who made a negligent misstatement to a person with whom he had a special relationship. Insofar as a 'special relationship' is capable of definition, the words of Lord Morris,[2] 'if someone possessed of a special skill undertakes, quite irrespective of contract, to apply that skill for the assistance of another person who relies on such skill, a duty of care will arise', seem most apt. The law had previously admitted the existence of liability for a negligent misstatement which caused physical damage[3] but not, until this decision, liability for such a statement causing economic loss. An architect, like any other professional man, would seem clearly to be a person possessed of a special skill, and therefore capable of incurring liability to his employer for loss suffered as a result of reliance by the employer on a negligent misstatement made by the architect.[4] Thus, for example, if during the course of pre-contract discussions the architect carelessly misrepresented himself as being qualified to make a particularly specialised design which the employer wished to have drawn up, and as a result of this misstatement the employer engaged the architect, who made the design, which turned out to be faulty and caused the employer economic loss, the employer could claim damages from the architect under *Hedley Byrne v Heller.*[5]

1 [1964] AC 465, [1963] 2 All ER 575. See para 1.47, above.
2 Ibid at 502–503 and 594.
3 See *Clayton v Woodman & Son (Builders) Ltd* [1962] 2 QB 533, [1961] 3 All ER 249; revsd [1962] 2 QB 533, [1962] 2 All ER 33 (the ruling on the principle that liability for negligent misstatement could be imposed was not impugned in the reversal).
4 In the light of the decision in *Midland Bank Trust Co Ltd v Hett Stubbs and Kemp* [1979] Ch 384,

[1978] 3 All ER 571 (see para 4.50, above) that the existence of a contractual relationship between representor and representee does not prevent the imposition of a duty under *Hedley Byrne v Heller*. See also *Esso Petroleum Co Ltd v Mardon* [1976] QB 801 at 819, [1976] 2 All ER 5 at 15, per Lord Denning MR.
5 Alternatively the employer might be able to claim damages from the architect for breach of contract.

4.71 As professional men, surveyors and solicitors may also be liable under *Hedley Byrne v Heller* to those employing them, in appropriate circumstances. It should be noted that the Privy Council in *Mutual Life and Citizens' Assurance Co Ltd v Evatt*[1] limited the duty of care in cases of negligent misstatement essentially to persons carrying on or holding themselves out as carrying on the business or profession of giving the kind of advice that has been furnished. Thus in that case an insurance company was held not to be liable to a policyholder for incorrect information concerning the financial soundness of another company that it furnished to him. On that basis if, for example, a purchaser of premises asked his solicitor whether the presence of poplars in the grounds of the house that he was contemplating buying posed any threat to the structure of the building, erroneous advice by the solicitor would not entail liability for negligent misstatement unless he held himself out as having equivalent skill or knowledge in giving that advice to a person in the business of providing such advice. However, on the one hand such a holding out might be implied from the making of the statement; on the other hand post-*Evatt* cases have reasserted the broader ratio of *Hedley Byrne v Heller*.[2]

1 [1971] AC 793, [1971] 1 All ER 150.
2 See *Esso Petroleum Co Ltd v Mardon* [1976] QB 801, [1976] 2 All ER 5; *Argy Trading Development Co Ltd v Lapid Developments Ltd* [1977] 3 All ER 785, [1977] 1 WLR 444; *Howard Marine and Dredging Co Ltd v A Ogden & Sons (Excavations) Ltd* [1978] QB 574, [1978] 2 All ER 1134.

4.72 Lord Denning MR in the important case of *Esso Petroleum Co Ltd v Mardon* said:[1]

It seems to me that *Hedley Byrne & Co Ltd v Heller & Partners Ltd* [1964] AC 465, [1963] 2 All ER 575 properly understood, covers this particular proposition: if a man, who has or professes to have special knowledge or skill, makes a representation by virtue thereof to another – be it advice, information or opinion – with the intention of inducing him to enter into a contract with him, he is under a duty to use reasonable care to see that the representation is correct, and that the advice, information or opinion is reliable.

This at least makes the argument that the solicitor in such circumstances would be liable to the client more tenable.
1 [1976] QB 801 at 820, [1976] 2 All ER 5 at 16.

4.73 As mentioned above, a negligent misrepresentation which causes physical damage will render the representor liable to the injured representee. Thus if, in the example above of the architect carelessly misrepresenting himself as being qualified to make a particular design, the employer suffered personal injury as a result of the later collapse of the building, damages in tort would be obtainable from the architect, though again damages could be awarded for such injury in an action for breach of the contractual duty to provide a competent and workable design.

4.74 Where a professional man has made a negligent misrepresentation to his

client he may be liable under section 2(1) of the Misrepresentation Act 1967.[1]
This provides:

> Where a person has entered into a contract after a misrepresentation has been made
> to him by another party thereto and as a result thereof he has suffered loss, then, if
> the person making the misrepresentation would be liable to damages in respect
> thereof had the misrepresentation been made fraudulently, that person shall be so
> liable notwithstanding that the misrepresentation was not made fraudulently, unless
> he proves that he had reasonable ground to believe and did believe up to the time the
> contract was made that the facts represented were true.

This in effect imposes liability in damages on the perpetrator of a negligent misrepresentation which induces another person to enter into a contract with him.
Liability under *Hedley Byrne v Heller* does not depend on the existence of an
ensuing contract between representor and representee, whereas there must be
this causal link between the making of the statement and the entering into a
contract under section 2(1). Thus in certain circumstances the only available
cause of action will be under *Hedley Byrne v Heller*. For example, an architect
might, prior to his appointment, recommend a particular material as being especially suitable for the employer's purpose. This could not be a breach of a contractual duty owed to the employer, as he has not yet engaged the architect, nor
would it fall under the Misrepresentation Act, as the recommendation of the
architect leads the employer to contract not with him but with the manufacturer or supplier of the recommended material. An action under *Hedley Byrne v
Heller* would, however, stand a good chance of success. However, in those cases
where there is concurrent liability under *Hedley Byrne v Heller* and section 2(1)
of the Misrepresentation Act it will often be to the advantage of the client to
claim under section 2(1) because of the reversed burden of proof created by the
Act. It should further be noted that rescission of the contract is available where
the misrepresentation induced the making of the contract, unless one of the
various bars to the right to rescind exists,[2] and it seems that where the misrepresentation was made negligently or fraudulently this will be in addition to the
right to damages. Only in those cases where a misrepresentation which induces
the making of a contract is made without fraud or negligence will there be no
remedy of damages; in such cases rescission of the contract (assuming the right
to do so is not barred) and an indemnity[3] constitute the available remedy.

1 See paras 1.48–1.50, above.
2 See para 6.29, below.
3 See *Whittington v Seale-Hayne* (1900) 82 LT 49 and para 1.51, above.

3   COLLATERAL CONTRACT

4.75   In addition the professional man may be liable on a collateral contract. If,
for example, an architect states to his employer, prior to his appointment, that a
particular design of his will be suitable for the purposes of the employer, the
court might be prepared to consider this to be a collateral contract. It would
have to be established that the statement was intended to have contractual
effect, and there must be some indication that the parties intended it to take
effect as a collateral contract and not simply as a term in the main contract (or
alternatively that it be not regarded simply as a representation). A statement
may at the same time constitute a misrepresentation and a collateral contract,[1]
though there may be advantages to the client vis-à-vis the professional man in
establishing that the essential nature of a statement was contractual rather than
tortious.[2] However, as stated by Lord Moulton in *Heilbut, Symons & Co v*

Buckleton:[3] 'Such collateral contracts . . . are . . . viewed with suspicion by the law . . . Not only the terms of such contracts but the existence of an *animus contrahendi* on the part of all the parties to them must clearly be shewn.'

1 See *Esso Petroleum Co Ltd v Mardon* [1976] QB 801, [1976] 2 All ER 5 (but note *International Broadcasting Authority v EMI Ltd and BICC Ltd* (1980) 14 BLR 1).
2 See paras 4.54 ff, above.
3 [1913] AC 30 at 47. See also para 6.10, below.

4 FRAUDULENT MISREPRESENTATION

4.76 If the professional man makes a fraudulent misrepresentation, to the client, this being a representation of fact made with knowledge of its falsity or with indifference as to whether it is true or false,[1] upon which the representee acts, and in so doing suffers loss, then the professional man will be liable to the client for damages in the tort of deceit. The absence of honest belief is difficult to establish, but it seems that, once established, the representor may be liable for all damage flowing directly from the fraudulent misrepresentation[2] rather than for all reasonably foreseeable loss (the rule for negligence).[3]

1 See e g *Derry v Peek* (1889) 14 App Cas 337.
2 See *Doyle v Olby (Ironmongers) Ltd* [1969] 2 QB 158, [1969] 2 All ER 119.
3 *The Wagon Mound* [1961] AC 388, [1961] 1 All ER 404.

B LIABILITY TO THIRD PARTIES

4.77 The decision of the Court of Appeal in *Dutton v Bognor Regis UDC*[1] has proved to be the progenitor of a remarkable expansion of tort liability. We have described above the scope of the case in relation to limitation of actions,[2] and it will be examined in detail in the context of local authority liability in due course. Certain remarks by Lord Denning MR in particular have been used as a basis for extending the potential liability of a local authority to all parties concerned with building works, at least where they have been negligent and there is a threat to health or safety. In considering the position of professional men in the context of liability for defective premises, Lord Denning MR said:[3]

> Nowadays since *Hedley Byrne & Co v Heller & Partners Ltd* [1964] AC 465, [1963] 2 All ER 575 it is clear that a professional man who gives guidance to others owes a duty of care, not only to the client who employs him, but also to another who he knows is relying on his skill to save him from harm.

He later said:[4]

> I can well see that in the case of a professional man who gives advice on financial or property matters – such as a banker, a lawyer or an accountant – his duty is only to those who rely on him and suffer financial loss in consequence. But in the case of a professional man who gives advice on the safety of buildings, or machines, or material, his duty is to all those who may suffer injury in case his advice is bad . . . If [an architect or engineer] designs a house or a bridge so negligently that it falls down, he is liable to every one of those who are injured in the fall: see *Clay v A J Crump & Sons Ltd* [1964] 1 QB 533, [1963] 3 All ER 687.[5] None of those injured would have relied on the architect or the engineer. None of them would have known whether an architect or engineer was employed or not. But beyond doubt, the architect and engineer would be liable. The reason is not because those injured relied on him, but because he knew, or ought to have known, that such persons might be injured if he did his work badly.

Later, Lord Denning refused to characterise the damage in the case as economic loss, but as physical damage to the house,[6] though seemingly his colleagues (especially Sachs LJ) were prepared to accept that liability could be imposed for economic loss.[7]

1 [1972] 1 QB 373, [1972] 1 All ER 462. For facts see paras 5.6–5.7, below.
2 See para 1.37, above.
3 [1972] 1 QB 373 at 394, [1972] 1 All ER 462 at 473.
4 Ibid at 395 and 473.
5 See also *Voli v Inglewood Shire Council* [1963] ALR 657, 110 CLR 74.
6 [1972] 1 QB 373 at 396, [1972] 1 All ER 462 at 474.
7 See para 1.30, above.

4.78 As an illustration of the implications of Lord Denning's words for professional men (in the particular case, architects) there is the case of *Brook Enterprises Ltd v Wilding*[1] decided by the British Columbia Supreme Court. The defendants were architects who, under a contract with NI Ltd, prepared the architectural plans for the construction of a motel, between October 1963 and February 1964. The motel was later built, in accordance with the plans, and was purchased by the plaintiffs from NI Ltd under an agreement in March 1967. At this stage there was at no time any communication between the plaintiffs and the defendants.

1 (1973) 38 DLR (3d) 472.

4.79 In July 1972 the plaintiffs issued a writ against the defendants for loss and damage suffered as a result of damage to the motel building, caused by alleged defects in its design and construction. The defendants denied negligence and the question of whether the claim was time barred was tried on an agreed statement of facts. On the basis of *Dutton* the court was satisfied that, if the evidence adduced at trial was sufficient, the plaintiffs had a cause of action against the defendants, although there was no contractual relationship between them. It was held that the plaintiffs' cause of action did not accrue until they acquired the building, rather than when the defendants' negligence (if any) occurred. Presumably because the case was argued on the limitation question alone, the court did not examine the arguments for employing *Dutton* to impose liability on architects, though it can perhaps be assumed that the court's readiness to accept that such liability could be imposed indicates that it saw no difficulty on this point.

4.80 The liability of a consulting engineer, employed by an architect to design and supervise the structure of a sports centre, to the building owner who had employed the architect, fell to be considered in the New Zealand case of *Bevan Investments Ltd v Blackhall and Struthers*.[1] The plaintiffs employed the first defendant, an architect, to design the centre, and he employed the second defendant; in the course of construction, structural defects in the design were discovered, and the contractors were instructed to cease work on the building. The plaintiff claimed damages against the first defendant in contract and tort, and against the second defendant in tort. In the Supreme Court Beattie J held[2] that the architect was liable in contract and held the engineer liable in tort, quoting with approval Lord Denning's words in *Dutton*: 'The time has come when in cases of new import, we should decide them according to the reason of the thing.'[3] The engineer was experienced, and held himself out as having experience. 'He knew or ought to have known the particular risks involved in his design proposals . . . As a professional man engaged to carry out a professional task he assumed an obligation to perform that task in a manner appropriate to his qualifications and status. That state of affairs, in my opinion, clearly discloses a duty situation and I can find no reason for declining to apply the neighbour principle of Lord Atkin to the facts of the present case.'[4] Beattie J did however emphasise that he was not trying to establish any broad principle beyond the facts of the case.

1 [1978] 2 NZLR 97. See paras 4.63–4.67, above.
2 [1973] 2 NZLR 45. See n. 4, below.
3 [1972] 1 QB 373 at 397, [1972] 1 All ER 462 at 475.
4 [1973] 2 NZLR 45 at 80–81. The case went on appeal to the Court of Appeal on the question of damages. The Court did not find it necessary to decide whether it agreed with the trial judge that the engineer was liable to the plaintiffs in tort, as it was agreed that the engineer was liable to the architect in such broad terms as to cover the architect's separate liability to the plaintiffs.

4.81 *Surrey District v Church*[1] is another case in which the liability of consulting engineers to third parties fell to be considered. The first defendant, an architect, was employed by the plaintiff to design a police station. The architect engaged a firm of consulting engineers to examine the soil exposed by the digging of 4 foot test pits. The engineers examined the soil, and recommended a deep soils investigation to be made by a geotechnical engineer, but were told by the architect that the plaintiff would not authorise this. This was not true; the plaintiff had been never asked for permission to make a deep soils investigation. If such an investigation had been made it would have revealed that the subsoil was thoroughly unsuitable for a load such as that of the building which was ultimately constructed, for it consisted of 100–150 feet of soft compressible marine clay. Indeed, such information could have been obtained from a published government geological survey. The engineers made a foundation and structural design, based simply on their final estimate of the load-bearing capacity of the site, as estimated from their examination of the soil on the test pits. Later the building inspector required a soils report before he would issue a building permit. The engineers were persuaded to write a letter in which they described what they had seen in the test pits and estimated that the soil had a considerable load-bearing capacity. Later, after construction of the police station differential settlement took place. The British Columbia Supreme Court held that the architect was clearly liable in contract to the employer. He had failed to have appropriate deep soils investigations carried out by an expert, and knew that the defendant engineer was not a soils expert. He knew that the plaintiff would authorise him to engage specialists and had failed to carry out his responsibility to design a building that was reasonably fit for the purpose intended.

1 (1977) 76 DLR (3d) 721.

4.82 The engineers were held to be liable in tort to the plaintiff. They had failed to inform the plaintiff directly of the need for deep soil tests. They knew that the plaintiff would rely on their skill and knowledge and had represented in the letter that adequate soils investigation had been done. Their communication to the architect of the need for a deep soils investigation was not notice to the plaintiff: nothing short of actual communication of their recommendations would have sufficed.

4.83 More recently, in *Eames London Estates Ltd v North Hertfordshire District Council*[1] the implications of the expansion of tort liability for architects were compellingly brought home to members of that profession. The plaintiffs purchased two factory units from the second defendants, Barker, who were the original developers of the sites and let them.[2] Serious cracks appeared in the fabric of the buildings following the drought of 1976, and the plaintiffs claimed against the first defendants, the successors to Hitchin UDC which had been the planning authority at the time (1964–65) when the units were built, the developers, the foundation contractor and the architect. Before the Official Referee, Judge Fay QC, expert witnesses agreed that the foundations as designed and constructed for the building were inappropriate for the site conditions as they were now known to be. The entire site was in fact underlaid by filled material, up to 4 metres in depth, and including timber, glass and old bottles. The settlement of the building resulted from settlement of the filling. The architect, who had designed the buildings, was found to be negligent. The building control officer had told the architect that foundations to carry three-quarters of a ton per square foot would be adequate for the site, but it was held that an architect could not avoid his responsibility for foundations 'by ascertaining what will get by with the local authority as this architect seems to have done'.[3] The architect was put on inquiry as to the inferior nature of the ground by the fact that three-quarters of a ton per square foot was a relatively light load, and he should have investigated the load-bearing capacity of the site himself. The builder queried the load-bearing capacity of the site, but the architect put the query aside. The architect knew or should have known that he was on made ground; even if he did think, as he claimed, that the whole site was an old railway embankment rather than, as was actually the case, part railway embankment, part filling to bring the site to the level of the top of the embankment, he should nevertheless have satisfied himself as to the site's load-bearing capacity. The architect's contention that the design was satisfactory in all but the extreme climatic conditions of 1976 was rejected.[4] Those conditions merely accelerated inevitable settlement. Accordingly the architect was prima facie liable in negligence to the plaintiffs. The fact that the architect had been employed by the developers, not the plaintiffs, was quite irrelevant to his liability; he owed a duty of care to a third party reasonably foreseeable as likely to suffer damage resulting from his defaults quite apart from his contractual duties owed to his employer.

1 (1980) 259 Estates Gazette 491.
2 The tenants brought separate actions against Eames, all the other parties and the Hertfordshire County Council, the planning authority at the time when permission was granted, but these actions were consolidated into the main action.
3 (1980) 259 Estates Gazette 491 at 495.
4 However, it is suggested that the effect of the drought conditions of that year could cause difficult problems of causation in other cases.

4.84   This is unlikely to be an isolated instance of the expanded liability of the architect. It is no longer open to the architect to argue that his duties are owed only to his client; quite separate from those contractual duties he owes the client a duty of care in tort. He is now potentially liable not only to his client, but also to any third party, such as an occupier or tenant of a building which he has designed, or whose construction he has supervised, where damage to that third party is reasonably foreseeable as a result of the architect's defaults. As the limitation period in tort does not begin to run until the damage could have been discovered, there will never be a time when the architect can sit back, safe in the knowledge that no future claims can be brought, though inevitably the passage of time carries its own problems of proof of causation for the would-be plaintiff. The need to keep detailed records and to ensure that he is backed by insurance must constantly be borne in mind by the architect. No doubt there will be renewed pressure for a fixed limitation period for latent defects, to run from the date of completion of the work.

C LIABILITY OF THE ARCHITECT TO THE BUILDER

4.85 In the context of the liability of professional men to third parties for defective premises, it is worth a brief examination of the case law concerning the liability of the architect (or engineer) to the builder and his employees, given the uncertainty that sometimes exists concerning the relationship between the functions of the architect and those of the builder. In *Townsends (Builders) Ltd v Cinema News and Property Management Ltd*[1] a contractor was under a statutory duty to serve notice on a sanitary authority before carrying out certain work. There was however shown to be a clear practice that the contractor relied upon the architect to see that notices were given and regulations complied with.[2] The architect failed to do so, and there was a breach of the byelaws. The employer was occasioned loss thereby; he claimed, as he was entitled to do, from the contractor, who in his turn succeeded in a claim against the architect who was liable for the negligent performance of a duty that he had (though gratuitously) undertaken.

1 [1959] 1 All ER 7, [1959] 1 WLR 119. See para 4.91, below.
2 This does not appear in the report, but can be found at p. 22 of the transcript of the case in the Bar Library, Royal Courts of Justice.

4.86 In *Clayton v Woodman & Son (Builders) Ltd*[1] builders were employed to carry out certain works at a hospital. Under the contract, which was in the RIBA form, the work was to be carried out under the direction of an architect but it was for the builders to make arrangements for the manner in which it was to be done including making all necessary provisions for shoring up and supporting walls and floors. The plaintiff, who was an experienced bricklayer employed by the builders, suggested to the architect that, rather than incorporating a certain gable into the new work (which it was planned to do if it was safe to do so) it would, because of the difficulties that that would entail, be better to pull the gable down and build a new wall. The architect examined the gable and, being satisfied that it was safe, decided to continue with the original plan. The plaintiff was injured when the work was carried out without support being arranged for the wall. At first instance the architect was held liable in negligence, but this was reversed on appeal. The Court of Appeal held that no duty of care was owed by the architect to the workman. On the facts the architect had done no more than to refuse to vary the contract. He had not taken on himself the responsibility of giving an order to the plaintiff to do work that was necessarily dangerous. If he had done so, he would have usurped the function of the builder, and very different considerations would have arisen. As it was, responsibility for the accident rested solely on the builders. Pearson LJ said:[2]

> It is quite plain, in my view, both as a general proposition and under the particular contract in this case, that the builder, as employer, has the responsibility at common law to provide a safe system of work . . . The architect, on the other hand, is engaged as the agent of the owner for whom the building is being erected, and his function is to make sure that in the end, when the work has been completed, the owner will have a building properly constructed in accordance with the contract, plans, specification and drawings and any supplementary instructions which the architect may have given. The architect does not undertake (as I understand the position) to advise the builder as to what safety precautions should be taken or, in particular, as to how he should carry out his building operations.

1 [1962] 2 All ER 33, [1962] 1 WLR 585.
2 Ibid at 39 and 593.

4.87   In *Clay v A J Crump & Sons Ltd*[1] the owner of a site appointed an architect to plan and supervise its redevelopment, and instructed demolition contractors to clear the site in accordance with the architect's plan. Some weeks before the building contractors came onto the site, the architect, after a telephone discussion with the demolition contractors, gave his approval to their leaving on the site a wall which was standing without support in a dangerous condition. The architect had accepted the word of the demolition contractors that the wall was safe and, though he later visited the site and had an opportunity to examine the wall, he did not do so. The building contractors made only a cursory examination of the wall and, a couple of weeks after they had come onto the site, it collapsed, causing personal injuries to the plaintiff, a labourer employed by the building contractors. It was held by the Court of Appeal that the architect, the demolition contractors and the building contractors were all liable to the plaintiff in negligence. The fact that the building contractors had had an opportunity to inspect the wall, and had done so carelessly, did not absolve the architect and the demolition contractors from their duty to the plaintiff to make a careful inspection of the wall, as they should reasonably have foreseen that if they left a dangerous wall standing it might fall and injure the building contractors' employees.

1   [1964] 1 QB 533, [1963] 3 All ER 687. See also *Driver v William Willett (Contractors) Ltd* [1969] 1 All ER 665.

4.88   In *Oldschool v Gleeson (Construction) Ltd*[1] the first defendants, building contractors, were employed by the plaintiffs to carry out certain building works on two houses. The second defendants were the consulting engineers. The works involved the total demolition of one of the houses and, shortly before this was completed, the party wall separating that house from a neighbour's house collapsed. The plaintiffs sued the first and second defendants seeking an indemnity against all damages that might be awarded against them to the neighbours or their tenants. The first defendants admitted their liability to indemnify the plaintiffs, and brought third party proceedings against the second defendants claiming an indemnity or contribution in respect of the plaintiffs' claim and damages for the loss they had suffered by reason of the delay of their contract works. In those proceedings they alleged that they were owed a duty of care by the second defendants in relation to the design and/or supervision of the works, which had been breached because the design could not have been constructed without causing the collapse of the party wall and/or failing to provide adequate supervision.

1   (1976) 4 BLR 103.

4.89   Judge Stabb QC held that the design was not fundamentally unsound, the collapse of the party wall was not due to any fault of the design, and the second defendants owed no duty to the first defendants and had no right to instruct them as to the manner of execution of the contract works.[1] Even if (which he did not accept) it was the law that a consulting engineer, who knows or should know that a contractor is failing to take proper precautions in the absence of which there is a risk of damage to property, would be under a duty to the contractor to take care to prevent such damage occurring, the duty would not extend beyond warning the contractor to take the necessary precautions, and this had been done.

1   See *Clayton v Woodman & Son (Builders) Ltd* [1962] 2 QB 533, [1962] 2 All ER 33. See para 4.86, above.

4.90 Judge Stabb said that if 'the design was so faulty that a competent contractor in the course of executing the works could not have avoided the resulting damage, then on principle it seems to me that the consulting engineer responsible for that design should bear the loss'.[1] This leaves open the question whether any losses suffered by the builder consequent upon the defective design are recoverable by him from the engineer, for example, losses caused by delay, as in the instant case Gleeson claimed they had suffered. Damages for such losses were in fact claimed in the Canadian case of *Vermont Construction Inc v Beatson*[2] where, as a result of defective design by the respondent architect, a change during construction was necessitated. The appellant builders received the compensation specified in their contract with the building owners for the change, but claimed that this was no compensation for the loss caused by the delay in the work and sued the architect in delict (the case was governed by Quebec law) for the difference between the amount awarded under the contract and the expenses actually caused by the change. The Supreme Court of Canada held that no action lay against the architect.[3]

1 (1976) 4 BLR 103 at 131.
2 (1975) 67 DLR (3d) 95.
3 As Duncan Wallace points out (*Hudson's Building and Engineering Contracts* (10th edn, 1st supplement) pp. 65–75), the report leaves it unclear to what extent liability was denied on the basis of special provisions of Quebec law which concern the joint responsibility of the builder with the architect for design. Arguably the kind of economic loss suffered by the builder would only be recoverable under the common law in a *Hedley Byrne v Heller* claim or by accepting that the loss suffered in many of the recent defective premises cases is more accurately characterised as economic loss rather than physical damage, thereby facilitating a claim in circumstances such as those in the *Vermont Construction* case under English law.

D LIABILITY TO THIRD PARTIES FOR MISREPRESENTATION

4.91 It is quite possible for the professional man to incur liability to third parties for loss suffered in reliance on a negligent misstatement under *Hedley Byrne v Heller*.[1] For instance, to use an example from Hudson,[2] a builder undertakes that his work will conform with the relevant byelaws. He is provided with plans of the work by the architect, who represents that he is satisfied that the design conforms to the byelaws. Later on it is discovered that the byelaws have been breached, and the builder has to demolish the building and rebuild at his own expense. The builder would, it is suggested, be able to claim against the architect under *Hedley Byrne v Heller*.[3]

1 See para 4.70, above.
2 *Building and Engineering Contracts.*
3 See *Townsends (Builders) Ltd v Cinema News and Property Management Ltd* [1959] 1 All ER 7, [1959] 1 WLR 119. See para 4.85, above.

4.92 This will also apply to other professional men. For example, liability may be imposed on an estate agent under *Hedley Byrne v Heller* on the basis that a special relationship exists between the estate agent of a vendor of property and a prospective purchaser. Thus, liability was imposed by the British Columbia Supreme Court in *Dodds and Dodds v Millman*[1] where a purchaser relied on negligent misstatements made by an estate agent concerning the profit-making capabilities of an apartment house that he subsequently purchased. To similar effect was the decision of the New Zealand Supreme Court in *Barrett v J R West Ltd*.[2] In this case an estate agent was showing prospective purchasers round a property when they pointed out a mushroom object on the back lawn and asked if this were evidence of a septic tank. The estate agent, aware that he was being trusted and relied upon by the prospective purchasers, replied that the house had formerly been on a septic tank but was now on mains sewage. The appellants subsequently bought the property, but later discovered that the only means of drainage was a septic tank. They claimed damages from the estate agent, and it was held that he had failed to use reasonable care in providing the information about drainage to the appellants and was consequently liable to them. The element of reliance should be emphasised: liability under *Hedley Byrne v Heller* depends upon reliance by that person on the skill of the maker of the statement and thereby on the statement itself.

1 (1964) 45 DLR (2d) 472.
2 [1970] NZLR 789. See also *Presser v Caldwell Estates Pty Ltd* [1971] 2 NSWLR 471 (see para 6.20–6.23, below); *Richardson v Norris Smith Real Estate Ltd* [1977] 1 NZLR 152.

4.93 Until recently it was thought that it was not possible for a purchaser of premises to claim damages from a building society surveyor in respect of a negligent survey, but in the recent decision in *Yianni v Edwin Evans & Sons*[1] it was held by Park J that liability in such circumstances could be imposed. A building society requested the defendants to value a property which the plaintiffs wished to purchase by means of a loan from the building society. The property was valued at £15,000 by the defendants, having carried out a survey, and they stated to the building society that the property was suitable for maximum lending (80 per cent of the purchase price); this recommendation was accepted, and the building society offered to advance £12,000 to the plaintiffs who accepted. The plaintiffs were aware that the property had been valued, and the court was satisfied that the statement that the society was willing to advance £12,000 on the security of the property served to confirm in the plaintiffs' mind that the house was worth at least that amount. In fact the defendants' report and valuation were the result of a grossly incompetent and negligent survey which failed to disclose the existence of serious faults in the property.

1 [1981] 3 All ER, 592. See also *Odder v Westbourne Park Building Society* (1955) 165 Estates Gazette 261, where it was held that a building society which surveyed premises prior to advancing £3,000 to the plaintiff to assist in the purchase of the premises, owed her no duty of care, in that the survey was made for the confidential information of the society's directors, and did not represent advice to her concerning the value of the property. This is, of course, a pre-*Hedley Byrne v Heller* decision.

4.94 Park J held that, following *Hedley Byrne v Heller* and *Anns v Merton London Borough Council*, a duty of care arose if on the evidence a court was satisfied that the defendants knew that the valuation of the property would be passed on to the plaintiffs who would, in the defendants' reasonable contemplation, place reliance on the accuracy of the valuation in deciding to buy the property. This was despite the fact that the plaintiffs were informed by the building society that the valuers' report was confidential information for the use of the society in determining whether an advance should be made and if so how much, and that the plaintiffs should instruct an independent surveyor if they wanted a survey (this was recommended). The defendants knew that the part of their report which said that the property was suitable security for a loan of £12,000 would be passed on to the plaintiffs, and it was not unreasonable for the plaintiffs to believe that the property was sufficiently valuable to cause the society to advance 80 per cent of its purchase price. Like 85–90 per cent of the population[1] the plaintiffs had not had a private survey, relying on the skill and judgment of the building society valuers to make a competent valuation of the property, and hence they were not guilty of contributory negligence.

1 RICS figures quoted in the judgment.

4.95 This decision clearly has serious implications for surveyors and valuers, and seems to take a generous view of reasonable reliance. In addition, as Margaret Brazier notes,[1] 'The inspection could be satisfactory for the society's purposes but still overlook defects which cover the value of the property to the mortgagor. The imposition of a duty to the mortgagor might then result in a move towards every building society survey becoming a full structural survey probably doubling the price to the mortgagor.' The latter point is certainly one way (and probably the safest way) for surveyors and building societies to proceed, in effect requiring the recalcitrant 85–90 per cent to have a structural survey of premises that they intend purchasing. This may be especially important in those cases where (as is beginning to occur) building societies disclose mortgage valuations to mortgage applicants, for in such instances the argument that reliance exists is strengthened. The other means of protection is the exclusion clause, and this is considered in detail below.[2]

1 (1981) Conv 96 at 104 (written prior to the decision in *Yianni*). The discussion on pp. 102–105 is particularly interesting and persuasive.
2 See paras 4.100–4.109, below.

4.96 In other circumstances also, a surveyor may be liable under *Hedley Byrne v Heller* to a third party, provided that the necessary special relationship can be established. Normally, of course, a private survey commissioned by a would-be purchaser will be made for that person only and if, later, that purchaser disclosed the surveyor's report to a person seeking to purchase from him, that second purchaser would have no claim against the surveyor if ultimately it transpired that the report had been prepared negligently. But if a would-be vendor commissioned a survey of his premises with the intention of using the surveyor's favourable report as an inducement to would-be purchasers, and informed the surveyor, before he made his report, that such use would be made of the report, then prima facie a purchaser who relied upon the report in making his purchase, and later discovered defects which the surveyor had carelessly failed to discover, would have a claim against the surveyor for negligent misstatement.[1]

1 See *Bourne v McEvoy Timber Preservation Ltd* (1975) 237 Estates Gazette 496.

4.97 Solicitors also may be held to owe a duty of care to third parties under *Hedley Byrne v Heller*. Recently, in *Wilson v Bloomfield*[1] a firm of solicitors appealed to the Court of Appeal against the decision of a registrar refusing to strike out a claim in negligence against them, on the basis that the particulars disclosed no reasonable cause of action. It was alleged that a representation contained in a reply to enquiries before contract, that the vendor was not aware of any disputes at any time relating to the land which was later purchased by the plaintiff, was untrue. It was asserted that the first defendant, the vendor, was in fact aware that there had been a dispute as to the ownership of the land, and also that the second defendants, the solicitors, aware that the plaintiff was relying on the accuracy of the answers to the enquiries, were aware or ought to have been aware of the dispute. The Court of Appeal refused to strike out the claim, and remitted the case to another county court judge. Apparently, the basis of the allegation was knowledge of an earlier dispute which had been acquired by the solicitors when acting for previous owners of the property. Though the decision is not concerned with liability for knowledge of a defect of the kind with which this book is concerned, knowledge of previous and continuing structural defects, if the subject of an enquiry and reply, could easily be substituted for awareness of a previous ownership dispute. It seems reasonable to infer, as Professor Adams does,[2] that this decision was the motivating force behind the initiative of the Law Society to secure an amendment to the disclaimer on the standard enquiries before contract form published by Oyez Publishing Ltd to disclaim expressly responsibility on the part of the vendor's solicitors, partners or employees for the replies. Whether or not such a disclaimer, insofar as it purports to protect the solicitor from liability under *Hedley Byrne v Heller*, will be effective, depends upon whether it satisfies the requirement of reasonableness as laid down in section 11(3) of the Unfair Contract Terms Act 1977.[3] The decision in *Wilson v Bloomfield* does not of course mean that the solicitor is necessarily liable to a third party in such circumstances: the necessary requirements of *Hedley Byrne v Heller*, discussed above, in particular the question of reliance, would not be easy to satisfy.[4] The decision raises difficult questions concerning professional privilege where the knowledge which the solicitor is alleged to possess was gained while he was acting for a previous owner of the premises, and also poses problems for firms of solicitors where the knowledge is that of a partner who dealt with the property previously but which is completely unknown to the partner presently dealing with the case.

1 (1979) 123 Sol Jo 860.
2 [1980] Conv 401.
3 See para 4.102, below.
4 As regards replies to pre-contract enquiries concerning structural defects, we have noted elsewhere (see para 6.12, below) that such enquiries will not be usual, and where they are made the prudent solicitor will suggest that the purchaser makes his own investigations. Nevertheless, the possibility of liability exists.

4.98   Further, it has been suggested[1] that the wording of section 2(1) of the Misrepresentation Act[2] is capable of including the liability of an agent in his personal capacity. On the basis that a statement made by an agent within the scope of his authority should be treated as being made by his principal, the representee would be a person 'who has entered into a contract after a misrepresentation has been made to him by another party thereto'. The agent would clearly be liable to damages if he had made the statement fraudulently, and thus would be liable unless he could establish that he had reasonable grounds for believing the facts represented and continued in this belief up to the time when the contract was made. Arguably therefore, in those cases where a professional man is acting as an agent, for example an estate agent making representations about a property on his client's behalf, he may be liable under section 2(1). Another example of this might be a solicitor, as in *Wilson v Bloomfield*[3] where he replies on the client's behalf to enquiries before contract. On the agent's behalf it would be argued that 'party' does not extend to an agent, but is limited to the principal, albeit via his agent, but it is at least an open question whether a court would regard the subsection as broad enough to cover an agent's liability.

1 *Chitty on Contracts* (24th edn) vol 1, p. 174.
2 See para 4.74, above.
3 (1979) 123 Sol Jo 860. See para 4.97, above.

4.99   Finally, as outlined above[1] liability may be imposed on a professional man for fraudulent misrepresentation, as much vis-à-vis a third party as vis-à-vis his client.

1 See para 4.76, above.

E EXCLUSION/LIMITATION OF LIABILITY[1]

4.100   Attempts by a professional man to exclude his liability, whether contractual or tortious, will be subject to the Unfair Contract Terms Act 1977. One of the main purposes of the Act is to control attempts to exclude 'business liability'. It is provided in section 14 of the Act that 'business' includes a profession, and hence the architect, engineer, surveyor or other professional man falls clearly within the controls of the Act that we shall now discuss. Section 2(1) of the Act places an absolute ban on purported exclusions of liability for death or personal injury resulting from negligence, whether such an exclusion is contained in a contract term or a notice given to persons generally or to particular persons. However, it is possible for the professional man to exclude his liability for other loss or damage resulting from his negligence,[2] provided that the excluding term or notice satisfies the requirement of reasonableness set out in section 11 of the Act.[3] Similarly subject to the requirement of reasonableness, according to section 3, are attempts by a person with whom another deals as consumer or on that person's written standard terms of business to exclude his liability or to render a different contractual performance or no performance at all, by reference to any contract term.[4] This, it is suggested, is likely to apply to the RIBA Conditions of Engagement.

1   For the purpose of brevity the term 'exclusion' will be used to cover both exclusion and limitation of liability, unless the context dictates otherwise. On exclusion generally, see paras 1.53–1.57, above.
2   Negligence will include breach of contractual duties of care. It will also, of course, include liability under *Hedley Byrne v Heller*.
3   See paras 4.101–4.103, below.
4   See paras 3.37–3.41, above.

4.101   Section 3 of the Misrepresentation Act 1967[1] requires contract terms seeking to exclude liability for misrepresentation to satisfy the requirement of reasonableness as stated in section 11(1) of the Act. This lays down the test that the term shall have been a fair and reasonable one to be included having regard to the circumstances which were, or ought reasonably to have been, known to or in the contemplation of the parties when the contract was made. The same test is applied to contract terms which seek to exclude liability for loss or damage other than personal injury. This then is the test which will govern attempts by professional men to exclude liability to their client for negligent misrepresentation or professional negligence by means of a term in the contract.

1   As amended by s. 8 of the Unfair Contract Terms Act.

4.102   Under section 11(3), the applicable test, where it is sought to exclude liability by means of a notice which does not have contractual effect, requires that it be fair and reasonable to allow reliance on the notice having regard to the circumstances which existed when the liability arose or would have arisen but for the notice. Thus under section 11(3) it is the reliance that must be reasonable in the light of the circumstances existing when the liability arose or would otherwise have arisen; under section 11(1) it is the term that must be reasonable, in the light of the circumstances known of or contemplated by the parties when the contract was made. These distinctions may be of particular importance to the client of a professional man in choosing between a contractual and a tortious claim.

4.103   At the heart of section 11 is the element of fairness and reasonableness. Particular guidance in cases where a person seeks by reference to a contract term or notice to restrict liability to a specified sum of money is given in section 11(4); in such cases especial regard is to be had to the resources he could expect to be available to him to meet such liability if it arose, and how far it was open to him to cover himself by insurance, in determining the reasonableness of the term or notice restricting liability. The difficulties faced by the architect today in obtaining liability insurance may mean that he can only afford (or indeed obtain) limited cover, and he may hence have to restrict his potential liability in the way foreseen by the subsection, and it is clearly sensible that the damages for which he is to be liable if negligent should be no greater than the insurance cover available to him. It is suggested that the factors of available resources and insurance should not be limited, in assessing the reasonableness of a clause, to cases where liability is purportedly restricted; they should be taken into account also in cases where total exclusion of liability is sought.

4.104 It is perhaps trite to point out that the absence of reported case law on the Unfair Contract Terms Act leaves its interpretation very much open to speculation. However, general exclusions of all the liabilities of a professional man in a contract term or notice are arguably unlikely to be regarded as fair or reasonable, on the basis that the client is paying his money for nothing if not for the very professional services for which the exemption clause seeks to avoid liability in the event of negligent performance. The professional man might stand a greater chance of success if he purported to exclude liability only for certain aspects of his duties but ideally, it is suggested, he will make quite clear to the client from the outset precisely what services he is proposing to offer, and ensure that the contract is unequivocal in its description of the duties he is to perform. For example, an architect who fears that he will be unable to undertake his duty to supervise adequately, because the number of visits he will be able to make to the site is likely to be severely limited, will do better to incorporate a term in the contract spelling out the fact that supervision will be limited, rather than purporting to exclude liability for breaches of the duty to supervise. Similarly, a surveyor who is not planning to inspect the drains of a house he is commissioned to survey would be better advised to indicate this clearly from the outset rather than fail to inspect the drains and hope that an exclusion clause will protect him from liability if the drains are defective. It should be emphasised that the duties incumbent on a professional man are not absolute, but require him to act as a reasonably competent member of his profession would. Thus, for example, a failure by a surveyor to inspect inaccessible parts of a house coupled with a clear statement that such inspection was impossible may not constitute a breach of his duties. If it does not, the applicability of an exclusion clause does not arise.[1]

1 See M Brazier [1981] Conv 96 at 106.

4.105 The professional man may be thought to have a better chance of persuading a court that his reliance on an exclusion clause vis-à-vis a third party was fair and reasonable, as such a person has not paid for the advice which is alleged to be negligent. Again, however, it is quite open to the court to deem, for example, a purported exclusion of an architect's liability for negligent design inoperative as regards a subsequent purchaser, particularly since section 11(5) of the Unfair Contract Terms Act provides that it is for the person claiming that a contract term or notice satisfies the requirement of reasonableness to show that it does, and the argument that the injured party did not pay for the advice may not be sufficient in itself, given the expansion over the past decade of the professional man's liability towards those who have not paid for his services.

4.106 As regards the liability of solicitors, seemingly as a result of *Wilson v Bloomfield*,[1] the disclaimer of liability for replies to pre-contract enquiries on the most commonly used standard form, published by Oyez Publishing Ltd, now reads: 'These replies are given on behalf of the proposed Vendor and without responsibility on the part of his solicitors their partners or employees. They are believed to be accurate but the accuracy is not guaranteed and they do not obviate the need to make appropriate searches, enquiries and inspections.' Whether or not this would be deemed to be reasonable, it should be noted[2] that, as the disclaimer does not appear appropriate to protect the vendor, in cases where the replies are the joint product of the vendor and his solicitor, the solicitor may (if the disclaimer is reasonable) evade liability to the purchaser, but (if the error was the solicitor's) be subject to a claim by his client.

1 (1979) 123 Sol Jo 860. See para 4.97, above.
2 See (1980) 124 Sol Jo 581, [1980] Conv 401–402.

4.107 In the case of a surveyor it will be advisable for him to restrict as far as possible the circulation of his report and, whether or not this can be done, to indicate clearly the exact purpose of the report so as at least to ensure that he will only be liable in negligence for performing the particular function that he is called upon to carry out, and not for advice which he did not intend to give but which might otherwise be implied by reason of the usual tasks of his profession.[1]

1 See Murdoch (1981) 257 Estates Gazette 1129 at 1132.

4.108 As we have noted[1] a practice is developing whereby building societies are disclosing mortgage valuations to mortgage applicants. The innovators here were the Abbey National Building Society, and the Royal Institute of Chartered Surveyors has negotiated a form of wording with the Society whose purpose is to allow the Society and its surveyor to avoid liability.[2] In his mortgage application, the aspirant borrower is obliged to acknowledge that neither Society nor Surveyor 'warrant, represent nor give any assurance . . . that the statements, conclusions and opinions expressed or implied in the report and mortgage application will be accurate or valid and the surveyor's report will be supplied without any acceptance of responsibility on their part to me'. The disclaimer of accuracy or validity and the denial of responsibility are to be repeated in the valuation report. The fact that this exclusion of liability has been deemed necessary suggests that the existence of reliance might otherwise be recognised to exist, which, in the light of *Yianni v Edwin Evans & Sons*[3] seems a fair conclusion. Whether the exclusion will be deemed reasonable by the courts remains an open question.

1 See para 4.95, above.
2 See Adams [1980] Conv 401 at 402–403.
3 [1981] 3 All ER 592. See paras 4.93–4.95, above.

4.109 The possibility also exists of restricting the duration of the professional man's liability. Arguably a term or notice providing that the professional man will not be liable beyond, for example, seven years from the completion of his work, would be reasonable, on the basis that insofar as he could be liable under the Defective Premises Act,[1] the limitation period under that Act is six years from the date when the dwelling is completed, and surely a limitation period longer than that provided by the Act could not be said to be unreasonable.[2]

Against this it may be argued that even a seven year limitation period appears unreasonable compared with the 'extended' limitation period available under a tort claim, though it is suggested that the longer the period of limitation contained in a professional man's exclusion clause, the more likely a court is to regard it as fair and reasonable, bearing in mind the burden on the professional man of claims arising long after his work was done.

1 See para 4.110, below.
2 We are indebted to Mr John Parris for this idea.

F DEFECTIVE PREMISES ACT 1972

4.110   Section 1(1) of the Defective Premises Act 1972 provides:

> A person taking on work for or in connection with the provision of a dwelling (whether the dwelling is provided by the erection or by the conversion or enlargement of a building) owes a duty—
> (a) if the dwelling is provided to the order of any person, to that person; and
> (b) without prejudice to paragraph (a) above, to every person who acquires an interest (whether legal or equitable) in the dwelling;
> to see that the work which he takes on is done in a workman-like or, as the case may be, professional manner, with proper materials and so that as regards the work the dwelling will be fit for habitation when completed.

4.111   Thus a statutory duty is imposed on, inter alios, architects, and engineers who undertake work for, or in connection with, the provision of a dwelling, to carry out their work in a professional manner so that the house is fit for habitation. Under section 1(2) the duty imposed by section 1(1) is discharged by a person who takes on work in accordance with another's instructions and carries out that work properly, though this is qualified by section 1(3) which provides that section 1(2) does not apply where the person taking on the work has himself issued instructions which constitute the terms governing the doing of the work. The duty is owed to the first owner and successors in title.

4.112   However, section 2 of the Act drastically limits the effectiveness of section 1 by providing that the statutory remedy under section 1 is excluded where the dwelling is constructed or first sold with the benefit of a scheme approved by the Secretary of State, which provides cover for defects in the state of the building. The only approved scheme is the National House Building Council scheme,[1] which covers nearly all new houses, and therefore the scope of section 1 of the Act is effectively limited to conversions and alterations which are not covered by the scheme.

1 See paras 3.49 ff, above.

4.113   Where the duty exists, it would appear to be stricter than the duty of care in negligence. It is modelled on the duty owed by the builder which is implied at common law in an ordinary building contract.[1] The stricter nature of the duty has led one commentator[2] to suggest that, 'the new statutory duty is no more onerous on the builder than his common law duties, but it may be considerably more burdensome on the architect, whose common law duties are duties of care rather than strict duties'. Thus, for example, where an architect is employed on a contract for the building of a house not covered by the NHBC scheme, he may be held under section 1 to be guaranteeing the suitability of his design, the builder whom he recommends, the materials that he recommends etc., rather than undertaking to employ reasonable care in the exercise of these various obligations which, as we have seen, is the position at common law. The logic behind imposing different obligations on him depending on whether the house is built under the NHBC scheme or not seems a little questionable. Further, insofar as the architect or engineer may be liable in tort for defective design or supervision, this will apparently be on the basis that there is a present or imminent threat to health or safety; whereas the Act imposes liability for defects of quality whether or not they pose a threat, provided they render the house unfit for habitation; and there is not necessarily a complete overlap between these two criteria.

1 See paras 3.8–3.11, above.
2 J R Spencer in [1974] CLJ 307 at 317.

4.114 The limitation period under the Act runs for six years from the time when the building is completed, unless further work is carried out later.[1] This is clearly likely to be less beneficial to a plaintiff than is the case where he is claiming in tort.[2] On the other hand, section 6(3) provides that the provisions of the Act cannot be excluded or restricted by any agreement, by contrast with the rules relating to exclusion or restriction of a contract or tort claim discussed elsewhere.[3]

1 S. 1(5).
2 See para 4.54, above.
3 See paras 4.100 ff, above.

4.115 It should be noted that a surveyor for valuation and condition purposes is not normally concerned with the provision of a dwelling within the meaning of section 1 of the Act, and therefore claims against such a person must be in contract and/or tort only.

Chapter 5

Local authority negligence

5.1 The purpose of this chapter is to examine the liability of local authorities in damages for negligent exercise or non-exercise of their statutory functions. Chapter 8 considers the content of the obligations owed by local authorities in respect of defective premises generally, where remedies other than damages are available for breach of those obligations. Where a local authority may be liable in damages when acting in a particular capacity, such as landlord or occupier, discussed elsewhere in this book, reference should be made to the appropriate chapter.

5.2 Ten years ago it might have been considered remarkable to devote detailed attention to the tort liability of local authorities for the negligent exercise or non-exercise of their statutory functions, but the developments in this area over the last decade, commencing with *Dutton v Bognor Regis UDC*,[1] seem to us to merit such an examination and we have deemed it appropriate, given the expanding and still very uncertain scope of local authority liability in this area, to examine the case law in some detail.

1 [1972] QB 373, [1972] 1 All ER 462.

5.3 Where a local authority has a duty to act[1] imposed on it by a statute, certain criteria must be fulfilled if liability in damages to an injured person is to be imposed for negligence in carrying out the duty.[2] In general, if the statute provides a specific remedy for the injury, this will exclude the possibility of a tort action.[3] If the duty is an imperative one, it must be determined whether the duty is owed to individuals, of which the plaintiff is one, in which case an action, subject to the other criteria, will lie; if the duty is owed to the community at large, an individual may not sue for damages.[4] These principles are as true of a local authority's duties with regard to premises as of any of its other functions. Thus, in *Reffell v Surrey County Council*[5] a schoolgirl cut her hand on a glass panel in a door at her school. It was held that the local education authority was in breach of its duty under section 10 of the Education Act 1944 and regulation 51 of the Standards for School Premises Regulations 1959 to secure the safety of the occupants of the school. The plaintiff was therefore a member of the class the statute was designed to protect. The special remedy of mandamus, provided to the Minister under section 99 of the Act, was inadequate to protect the plaintiff, and the authority was held to be liable for breach of statutory duty and also in negligence.

1 See Cross *Principles of Local Government Law* (4th edn) pp. 158–161.
2 Liability may also be imposed in certain cases for failure to carry out a duty: *Dawson & Co v*

Bingley UDC [1911] 2 KB 149; *Rider v Rider* [1973] 1 QB 505, [1973] 1 All ER 294.
3 See *Hesketh v Birmingham Corpn* [1924] 1 KB 260; *Read v Croydon Corpn* [1938] 4 All ER 631; the latter case emphasises the need for detailed consideration of the relevant Act in determining whether the statutory remedy excludes a tort claim.
4 *Cross* (p. 160) uses the examples of a duty to remove refuse as being a duty owed to occupiers of dwellings (one of whom may therefore prima facie bring a claim), and a duty to cleanse public sewers as being a duty owed to the community at large.
5 [1964] 1 All ER 743, [1964] 1 WLR 358. See also *Ministry of Housing and Local Government v Sharp* [1970] 2 QB 223, [1970] 1 All ER 1009.

5.4 Liability in damages for the negligent exercise of a statutory power raises, as we shall see, a number of difficult problems.[1] During the nineteenth century, the principle became established that liability could be imposed where a statutory power was exercised negligently.[2] Thus, it was said by Lord Blackburn in *Geddis v Bann Reservoir Proprietors*:[3] 'for I take it without citing cases, that it is now thoroughly well established that no action will lie for doing that which the legislature has authorised, if it be done without negligence, although it does occasion damage to anyone; but an action does lie for doing that which the legislature has authorised, if it be done negligently'.

1 See Craig (1978) 94 LQR 428; Ganz [1973] PL 84; Harlow (1976) 39 MLR 516.
2 See e g *Mersey Docks and Harbour Board Trustees v Gibbs* (1864–66) 11 HL Cas 686; *Coe v Wise* (1866) LR 1 QB 711.
3 (1878) 3 App Cas 430 at 455–456.

5.5 In *Sheppard v Glossop Corporation*[1] the plaintiff relied upon this dictum in his claim against a local authority stemming from injuries he suffered when he fell over a retaining wall. The authority had power to install street lighting, and had placed a lamp upon the wall but, following a resolution of the corporation the light had been turned off at 9 p.m. The Court of Appeal found in favour of the corporation. If the corporation had been negligent in carrying out the lighting, for example allowing gas to escape into someone's house, they would have been liable, but they were not liable for deciding, in the exercise of their discretion, not to light, or to light for a certain period of time only.[2] This reasoning was followed in *East Suffolk Rivers Catchment Board v Kent*[3] and raises the important and difficult distinction between policy and operational decisions which, as we shall see, plays a significant role in those cases which deal directly with local authority liability for defective premises resulting from negligent exercise of a statutory power. Bearing this brief introductory background in mind, we turn to those cases, beginning with *Dutton v Bognor Regis UDC*,[4] in which it was said by Lord Denning MR:[5] 'Never before has an action of this kind been brought before our courts. Nor, so far as we can discover, before the courts of any other countries which follow the common law. It raises issues of far-reaching importance.'

1 [1921] 3 KB 132.
2 Ibid at 143.
3 [1941] AC 74, [1940] 4 All ER 527. See Craig (1978) 94 LQR 428 at 432–436. See also para 5.21, below.
4 [1972] 1 QB 373, [1972] 1 All ER 462.
5 Ibid at 390 and 469.

5.6 The facts of *Dutton v Bognor Regis UDC* are fairly straightforward. In 1958 a builder purchased land in Bognor Regis with a view to developing it as a housing estate. He applied to the local authority for permission to build a house on a numbered plot and for approval under the council's building byelaws made under the Public Health Act 1936. Approval was duly notified on a form

177

which stated that: 'All foundations and drains must be first examined by the surveyor before being covered up.' In 1959 one of the council's building inspectors
inspected the excavations for the foundations and passed them. The foundations were then covered up with concrete, and the house was built and sold early
in 1960 to a Mr Clark, who resold it a few months later to the plaintiff,
Mrs Dutton. She did not have a private survey, but the surveyor of the building
society which was lending her money for the house purchase passed the house.
Mrs Dutton moved into the house in early 1961 and soon became disturbed as a
result of observing cracks in walls and ceilings, and by the fact that doors and
windows would not close. She called in a surveyor, who reported that an
internal wall had subsided, because of inadequate foundations. It transpired
that the foundations had been built on the site of an old rubbish tip. The expert
surveyor who discovered this was of the opinion that the nature of the site could
easily have been detected at the time when the house was built.

5.7 In February 1964, Mrs Dutton issued writs against the builder and the
local authority. The builder claimed to be exempted from liability by *Bottomley
v Bannister*[1] and *Otto v Bolton and Norris*[2] and Mrs Dutton settled her claim
against him for £625 (her total damage was £2,740 : £2,240 for cost of repair,
£500 for diminution of value). She claimed that the local authority, through
their inspector, owed her a duty of care in approving the building works under
the byelaws and that this duty had been breached by reason of the negligent
inspection. The trial judge found in favour of Mrs Dutton, and the Court of
Appeal dismissed the appeal of the local authority.

1 [1932] 1 KB 458. See para 3.87, above.
2 [1936] 2 KB 46, [1936] 1 All ER 960. See para 3.87, above.

5.8 The Court of Appeal considered the potential liability of the local
authority within the context of the Public Health Act 1936. Section 1 of the
Act imposes a duty upon the local authority to carry the Act into execution, and
section 61(1) provides that:

> Every local authority may and, if required by the Minister, shall make byelaws for
> regulating all or any of the following matters:
> (i) as regards buildings—
>   (a) the construction of buildings, and the materials to be used in the construc-
>   tion of buildings . . .[1]

The council had made byelaws under this authority. They argued that there was
no duty to enforce the byelaws; they had power to inspect the site and impose
penalties, and to require work to be done or redone, but they were under no
duty to do so. They claimed that the decision of the House of Lords in *East
Suffolk Rivers Catchment Board v Kent*[2] supported their contention that
'where a local authority or other body X has power or authority to do something
which if done competently would benefit Y, X is not liable in negligence to Y if
he exercises that power so incompetently that Y sustains damage which would
have been arrested if X had exercised reasonable skill and care'.[3] The Court of
Appeal did not accept this argument. Lord Denning MR identified three
categories of local authorities' functions: power, duty and control. In his view
the extensive control over building work given by the legislature to the local
authority carried with it a duty, which required the local authority to exercise
that control properly and with reasonable care. In the instant case the local

authority had not exercised reasonable care, and was therefore liable to the plaintiff. Sachs LJ distinguished the *East Suffolk Rivers Catchment Board* case on the basis that that case 'is one in which the failure to proceed with the building work sufficiently quickly was held to be in essence a case of non-feasance ... In the present case, on the contrary, the negligence plainly occurred in the course of a positive exercise by the council of its powers.'[4] By exercising its power under section 61 of the Public Health Act 1936, the council assumed control over building operations within its area, including Mrs Dutton's house, and this assumption of control was a positive act. Stamp LJ adopted a rather different line. He interpreted the problem as being essentially one of causation. In the *East Suffolk Rivers Catchment Board* case the House of Lords had on the facts concluded that the board had not caused any injury; in the instant case he took the view that, on a balance of probabilities, the house would not have been built upon its unstable foundation if the council had not been careless; the careless act caused the injury and therefore the council was liable. To the argument that if, on the authorities, the builder was not under a duty to a purchaser of the house, the council should not be liable for the negligence of their inspector in passing the bad work, Lord Denning MR and Sachs LJ responded by disapproving of *Bottomley v Bannister*[5] and *Otto v Bolton and Norris*,[6] which comprised the authorities relied upon by the council, stating that an action in negligence could now be brought against a builder or builder/owner who put a defective house on the market.[7]

1 Since 1965 building work has been subject to Building Regulations made by the Minister under section 4 of the Public Health Act 1961. See paras 3.110 ff, above.
2 [1941] AC 74, [1940] 4 All ER 527. The board had a statutory power to repair sea walls. A high tide broke a sea wall and flooded the plaintiff's land. The board sent a man to carry out repairs which were effected very tardily. It was held that the board was not liable in tort.
3 [1972] 1 QB 373 at 380–381.
4 Ibid at 402–403.
5 [1932] 1 KB 458.
6 [1936] 2 KB 46, [1936] 1 All ER 960.
7 Stamp LJ did not consider that it was open to the court to question the line of authority which seemingly held that the builder was not liable but he saw no inconsistency in finding the local authority liable for negligence where the builder could not be liable.

5.9 The council argued further that if a duty of care did exist in the circumstances of the case, it could only be owed to a person who had acted in reliance on the misstatement, as in *Hedley Byrne & Co Ltd v Heller & Partners Ltd*.[1] Lord Denning drew a distinction between professional men who give advice on financial or property matters, such as lawyers, bankers or accountants, who owed a duty only to those who relied on them and suffered financial loss in consequence; and professional men giving advice on the safety of buildings, or machines, or material: their duty was owed to persons who might suffer loss if the advice were bad. A person in the latter category was liable, not because of reliance by the injured person, but because he knew, or ought to have known, that such people might incur injury if he did his work badly. According to Stamp LJ, in *Hedley Byrne* only a person who relied upon what the defendant did and said could suffer damage, and the defendant could only be held to have contemplated as someone who might be injured by his carelessness a person who might rely upon his statement. The instant case was not one where only a person relying upon the statement of the defendants might suffer loss, and Mrs Dutton was a person who was so closely and directly affected by the

act of the defendants that they ought reasonably to have had her in contemplation as being thus affected.
1 [1964] AC 465, [1963] 2 All ER 575.

5.10   A further argument raised by the council was that, if they were liable,
such liability was restricted to physical injury to person or property. They
claimed that the ground of the plaintiff's complaint was that, as a result of the
inspector's carelessness, she had a house whose value was consequently
reduced: this was economic loss and not recoverable. Lord Denning did not
accept this, characterising the damage in the case as being physical damage to
the house. Sachs LJ was of the view that there was ample evidence of physical
damage to the property, but in any case he regarded attempts to decide whether
damage were physical or economic as fallacious; the correct test was: 'What
range of damage is the proper exercise of the power designed to prevent?'[1]
Stamp LJ, in considering this, 'the most difficult point for decision in this case',[2]
returned to his earlier doubts as to the builder's liability, while finding the
authority liable. He seemed to regard the loss as being purely financial, but
'there is in my judgment nothing illogical or anomalous in fixing the former [the
authority] with a duty to which the latter [the builder] is not subject. The former
by undertaking the task is in my judgment undertaking a responsibility at least
as high as that which the defendant in the *Hedley Byrne* case would in the
opinion of the majority in the House of Lords have undertaken had he not
excluded responsibility.'[3]
1 [1972] 1 QB 373 at 404, [1972] 1 All ER 462 at 484.
2 Ibid at 414 and 489.
3 Ibid at 415 and 490.

5.11   Quite apart from its potential impact upon builders[1] this decision clearly
had great significance for local authorities. In a sense, though, the fact that the
courts seemed to have shifted in favour of imposing liability on the negligent
builder (and Parliament effected a similar shift in the Defective Premises Act
1972) indicated that, even in those cases where a local authority might be held
liable, as long as there was a builder to be claimed against, he presumably would
bear the major burden of the liability in any contribution proceedings.[2] This was
of consolation to the Court of Appeal in rationalising their decision,[3] as also was
the fact that practical problems of proof would militate against any risk of a
flood of claims.[4] Nevertheless, the fact remained that there was now a cause of
action against a local authority where their inspector had been negligent in
inspecting the foundations of a house pursuant to byelaws (or, since 1965,
regulations made by the Minister) under public health legislation.
1 See para 3.89, above.
2 See ch 9, below.
3 [1972] 1 QB 373 at 398, [1972] 1 All ER 462 at 476, per Lord Denning MR.
4 Ibid at 407 and 484, per Sachs LJ.

5.12   In *Dutton* the council had also expressed anxiety that they would be
exposed to endless claims, as the period of limitation would only begin to run
when the damage was done, i e when cracks initially appeared in the premises.
However, Lord Denning MR reassured them on this point. He quoted
Diplock LJ in *Bagot v Stevens Scanlan & Co Ltd*[1] as authority for the proposition that the damage was done when the foundations were badly constructed
and the limitation period began to run from that time.[2] The practical effect of
that was that the limitation period could pass with the owner of the property in

blissful ignorance as to the state of the foundations, as the damage might not manifest itself until more than six years after it was done. However, this might not protect the builder; following *Applegate v Moss*,[3] if he covered up his own bad work, he would be guilty of concealed fraud, and the limitation period would not begin to run until the fraud was discovered.

1 [1966] 1 QB 197, [1964] 3 All ER 577. See also para 4.47, above.
2 Though Sachs LJ ([1972] 1 QB 373 at 405–406, [1972] 1 All ER 462 at 482) reserved the question of the correctness of Diplock LJ's dictum for further consideration.
3 [1971] 1 QB 406, [1971] 1 All ER 747. See para 1.43, above.

5.13 As regards the local authority, it was not long before these dicta fell to be considered. In *Higgins v Arfon Borough Council*[1] a firm of builders started to construct a bungalow within the area of the defendant local authority. Contrary to the byelaws, the bungalow was built on the earth as it stood, within the area of the walls, and no provision was made for holes to drain away standing water, and the underfloor area was inadequately ventilated. The builders duly gave the local authority notice of the dates when they intended to cover the various underfloor areas, so that the local authority would be able to inspect them, and check that the builders had complied with the byelaws, but there was no evidence that inspections were ever carried out. The premises were originally purchased by a Mr and Mrs Williams in March 1966, and the plaintiff bought the bungalow from them in 1969. In January 1970, a plumber installing central heating noticed standing water under the floorboards, which, not surprisingly, were affected by wet-rot.[2] The cost of the necessary remedial work plus architect's fees came to over £2,000, and the plaintiff claimed damages in negligence from the defendant local authority. The central argument in the case turned on the question of limitation, for the plaintiff did not serve his writ until 30 May 1972. He argued that the period of limitation began to run from the time when he discovered the damage; the defendant contended that the period ran from the time when the damage occurred. It then became necessary to establish when the damage occurred. The dicta of Diplock LJ and Lord Denning MR outlined above were applied. It was consequently held that the cause of action accrued not later than 22 March 1966, when the bungalow was conveyed to the first owner-occupiers, who were then potential plaintiffs, and that consequently the action was statute-barred. The fact that further damage was sustained by reason of the development of the wet rot did not, it was held, constitute a fresh cause of action.

1 [1975] 2 All ER 589, [1975] 1 WLR 524.
2 Perhaps not inappropriately the action was heard at Mold.

5.14 Presumably local authorities received a certain amount of consolation from this decision. At least it appeared that the threat of the limitation period running from the date when damage first manifested itself had receded. This respite did not last long. In *Sparham-Souter v Town and Country Developments (Essex) Ltd*[1] the question of limitation fell to be reconsidered. The defendant developers, who in 1964 wished to build a new housing estate, applied to the relevant local authority for planning permission. The authority granted permission and passed the plans, subject to the builders complying with the building byelaws. In May 1965, the developers, who were themselves the builders, began work on the houses which were later purchased by the plaintiffs, and the council surveyor inspected the work and passed it. The houses were completed by the end of September and were again inspected and passed by the surveyor. In October and November the developers agreed to sell the houses to the plaintiffs. In December the council certified that the two houses had been inspected and they found no reason to question the legality of the work carried out under the building byelaws. The conveyances were completed in November and January.

1 [1976] QB 858, [1976] 2 All ER 65.

5.15 Cracks appeared in the brickwork of the houses two or three years later, allegedly because the foundations were inadequate to support the load. The plaintiffs issued a writ against the builder/developers and the council on 22 October 1971, claiming damages for negligence. A preliminary issue was tried on the question whether the plaintiffs' cause of action was brought within six years from the date on which the cause of action accrued. The Court of Appeal agreed that the action was not statute-barred. For the local authority's defence to have succeeded, the act or acts of negligence which constituted the cause of action had to have taken place before 22 October 1965. Clearly this negligence would thus have to antedate the conveyance of the premises. The local authority argued that the act of negligence (assuming there had been negligence) took place when the houses were inspected and passed as complying with the byelaws, i e in May and September 1965, but it was conceded at the outset of the Court of Appeal hearing[1] that the last negligent act alleged by the plaintiffs, the certificate of December 1965, fell within the limitation period running back six years from October 1971. This effectively disposed of the appeal. However, the Court of Appeal considered the argument of the local authority that when the plaintiffs acquired the property they acquired an existing cause of action against the local authority, which arose when the negligent act took place and the foundations were laid. This cause of action, it was argued, arose at that time in favour of the person who then held title to the land, and there then existed the necessary breach of duty and damage to the then owner which caused the limitation period to begin to run from that time. The cause of action 'came with the property', in the words of counsel for the local authority, and was taken over by the plaintiffs when they purchased the property. The Court of Appeal was not prepared to accept this argument, on the basis that a cause of action could not accrue to the plaintiffs, and time begin to run against them, before they had any interest in the property. The earliest moment at which it could possibly be said that damage was suffered, and thus when a cause of action accrued, was when the plaintiffs acquired an interest in the property by contracting to buy it. The Court did not consider, however, that it was at that time that the plaintiffs necessarily suffered damage. If no defects appeared in a building during the time when it was in a person's ownership, he would have suffered no damage: it was 'the emergence of the faults not the purchase of the house which has caused him the damage'.[2] The Court therefore disapproved of the dicta of Lord Denning MR in *Dutton* and Diplock LJ in *Bagot*, holding (though technically this in its turn was obiter) that the period of limitation in such a case as the instant one began to run from the time when the owner discovered, or with reasonable diligence ought to have discovered the defective state of the property.

1 Because of fresh evidence that had come to light as to the date of that certificate.
2 [1976] QB 858 at 880, [1976] 2 All ER 65 at 80, per Geoffrey Lane LJ.

5.16 Roskill LJ referred[1] to the risk that the time when the period of limitation began to run might be postponed indefinitely, as time would, at the earliest, begin to run when each subsequent purchaser acquired his title; and, as new defects emerged, so would new causes of action. The position was viewed with no particular enthusiasm by Roskill LJ and Geoffrey Lane LJ, but they were of the view that the decision in *Dutton* led them inevitably to it. The fact that ultimately litigation might fail because the time between the inspection and the claim was so lengthy did not remove the objections to such litigation being brought, and the need for local authorities to prepare themselves accordingly for the risk of such litigation. However, only the House of Lords could overrule *Dutton*.

1 [1976] QB 858 at 873–874, [1976] 2 All ER 65 at 74.

5.17   This the House of Lords very soon had the opportunity to do. In fact, just seven days after the decision in *Sparham-Souter* a Mr Anns, together with seven other plaintiffs, appealed to the Court of Appeal from a decision of Judge Edgar Fay QC which (correctly) followed Lord Denning's dictum in *Dutton*. The Court of Appeal followed *Sparham-Souter* and allowed the plaintiff's appeal. The Court of Appeal gave leave to appeal to the House of Lords. Before the appeal was heard, the London Borough of Merton, the defendants in the case, presented a petition to the House, asking for leave to argue not only the preliminary issue of limitation but also the question of whether they were under any duty of care at all to the plaintiffs. The petition was acceded to, thus providing an ideal opportunity for guidance from the House of Lords on the difficult questions of duty of care and limitation that the previous case law had posed.[1]

1 *Anns v London Borough of Merton* [1978] AC 728, [1977] 2 All ER 492.

5.18   In February 1962, the Mitcham Borough Council (the predecessors in title of the defendants) passed building plans for a block of seven maisonettes to be built by the Walcroft Property Co Ltd. The builders, who were also the owners, granted long leases of the maisonettes in 1962 (by the time the case was heard only two of the plaintiffs were original lessees; the other six acquired their leases by assignment in 1967 and 1968). In February 1970 cracks in the walls and sloping of floors were noticed. The cracks and sloping were caused by structural movements. The plaintiffs claimed that this was due to a failure to build the block of maisonettes on adequate foundations. The deposited plans required the foundations to be 3 feet or deeper; it was alleged that there was a depth of only 2 feet 6 inches. The plaintiffs claimed damages for breach of contract against the builders, and also for breach of the implied undertaking under section 6 of the Housing Act 1957. The builders did not put in a defence, but undertook to carry out certain work. They did not appear in the various proceedings. The action against the local authority was for negligence in approving the foundations or failing to inspect the foundations. The writs were issued in February 1972.

5.19   The context in which the local authority exercised its duties and powers was, as in *Dutton*, considered to be of great importance. This context, the Public Health Act of 1936, was considered in detail. Lord Wilberforce, who delivered the leading judgment, underlined the emphasis in the sections of the Act dealing with construction and repair of buildings, on health and safety. Building byelaws had been made by the authority under the enabling powers of section 61,[1] and the builders complied with those byelaws which required them to inform the authority of their intention to erect a new building in accordance with the accompanying plans, which inter alia stated, in relation to the depth from ground level to the underside of the concrete foundations, 'three feet or deeper to the approval of local authority'. The plans were duly approved; the approval drew attention to the requirements of the byelaws that notice was to be given to the surveyor before the work was begun and when the foundations were ready to be covered up. The plaintiffs claimed that in fact the builders only took the foundations down to a depth of 2 feet 6 inches; at the time of the hearing it was not established whether the authority's inspector did in fact ever make an inspection.

1 Quoted at para 5.8, above.

5.20   Clearly supervision at this stage was vital, given the fact that, as the foundations would thenceforth be covered up, there was no opportunity for intermediate inspection, and thus a failure to inspect, or a negligent inspection, which resulted in a breach of the byelaws going undetected, might well result in a hidden defect which could later cause damage to the building and adversely affect the health and safety of the occupants. However, the authority argued that, since they were not under a duty to inspect, but merely had a power to do so, they could not be liable for a failure to inspect, and therefore could not be liable for a negligent inspection; if they could be so liable, local authorities would simply in each case decide not to inspect. Lord Wilberforce[1] drew a distinction between policy and operational decisions. Essentially the policy decision covers such matters as the scale of resources that the local authority decides it can make available – the number of inspectors to be appointed and the types of inspection to be made. The operational decision is concerned with the way in which the inspection is carried out bearing in mind the limits created by the policy decision. Thus to use an example suggested by Craig[2] if as a result of a policy decision an authority were to decide that their inspectors could only carry out certain limited tests since the cost of more detailed tests would be prohibitive, it would not be open to an individual to claim compensation simply on the grounds that a further test would have revealed the defect.[3] It did not follow from this that a fixed policy never to inspect was permissible. Lord Salmon, for example, said,[4] 'this would, in my view, amount to an improper exercise of discretion which, I am inclined to think, might be corrected by certiorari or mandamus'.[5] The Law Lords were not prepared to accept that, though there was no duty to inspect, there could be no liability for failure to inspect. The council was, in the words of Lord Wilberforce,[6] 'under a duty to give proper consideration to the question whether they should inspect or not', and if a plaintiff could establish that a council had not given due consideration in such a case as the instant one, the council would be in breach of the duty of care that it owed.

1 [1978] AC 728 at 754–755, [1977] 2 All ER 492 at 500–501.
2 (1978) 94 LQR 428 at 440.
3 However, carelessness by the inspector in carrying out the tests would constitute operational negligence.
4 [1978] AC 728 at 762, [1977] 2 All ER 492 at 507.
5 Unlike the other Law Lords, Lord Salmon doubted whether a failure to inspect would allow an individual to sue the authority for damages in respect of such a failure to inspect.
6 [1978] AC 728 at 755, [1977] 2 All ER 492 at 501.

5.21   Where an inspection was made, it was argued by the authority that, whereas a statutory duty gave rise to possible liability, a statutory power, as in the case, could only give rise to liability where the exercise of the power involved a positive act which created fresh or additional damage. In disagreeing with this proposition, the Lords had to examine the difficult case of *East Suffolk Rivers Catchment Board v Kent*[1] which had already been analysed in *Dutton*. The *East Suffolk* case, it was said, was to be considered in the light of the later recognition, which did not come perhaps until *Home Office v Dorset Yacht Co Ltd*,[2] of the existence of 'a general duty of care, not limited to particular accepted situations, but extending generally over all relations of sufficient proximity, and even pervading the sphere of statutory functions of public bodies'.[3] Quite apart from the fact that the consequences that resulted from an examination of the duties that the particular statute laid down might well differ from case to case, the general principle was that a duty of care at common law could exist even where what was created by the statute was a power rather than a duty. The difference was that where it was a power created by the statute, liability could only ensue where the act complained of lay outside the ambit of the power. If therefore a local authority with a power to inspect building foundations failed to do so without duly considering whether it should inspect or not, or carried out an inspection, but did so carelessly, a duty of care could arise, and the local authority could be liable in tort. This duty was a duty to take reasonable care to secure that the builder did not cover in foundations which did not comply with byelaw requirements. Their Lordships agreed with the majority of the Court of Appeal in *Dutton* that it would be inconsistent to impose liability for defective foundations on the council if the builder were allowed to escape liability. The fact that a builder of a house was also the owner of the house did not render him immune from liability in negligence for defects in the house towards someone who later acquired it. In the alternative, as the builder (whether owner or not) was under a duty to comply with the byelaws, he could be sued for breach of statutory duty by any person for whose benefit or protection the byelaw was made.

1 [1941] AC 74, [1940] 4 All ER 527.
2 [1970] AC 1004, [1970] 2 All ER 294.
3 [1978] AC 728 at 757, [1977] 2 All ER 492 at 503, per Lord Wilberforce.

5.22 The House of Lords discounted the risk of a multiplicity of actions. In holding that the duty of care was owed to owners and occupiers of the house,[1] who must be such when the damage occurred, it was assumed that 'this disposes of the possible objection that an endless, indeterminate class of potential plaintiffs may be called into existence'.[2]

1 The case of users was left open, as they might have a remedy against the occupier under the Occupiers' Liability Act 1957. See ch 2, above.
2 [1978] AC 728 at 758, [1977] 2 All ER 492 at 504, per Lord Wilberforce.

5.23 The damage was classified as material physical damage and the damages recoverable included all those foreseeably arising from the breach of duty of care – a duty to take reasonable care to secure compliance with the byelaws. These damages comprised the amount of expenditure necessary to restore the dwelling to a condition in which it was no longer a danger to the health or safety of the persons occupying it and possibly (depending on the circumstances) the expenses arising from necessary displacement. Subject to adequate proof of causation the damages might include compensation for personal injury and property damage, and also, given the purpose of the byelaws to secure the health and safety of occupants, damage to the dwelling house itself.

5.24 On the question of limitation, their Lordships agreed with the Court of Appeal in *Sparham-Souter* that time could not begin to run on conveyance of the property. However, they differed from the Court of Appeal in holding that in respect of damage to the house the cause of action arose when the state of the building was such that there was present or imminent danger to the health or safety of persons occupying it, rather than when the owner discovered, or with reasonable diligence ought to have discovered, the defective state of the property.[1]

1 See para 5.29, below.

5.25 A variety of criticisms have been levelled at this decision, which we shall examine before moving on to consider the post-*Anns* case law. Not surprisingly, local authorities are particularly reluctant to act as insurers for house purchasers who buy defective premises and are unable to sue a builder who may be insolvent. The contrary argument to this is that since the major purchase in most people's lives is likely to be their house, if as a result of a defect which was quite undetectable at the time of purchase, the house is seriously defective, and the builder is insolvent, it is important that there be someone from whom they can claim damages, if that someone is at fault. As against this, of course, the same loss would be suffered if the local authority chose not to inspect on good policy grounds and avoided placing itself in the position of a potential defendant.

5.26 The fact that *Anns* was decided on a preliminary point of law raises further difficulties.[1] The liability declared to exist was inevitably stated at a fairly generalised level, given the assumptions that had to be made about the acts (or omissions) of the local authority. This left open the limits that might be sought to be imposed in future cases where the facts were concrete and ascertained. The tenor of this argument is that a precedent based on a preliminary point of law is of necessity, particularly in a negligence action, a particularly nebulous and unhelpful one, likely to leave the law still with many questions unanswered. Although it is too early to be categorical about this, the indications from the few post-*Anns* cases that we have are that the courts are not as yet finding this to be a problem.[2]

1 Buxton (1978) 41 MLR 85 at 86.
2 See paras 5.32 ff, below.

5.27 More specifically, much discussion has inevitably ensued over the characterisation of the damage in *Anns* as 'material, physical damage'[1] following a similar characterisation of the damage in *Dutton*. The essence of the objections to this is that as a matter of policy it is only physical damage to person or property which is compensable damage under *Donoghue v Stevenson*, and a negligent act whose consequence is pure economic loss is not in general compensable unless, on strict policy grounds as in *Hedley Byrne v Heller*, compensation is deemed appropriate within some more restricted rubric than a foreseeable duty of care, such as the 'special relationship' in that case.[2] To suggest that the damage caused to the premises in *Anns* is physical damage is, it is argued, akin to claiming that the plaintiff in *Donoghue* could have claimed for replacement of the ginger beer bottle, which would not have been possible; all that could be recovered in that case was damage to the person or to property other than the item itself. Claims for compensation for the damage done to the bottle/house are, on this argument, contractual only. Duncan Wallace[3] argues that where there is cracking, this is only a symptom of past movement, 'but for practical purposes the repair costs claimed would be for remedying the underlying cause of further future movement or failure'. In so far as the characterisation by the

Court of Appeal and the House of Lords can be justified, it is on the basis that the damages are awarded to cover the cost of avoiding potential physical damage from the collapse of the premises, and thus rather than waiting until such time as personal injury or property damage is occasioned by the collapse, damages are awarded at an earlier stage, when no injury has yet occurred, but the cost of remedying the defects is likely to be less than will be the case if the plaintiffs, with an unsaleable property on their hands, are compelled to wait until the inevitable occurs.

1 [1978] AC 728 at 759, [1977] 2 All ER 492 at 505, per Lord Wilberforce.
2 See Craig (1976) 92 LQR 213; Duncan Wallace (1977) 93 LQR 16. See paras 1.22–1.23, above.
3 (1978) 94 LQR 60 at 64.

5.28 The emphasis on 'present or imminent danger to the health or safety of occupiers' in relation to the time when the limitation period begins to run and also the measure of damages awardable also raises certain problems. How likely must it be that this kind of ultimate threat exists: how imminent must it be? Also, not every house built defectively as a result of a negligent or non-inspection will, even in the long term, contain such faults that the occupiers' health or safety will ever be threatened, yet the property may well have its marketability severely diminished. Clearly the authority's liability is not absolute, but this is inevitable, if consistency with the content of the relevant legislation (i e the Public Health Act 1936) is to be maintained.

5.29 A further problem is the distinction, in terms of limitation, between the *Anns* formula of present or imminent danger, and the *Sparham-Souter* test under which time begins to run from when the owner discovers, or with reasonable diligence ought to discover, the defective state of the property. Can it be assumed that the present or imminent danger must have manifested itself, or have been reasonably discoverable, for time to begin to run, or is it possible for time to run while the damage is latent? Can damage be imminent, and yet latent, for over six years, or does imminence presuppose some kind of manifestation? Lord Salmon addressed himself to this problem in *Anns*. Bearing in mind the fact that, since the writ was issued in February 1972, if it could be proved that damage occurred prior to February 1966, which endangered the safety of the occupants, the claim would be time-barred, he said: 'It seems to me, however, that since in fact no damage manifested itself until February 1970 it may be very difficult to prove that damage had in fact occurred four years previously. In the unlikely event of the defendants overcoming this difficulty, the fact that the damage went undetected for four years would not prevent the statute running from the date when the damage first occurred.'[1] This clearly suggests, on the one hand, the fact that the limitation period can be running while the plaintiff remains in blissful ignorance of the damage, and on the other hand that it will be far from easy for a local authority to establish that damage had occurred prior to the time it manifested itself or, if it could so establish, how long before the manifestation the damage occurred. We have suggested[2] that the formula in *Anns* should be seen in the light of the *Sparham-Souter* test, and consequently that the limitation period should only begin to run when the plaintiff realises, or ought reasonably to realise that the state of the building constitutes a present or imminent threat to the health or safety of occupiers. This seems consistent with the general approval of *Sparham-Souter* expressed by the House of Lords in *Anns*, and avoids the risk of time running against an occupier who is not, and could not be, aware of the existence of the defects.

1 [1978] AC 728 at 770, [1977] 2 All ER 492 at 514.
2 See para 1.39, above. See *Emden's Building Contracts and Practice* (8th edn) pp. 508–509.

5.30 Further concern has been expressed by and on behalf of local authorities concerning the duration of potential liability. The fact that the six year limitation period begins to run from the time when the state of the building is such that there is reasonably discoverable present or imminent danger to the health or safety of persons occupying it entails the need for local authorities to retain records of inspections almost indefinitely, quite apart from the problems of insurance that this will pose. In *Anns*, over thirteen years elapsed between the inspection (if any) and the date of trial; in *Dutton* twelve years; and memories inevitably become dim over such a period, though arguably this factor might operate to the advantage of the local authority, as it would become increasingly difficult for plaintiffs to prove causation.

5.31 Against this, it can be argued that all the local authority has to do is to give thought to the question of whether or not to inspect, and, if an inspection is carried out, to make this inspection with due care. Unless the decision not to inspect is made in a way which on its face indicates a total lack of proper consideration given to the question, the court is not likely to delve more deeply into the basis for the decision not to inspect, for this is a policy matter which it is for the local authority to decide. 'As was well said, public authorities have to strike a balance between the claims of efficiency and thrift (du Parcq LJ in *Kent and Porter v East Suffolk Rivers Catchment Board*): whether they get the balance right can only be decided through the ballot box, not in the courts.'[1] If the decision is to inspect, the inspection will be carried out by a qualified man doing his job. How difficult will it be for the local authority to satisfy the requirements of *Anns*?

1 [1978] AC 728 at 754, [1977] 2 All ER 492 at 501, per Lord Wilberforce.

5.32 Some encouragement for local authorities can be derived from the recent decision of Sir Douglas Frank QC[1] in *Stewart v East Cambridgeshire District Council*,[2] it was claimed that a local authority inspector had been negligent in inspecting foundation trenches. Following recommendations made by consulting engineers, the council had required the owner of a plot of land who wished to build on it to dig foundations no less than 4 feet in width with reinforcement. Foundation trenches were dug, inspected and passed and a house was built, but later the plaintiff, who was the second assignee of the house, discovered very serious cracking in the walls, which was due to settlement of the site.

1 Sitting as a deputy judge of the Queen's Bench Division.
2 (1979) 252 Estates Gazette 1105.

5.33 The court found that the inspector had inspected the trenches, and had found no reason to change the requirements that he had made, based on the advice of the consulting engineers. The court also found that, despite this advice, settlement could not have been avoided by the strip foundations that had been dug, but that deep piling to firm ground would have been necessary. Counsel for the plaintiff conceded that the only way the inspector could have satisfied the duty on him was to have had boreholes sunk to a depth of 20 feet (for the engineers' report had indicated that the ground was filled to that depth with sand, flints, chalk and other material; hence their recommendation concerning the foundations) for otherwise he could not be sure of there being firm ground. The case thus turned on whether the inspection made by the inspector was made with reasonable care, in these particular circumstances.

5.34 As with the *Acrecrest case*[1] (considered in detail below) the court was concerned to bear in mind the qualifications of the building inspector. As was pointed out by the judge,[2] the building inspector is not usually a civil engineer, architect or chartered surveyor, and consequently he cannot be expected to possess the expertise of members of those professions. The inspector relied on the advice of those qualified to give it, the consulting engineers, who had made a soil exploration and analysed the soil. They had recommended full inspection of the foundation trenches, and these he had duly inspected, examining the soil, and checking that the levelling pegs were rigid, and he had found nothing to cause him to believe that 4 feet wide foundations would not be safe. The judge considered the submission of counsel for the plaintiff, that the inspector should have sunk boreholes to the bottom of the site, to amount effectively to saying 'that it is the function of the local authority to carry out for a developer the functions of a civil engineer in ascertaining the suitability of a site for building and advising on the design of that building. It puts the building inspector in the position of consulting engineer, insurer and warrantor.' The court was not prepared to accept this. Consequently, the plaintiff's claim failed.[3]

1 (1979) 252 Estates Gazette 1107.
2 Ibid at 1107.
3 If he had succeeded, the court would have awarded him £8,350, being the cost of the repairs as soon as it was reasonable to execute them, irrespective of personal financial circumstances.

5.35 Clearly this is a satisfactory decision from the point of view of local authorities. Admittedly it does nothing to clarify the problems inherent in the decision not to inspect, and the extent to which that decision may be treated as inadequate by the court: but where an inspection is made, the court's realistic approach to the qualifications of the inspector as defining the duty owed by his employers through him is likely to be received with enthusiasm. The decision entirely accords with the spirit and reasoning of *Anns*: the local authority is not to be the automatic filler of the gap left by the builder who cannot be proceeded against, but will only be liable where a reasonably imposed duty of care has been breached. What, though, will be the position where it can be shown that the inspector in question was particularly highly qualified? If, for example, the inspector in *Stewart* had been a qualified consulting engineer, would the duty imposed on him have been different? The answer to this depends upon the weight attached to the matter of cost to the ratepayer as a factor in determining the existence of a duty. If the inspector is a qualified consulting engineer, is it reasonable to expect the ratepayer in a case of this sort to bear the cost of sinking boreholes or making whatever other tests a consulting engineer might regard as necessary, but an unqualified inspector would not? It may be argued that the implication of the judgment in *Stewart* is that the typical building inspector is to be regarded as the norm, and any extra qualifications are likely to be regarded as irrelevant, given the emphasis in that judgment on the cost to the ratepayer of a finding of liability. On the other hand, the normal rule is that, whereas usually the standard of care expected of a practitioner of a particular profession or trade is that of the reasonably competent practitioner, where it can be shown that the particular defendant is an especially well-qualified member of his profession or trade, the standard required will be that of the reasonably competent person with those extra qualifications. Hence it is likely that in a case where the inspector has particular qualifications that might put him on his guard to make extra checks or carry out extra tests, the court will have to decide whether the reasonably competent inspector/civil engineer (or inspector/architect, as the case may be) would have carried out those extra tests, irrespective of whether the ratepayers might incur extra expense as a result of, for example, sinking boreholes. Does the authority have the discretion to limit the functions of the inspector in carrying out inspections, so as to save money for the ratepayers? The Law Lords in *Anns* emphasised that the public law context of this line of cases allows for an area of discretion which will be lacking in the typical negligence action, and it is submitted that the discretion of the local authority would render reasonable a decision to circumscribe the activities of a well-qualified building inspector in the interests of the ratepayers' pockets.

5.36 Shortly afterwards the same judge had to decide another case concerning alleged negligence of a local authority: *Acrecrest Ltd v W S Hattrell & Partners*.[1] The plaintiffs were a company which owned certain blocks of flats which had been designed, and whose construction had been supervised, by the defendant architects, whom the plaintiffs employed for this purpose. The plaintiffs' claim for damages for negligent design and supervision against the architects was settled early in the hearing, and the decision to be discussed relates to the third party claim by the architects for a contribution from the local authority (the London Borough of Harrow) whose inspector had inspected the foundations of the blocks, on the ground that the authority were joint tortfeasors.

1 (1979) 252 Estates Gazette 1107.

5.37 The blocks of flats were built on a site which originally contained a number of trees, mainly elms and fruit trees. A number of trees, mainly fruit trees, were removed before or during the building operations; the elms were later discovered to be suffering from Dutch Elm disease and were therefore felled. The architects originally specified strip foundations approximately 3 feet 6 inches deep. These were duly dug, in early 1972, but the local authority inspector, when he examined the trenches, found tree roots and therefore required the builders to take the foundations in parts down to a depth of 5 feet minimum. This was duly done, and the building was completed at the end of 1972. Cracks and movement were noticed and complained of by tenants in the summer of 1973, and, though repair work was carried out, further cracks occurred, and it became clear that the plaintiffs would have to undertake the expensive task of underpinning the foundations.

5.38 The judge found that the cause of the cracks was 'heave' i e swelling of the subsoil caused by water which, but for their removal, would have been absorbed by trees. Instead, the subsoil (London clay) absorbed the water and the consequent 'heave' pushed up the building from under the foundations. The architects, who, having regard to the nature of the subsoil had anticipated the risk of settlement rather than heave, admitted that they were negligent (and in breach of contract) in failing to design uniform foundations to a depth of 5 feet, and they alleged that the building inspector was likewise negligent in that he should have required all foundations to be to a depth of 5 feet.

190

5.39 The local authority argued that the only duty owed by them was to an owner or occupier whose health or safety was likely to be affected, rather than to a person such as the plaintiffs, commercial developers, whose health and safety would be unaffected even if the building collapsed. The court did not accept this argument, on the basis that the plaintiffs did not constitute negligent building owners, who, according to Lord Wilberforce in *Anns*[1] are the source of their own loss. Clearly it was not alleged that the plaintiffs had been negligent, and thus the inspector was under a duty to ensure that the building complied with the building regulations. With respect, this reasoning may be questioned. Simply because the plaintiffs were not negligent it does not follow that a duty was owed to them. The essence of *Anns* is that there is a threat to the health or safety of the owner or occupier, rather than simply that economic loss will ensue to the owner or occupier. If the essence of the judge's argument is that 'health and safety' explains why the law imposes a duty, and that this does not prevent reliance on the duty by a person or body whose interests are adversely affected by a breach of the duty:[2] this would appear to be beyond the ratio of *Anns* and further extend the range of persons to whom the duty is owed, the proper plaintiffs, as against the local authority, are surely the lessees.[3]

1 [1978] AC 728 at 758, [1977] 2 All ER 492 at 504.
2 (1979) 252 Estates Gazette 1107 at 1113.
3 A further argument put forward by the authority was that they did not owe a duty of care to the plaintiffs because of the statutory duty of the plaintiffs to ensure compliance with the Building Regulations. The court was not of the view that the existence of such a duty could excuse the authority from failing to exercise due care, even if such a duty required the plaintiffs to protect the health and safety of the lessees by ensuring that there had been no breach of the Building Regulations. Although admittedly negligence was not alleged against the plaintiffs, if it is accepted that the building owner owes a duty to the lessees, in a case such as this, to secure compliance with the Building Regulations, and fails to do so, this comes perilously close to the negligence referred to by Lord Wilberforce above.

5.40 Having decided that the local authority owed a duty, the learned judge went on to consider whether they were in breach of that duty. He held that the inspector was negligent in failing to require the foundations to be taken down to 5 feet all round, and consequently the authority were liable for the damage resulting from the removal of the fruit trees, the cause of the initial damage. In addition they were liable for the damage resulting from the removal of the elms. Though there was no reason to attribute greater knowledge or means of knowledge to the building inspector than to the architect,[1] and though it was common ground that no reasonable architect could have foreseen that the elms would have to be removed as a result of the disease, nevertheless the judge was persuaded that, since the breach of duty of the local authority was a failure to require adequate foundations, the foreseeable damage was damage resulting from movement of the buildings, and the fact that the manner and extent of the movement was unforeseen was irrelevant. Thus, if the inspector had required 5 foot foundations all round, his employers would not have been liable for this particular unforeseeable damage; as it was, the fact that the (unforeseeable) damage resulted from the failure to require such foundations rendered them liable. This certainly creates another rod for the local authority's back, and raises potentially difficult questions concerning which the unforeseeable events will or will not render the authority liable or not liable for it. Arguably, if damage as a result of movement is foreseeable, then whatever the cause of the movement, if there has been a breach of duty by the authority, they will be responsible for the damage, though it has been suggested[2] that some events which cause the damage may be so independent and unusual as to fall outside the responsibility of the authority.

1 'I bear in mind that the building inspector may not have any professional qualifications and, if he has they are unlikely to be of such a high standard as those of an architect; and I think it would be unreasonable to expect the building inspector to have a greater knowledge of Dutch Elm disease than the architects': (1979) 252 Estates Gazette 1107 at 1112, per Sir Douglas Frank QC.
2 Ibid at 1113.

5.41 Assuming that a duty does exist in the circumstances of a case like *Acrecrest* the decision is perhaps unremarkable. The difficulty though lies in the question of whether a duty is owed to someone whose health and safety will not be affected as a result of a negligent inspection. On a strict reading of *Anns* the duty is limited to those who will be so affected. Lord Wilberforce in *Anns* said:[1] 'A reasonable man in the position of the inspector must realise that if the foundations are covered in without adequate depth or strength as required by the byelaws, injury to safety or health may be suffered by owners or occupiers of the house. The duty is owed to them, not of course to a negligent building owner, the source of his own loss.' This would not appear to extend to a developer such as the plaintiff whose health and safety is not thus hazarded. The prudent developer/reversionary might insert in the lease a term requiring the lessee to pass on to him any compensation obtained as a result of a successful action against a local authority, but if this has not been done, should the court make the extension of allowing the lessor a cause of action? In any event, the interests of the lessee and lessor in the property, being those of possession and ownership respectively, will not necessarily overlap, and so a clause requiring payment to the lessor of all compensation obtained may well be regarded as unconscionable. On grounds of convenience, it may be that the *Acrecrest* solution will be deemed to be the most acceptable, but insofar as it opens the way for further extensions beyond the limits of *Anns* it should be regarded with caution.

1 [1978] AC 728 at 758, [1977] 2 All ER 492 at 504.

5.42 Alarm at this new liability whose potential existence was hardly imagined before 1972, together with uncertainty as to what precisely was required of them, caused local authorities to fear that many extensive claims would be brought against them. This fear does not, so far, appear to be justified. For example, although quite a large number of claims was threatened against the London Borough of Merton, no claims have as yet actually been made since *Anns*. Obviously the frequency of inspections and the quality of those inspections will vary, depending upon the resources of the authority in question, but it is suggested that, where an inspection is made, it will generally have to be made not only of the foundation trenches, but of all parts of the building which are later covered up. The court is unlikely to regard as acceptable a decision to inspect which is not followed by, at the least, inspection of those areas which cannot later be examined by a surveyor or other adviser. The quality of the inspection required, as regards testing the soil or considering any expert reports, will depend upon the view taken of what can reasonably be expected of the inspector in the particular circumstances.

5.43 Local authorities have many powers relating in one way or another to premises, other than the power to inspect foundations. How far (if at all) can *Anns* be used by analogy to impose civil liability in respect of the exercise or non-exercise of these? Before examining some of these powers, and considering the potential liability of local authorities, it is worth returning to *Anns* so as to see how far the judgments therein provide guidance on this difficult matter. Lord Wilberforce stated:[1]

> Part II of the [Public Health] Act [1936] is headed 'Sanitation and Buildings' and contains provisions in the interest of the safety and health of occupiers of dwelling-houses and other buildings such as provisions about sewage, drains and sanitary conveniences. From section 53 onwards, this part of the Act is concerned with such matters as the construction of buildings (section 54), repair or removal of dilapidated buildings (section 58) and fire escapes. The emphasis is throughout on health and safety. The directly relevant provisions start with section 61.

After describing the byelaws that were made, and the facts of the case, Lord Wilberforce summarised the statutory position.[2]

> The Public Health Act 1936, in particular Part II, was enacted in order to provide for the health and safety of owners and occupiers of buildings, including dwelling houses, by, inter alia, setting standards to be complied with in construction, and by enabling local authorities, through building byelaws, to supervise and control the operations of builders. One of the particular matters within the area of local authority supervision is the foundations of buildings, clearly a matter of vital importance, particularly because this part of the building comes to be covered up as building proceeds. Thus any weakness or inadequacy will create a hidden defect which whoever acquires the building has no means of discovering: in legal parlance there is no opportunity for intermediate inspection.

In similar vein Lord Salmon stated:[3]

> We are concerned particularly with the safeguards relating to building foundations; these foundations are of the greatest importance because the stability of the building depends on them and they are covered up at a very early stage.

1 [1978] AC 728 at 752, [1977] 2 All ER 492 at 499.
2 Ibid at 753 and 500.
3 Ibid at 761–762 and 506.

5.44 The fact that the context of health and safety of owners and occupiers of buildings was regarded as being of great importance in *Anns* does not mean, it is submitted, that where a local authority exercises or fails to exercise a power in this context a duty of care can be said inevitably to arise. The emphasis in both the above quotations[1] suggests that the fact that the foundations were covered up after the inspection, and thus could not be examined again, was of great significance, and that some parallel factor may be necessary in relation to other local authority powers for liability to be imposed. The remarks of Lord Wilberforce concerning the particular nature of a local authority as a public body are of significance here.[2]

> I do not think that a description of the council's duty can be based on a 'neighbourhood' principle alone or on merely any such factual relationship as 'control' as suggested by the Court of Appeal. So to base it would be to neglect an essential factor which is that the local authority is a public body, discharging functions under statute: its powers and duties are definable in terms of public not private law. The problem which this type of action creates, is to define the circumstances in which the law should impose, over and above, or perhaps alongside, these public law powers and duties, a duty in private law towards individuals such that they may sue for damages in a civil court.

In *Anns*, despite the fact that a public body was involved, the context of health and safety to owners and occupiers, the fact that foundations would be covered up after inspection, the 'operational' nature of the power, involving the practical execution of a policy decision to inspect, all militated in favour of the imposition of a duty of care. All this, as well as the need for a plaintiff to establish that 'action taken was not within the limits of a discretion bona fide exercised'[3] must be borne in mind when examining other relevant local authority powers.

1 See the further remarks by Lord Wilberforce at 755e and 501g.
2 Ibid at 754 and 500.
3 Ibid at 755 and 501, per Lord Wilberforce.

5.45   Claims that a local authority is liable for defective premises as a result of its failure to carry out its function of seeing that the Building Regulations are enforced are unlikely to be restricted to claims concerning inadequate foundations. An example of this can be seen in the decision of Judge Fay QC in *Haig and Haig v Hillingdon London Borough*.[1] Following the construction in 1974 of an extension to a terraced house, defects, in the form of sagging of a bedroom floor, cracking of the ceiling below and incursions of rain water through a french window, were soon discovered. This, it transpired, was due to the use of wooden rather than rolled steel joists to support the bedroom floor, and the fact that the roof outside the french window sloped towards it rather than away from it. There had been a breach of building regulations C10 and D8,[2] but the builder was a man of straw, and consequently the plaintiffs sought damages from the local authority, on the basis that they provided insufficient inspections, and when they did inspect they should have discovered the defects and required the Regulations to be complied with.

1 (1980) 9 May (unreported).
2 The Regulations in force at the time were the 1972 Building Regulations, but the wording of the relevant Regulations was not changed in the 1976 Regulations.

5.46   Judge Fay, criticising in passing the absence in the Regulations of the imposition of a requirement that the builder give an opportunity of inspection before covering up structural steelwork, examined the inspection history and held that the inspectors had not visited as the occasion required and had thus not discovered the breaches of the Building Regulations. He considered that Lord Wilberforce's words in *Anns v London Borough of Merton* stressing the vital importance of inspection of foundations because that part of the work would be covered up and any defects would be hidden, applied equally to a beam upon which the structure rested. The fact that the plaintiffs had not employed a private surveyor did not break the chain of causation:[1] firstly, because it was in evidence that purchasers of that class of property rarely employed surveyors; secondly, because the survey in such cases would be carried out by a building society surveyor, who would be conducting a valuation and would not open up floorboards; thirdly, even a private surveyor would be unlikely to open up floorboards, as would have been necessary to uncover the defect. It might however have been different if the case had concerned a large mansion, in which case there might well have been a reasonable expectation that there would be a survey before a sale.

1 See para 6.54, below.

5.47   It was held that the local authority had not been negligent with respect to the roof, for, though when the drains test was done the opportunity should have been taken to examine the roof, there was no evidence that the inspector would then have found the roof and french window in their final condition. A final examination might have revealed the defects but because of staff shortage and the absence of urgency or case of materials being covered up known to the authority, the failure to examine was not held to constitute negligence.

5.48 Liability was imposed in respect of the beam: the damages constituted the costs to which the plaintiffs had been put and compensation for disruption and inconvenience while repairs to the beam were carried out. A claim for interest on loans which the plaintiffs had to pay to finance the building works was disallowed as being attributable to the plaintiffs' impecuniosity rather than the defendants' negligence.

5.49 There is a clear parallel between liability for foundations and liability for beams; both are potentially hazardous and are covered up, and in addition it is worth noting that Judge Fay did not discount the possibility of liability for failure to discover a breach of regulation C10 concerning the roof. Local authorities may however derive some comfort from the court's realistic attitude to local authorities' priorities and the effects of staffing shortages, though the inference is that where building work is actually covered up the criteria imposed by the court will be stricter, and it will be less inclined to accept that circumstances render inspection impossible.

5.50 The local authority also has duties under the Public Health Act 1936 concerning plans. Section 64 of the Act (as amended) provides:

> Where plans of any proposed work are, in accordance with building regulations, deposited with a local authority, the local authority shall, subject to the provisions of any other section of this Act which expressly requires or authorises them in certain cases to reject plans, pass the plans unless they either are defective, or show that the proposed work would contravene any of those regulations, and, if the plans are defective or show that the proposed work would contravene any of those regulations, they shall reject the plans.

5.51 This fell to be considered by Phillips J in the recent case of *Grice v Williams Jehu Ltd.*[1] A house was built in or about 1970 by the first defendants. The house was built upon a raft foundation, on the site of a disused quarry which had formerly been a tip. In 1975 internal and external cracks in the house were discovered and the plaintiff caused remedial work to be done. He sought to recover the cost of this, together with certain consequential loss, from the builders and the second defendants, the Ogwr Borough Council, who were the successors to the district council that had passed the plans and carried out the inspections.

1 (1980) 16 May (unreported).

5.52 The cracks were held to be due to two factors. Firstly subsidence had been caused by the downrush of water not being properly accommodated in soakways away from the building. This created voids beneath the building, and the raft foundation was unable to stand the strain thus created and became distorted. Secondly, the method of roof construction employed was unsatisfactory. Phillips J stated that the primary duty of a local authority under section 64 was to pass plans unless they were defective or contravened the Regulations. The authority was under a duty to examine the plans before passing them; the extent of the duty was to be determined in accordance with the principles laid down in *Anns v London Borough of Merton*. The duty was one of reasonable care, but even allowing a local authority the wide measure of freedom of policy or discretion referred to in *Anns*, a local authority could not discharge its duty under section 64 if it passed a plan without any examination or with only a formal one. What was needed depended upon the circumstances of the case.

5.53 The learned judge examined in detail the efforts by the local authority to discharge its duty under section 64. He held that those efforts had failed, and consequently it was liable. Although the authority was a small one, with limited resources, its officers had been aware that the site was unusual and difficult and, while they had not directed or imposed the use of a raft foundation (which, unless the raft was of enormous thickness, was unsuitable for a foundation on made ground), they had encouraged it, and had been instrumental in approving the plans without sufficient examination. The officers should have required the opinion of an expert or at least discussed the matter with the architect to see whether he approved the plan and was qualified to do so. Though aware of the problem they had failed to give it proper and sensible consideration.

5.54 In addition the authority was held to be liable for negligent inspection of the foundations and the surface water drainage system. The raft foundation was not constructed as drawn which made it even less useful as a foundation (even if it had been constructed according to the plans, as we have noted, it was inadequate and would sooner or later have become distorted). There was a serious failure by the builders to comply with the drainings of the surface water drainage system, such that in the event there was really no system at all.

5.55 The evidence as to whether or not there had been an inspection was unclear, and Phillips J, while finding that an inspection had taken place, and that a reasonable inspection would have revealed the defects, also stated that even if there had not been an inspection the local authority would still be liable, since this was a case where in accordance with its own system it would have been necessary to inspect the drains and foundations. In conclusion he said, 'in my judgement a local authority is equally liable for the negligent failure to carry out inspections in a case where its own system requires it to inspect as it is for an inspection carried out negligently' and this, it is suggested, is entirely consistent with *Anns*.

5.56 To sum up thus far, it would appear that the statutory function of local authorities to enforce the Building Regulations in their district entails the risk of liability in the tort of negligence if their failure to enforce, or to enforce adequately, the Regulations is held to fall within the criteria laid down by the House of Lords in *Anns v London Borough of Merton*. Clearly this is very far from meaning that damage ensuing from breach of the Regulations can automatically be laid at the door of the local authority; instances of liability will be very much the exception rather than the rule.

5.57 Beyond the decided cases, it is impossible to do more than speculate about further potential civil liability of local authorities for defective premises in relation to which they exercise powers. Much, as we have seen, will depend upon factors such as the nature of the power in question, the context within which it operates, and the manner of its exercise or the validity of the reasoning behind a decision not to exercise it. Craig[1] sums up the position thus:

> The public body should not be liable when the alleged negligence attacks a conscious choice as to the use of scarce resources, or a deliberate balancing of thrift and effi- ciency or when it results from a risk consciously taken by that body to achieve a policy pursuant to a discretionary power in a statute. These are policy or planning determinations because the court cannot or should not re-assess or 'second-guess' the authority's choice. Operational decisions are subject to the ordinary common law principles of duty of care. The question may be put as follows: given the policy choice made by the public body, did the authority take reasonable care in applying it. For example, given that the local authority has decided to carry out only two tests, has it done these carefully?

This illustrates well the distinction between the type of case in which prima facie liability of local authorities for negligent exercise of their powers will be imposed, and that in which it will not. It should be emphasised that where a deci- sion is taken, for example, not to inspect premises in a case where a power to inspect exists, the authority must exercise reasonable care in making the deci- sion not to inspect.

1 (1978) 94 LQR 428 at 454–455.

5.58 One or two aspects of the powers of local authorities concerning premises suggest themselves as particularly likely to engender potential civil liability, but it must be emphasised that the matters discussed below by no means constitute an exhaustive list, and it may be a long time before any clear picture of the extent of local authority liability in damages for negligent exercise of their powers in connection with defective premises emerges.

5.59 Local authorities outside London[1] have certain statutory powers in rela- tion to dangerous buildings.[2] Section 58 of the Public Health Act 1936 empowers a local authority to which it appears that any building or structure or part of a building or structure is in such a condition, or is used to carry such loads, as to be dangerous, to apply to a court of summary jurisdiction. The court may make an order, where the condition of the building is dangerous, requiring the owner to do work obviating the danger or, if he chooses to, demolish the building and clear the rubble: if the danger arises from overloading the court may make an order restricting the use of the building until a court of summary jurisdiction, satisfied that any necessary works have been done, withdraws or modifies the restriction. If the person fails to comply with the court order the local authority may do the necessary work and recover their expenses from him.

1 As regards London, see London Government Act 1963, s. 40(1) and Sch 11, Part 1; also London Building Acts (Amendment) Act 1939, ss. 61–68.
2 See Cowen [1980] LS Gaz 487.

5.60 Section 25 of the Public Health Act 1961, envisages a more serious state of affairs, and empowers a local authority to which it appears that a building or structure or part of a building or structure is in such a state or is used to carry such loads as to be dangerous and that immediate action should be taken to remove the dangers, to take the necessary steps, i e to do the work themselves, rather than persuading a court to order the owner to do it. Notice, if reasonably practicable, should be given to the owner and occupier, of the authority's intention and expenses if reasonably incurred, may be recovered from the owner by the authority.

5.61   If a local authority were to decide not to inspect any buildings or structures which might be dangerous, and a building in relation to which it had power to act under section 58 or section 25 were to collapse and cause damage, prima facie unless the authority exercised reasonable care[1] in deciding not to inspect at all, liability could be imposed. Again, if an authority were to decide that in all cases where buildings or structures appeared to be dangerous it would always act under section 58 rather than section 25, and a building were to collapse at such time after the authority realised it was dangerous that it could be shown that acting under section 25 would have led to the demolition of the building before its collapse, if the authority did not exercise reasonable care in reaching its decision, they could be liable. Also they could be liable if they inspected a building negligently and decided it was not dangerous when in fact it was, and it collapsed, causing damage. It would of course be necessary to bear in mind the criteria discussed above, the need, as the post-*Anns* case law underlines, to consider in detail the precise circumstances of each case, and of course the practical problems, such as proof of causation, that a negligence action always involves.

1 See Craig (1978) 94 LQR 428 at 449.

5.62   Section 26 of the 1961 Act empowers a local authority to which it appears that any premises are in such a state as to be prejudicial to health or a nuisance, and that the procedure laid down by sections 93–95 of the 1936 Act for dealing with statutory nuisances would be too slow, to remedy the defective state of the premises. Nine days notice must be given to the owner, occupier or person responsible. Again a case can be made for liability if, for example, a local authority decided that in all cases in which it appeared to the authority that premises were in a state prejudicial to health, it would act under sections 93–95 and not under section 26, and a case arose where it could be shown that action under section 26 would have avoided the damage to health resulting from the state of the premises that occurred. The power given to a local authority by section 72 of the Housing Act 1957, to order the demolition of an obstructive building (defined by section 72(4) as a building which, by reason only of its contact with, or proximity to, other buildings, is dangerous or injurious to health) again raises the spectre of liability under *Anns*, as does section 8 of the Local Government (Miscellaneous Provisions) Act 1976, which empowers local authorities[1] to which it appears certain[2] unoccupied premises, are, or are likely to become, a danger to public health to do such works (after giving notice to the owner of the premises) in connection with the premises as the authority thinks fit for the purpose of preventing the premises from being a danger to public health.

1 Other than county councils and the GLC.
2 See s. 8(1)(a), 8(1)(b).

5.63   A novel situation presented itself in 1979 in the form of *Ainsworth v Halton District Council.*[1] In 1972 the Runcorn UDC, the predecessors of the defendants, served a notice under either the 1957 or the 1964 Housing Act (the notice was not produced by either side) upon the plaintiff requiring her to do work on her house. The plaintiff applied to the local authority for an improvement grant (under the Housing Act 1969), a grant was promised upon satisfactory completion of the work, and the authority's officials visited and approved the work. The authority paid three-quarters of the cost of the work, and the plaintiff a quarter, which she raised by means of a loan from the authority by way of a mortgage on the security of her house.

1 (1979) 20 March (unreported), Runcorn CC.

5.64 Despite the approval of the authority, it later transpired that the damp-proof course which should have been built by the contractor[1] was wrongly made and quite inadequate. The plaintiff claimed the cost of remedial work (and general damages for discomfort and inconvenience) from the authority, in that the authority owed her a duty of care which, by means of their negligent inspection, they had broken.

1 Who apparently thereafter went out of business.

5.65 The learned judge found that the defendants' surveyor had been negligent in his inspection, that the plaintiff had suffered loss and damage, and that although the plaintiff had not directly received the surveyor's advice, she had relied upon his findings and, relying upon his approval, she had paid the builder. It does not emerge clearly from the judgment whether it was based upon *Hedley Byrne v Heller* or upon *Anns v London Borough of Merton*.[1] If the former was the basis, there would have to have been a special relationship between the plaintiff and the defendant, with reasonable reliance, and with no need to establish that the damage suffered was physical damage. The absence of discussion in the judgment as to the existence of a present or imminent threat to the health or safety of the occupier (unless this was assumed) supports the idea that *Hedley Byrne v Heller* rather than *Anns v London Borough of Merton* was the basis of the judgment. Section 6(3) of the Housing Act 1969 provides that the payment of an improvement grant shall be conditional on the works being executed to the satisfaction of the local authority. If *Anns v London Borough of Merton* was the basis of the judgment, liability would be founded on a negligent inspection, a failure by the authority to act reasonably in satisfying itself that the work was properly executed. Either way an interesting further avenue of local authority liability has opened up.

1 Both cases are referred to in the judgment.

5.66 It should finally be noted that, in the appropriate circumstances, local authorities as much as other parties who, through their negligence, are liable for defective premises, may, in addition to compensating the plaintiff for their responsibility concerning the defect itself, (generally on a cost of repair basis in the case of local authorities) also be liable to damages for upset and/or inconvenience[1] suffered by the plaintiff as a result of their breach of duty. In an appropriate case, damages might also be awarded for any diminution in value following repair[2] and, since *Dodd Properties (Kent) Ltd v Canterbury City Council*,[3] damages may be assessed as at the date of the trial, rather than when the breach of duty occurred.

1 See paras 3.93 and 4.38, above.
2 See para 3.95, above.
3 [1980] 1 All ER 928, [1980] 1 WLR 433. See paras 1.13–1.17, above.

5.67 It is arguable that, in addition to their liability at common law for negligent inspections, local authorities may also be liable under section 1 of the Defective Premises Act 1972, which imposes a duty upon persons who take on work for or in connection with the provision of a dwelling to see that the work taken on is done in a workmanlike or professional manner, with proper materials, and so that as regards the work the dwelling will be fit for habitation when completed.[1] It would not appear inappropriate to categorise Building Regulation inspections as 'taking on work', though Lord Denning MR in *Sparham-Souter v Town and Country Developments (Essex) Ltd*[2] was unsure whether the local authority inspector takes on work 'in connection with' the provision of the house inspected, and Roskill LJ thought the position was very far from clear.[3] In any event the operation of section 2 of the Defective Premises Act[4] is likely to prevent liability from arising under section 1 save in the exceptional case.

1 Insofar as they act, in effect, as developers, pursuant to statutory powers, for the provision of dwellings, local authorities will fall within section 1(4) of the Act, but this is of course different from their powers of inspection to ensure that the Building Regulations are complied with.
2 [1976] QB 858 at 870, [1976] 2 All ER 65 at 70.
3 Ibid at 877 and 77.
4 See para 3.106, above.

5.68 The recently published White Paper entitled 'The Future of Building Control in England and Wales'[1] has important implications for local authorities. Quite apart from the proposed recasting of the Building Regulations described elsewhere,[2] and the recognition of the present concern of those involved in building control and construction generally regarding the problems of open-ended liability in cases involving latent damage and the referral of this to the Law Reform Committee,[3] the proposal of a system of private certification of building work by approved experts as an optional alternative to local authority inspection of plans and construction[4] work is of especial interest.

1 Cmnd 8179, 1981.
2 See para 3.125, above; Cmnd 8179, paras 6–10.
3 Cmnd 8179, paras 40–42.
4 Ibid, paras 19–38.

5.69 The system envisages the supply by an approved certifier to a developer of two separate certificates to be lodged with his building control authority; the first to be submitted before construction starts, confirming that the design accords with the Building Regulations, the second to be submitted before the building is occupied, confirming that the construction work has been duly inspected and the building complies with the Regulations. Local authorities will check that the certificates are issued by approved persons, cover the necessary points and are supported by evidence of proper insurance coverage. Authorities will not be liable in damages to any person on account of certifiers' negligence.[1] Authorities will, because of their general public law duties, remain responsible for taking any enforcement action; they will retain their powers to prosecute for contraventions of the Building Regulations and to require the removal of works that do not comply.

1 Though it may be argued that in a particular case an authority was negligent in accepting a certificate from a person whom they should have realised was not approved.

5.70 The criteria for approval of certifiers will be professional qualifications, practical experience, and the possession of indemnity insurance. The White Paper recognises that in most cases the inspection of works to be carried out by certifiers will have to be prescribed in some detail, because private certifiers can not have the discretion accorded to public authorities and also the availability of redress for damage as a result of negligence should be no less when buildings have been certified than when they have been inspected by the local authority. A person alleging negligence in certification would appear to have at his disposal a much more straightforward claim vis-à-vis a private certifier than is the case vis-à-vis a local authority inspection (or failure to inspect). No doubt he will indirectly pay for this, as no centrally prescribed scale of charges will restrict the private certifier; he will be able to choose the level at which he sets his fees, and no doubt the developer will pass the cost of this on. Such a scheme seems likely to satisfy on the one hand the wish expressed in the White Paper to provide the opportunity for maximum self-regulation by the building industry, and on the other hand, the need to safeguard public health and safety. The fact that in response to the Consultation Document, comments on which formed the basis for the proposals contained in the White Paper, a significant minority argued that control should remain solely with local authorities, suggests that such control will continue to be of importance. From the point of view of liability for negligent inspection/certification it will be interesting to contrast the courts' attitude to liability of local authorities with that of private certifiers. It is suggested that that attitude should, and will clearly reflect the important difference in nature and function between the two. In the meantime it should be noted that since April 1980 payment has had to be made for Building Regulation inspections by local authorities, though this would not appear to affect local authority liability. However, it will surely not be open to an authority which has received payment to argue that on policy grounds inspection was not possible: in such circumstances a discretion can hardly still be said to exist, and failure to inspect would constitute negligence (assuming the existence of defects which the inspection should have revealed); indeed it could almost be argued that the local authority is in a contractual relationship with the building owner, and is liable to him for breach of a contractual duty to inspect.

Chapter 6

Vendor

6.1 Traditionally the only possible civil liability of the vendor of defective premises has been in contract or in misrepresentation. The expansion of liability for premises over the past decade has, as we shall see, had its effect in imposing liability in tort on the vendor in certain circumstances, and suggestions have been made that civil liability may yet be further expanded, but in general the vendor has emerged, at least thus far, relatively unscathed. However, it is worth not only examining the existing liability of the vendor but also speculating as to possible future trends for, if tort liability is not to be imposed on the vendor as widely as on, for example, the builder or the architect, there must be good reasons for this; if there are not, then speculation may become reality.

Contract

6.2 The basic principle is that of *caveat emptor*; there is no implied term in a contract for the sale of land that the property on that land is free from defects.[1] The burden is on the purchaser to discover, by himself or through his professional advisers, whether defects exist and, subject to the exceptions to be examined below, he will have no claim against the vendor. The Law Commission, in their Report on the Civil Liability of Vendors and Lessors for Defective Premises,[2] described the traditional justification for the basic principle as being 'that a purchaser[3] of a completed building can see what he is buying and does not rely upon the skill or knowledge of the vendor. If he wishes to satisfy himself as to its condition he is as well able as the vendor to have it surveyed and to ascertain its condition. Moreover, he knows, and the vendor may not, to what use he intends to put the premises. He can judge their suitability for his purpose and negotiate the price accordingly.'[4] The Law Commission saw no reason to recommend departure from this long-standing principle by means of the statutory imposition of an implied warranty as to the condition of the premises or their suitability for any particular purpose. Especially in the case of private dwelling houses[5] there would be a risk of duplication of expense, as, even if there were a warranty by the vendor, the purchaser might still consider it necessary to have a survey. A private survey was preferable to a possible claim against a vendor, if traceable, when a defect manifested itself perhaps some years later. It would be contrary to the public interest to encourage purchasers to dispense with a proper survey. The parties in all cases of sale of dwellings based their arrangements on the fact that, in the absence of fraud or misrepresentation, the risk lay with the purchaser. It may be questioned whether this is as true of the parties as of their advisers. The fact that many purchasers do not arrange to have a private survey of premises is perhaps some indication that it is not so, though in many cases no doubt the enormous assumption is made that the survey carried out on the mortgagee's behalf, in cases where there is a mortgage involved, will reveal the existence of defects. This is by no means necessarily the case though the purchaser may now be able to obtain damages in an action against a negligent building society surveyor.[6]

1 See e g *Greenhalgh v Brindley* [1901] 2 Ch 324.
2 Law Com No 40, 1970.
3 Defined as 'any person who acquires an interest in property on a sale, a letting or a charge'.
4 Para 15.
5 Paras 17–19.
6 See *Yianni v Edwin Evans & Sons* [1981] 3 All ER 592.

6.3 Nevertheless, on grounds of general convenience, there is no reason to suppose that the *status quo* will not remain. It seems right to encourage purchasers to have premises surveyed, given the importance of the transaction, and the risk of duplication of expense if the vendor were deemed to warrant the premises free from defects would in a number of cases be a real one. The limited circumstances in which a solicitor may be liable for failing to advise his client to have an independent survey are described elsewhere.[1] All that need be reiterated here is the desirability of a solicitor recommending such a survey to every purchaser whom he advises.

1 Para 4.40, above.

6.4 It is, of course, always possible for the purchaser to secure warranties in the contract that the premises are free from particular or general defects but needless to say, the prudent vendor is highly unlikely to accede to a request for such warranties, still less to volunteer them of his own initiative. In the particular case of a contract for the purchase of a house which is to be constructed by a builder/vendor, there is an implied warranty that the builder will do his work in a good and workmanlike manner; that the builder will supply good and proper materials and that the house will be reasonably fit for human habitation.[1]

1 For detailed discussion of these see paras 3.8–3.10, above.

6.5 Occasionally it may be found that an express warranty has been given. Thus, in the Canadian case of *Fraser-Reid v Droumtsekas*[1] the plaintiff purchased a new house from the defendant, a builder. The contract of sale contained a clause which stated: 'providing that the vendor has disclosed to the purchaser all outstanding infractions and orders requiring work to be done on the premises . . . herein'. Some months later, after the plaintiff had moved into the house, serious basement flooding occurred, and further water entered the basement after very heavy rain. The leakage was caused by improper foundation drainage in contravention of the relevant municipal building law. The plaintiff argued that the clause referring to infractions amounted to an express warranty that the house was built in accordance with all applicable byelaws unless the contrary was disclosed. The Supreme Court of Canada agreed, and awarded damages to the plaintiff for breach of the express warranty, though they held, contrary to his claim, that there was no implied warranty on the sale of a completed house, only where an uncompleted house was sold. It was further held that the warranty was not merged in the conveyance and thereby extinguished: merger depended in every case upon the intention of the parties and in this case it could not reasonably be supposed that the parties intended the warranty to be merged in the deed.

1 (1980) 103 DLR (3d) 385. See also *Batty v Metropolitan Realisations Ltd* [1978] QB 554, [1978] 2 All ER 445.

6.6 Where a term of the contract contains an error or a misstatement concerning the quality of the property, this amounts to a misdescription.[1] Thus if it is provided in the contract that the property is free from structural defects, or dry rot (though as we have seen the likelihood of such a term being included is remote), if defects do exist there is a breach of contract, and common law remedies are available.[2] The effect of a substantial misdescription is, as with rescission for misrepresentation, to terminate the contract *ab initio*, and to allow the purchaser to recover his deposit in an action for money had and received.[3] A decree of specific performance may not be made against the purchaser. If the misdescription is not substantial, so the purchaser would in effect get what he wanted, then he will not be entitled to rescind, and specific performance can be decreed against him. However, he may claim damages,[4] which will generally consist of an abatement, by the appropriate amount, of the purchase price.[5]

1 See Barnsley *Conveyancing Law and Practice* pp. 564–570; Farrand *Contract and Conveyance* (3rd edn) pp. 52–56.
2 See *Barnsley* p. 564.
3 E g *Flight v Booth* (1834)1 Bing NC 370 at 377, per Tindal CJ: 'where the misdescription is in a material and substantial point, so far affecting the subject matter of the contract that it might reasonably be supposed that, but for such misdescription the purchaser might never have entered into the contract at all, in such a case the contract is avoided altogether'. See also *Bellotti v Chequers Developments Ltd* [1936] 1 All ER 89.
4 E g *Belworth v Hassell* (1815) 4 Camp 140.
5 E g *Jacobs v Revell* [1900] 2 Ch 858.

6.7 Inevitably vendors have sought to reinforce their position by means of conditions of sale, the most common examples of which are as follows. Condition 7 of the Law Society's General Conditions of Sale[1] provides as follows:

7. *Errors, omissions and misstatements*
   (1) No error, omission or misstatement herein or in any plan furnished or any statement made in the course of the negotiations leading to the contract shall annul the sale or entitle the purchaser to be discharged from the purchase.
   (2) Any such error, omission or misstatement shown to be material shall entitle the purchaser or the vendor, as the case may be, to proper compensation, provided that the purchaser shall not in any event be entitled to compensation for matters falling within conditions 5 (2) or 6 (3).
   (3) No immaterial error, omission or misstatement (including a mistake in any plan furnished for identification only) shall entitle either party to compensation.
   (4) Sub-condition (1) shall not apply where compensation for any error, omission or misstatement shown to be material cannot be assessed nor enable either party to compel the other to accept or convey property differing substantially (in quantity, quality, tenure or otherwise) from the property agreed to be sold if the other party would be prejudiced by the difference.
   (5) The purchaser acknowledges that in making the contract he has not relied on any statement made to him save one made or confirmed in writing.

The National Conditions of Sale[2] contain the following condition:

17. *Immaterial errors*
   (1) Without prejudice to any express right of either party, or to any right of the purchaser in reliance on section 24 of the Law of Property Act 1969, to rescind the contract before completion, no error, misstatement or omission in any preliminary answer concerning the property, or in the Special Conditions, shall annul the sale, nor (save where the error, misstatement or omission is in a written answer and relates to a matter materially affecting the description or value of the property) shall any damages be payable, or compensation allowed by either party, in respect thereof.
   (2) In this condition a 'preliminary answer' means and includes any statement made by or on behalf of the vendor to the purchaser or his agents or advisers, whether in answer to formal preliminary enquiries or otherwise, before the purchaser entered into the contract.

Both of these will also be considered below in the context of liability for misrepresentation.

1 1980 edn.
2 19th edn, 1976.

6.8 The attempt made in each condition (and in any other contractual condition) to provide that no misdescription shall annul the sale does not alter the common law position : where the misdescription is substantial, as we have seen, the contract is terminated *ab initio*. The Law Society's Condition 7(4) provides that, for the purchaser to be able to avoid the contract, the misdescription, in addition to being substantial, must also prejudice him. As Professor Barnsley[1] points out, this probably adds little, as where there is a substantial misdescription, the purchaser is likely to be prejudiced in any case. Insofar as it is provided that the purchaser is not entitled to compensation for any misdescription, the practical effect of this is that the purchaser will be prevented from obtaining compensation if he seeks specific performance[2] and that he will not be able to claim damages for breach of contract.[3]

1 Barnsley *Conveyancing Law and Practice* p. 569.
2 See *Re Terry and White's Contract* (1886) 32 ChD 14.
3 See *Curtis v French* [1929] 1 Ch 253.

Collateral contract

6.9 In certain circumstances liability for defects may be imposed if the existence of a collateral warranty or a collateral contract to the effect that the premises are not defective can be established. In *De Lassalle v Guildford*[1] the plaintiff and the defendant agreed terms for the lease of a house by the defendant to the plaintiff. The plaintiff refused to hand over the counterpart that he had signed unless the defendant assured him that the drains were in good order. He was given a verbal assurance to that effect, and handed over the counterpart. The lease contained no reference to drains. The drains were not in good order, and the plaintiff succeeded in a claim for damages for breach of a collateral warranty. A L Smith MR said in *De Lassalle v Guildford*,[2] 'to create a warranty no special form of words is necessary. It must be a collateral undertaking forming part of the contract by agreement of the parties express or implied, and must be given during the course of the dealing which leads to the bargain, and should then enter into the bargain as part of it.' This passage was quoted with approval by Atkinson J in *Otto v Bolton and Norris*.[3] In that case a builder/vendor assured a prospective client that a house which she was considering buying was well built. The builder admitted that this was a serious statement, which he knew would influence her mind, and that he intended her to believe that he was selling a well built house and intended her to think that he was promising that it was a well built house. In fact the first floor ceilings were badly built, so that on several occasions they fell. The court awarded the plaintiff £340 by way of damages to compensate for the cost of reconstructing the ceilings, repairing the damage to furniture and renting other premises.

1 [1901] 2 KB 215.
2 Ibid at 221.
3 [1936] 2 KB 46 at 50–51, [1936] 1 All ER 960 at 962. See also *Terrene Ltd v Nelson* [1937] 3 All ER 739 at 744–745.

6.10 Usually, however, the dealings between vendor and purchaser will not be such that the existence of collateral warranties as to the state of the premises can be established, for the prudent (and even, generally, the imprudent) vendor is unlikely to go beyond the usual 'puffs' that are part of the thankless process of purchase of premises. However, it may well be asked whether replies to the standard pre-contract enquiries are capable of constituting collateral warranties. In *Gilchester Properties Ltd v Gomm*[1] the vendor's solicitors, in a reply to pre-contract enquiries, innocently misrepresented the value of rents payable by the tenants of premises which the plaintiffs were proposing to purchase. Romer J[2] quoted Lord Moulton in *Heilbut, Symons & Co v Buckleton:*[3]

> It is evident, both on principle and on authority, that there may be a contract the consideration for which is the making of some other contract. 'If you will make such and such a contract I will give you one hundred pounds', is in every sense of the word a complete legal contract. It is collateral to the main contract, but each has an independent existence, and they do not differ in respect of their possessing to the full the character and status of a contract. But such collateral contracts must from their very nature be rare ... they must be proved strictly. Not only the terms of such contracts but the existence of an *animus contrahendi* on the part of all the parties to them must be clearly shown. Any laxity on these points would enable parties to escape from the full performance of the obligations of contracts unquestionably entered into by them and more especially would have the effect of lessening the authority of written contracts by making it possible to vary them by suggesting the existence of verbal collateral agreements relating to the same subject-matter.

It was held that the statements contained in the replies were simply information given in response to a request for information in the course of negotiations leading up to the contract, and that they neither constituted part of the contract itself nor a warranty collateral to it.

1 [1948] 1 All ER 493. For discussion of this case on the misrepresentation aspects, see para 6.27, below.
2 [1948] 1 All ER 493 at 495–496.
3 [1913] AC 30 at 47.

6.11 In *Mahon v Ainscough*[1] before a contract for the purchase of a dwelling house was entered into, the purchaser's solicitor sent preliminary enquiries to the vendor's solicitor, one of which was: 'Has the property suffered war damage? If so, please state the date and nature of the damage, the steps which have been taken under the War Damage Acts, and the reference number of any claim made.' The vendor's solicitor replied, in good faith, 'I understand not'. At the end of the form was a note which stated, 'It is still necessary to make inspection of the property, inquiry of the local authority, the local planning authority, and of any occupier, and the usual searches.' After the contract was signed, requisitions on title were sent, the second of which asked, 'Will the vendor confirm that, if the preliminary inquiries made on behalf of the purchaser and replied to on March 31, 1950, were repeated herein, the replies at the present date would be the same as those already made. If not, please give full particulars of any variation.' The vendor's solicitor replied 'Confirmed'. The sale was completed, and it was later discovered that the premises had in fact suffered considerable war damage. The purchaser claimed damages for breach of a collateral warranty. This argument did not appeal to the Master of the Rolls, Sir Raymond Evershed. He said,[2] 'I confess that anything less like asking for a warranty or the giving of a warranty than this document would be difficult to imagine.' If it was the case that a warranty had been given concerning war damage, all the other answers to the other questions about the local authorities must have constituted warranties. It was also difficult to reconcile the suggestion that any of these answers amounted to warranties with the fact that in the second requisition the purchaser in effect repeated the questions already asked and requested the vendor's solicitor to confirm (which he did) that the conditions were unchanged. According to Jenkins LJ,[3] 'the inquiries and answers are intended simply to provide preliminary information to assist in the attainment of the object I have mentioned [to enable the proposed purchaser's solicitor to consider whether the contract for sale should be proceeded with, and, if so, what would be the appropriate form for it to take], and not in themselves to have any contractual force'. This was further indicated by the note reminding the purchaser of the need to make the usual inspection, inquiries and searches. There was no indication in the evidence of 'any intention to make such a separate contract as a warranty must necessarily import'.[4]

1 [1952] 1 All ER 337.
2 Ibid at 339.
3 Ibid at 340.
4 Ibid per Sir Raymond Evershed MR at 340. See also *Esso Petroleum Co Ltd v Mardon* [1976] QB 801 at 817–818 and 824–827, [1976] 2 All ER 5 at 13–14 and 19–21, per Lord Denning MR.

6.12 In any case, as regards liability on the basis of breach of a collateral warranty (or indeed for misrepresentation) in connection with replies to preliminary enquiries, it should be noted that the current version of the most commonly used form of enquiries before contract, published by Oyez Publishing Ltd, does not contain an enquiry concerning the existence of defects such as damp, subsidence, rot etc. Unless a form containing a defects enquiry is used, therefore, or an additional enquiry to that effect is added to the Oyez form, no liability for breach of a collateral warranty or misrepresentation contained in a reply to pre-contract enquiries will arise in respect of defects (of the kind with which this book is concerned). In any event, the prudent solicitor acting for a vendor would be likely to respond to a defects enquiry by suggesting that the purchaser make his own enquiries with respect to such matters. Nevertheless, the potential liability arising from an erroneous reply to a defects enquiry cannot be ignored.

6.13 As a final point on liability on a collateral contract, the case of *Ware v Verderber*[1] covers a further aspect of vendor's liability. Purchasers claimed damages for items removed from the property by the vendors, including a freezer and a washing-machine, and for items such as a telephone that had been damaged. The vendors were said to be under a duty not to remove anything fixed to the realty and to take reasonable care of chattels that they had contracted to sell. The contract did not list the chattels included in the sale, but liability was imposed on the basis of a collateral contract founded on agents' particulars, which stated what was included in the sale, and which negotiations between the vendor and the purchasers had confirmed.

1 (1978) 247 Estates Gazette 1081. See (1978) 122 Sol Jo 718.

6.14 If the courts, with their long-standing opposition to awarding damages for an innocent misrepresentation,[1] had set their faces against finding warranties in the replies to pre-contract inquiries before the Misrepresentation Act 1967, now that the Act provides a right of damages to the victim of a non-fraudulent misrepresentation, the judicial attitude is scarcely likely to relax at this stage. The extent to which the vendor of defective premises may be liable for misrepresentation needs consideration, both in the light of the Act and the common law as well.

1 See e g Lord Moulton in *Heilbut Symons & Co v Buckleton* [1931] AC 30 at 51.

Fraudulent misrepresentation

6.15 Where the contract is induced by a fraudulent misrepresentation, i e one made with an absence of honest belief or recklessness as to its inaccuracy,[1] the representee may rescind the contract and claim damages in the tort of deceit.[2] In *Ridge v Crawley*[3] the defendant, a builder, was held liable in damages to the plaintiff to whom he sold a house whose foundations had suffered settlement. It was held that fraudulent statements and conduct (filling up and wallpapering over cracks) of the defendant constituted a false representation. The plaintiff was awarded £955, the cost of underpinning, and £200 in respect of inconvenience for eight weeks while the underpinning work was done. In *Doyle v Olby (Ironmongers) Ltd*[4] it was established that the measure of damages is designed to effect a *restitutio in integrum*, though all damage directly flowing from the act of deceit is recoverable, rather than the rule in negligence cases that all reasonably foreseeable damage may be recovered.[5] Rescission may theoretically be effected at any stage, even after completion, though the representee is faced with the usual risk that the later rescission is sought, the more likely it is that third party rights may have intervened, thus making rescission impossible.[6]

1 *Derry v Peek* (1889) 14 App Cas 337.
2 It has been long established that rescission for a fraudulent misrepresentation is available even after completion: *Hart v Swaine* (1877) 7 Ch D 42, unlike the position regarding innocent misrepresentation, where rescission after completion has only been available since the Misrepresentation Act 1967, s. 1 (see para 6.29, below.) Alternatively, the representee may affirm and seek damages only: *London County Freehold and Leasehold Properties Ltd v Berkeley Property and Investment Co Ltd* [1936] 2 All ER 1039. See Wilkinson (1967) 117 NLJ 975 on rescission.
3 (1959) 173 Estates Gazette 959. See also *Rowley v Isley and W G Switzer Ltd* [1951] 3 DLR 766.
4 [1969] 2 QB 158, [1969] 2 All ER 119.
5 *The Wagon Mound* [1961] AC 388, [1961] 1 All ER 404.
6 See para 6.29, below.

6.16 The difficulty of establishing fraud and the fact that no damages could be awarded for an innocent misrepresentation were no doubt factors motivating the frequent attempts to establish collateral contracts and collateral warranties,[1] but such attempts have been rendered largely unnecessary by the decision of the House of Lords in *Hedley Byrne & Co Ltd v Heller and Partners Ltd*.[2] This decision, imposing a duty of care in certain circumstances to refrain from making negligent misstatements leading to economic loss, followed three years later by the Misrepresentation Act 1967,[3] opened up further possibilities for the purchaser to obtain damages for misrepresentation.

1 See e g the remarks of Lord Denning MR in *Esso Petroleum Ltd v Mardon* [1976] QB 801 at 817, [1976] 2 All ER 5 at 13.
2 [1964] AC 465, [1963] 2 All ER 575; see para 4.70 and paras 1.22, 1.47, above.
3 See paras 6.25–6.26, below.

Negligent misstatement under *Hedley Byrne v Heller*

6.17   The circumstances in which liability for loss resulting from a statement will be imposed were limited by the House of Lords to cases where there was a special relationship between the parties. The policy arguments behind restricting the duty of care in some way in cases involving economic loss have some force,[1] though the court did not specify the precise circumstances in which a special relationship would be deemed to arise. Generally speaking, the duty may be said to arise where the defendant makes an undertaking, whether expressly or impliedly, that he will exercise care in giving information or advice, and the person to whom he gives that information or advice, or to whom he can reasonably apprehend such information or advice will be passed on, places reliance on it, irrespective of whether there is a contract between the maker of the statement and its receiver. The defendant must, it seems, be possessed of a special skill such that others may reasonably rely upon it.

1 See Craig (1976) 92 LQR 213 for discussion of this and related issues.

6.18   Though the scope of the principle remains somewhat unclear, it has been established, as we have seen,[1] that architects and other professional men exercising their professional functions may be liable under it. It will be possible to claim against the vendor's solicitor or estate agent under *Hedley Byrne v Heller* in the appropriate circumstances,[2] but the position is rather less certain as regards the vendor. A decision of the County Court of York, Ontario, *Smith v Mattacchione*,[3] favours the applicability of *Hedley Byrne v Heller* to the vendor, though the analysis of the nature of the vendor's liability and the scope of *Hedley Byrne v Heller* is minimal. In the case, there was an untrue statement in the contract of sale that a third party was responsible for improvement charges, and the defendant was held liable in damages for negligent misstatement.

1 See para 4.70, above.
2 See *Dodds and Dodds v Millman, Warwicker, Lister and Merlin M Lister Ltd* (1964) 45 DLR (2d) 472; *Barrett v J R West Ltd* [1970] NZLR 789; *Bango v Holt* (1971) 21 DLR (3d) 66; *Richardson v Norris Smith Real Estate Ltd* [1977] 1 NZLR 152 and paras 4.71, 4.92, 4.97.
3 (1971) 13 DLR (3d) 437.

6.19   There was no reference in *Smith v Mattacchione* to the decision of the Privy Council in *Mutual Life and Citizens' Assurance Co Ltd v Evatt*,[1] which may give some grounds for doubting *Smith*. In *Evatt* the plaintiff, a policy-holder in the defendant's insurance company, claimed damages for the company's negligence in furnishing him with gratuitous information and advice on the financial stability of an associated company. Acting on this advice the plaintiff had invested in the associated company and had suffered a financial loss. The Privy Council held that the duty of care under *Hedley Byrne* was limited to cases where the person or body giving advice or information carried on the business of giving the advice in question or in some way let it be known that they claimed to possess the necessary skill and competence of a person engaged in such a business, or perhaps where they had a financial interest in the transaction.[2] Consequently the insurance company owed the plaintiff a duty merely to give him an honest answer and they were not liable to him in the absence of proof of dishonesty.

1 [1971] AC 793, [1971] 1 All ER 150.
2 As e g in *W B Anderson and Sons Ltd v Rhodes (Liverpool) Ltd* [1967] 2 All ER 850.

6.20   As we shall see, this decision has been doubted in later cases, but it fell to be considered very soon afterwards, as regards the liability of a vendor for defective premises, in the Australian case of *Presser v Caldwell Estates Pty Ltd*.[1] In about 1960 the defendant began to develop an estate, to be sold in lots to home-builders. The development involved contouring of the land and providing roads, drains, kerbs and gutters. In the course of the work a substantial amount of filling[2] was deposited on parts of the estate, this work being supervised by W, a licensed surveyor employed by the defendant. In 1963 the defendant appointed S Co, a firm of estate agents, as agent for the sale of the lots, without any apparent limitation on its ability so to act. S Co was entitled to commission on sales and also to a 'management fee' in respect of each lot sold. The plaintiff and his wife began negotiations in 1965 with S Co. The plaintiff's builder examined the lot which they eventually purchased; he sunk a test hole and recommended the site, but also suggested that they inquire whether there was any filling on the land. The plaintiff was assured by a salesman employed by S Co that he had been told by a director of S Co that there was no filling on the land the plaintiff wished to purchase. The plaintiff bought the lot in the same year and built a house thereon. He moved in in 1966, and in 1967 cracks appeared in the dwelling caused by subsidence of filling in the lot.

1 [1971] 2 NSWLR 471. See note in (1972) 46 ALJ 466.
2 'Filling' is soil artificially brought onto a lot.

6.21   The trial judge found that there was a special relationship within the doctrine of *Hedley Byrne v Heller* between the plaintiff and the defendant, and that the defendant was in breach of this duty in not ensuring that its agent S Co had all necessary information to enable it to answer correctly any question asked with respect to filling. On appeal to the Court of Appeal of New South Wales, it was held that, following *Mutual Life v Evatt*, all that was required of the defendant's agent in the circumstances was to answer honestly the plaintiff's questions, based on the knowledge that S Co had. The court held that S Co was authorised only to perform acts in the ordinary course of business of estate agents selling land, or reasonably incidental thereto and, since this did not extend to the answering of questions about the structure of the subsoil, the defendant could not be vicariously liable, even if the estate agent owed a duty of care which it had broken. No duty of care was owed by the vendor, for he made claim to no particular qualification to speak as to the structure of the subsoil and this qualification could not be implied from the fact of ownership of the land, though the court did not exclude the possibility of the vendor of land ever being liable under *Hedley Byrne v Heller*.

6.22   The decision in *Mutual Life v Evatt* has not met with universal approval,[1] as being unduly restrictive of the broad principle enunciated in *Hedley Byrne v Heller* and in any case, as a decision of the Judicial Committee of the Privy Council, it is not binding on the English courts, merely persuasive. The decision in *Presser v Caldwell*, based heavily as it is on *Mutual Life v Evatt*, is therefore by no means necessarily authoritative on the question of vendor's liability for negligent misstatement at common law, bearing in mind that in any case it, like *Mutual Life v Evatt*, is of merely persuasive authority as regards an English court, and only purports to deal with the particular instance of potential liability for statements concerning the structure of the subsoil, rather than attempting to lay down a broader principle.

1 See e g *Esso Petroleum Co Ltd v Mardon* [1976] QB 801 at 827, [1976] 2 All ER 5 at 22, per Ormrod LJ; *Howard Marine and Dredging Co Ltd v A Ogden & Sons (Excavations) Ltd* [1978] QB 574 at 591, [1978] 2 All ER 1134 at 1141, per Lord Denning MR.

6.23 A vendor is not in the business of giving advice or information on the quality of premises (unless he is an architect, builder or surveyor, in which case presumably a duty of care for negligent misstatement may be imposed on him). According to *Presser v Caldwell* he does not, at least in the particular instance of statements made about the structure of the subsoil, ordinarily hold himself out as having the skill or competence of a person engaged in such a business. If however the broader ratio of *Hedley Byrne v Heller* rather than that of *Mutual Life v Evatt* is used as the basis of liability, the possibility of a successful action against the vendor is seen as more likely. Certainly the element of reliance by the purchaser is likely to exist, and, in regard to less technical matters than the structure of the subsoil, it may perhaps be implied in a sufficiently precise statement that the vendor is qualified to make such a statement. For example, if a vendor represents to a purchaser or to the agent of a purchaser (e g a surveyor) that there is no reason to lift the carpets or to go into the loft of the house because there is no woodworm, if this statement is made carelessly, liability might well be imposed under *Hedley Byrne v Heller* on the vendor if it later transpired that there was in fact woodworm in the floors and attic. Some support for this can be gained from remarks of Lord Denning MR in *Esso Petroleum Co Ltd v Mardon*,[1] a case where the petroleum company was held liable, inter alia, under *Hedley Byrne v Heller* for negligently misrepresenting to a prospective tenant of a petrol filling station the throughput potential of the station. Lord Denning said :

> It seems to me that *Hedley Byrne*, properly understood, covers this particular proposition : if a man, who has or professes to have special knowledge or skill, makes a representation by virtue thereof to another – be it advice, information or opinion – with the intention of inducing him to enter into a contract with him, he is under a duty to use reasonable care to see that the representation is correct, and that the advice, information or opinion is reliable. If he negligently gives unsound advice or misleading information or expresses an erroneous opinion, and thereby induces the other side into a contract with him, he is liable in damages.

However, it should be noted that liability under *Hedley Byrne v Heller* does not depend upon an ensuing contract between representee and representor, but clearly such a contract will be good evidence at least of reliance by the representee and, perhaps, assumption of responsibility by the representor.

1 [1976] QB 801 at 820, [1976] 2 All ER 5 at 16. See also [1975] QB 819 at 830, [1975] 1 All ER 203 at 220, per Lawson J.

6.24 Once a special relationship under *Hedley Byrne v Heller* is established, it is clear that pure economic loss may be compensated. This may be of advantage to the plaintiff, although, given the characterisation by the Court of Appeal in *Dutton v Bognor Regis UDC*[1] and the House of Lords in *Anns v London Borough of Merton*[2] of the damage to premises caused by being built on unsafe foundations as physical rather than economic damage, it may be that only a case of cosmetic damage to premises where there is no threat to health or safety would show the advantage to the plaintiff of being able to claim damages for economic loss.

1 [1972] 1 QB 373, [1972] 1 All ER 462.
2 [1978] AC 728, [1977] 2 All ER 492.

Misrepresentation Act 1967

6.25 Section 2(1) of the Misrepresentation Act 1967, provides as follows:

> Where a person has entered into a contract after a misrepresentation has been made to him by another party thereto and as a result thereof he has suffered loss, then, if the person making the misrepresentation would be liable to damages in respect thereof had the misrepresentation been made fraudulently, that person shall be so liable notwithstanding that the misrepresentation was not made fraudulently unless he proves that he had reasonable ground to believe and did believe up to the time the contract was made that the facts represented were true.[1]

This in effect creates a right for the victim of a negligent misrepresentation to claim damages, for if the representor can prove that he reasonably believed what he said to be true, and continued in this belief until the contract was made, he will not have been negligent. It should be noted that the misrepresentation made by the representor (or his agent)[2] must lead to a contract between representor and representee and (since this is a feature of innocent misrepresentation at common law), the representation must induce the contract, and it must be a representation of fact.[3] Unlike *Hedley Byrne v Heller* there need be no special relationship between representor and representee and the advantages of the reversed burden of proof, once it has been established that the representor would have been liable to damages had the statement been made fraudulently, are likely to make this more attractive to the representee than the common law action, though of course there is nothing to bar a claim being brought based on both forms of liability (and indeed on breach of a collateral warranty as well).[4]

1 See Oakley [1980] CLJ 58 at 77–83.
2 See e g *Gosling v Anderson* (1972) 223 Estates Gazette 1743.
3 Though not necessarily: the Act does not define the term 'misrepresentation' or expressly incorporate the common law rules relating to misrepresentation. However, it can most probably be assumed that these rules apply to the Act.
4 E g *Howard Marine and Dredging Co Ltd v A Ogden & Sons (Excavations) Ltd* [1978] QB 574, [1978] 2 All ER 1134. But see *Independent Broadcasting Authority v EMI Ltd and BICC Ltd* (1980) 14 BLR 1.

6.26 This 'fiction of fraud' is one of the factors in the uncertainty over the measure of damages under section 2(1). It is far from clear whether the damages are tortious, and also whether they are the same as those in deceit, or based on the measure appropriate in negligence actions, or whether they are contractual. This matter is discussed in detail in the Introduction.[1]

1 See paras 1.48–1.50, above.

6.27 We have already canvassed the possibility that replies to pre-contract inquiries might be deemed to constitute collateral warranties, and indicated the likelihood of a court being disinclined so to deem. Could not such replies be regarded as representations which, if erroneous, could found liability in damages to a purchaser? Prima facie this would appear to be so, but in practice it is debateable. In *Gilchester Properties Ltd v Gomm*[1] the amount of rents payable by tenants of certain leasehold premises was innocently misrepresented to the plaintiff, who proposed to purchase the premises. Romer J stated:[2] 'I am not entirely satisfied that the replies to the preliminary enquiries did constitute sufficiently definite statements of fact to amount to a representation', primarily because the statements were qualified by the phrase 'so far as the vendor knows'. Such a phrase is likely to be used to qualify all replies made by solicitors. Romer J did go on to say:[3] 'I am prepared, however, to assume that the replies were sufficiently definite and that the purchasers acted on the faith of the statements contained in those replies', but as damages could not be awarded for an innocent misrepresentation, the form of relief claimed (specific performance and an abatement of £550 in the purchase price) was inapppropriate. It is not clear whether, if rescission had been sought, the judge would have been as prepared to assume that the statements made were material inducements, so the question must to a certain extent remain open. Now, of course, damages under the Misrepresentation Act could theoretically be awarded in such a case, but it is suggested that phrases such as 'so far as the vendor knows' at least afford the court the opportunity to find on the one hand that the statement made is insufficiently definite, and on the other hand that the necessary reliance by the purchaser is thereby precluded. However, it may be argued that a reply to a pre-contract inquiry is the kind of statement which involves the necessary implication that the maker of the statement knows facts which justify his opinion, and words such as 'so far as the vendor knows' are insufficient to avoid responsibility for such a statement.[4]

1 [1948] 1 All ER 493. The claim was by the purchaser against the vendor for specific performance and an abatement of the purchase price.
2 Ibid at 495.
3 Ibid.
4 See *Smith v Land and House Property Corpn* (1884) 28 ChD 7; *Brown v Raphael* [1958] Ch 636, [1958] 2 All ER 79; and the analysis of this point by Adams (1970) 67 LS Gaz 183.

6.28 If the representee is unable to establish that the representor was fraudulent or negligent, he is not entitled to damages, merely to rescission of the contract and an indemnity.[1] However, section 2(2) of the Misrepresentation Act empowers the court to award damages in lieu of rescission if it considers it equitable to do so, having regard to the nature of the misrepresentation and the position of both of the parties.[2] Although there is as yet no case law on this, it seems likely that the discretion will only be exercised in cases where the misrepresentation is fairly unimportant, though this, as well as the measure of damages under the subsection, remains speculative.[3] Certainly it seems likely that if the effect of allowing rescission would involve the need to unscramble a number of transactions, as would be the case where the perpetrator of the misrepresentation had himself bought a property with the proceeds of his sale, and there was a chain of transactions beyond him in one direction and beyond the purchaser in the other, the case for granting damages in lieu would usually be a strong one.

1 See para 6.29, below, para 1.51, above.
2 The actual wording of s. 2(2) is: 'Where a person has entered into a contract after a misrepresentation has been made to him otherwise than fraudulently, and he would be entitled, by reason of the misrepresentation to rescind the contract, then, if it is claimed in any proceedings arising out of the contract, that the contract ought to be or has been rescinded, the court or arbitrator may declare the contract subsisting and award damages in lieu of rescission, if of opinion that it would be equitable to do so, having regard to the nature of the misrepresentation and the loss that would be caused by it if the contract were upheld, as well as to the loss that rescission would cause to the other party.'
3 See para 1.52, above.

6.29 The basic remedy for misrepresentation is rescission of the contract.[1] In addition, where rescission is claimed, the representee is entitled to an indemnity in respect of liabilities necessarily incurred under the contract.[2] The effect of rescission is to set the contract aside for all purposes, so as to effect a *restitutio in integrum*. Misrepresentation renders the ensuing contract voidable rather than void, so the representee may elect to keep the contract alive. However, if the contract is not avoided, a third party can acquire rights in its subject matter and the right to rescind is lost. The right to rescind may also be lost if the subject matter of the contract has been so changed by the representee that he can no longer restore what he obtained under the contract, and also if he has affirmed the contract after discovering the untruth of the misrepresentation. Thus if a purchaser discovers that a representation concerning the state of the property is untrue, affirmation, whether express or by conduct, will bar his right to rescind, should he later wish to exercise it. Also, it appears that lapse of time, even without evidence of affirmation, will bar the right to rescind for misrepresentation.[3] Also, as we have seen, the court may, under section 2(2) of the Misrepresentation Act, decide to award damages in lieu of rescission, in appropriate circumstances, though it is not clear whether this can be done where the right to rescind has been lost. Before the Misrepresentation Act, the rule in *Angel v Jay*[4] precluded the right to rescind for an innocent misrepresentation for a purchaser after conveyance: he could only rescind before completion. However, under section 1(b) of the Act, performance of the contract no longer prevents rescission for innocent misrepresentation. If the misrepresentation has been reproduced as a term of the contract, section 1(a) of the Act provides that the contract may nevertheless be rescinded for misrepresentation. Where the misrepresentation is fraudulent, damages in the tort of deceit may be awarded, as well as rescission of the contract. If the misrepresentation is negligent, there is nothing in section 2(1) of the Misrepresentation Act to prevent rescission as well as the damages available under the subsection, though this is subject to the exercise of the court's discretion under section 2(2) to award damages in lieu of rescission in respect of any misrepresentation other than a fraudulent one.

1 See Treitel *The Law of Contract* (5th edn) pp. 274–291.
2 See *Whittington v Seale-Hayne* (1900) 82 LT 49, 16 TLR 181.
3 See *Leaf v International Galleries* [1950] 2 KB 86, [1950] 1 All ER 693.
4 [1911] 1 KB 666.

Exclusion of liability

6.30 In *Hedley Byrne v Heller*[1] the defendants were able to avoid liability by giving their advice 'without responsibility'. The Unfair Contract Terms Act 1977, which came into force on 1 February 1978, must be seen as at least potentially controlling attempts in the future to make such disclaimers. Section 2(2) of the Act provides that a person cannot by means of a contract term or notice exclude or restrict his liability for loss or damage (other than personal injury, in relation to which no exclusion of liability is permitted, by section 2(1) of the Act) caused by negligence, unless this term or notice satisfies the requirement of reasonableness laid down in section 11. However, this control applies only to 'business liability' and, though 'business' is not fully defined in the Act, it is hardly appropriate to describe the typical private sale of premises as involving a business activity of the vendor, but where a builder/vendor or a developer is involved the position will of course be different. Section 1(3) provides that 'business liability' is liability for breach of obligations or duties arising—

(a) from things done or to be done by a person in the course of a business (whether his own business or another's); or
(b) from the occupation of premises used for business purposes of the occupier.

Where the vendor is acting in the course of a business, for example if he is a builder/vendor, then prima facie the test of reasonableness established in section 11 will be applied to his disclaimer.[2] However, it may be possible for the vendor to argue that making a statement 'without responsibility' constitutes, given the voluntary nature of a *Hedley Byrne v Heller* statement, a denial that a duty is being undertaken at all. Certainly it is provided in section 13 of the Act that section 2 also prevents 'excluding or restricting liability by reference to terms and notices which exclude or restrict the relevant obligation or duty', but this arguably presupposes that there already exists a liability to be excluded, whereas our vendor would claim that his words prevented this voluntary duty from ever arising. As against this, it may be argued that 'without responsibility' admits potential liability: that the only type of formula to prevent liability from ever arising is something like that used in *Overbrooke Estates Ltd v Glencombe Properties Ltd*[3] where conditions of sale at an auction provided that the vendors did not make representations, and the auctioneers had no authority to make representations. This distinction between excluding liability and preventing liability from ever arising is a fine one, which will be examined in more detail in the discussion below of purported exclusions of liability under the Misrepresentation Act 1967. In conclusion though it should be emphasised that the Unfair Contract Terms Act will not apply to private vendors, as regards negligence liability, and thus the private vendor who might otherwise be liable under *Hedley Byrne v Heller* for a negligent misstatement will, subject to the common law rules governing the interpretation of exclusion clauses,[4] be able to avoid liability by means of an appropriate disclaimer.

1 [1964] AC 465, [1963] 2 All ER 575.
2 Though see Sch 1, para 1(b) if the exclusion is contained in the contract of sale.
3 [1974] 3 All ER 511, [1974] 1 WLR 1335. See para 6.32, below.
4 See paras 1.53–1.55, above.

6.31 Section 3 of the Misrepresentation Act, as amended by section 8 of the Unfair Contract Terms Act 1977, provides as follows:

If a contract contains a term which would exclude or restrict
(a) any liability to which a party to a contract may be subject by reason of any misrepresentation made by him before the contract was made; or
(b) any remedy available to another party to the contract by reason of such a misrepresentation,
that term shall be of no effect except in so far as it satisfies the requirement of reasonableness as stated in section 11(1) of the Unfair Contract Terms Act 1977; and it is for those claiming that the term satisfies that requirement to show that it does.[1]

1 For a general analysis of the section, see Treitel *The Law of Contract* (5th edn) pp. 291–294.

6.32 This, unlike disclaimers of *Hedley Byrne v Heller* liability, applies to both business and private liability, so that a private vendor, whether through his solicitor/agent or not, may find his purported exclusions or restrictions of liability controlled by the court. The requirement of reasonableness in section 11(1) of the Unfair Contract Terms Act is: 'that the term shall have been a fair and reasonable one to be included having regard to the circumstances which were, or

215

ought reasonably to have been, known to or in the contemplation of the parties when the contract was made'. As yet there has been no reported case under these provisions, and thus there is little indication of how the the courts will interpret the requirement of reasonableness.[1] It does appear however that in certain circumstances it will be possible to prevent liability from arising rather than excluding or restricting liability that has arisen by means of an appropriate term, as in *Overbrooke Estates Ltd v Glencombe Properties Ltd.*[2] In this case, as we have seen, conditions of sale of land at an auction provided that no representations were made by the vendors and the auctioneers who were their agents had no authority to make representations. This was regarded by the court as a public limitation of the otherwise ostensible authority of the agent rather than an exclusion or restriction of liability.

1 However, the decision in *Howard Marine and Dredging Co Ltd v A Ogden & Sons (Excavations) Ltd* [1978] QB 574, [1978] 2 All ER 1134 contains discussion of the old s. 3 in relation to a purported exemption clause. Each case will, though, depend very much upon its particular facts.
2 [1974] 3 All ER 511, [1974] 1 WLR 1335. Though decided under the old s. 3, the decision is unaffected by the changes in the section. See also *Collins v Howell-Jones* (1980) 259 Estates Gazette 331.

6.33 In *Cremdean Properties Ltd v Nash*[1] the Court of Appeal considered *Overbrooke Estates Ltd v Glencombe Properties Ltd* in interlocutory proceedings on a preliminary issue of whether a disclaimer was effective to exclude liability for misrepresentation. The case concerned an alleged misrepresentation concerning the amount of lettable office space which could be accommodated in the planning permission with which the property in question was sold. A disclaimer was contained in a footnote to the special conditions of sale. It stated, '(a) these particulars are prepared for the convenience of an intending purchaser or tenant and although they are believed to be correct their accuracy is not guaranteed and any error, omission or misdescription shall not annul the sale or be grounds on which compensation may be claimed and neither do they constitute any part of an offer of a contract; (b) Any intending purchaser or tenant must satisfy himself by inspection or otherwise as to the correctness of each of the statements contained in these particulars.' Bridge LJ agreed with the reasoning in the *Overbrooke Estates Ltd v Glencombe Properties Ltd* case[2] and went on to say:[3]

> It is one thing to say that section 3 does not inhibit a principal from publicly giving notice limiting the ostensible authority of his agents; it is quite another thing to say that a principal can circumvent the plainly intended effect of section 3 by a clause excluding his own liability for a representation which he has undoubtedly made.

The learned judge did not accept the defendant's arguments that the footnote was effective to nullify any representation in the document altogether and that it was effective to bring about a situation in law as if no representation had ever been made. Looking more broadly at the problem of distinguishing between clauses excluding liability and clauses preventing liability from arising, he said:[4]

> Supposing the vendor included a clause which the purchaser was required to, and did agree to in some such terms as 'notwithstanding any statement of fact included in these particulars the vendor shall be conclusively deemed to have made no representation within the meaning of the Misrepresentation Act 1967'. I should have thought that that was only a form of words the intended and actual effect of which was to exclude or restrict liability, and I should not have thought that the courts would have

been ready to allow such ingenuity in forms of language to defeat the plain purpose at which section 3 is aimed.

1 (1977) 244 Estates Gazette 547. See also *F and H Entertainments Ltd v Leisure Enterprises Ltd* (1976) 120 Sol Jo 331.
2 (1977) 244 Estates Gazette 547 at 549.
3 Ibid at 551.
4 Ibid. See also Treitel *The Law of Contract* (5th edn) p. 172.

6.34 Both the most commonly used sets of Conditions of Sale contain clauses which require examination in connection with section 3 of the Misrepresentation Act (as amended by section 3 of the Unfair Contract Terms Act).[1] Condition 17 of the National Conditions of Sale[2] provides:

> (1) . . . no error, misstatement or omission in any preliminary answer concerning the property, or in the sale plan or the Special Conditions, shall annul the sale, nor (save where the error, misstatement or omission is in a written answer and relates to a matter materially affecting the description or value of the property) shall any damages be payable, or compensation allowed by either party, in respect thereof.

In subsection 2 it is provided:

> In this condition a 'preliminary answer' means and includes any statement made by or on behalf of the vendor to the purchaser or his agents or advisers, whether in answer to formal preliminary enquiries or otherwise, before the purchaser entered into the contract.

Prima facie this falls foul of section 3, though it is worth noticing in passing that the purported exclusion may in any event not apply to information which is volunteered by the vendor or his agent.[3]

1 As regards liability under *Hedley Byrne v Heller*, insofar as the Conditions of Sale purports to exclude such liability, again, as we have seen, the Unfair Contract Terms Act does not control a purported exclusion by a private vendor; s. 2(2) requires a vendor in the course of a business to satisfy the requirement of reasonableness laid down in s.11(3) of the Act. See para 6.31, above.
2 19th edn, 1976.
3 This, it is suggested, will depend upon whether 'or otherwise' can be said to cover information that is volunteered.

6.35 Condition 7 of the Law Society's General Conditions of Sale[1] provides:

> (1) No error, omission or misstatement made in the course of the negotiations leading to the contract shall annul the sale or entitle the purchaser to be discharged from the purchase.
> (2) Any such error, omission, or misstatement shown to be material shall entitle the purchaser or the vendor, as the case may be, to proper compensation, provided that the purchaser shall not in any event be entitled to compensation for matters falling within conditions 5(2) or 6(3).
> (3) No immaterial error, omission or misstatement (including a mistake in any plan furnished for identification only) shall entitle either party to compensation.
> (4) Sub-condition (1) shall not apply where compensation for any error, omission or misstatement shown to be material cannot be assessed nor enable either party to compel the other to accept or convey property differing substantially (in quality, tenure or otherwise) from the property agreed to be sold if the other party would be prejudiced by the difference.
> (5) The purchaser acknowledges that in making the contract he has not relied on any statement made to him save one made or confirmed in writing.

1 1980 edn.

6.36 This is potentially broader, as it does not purport to restrict the disclaimer to errors, misstatements or omissions contained in preliminary answers or in the sale plan or Special Conditions but applies to all statements made in the pre-contract negotiations, or sale plan or Special Conditions. Again, though it is prima facie in conflict with section 3, it remains a matter of speculation whether such conditions of sale satisfy the requirement of reasonableness as stated in section 11(1) of the Unfair Contract Terms Act 1977. The subsection makes it clear that the knowledge or contemplation of the parties will be an important factor in determining whether or not the disclaimer is reasonable, with the burden of establishing sufficient reasonableness resting on the representor. The representor/vendor may argue, in the words of Professor Farrand,[1] 'could the purchaser's solicitor conceivably contend that he had approved a contract of sale on behalf of his client containing an unfair or unreasonable condition?' Though the approval by the purchaser's solicitor of a condition of sale is not conclusive proof of the condition's reasonableness, it is suggested that this argument is prima facie likely to commend itself to a court. If, though, there exists some inequality of bargaining power, for example, if there are few properties on the market and the purchaser is under pressure to buy, it might not be unreasonable for the purchaser's solicitor to approve a potentially onerous condition, and therefore be less open to the vendor to argue that acceptance of the condition was evidence of its reasonableness. If the vendor has represented that, for example, the property is free of dry rot, then the reasonableness of the disclaimer is likely to turn on whether he knew or could reasonably have contemplated that dry rot was present, though if in doubt, the court is likely to have recourse to the overriding principle of *caveat emptor*.

1 [1978] Conv 177. How (if at all) would it affect the reasonableness of the clause if the vendor's solicitor refused a request to delete it?

6.37 Condition 7(5) of the Law Society's conditions has met with some criticism.[1] It would appear to be fairly close to the type of clause castigated by Bridge LJ in *Cremdean Properties Ltd v Nash*[2] and probably prima facie falls foul of the Unfair Contract Terms Act, unless it can be said to satisfy the requirement of reasonableness. As is stated by Wilkinson:[3]

> The clause seems to put a duty on the purchaser's solicitor to find out from his client what representations have been made to him and either to warn his client not to rely on them or to insist that the vendor puts them into writing. If the solicitor does not do this and the clause bars the purchaser's action against the vendor for misrepresentation the purchaser could then turn to his own solicitor for damages. A careful purchaser's solicitor will delete the clause and an open vendor would let him.[4]

It must at least be arguable that acceptance by a purchaser's solicitor of any condition which prevents the purchaser from suing for misrepresentation, and which condition is later held to be reasonable by the court, leaves the solicitor open to a potential negligence action, unless the solicitor has clearly warned the client of, and the client has accepted, the risk of this.

1 Wilkinson [1980] Conv 404 at 406–407; Farrand [1981] Conv 4–5 ('the awful exclusion clause').
2 (1977) 244 Estates Gazette 547 at 551. See para 6.33, above.
3 [1980] Conv 404 at 406–407.
4 It must at least be an open question whether the solicitor of the open vendor would allow the deletion of the clause, however.

6.38 As we have seen,[1] the replies to pre-contract enquiries constitute a potential source of misrepresentations. The most recent version of the standard form of enquiries published by Oyez Publishing Ltd contains the following disclaimer at the head of the space for replies: 'These replies are given on behalf of the proposed Vendor and without responsibility on the part of his solicitors, their partners or employees. They are believed to be correct but the accuracy is not guaranteed and they do not obviate the need to make appropriate searches, enquiries and inspections.'[2] Insofar as replies to pre-contract enquiries can constitute negligent misstatements under *Hedley Byrne v Heller*, the disclaimer will be subject to section 2 of the Unfair Contract Terms Act 1977 which, as we have seen, does not apply to a private vendor, but which requires a vendor where the sale is in the course of a business to satisfy the requirement of reasonableness laid down in section 11 of the Act. As the disclaimer is a non-contractual notice, it falls under section 11(3), which requires 'that it should be fair and reasonable to allow reliance on it, having regard to all the circumstances obtaining when the liability arose or (but for the notice) would have arisen'. Much will depend upon the circumstances of the case, but it is suggested that prima facie the disclaimer, if effective to exclude the vendor's liability, is reasonable except insofar as it purports to exclude liability for statements about matters which the purchaser cannot usually find out from other sources.[3] However it is strongly arguable that the disclaimer is not appropriate to exclude the vendor's liability for misrepresentation.[4] Its wording seems rather to be geared towards protection of the vendor's solicitor vis-à-vis the purchaser.

1 See para 6.27, above.
2 See para 4.106, above.
3 See (1980) 124 Sol Jo 581.
4 Ibid.

6.39 If it is argued that the replies constitute negligent misrepresentation under section 2(1) of the Misrepresentation Act 1967, it should be noted that section 3 of the Unfair Contract Terms Act, which applies to terms in contracts which purport to exclude or restrict liability for misrepresentation, will be inapplicable, for the replies are not terms in a contract. Thus attempts by private and business vendors to exclude section 2(1) liability by means of a disclaimer in replies to pre-contract enquiries will fall altogether outside statutory and common law controls.

Vendor's liability in negligence

6.40 Here we shall consider instances where the vendor is, or arguably may be, liable in negligence (other than for misrepresentation or misstatement) for defects in the premises which he owns. Although the liability of the landlord will be considered separately[1] the relationship of landlord and tenant and that of vendor and purchaser were for many years assumed to be on a similar footing, and consequently authorities on the liability of a landlord were considered equally applicable to a vendor. Thus, in *Bottomley v Bannister*[2] an action under the Fatal Accidents Act 1846 was brought by the administrator of a couple who were poisoned by carbon monoxide gas in a house which they had agreed to purchase from the defendants, and which they were occupying as tenants at will. The Court of Appeal, relying on the authority of three cases concerned with the liability of a landlord,[3] assumed that it was, in the words of Scrutton LJ,[4] 'at present well established English Law that, in the absence of express contract, a landlord of an unfurnished house is not liable to his tenant, or a vendor of real estate to his purchaser, for defects in the house or land rendering it dangerous or unfit for occupation, even if he has constructed the defects himself or is aware of their existence'. It was held in *Otto v Bolton and Norris*[5] that this immunity had survived *Donoghue v Stevenson*.[6] Thus the builder of a new house was held not to be liable for injury caused to the purchaser's mother by the collapse of a ceiling which he had carelessly put up. On this the Law Commission said:[7]

> once the duty of care is accepted as being applicable to land as well as to chattels, the conclusion in *Otto v Bolton and Norris* does not seem to follow inescapably from the propositions expounded in *Robbins v Jones* and *Cavalier v Pope* . . . if the point were taken [to the House of Lords] it could be argued with some chance of success that the decision in *Otto v Bolton and Norris* was inconsistent with the true scope of the principles in *Donoghue v Stevenson* as they are now understood.[8]

How much truer this may be in the light of the developments of the subsequent decade will be discussed below.

1 See ch 7, below.
2 [1932] 1 KB 458.
3 *Robbins v Jones* (1863) 15 CBNS 221; *Lane v Cox* [1897] 1 QB 415; *Cavalier v Pope* [1906] AC 428.
4 *Bottomley v Bannister* [1932] 1 KB 458 at 468.
5 [1936] 2 KB 46, [1936] 1 All ER 960.
6 [1932] AC 562.
7 Law Com No 40, para 4.
8 See also the views of Glanville Williams (1941) 5 MLR 194 at 202 where he argues that there is nothing in the facts of *Cavalier v Pope*, *Robbins v Jones* or *Lane v Cox* to prevent the imposition of liability upon a vendor for failing to warn the purchaser of dangerous latent defects which he knows are present in the premises.

6.41 In their report the Law Commission drew a distinction between dangerous defects which the vendor created, and those which he did not create. In the case of the former the operation of the existing case law was regarded as indefensible.

> If, for example, a prospective purchaser is injured as a result of negligent work while he is inspecting a newly-built house he can sue the owner/builder; but if he is injured as a result of the same undetectable defect after he has bought the premises he will have no right of action. Again, vis-à-vis the builder, the rights of a customer who suffers injury in a newly-built shop, through a structural defect, will depend on whether the builder has sold or let the premises or still retains them.[1]

Consequently the Law Commission recommended that the vendor's immunity from liability for the consequences of his own negligent acts should be removed by a statutory provision to that effect, and this was done by section 3 of the Defective Premises Act 1972, which in effect provides that a vendor's duty of care in respect of work done on land is not abated by its subsequent disposal.[2]

1 Para 45.
2 S. 3(1) of the Act provides: 'Where work of construction, repair, maintenance or demolition or any other work is done on or in relation to premises, any duty of care owed because of the doing of the work to persons who might reasonably be expected to be affected by defects in the state of the premises created by the doing of the work shall not be abated by the subsequent disposal of the premises by the person who owed the duty.'

6.42 In their recommendations concerning liability of the vendor for dangerous defects which he did not create, the Law Commission drew a distinction between defects actually known to the vendor and those which are not. It was not considered necessary to impose liability on the vendor for defects not known, even if they were ascertainable by reasonable inspection. The vendor/purchaser relationship was not one in which the former undertook liability to the latter for such defects (*caveat emptor* was therefore regarded as of similar importance here to the question of a proposed statutory warranty in private sales discussed above).[1] The cost of the transfer of property would be likely to increase, as each side would consider it necessary to have the property surveyed. This factor of increased cost was an important factor militating against the imposition of liability on the vendor for unknown defects not due to his work, to third parties, coupled with the argument that the third party would normally have a remedy against the transferee or occupier.

1 See para 6.2, above.

6.43 However, the Law Commission recommended the imposition of liability on a vendor who knew of defects, not only to the purchaser but also to all persons who might reasonably be contemplated as likely to be endangered by them. It was suggested that this duty could be discharged by the vendor by showing that the purchaser had sufficient information concerning the defects to enable him to take precautions for his own safety and to discharge his duty of care as an occupier to others. For a warning to be adequate, it would have to be sufficiently specific to satisfy those purposes. Clause 3 of the Draft Defective Premises Bill attached to the Law Commission Report incorporated these recommendations. However, on account of the controversy it provoked, and with a view to securing the enactment of the Commission's other proposals,[1] no equivalent clause was included in the Bill which later became the Defective Premises Act 1972.

1 830 H of C Official Report (5th series) col 1823.

6.44 In this context it is interesting to note the decision of the Ontario Supreme Court in *Lock and Lock v Stibor*.[1] Workmen who were employed and supervised by the original owner and the builder of a house installed a kitchen cabinet in a house in a negligent manner. Following the purchase of the house by the first defendants, they were visited by the plaintiff, who sustained injuries when the cabinet fell off the wall and hit her. At the beginning of the trial the plaintiff's counsel agreed that the action could not succeed against the first defendants and the action proceeded against the vendor and the builder. The court applied *Donoghue v Stevenson*, distinguished *Otto v Bolton and Norris* and *Bottomley v Bannister* and agreed[2] with Glanville Williams that in a case where 'there are defects in the premises of which the [vendor] actually knows, and if he also knows that they are not likely to be discovered by the [purchaser] ... it is consistent with the general principles of the law of negligence to impose upon the [vendor] the duty to communicate the defects to the [purchaser]'.[3] The builder and the vendor, it was said, should have known of the defect due to the gross negligence of their employees, and that it was unlikely to be discovered, and should have brought it to the purchaser's attention. The defendants through their employees could or should have known that visitors would come to the house and go into the kitchen, and they owed a duty to such visitors not to expose them to such danger.

1 (1962) 34 DLR (2d) 704.
2 Ibid at 709.
3 (1941) 5 MLR 194 at 200.

6.45 The Canadian court's decision goes further than the recommendation of the Law Commission, in imposing liability where the vendor should have been aware of the defect rather than restricting liability to cases where the vendor was actually aware of the defect's existence. The Law Commission was of the view[1] that by limiting the duty to those defects of whose existence he is aware, the vendor would not be subjected to a heavy burden of surveying costs, and certainly a prudent vendor who is faced with potential liability for defects of which he should have been aware would be advised to employ a surveyor. On the other hand, proof of actual knowledge is likely to be very difficult to establish. Any imposition of liability for negligence on a vendor, however, represents such a striking inroad into *caveat emptor* that the Law Commission recommendation is the more likely to commend itself to Parliament or a court that felt free to depart from previous authority. As we have noted,[2] it has been suggested that there is nothing in the earlier case law to prevent the imposition of liability along the lines suggested by the Law Commission, on the basis that in none of those cases was there a finding that the lessor was aware of the defect at the time of the letting, and that, assuming that the purpose of such liability would be to protect the purchaser from latent defects, in two of the cases[3] it was apparent that the lessee was aware of the defect before the injury was incurred, and in the other[4] there was no finding as to whether the defect was latent or had been discovered by the lessee or the plaintiff prior to the injury.

1 Law Com No 40, para 51.
2 See para 6.40, n. 8, above.
3 *Robbins v Jones* (1863) 15 CBNS 221; and *Cavalier v Pope* [1906] AC 428.
4 *Lane v Cox* [1897] 1 QB 415.

6.46 The Defective Premises Act 1972, based upon recommendations of the Law Commission, came into force on 1 January 1974. By that time an expansion of the common law concerning liability for defective premises had commenced, to the extent that, in the light of the further developments of the ensuing years, the factors discussed in the preceding paragraph have assumed an increasing relevance.[1] The Court of Appeal in *Dutton v Bognor Regis UDC*[2] stated (obiter) that the principle of *Donoghue v Stevenson* applied not only to chattels but to real property as well, and consequently that the builder/vendor immunity as propounded in, for example, *Bottomley v Bannister* could no longer stand. This view was confirmed unanimously, by the House of Lords in *Anns v London Borough of Merton*.[3] Again this was obiter, but the unanimity of views, together with the decision of the Court of Appeal the following year in *Batty v Metropolitan Property Realisations Ltd*,[4] makes it quite clear that this now represents the law. Quite apart from the Defective Premises Act 1972, therefore, it is clear that the vendor is liable in tort for negligent work on the premises of which he disposes,[5] and will owe a duty in respect of defects caused by his careless work to all persons likely to be affected by the defects, e g purchaser, visitors. This is illustrated by the case of *Hone v Benson*.[6] The case was argued on a preliminary point of law and on the assumed facts that the defendants built a restaurant on their own land and employed a third party, who was their servant and/or worked to the defendants' design, to install a hot-water and central-heating system. Shortly after the system was installed the defendants sold the property to the plaintiffs, and not long thereafter the system went wrong and caused physical damage and financial loss, for which the plaintiffs claimed damages. Judge Edgar Fay QC, sitting as a deputy judge of the Queen's Bench Division, accepted the authority of the dicta in *Dutton v Bognor Regis UDC* and *Anns v London Borough of Merton* and found that where a builder has done building work negligently, he is liable to persons who suffer injury in consequence. The learned judge was not prepared to make a distinction between the duty owed by a professional builder and that owed by an amateur 'do-it-yourself' enthusiast such as the vendor in this case.

> A person who takes on skilled work holds himself out to be judged by the standard of skill of those able and qualified to do such work. I can see no reason in law or justice – indeed, I can see reasons for the contrary – why those who, it may be unskilfully, do do-it-yourself building work should[7] be held just as liable as a professional builder.[8]

1 See the valuable article by Newsome in [1980] Conv 287 entitled 'Pre-Contractual Disclosure of Dangerous Defects'.
2 [1972] 1 QB 373, [1972] 1 All ER 472.
3 [1978] AC 728, [1977] 2 All ER 492.
4 [1978] QB 554, [1978] 2 All ER 445.
5 And not only for negligent work. See, for example, the illustration provided by Street [1979] Conv 241 at 247 of a vendor who plants a tree near his house, and the tree's roots later cause subsidence and damage. If a court found that the vendor should have foreseen the act of damage by subsidence as a result of planting the tree, he would be liable to the purchaser.
6 (1978) 248 Estates Gazette 1013, and see (1978) 248 Estates Gazette 507. See para 3.99, above.
7 The word 'not' has clearly been omitted from the report at this point.
8 (1978) 248 Estates Gazette 1013 at 1014.

6.47 The defendants argued that the opportunity that a purchaser had to survey the property operated to break the chain of causation. This was rejected, as the learned judge took to be proved the allegation that it was within the defendants' contemplation that in the circumstances of the case (the fact that the work had been done so recently) the purchaser was unlikely to have a survey (the fact that the work had been done so recently). The judge was not deterred by the collision between the development of the law of negligence and the ancient principle of *caveat emptor*:

> the principles laid down in the Court of Appeal and the House of Lords which I follow . . . are said, in the judgment and opinions which I have cited, to apply to the case of the vendor and purchaser where the vendor is a builder and it seems to me that no valid distinction or no distinction of principle can be drawn between the case of the vendor who is a professional builder, or for that matter a professional estate developer, and a vendor who is a private individual who initially built for his own occupation.[1]

1 (1978) 248 Estates Gazette 1013 at 1014–1015.

6.48 A final point for consideration was whether Condition 4(2)(a) of the Law Society's General Conditions of Sale[1] afforded a defence. This read: 'The purchaser shall buy with full notice of the actual state and condition of the property and shall take it as it stands save where it is to be constructed or converted by the vendor.' Could this exempt the defendants from liability for negligence? The learned judge held that it could not. It was primarily a conveyancing condition whose purpose was to prevent a purchaser, where defects were discovered between contract and conveyance, from calling off the sale or asking for an abatement in price. Whether or not such a clause could survive the date of conveyance and operate as an exemption clause did not require to be answered in this case, because the decision of the House of Lords in *Smith v South Wales Switchgear Co Ltd*[2] made it clear that in order to disclaim liability for negligence, a contractual term must set this out in clear words referring expressly to negligence, and this had not been done in the instant case.[3]

1 1970 edn.
2 [1978] 1 All ER 18, [1978] 1 WLR 165.
3 On the question of exemption of negligence liability of vendors generally, see paras 6.30 ff, above.

6.49   Could liability in a case with facts similar to *Hone v Benson* also be imposed on the vendor under section 1 of the Defective Premises Act 1972? This section imposes a duty on a person who takes on work for or in connection with the provision of a dwelling to see that the work is done in a workmanlike manner, with proper materials and so that the dwelling will be fit for habitation. In *Alexander v Mercouris*[1] where a preliminary issue was tried in order to establish whether section 1 of the Act applied to an agreement dated 20 November 1972 (it was held that it did not, as the Act, which did not come into force until 1 January 1974, did not have a retrospective effect). Buckley LJ said:[2] '[the Act] is intended to apply not only to cases in which a contractual obligation to work exists, but also . . . to cases in which the work is done voluntarily without expectation of gain and, perhaps most importantly, to cases in which a building owner does the work himself'. Thus when a vendor has done work on a house which is not protected by an NHBC certificate,[3] he is potentially liable for such work if it fails to come up to the standard required by section 1. This is a stricter duty than the duty of care in negligence, and section 6(3) of the Act provides that its terms cannot be excluded. The limitation period runs for six years from the date of completion of the work. The duty will not be imposed upon the handyman who constructs cupboards or puts up shelves in his house which was constructed by someone else, for this is not work in conection with the provision of a dwelling. The householder who constructs an extension to his house would not, it is suggested,[4] fall within the section, unless the extension constituted a separate dwelling, for example a 'granny flat', rather than simply an extra room, for building on an extra room is not 'provision of a dwelling'; building a flat clearly is.

1   [1979] 3 All ER 305, [1979] 1 WLR 1270.
2   Ibid at 308 and 1273.
3   See Defective Premises Act 1972, s. 2.
4   See Barnsley *Conveyancing Law and Practice* p. 144.

6.50   The next question requiring consideration is whether the law has developed to the extent that a vendor can be said to be under a duty to disclose the existence of defects of which he is aware, but which he did not cause. A case which must briefly be considered here is that of *Batty v Metropolitan Property Realisations Ltd*.[1] A firm of builders sold land to a development company which 'sold' (leases of 999 years were granted) the houses constructed by the builders on the land, then the developers reconveyed the reversions to the builders. Representatives of the builders and the developers had thoroughly inspected the site, but had failed to realise that the hillside on which the plaintiff's house was built was unstable. Three years later a landslip occurred, which made it inevitable that within the next decade the house would be in ruins, as its foundations would slide down the hill. The developers were held liable to the plaintiffs in contract for breach of an express warranty which was couched in the following terms: 'The vendor hereby warrants that the dwelling has been built or agrees that it will be built: (1) in an efficient and workmanlike manner and of proper materials and so as to be fit for habitation . . .'. In addition they were held liable in negligence. Megaw LJ said:[2]

> I have no doubt that it was the duty of [the developers], in the circumstances of this case, including the fact of the joint responsibility which they undertook in arranging for the erection of this house on this site, apart altogether from the contractual warranty, to examine with reasonable care the land, which in this case would include adjoining land, in order to see whether the site was one on which a house fit for

habitation could safely be built. It was a duty owed to prospective buyers of the house. How wide or deep the examination had to be, to comply with the duty, would depend on the facts of the particular case, including the existence and nature of any symptoms which might give cause for suspecting the possibility of instability.

Though this case has no express significance for the private vendor, the implications for the vendor who is a developer are considerable, and are considered in detail elsewhere.[3]

1 [1978] QB 554, [1978] 2 All ER 445.
2 Ibid at 567 and 451.
3 See paras 3.92 ff, above.

6.51 The attitude of the courts towards liability for defective premises encapsulated in the decisions in *Dutton v Bognor Regis UDC*, *Anns v London Borough of Merton* and *Batty v Metropolitan Realisations Ltd* represents perhaps the best hope of the purchaser who seeks to impose liability for damage on a vendor who was aware of the defect but did not cause it. Before finally assessing the chances of such a purchaser's success, several potential difficulties and uncertainties attaching to this notional liability must be examined.

6.52 Should such liability be imposed only in cases where the vendor is aware of the defect itself or should it be extended to cover defects of whose manifestation he is aware? If, for example, a vendor discovers cracks in a wall and, assuming they are only minor settlement cracks, fills them and paints or wallpapers over them, is he to be liable to the purchaser, if it later transpires that the cracks are a manifestation of structural defects in the house, or should his liability be restricted to cases where he is aware that the cracks indicate such structural defects? This is reminiscent of the discussion above[1] on the question whether a vendor should be liable only for those defects of which he is aware, or for those of which he should have been aware. Arguably the prudent purchaser, having employed a surveyor, will discover through the surveyor the existence of the defects in either case. Since the reasoning behind imposing liability on the vendor in only the former rather than also the latter circumstance is that this does not increase the cost to the vendor of the sale transaction, as, if he is aware of the defect, he does not need a surveyor to confirm it, it should only be in those cases where he is aware of the defect itself, e g rotten floorboards, structural defects, that liability should be imposed, since in order to confirm whether, for example, a crack is a cosmetic or a structural defect, he would need a surveyor to advise him.

1 See paras 6.42 ff, above.

6.53 A potential difficulty with a change in the law along the lines of the Law Commission's recommendations would be that, since the duty imposed in clause 3 of the Draft Bill was to take reasonable care to see that those persons to whom the duty was owed were reasonably safe from personal injury or damage to property caused by any of the known defects, the vendor could discharge the duty without any cost to himself in that he could 'simply warn the purchaser of the rot or the mineshaft under the kitchen floor as the latter arrived to take up residence after completion of his purchase'.[1] The Law Commission recognised that this might lead to a sense of grievance on the part of the purchaser, but felt that it was inevitable (and in any case would only happen rarely if the purchaser had employed a surveyor).[2] However, it has been argued[3] that, in the light of the developments in the liability of builders and local authorities over the past few years, the duty need not be so limited. Since, as a result of *Dutton v Bognor Regis UDC, Anns v London Borough of Merton* and *Batty v Metropolitan Realisations Ltd*, the cause of the action against, for example, a builder who has been negligent, arises when the state of the premises represents a present or imminent danger to the health or safety of persons occupying those premises, and the damages awardable are designed to restore the premises to a state where they no longer present such a danger, then arguably a similar duty could be imposed upon the vendor, which would not be satisfied simply by warning of the danger, but would require financial compensation for the cost of remedying the defect.

1 Newsome [1980] Conv 287 at 297. See also *Barnsley* p. 140, n. 5.
2 Law Com No 40, para 531.
3 Newsome, above, 297–298.

6.54 As we have seen,[1] in *Hone v Benson* the argument that the purchaser's failure to have the premises surveyed broke the chain of causation was rejected. This is of course only a decision on the particular facts of that case, and it is suggested that the question whether or not the purchaser should have employed a surveyor is likely to be important in any case where it is sought to impose liability for known dangerous defects on a vendor, though of course if the defect, known to the vendor, is one which the reasonable surveyor could not have discovered (as e g in *Dutton v Bognor Regis UDC*) then there could be no break in the chain of causation. In *Higgins v Arfon Borough Council*,[2] a case concerning the potential liability of a local authority for failure to inspect a bungalow during the course of construction, Mars-Jones J said: 'Having regard to the comparatively low price of the property,[3] its age[4] and the fact that the purchaser knew that the building society had had the property inspected by an expert, I find it quite unreasonable to expect that plaintiff to have had an independent survey carried out by an expert on his own behalf.'[5] In addition, the plaintiffs' own inspection had revealed no indications that the house was defectively constructed. In the context of builders' liability, Cobb J in *Sutherland v C R Maton & Sons Ltd*[6] held that failure to have a private survey did not break the chain of causation. In this case, one manifestation of subsidence in made-up ground beneath a concrete slab below a bungalow was a crack in the lounge wall. The building society report advised the purchaser to investigate the cause and make good the crack, but the fact that they did not withhold any of the amount advanced and his own impecuniosity persuaded the purchaser not to employ a surveyor. The judge 'accepted that ordinary people relied on building society surveys and did not instruct surveyors'[7] and found the defendant builders liable to the plaintiff. On the other hand, Lord Denning MR in *Dutton v Bognor Regis UDC*[8] stated (obiter) on the question of a private survey: 'a subsequent purchaser often has the house surveyed. This intermediate inspection, or opportunity of inspection, may break the proximity. It would certainly do so when it ought to disclose the damage.' Insofar as an analogy can be drawn between liability for known defects in products and liability for known defects in premises, this question of the opportunity for intermediate examination is of great significance. Lord Atkin said in *Donoghue v Stevenson*:[9] 'A manufacturer of products, which he sells in such a form as to show that he intends them to reach the ultimate consumer in the form in which they left him with no reasonable possibility of intermediate examination, and with the knowledge that the absence of reasonable care in the preparation or putting up of the products will result in an injury to the consumer's life or property, owes a duty to the consumer to take reasonable care.' The reasonable possibility of intermediate examination will only defeat the claim if there is a real likelihood of the sort of examination which would or ought to reveal the defect.[10] With regard to premises, it may well be argued that even though a survey might well have revealed a particular defect, the fact that the vendor should have realised that the purchaser was unlikely to commission such a survey[11] means that there is no 'real likelihood' of intermediate examination.

1 See para 6.47, above.
2 [1975] 2 All ER 589, [1975] 1 WLR 524. See para 5.13, above.
3 Slightly below the national average at that time: Newsome [1980] Conv 287 at 297.
4 Three years.
5 [1975] 2 All ER 589 at 591–592, [1975] 1 WLR 524 at 526.
6 (1976) 240 Estates Gazette 135.
7 Ibid at 136. See also *Yianni v Edwin Evans & Sons* [1981] 3 All ER 592.
8 [1972] 1 QB 373 at 396, [1972] 1 All ER 462 at 474.
9 [1932] AC 562 at 599.
10 See e g *Evans v Triplex Safety Glass Co Ltd* [1936] 1 All ER 283.
11 Fewer than a third of house purchasers have a private survey, it seems: see Troop (1980) *Sunday Times* 27 January. See also *Yianni v Edwin Evans & Sons*, above, at 597.

6.55 As against this it may be argued that a private transaction, which the sale of a house usually is, is very different from the business liability involved in most of the chattel cases;[1] that, despite judicial criticism of the distinction between chattels and real property,[2] the principle of *caveat emptor* is still of fundamental importance in cases of sale of land; that it is inconsistent with the arguments that preclude the imposition of warranties on the vendor to allow a purchaser who is insufficiently prudent to employ a surveyor nevertheless to claim damages from a vendor in tort. On this last point the Law Commission[3] did not regard it as inconsistent that 'a vendor's duty in contract in respect of quality defects to . . .[4] a purchaser may in some respect be less exacting than his duty in tort towards the world at large (including the purchaser) as regards dangerous defects'. The purpose of the Commission's proposal was not to invalidate *caveat emptor* but if in some cases the effect of the proposal was to override that principle, the Commission did not regard this as undesirable.

1 Newsome [1980] Conv 287 at 294. But should there be a distinction where the house is sold in the course of business by a developer? Arguably, since the houses a developer sells are new, there is less reason to expect a purchaser to commission a private survey.
2 E g per Lord Denning MR in *Dutton v Bognor Regis UDC* [1972] 1 QB 373 at 393, [1972] 1 All ER 462 at 471; per Lord Salmon in *Anns v London Borough of Merton* [1978] AC 728 at 768, [1977] 2 All ER 492 at 512.
3 Law Com No 40, para 53.
4 The particular purchaser under discussion was the one who, under the Law Commission's recommendation, might find that he had negotiated a price only to be told of a dangerous defect at the time of completion, but it is suggested that the sense of the quoted passage is applicable to purchasers generally.

6.56 The fact that a purchaser did not commission a private survey is not in itself therefore likely to preclude the imposition of liability on the purchaser. But in the appropriate circumstances, for example, if the property is an elderly and/or expensive one, or if there is no mortgage and therefore no building society survey involved, a court may well regard the chain of causation as having been broken. The weight of authority suggests that in the typical case of a modern house bought on a mortgage, a court is unlikely to hold that the failure to have a private survey precludes a successful claim by the purchaser, assuming that in any case an action can lie against the vendor.

6.57 The kind of defects in relation to which liability might be imposed was limited to dangerous defects by the Law Commission, though they did not define 'dangerous' except insofar as the duty in clause 3(2) of the Draft Bill required the vendor to take 'reasonable care to see that they are reasonably safe from personal injury or from damage to property caused by any of those defects'. As we have seen in earlier chapters, structural defects in premises have been characterised by the courts as physical damage, provided that they present a 'present or imminent threat to the health or safety of persons occupying the property' (in cases involving the liability of builders and local authorities), and the limitation period begins to run from the time when such defects are known to present such a threat. If this definition were adopted for vendor's liability for known defects, then, unless the vendor provides the purchaser with adequate information concerning the defect, prior to exchange of contracts,[1] he will potentially be liable for damage caused by the defect and damage which the defect threatens to cause in the future.[2] If, for example, a vendor is aware that the premises which he is selling have structural defects, and yet he does not disclose this, the limitation period will not begin to run until the defects are known to pose a present or imminent threat to health or safety. The vendor might argue that, in order for him to be liable at all, such a threat must exist before contracts are exchanged, as his knowledge of the defects is the basis of his liability, and therefore if the defects remain latent for more than six years from exchange of contracts, any damage suffered thereafter is time-barred. This underlines the general uncertainty caused by the notion of a threat to health or safety. It is not clear whether time does run from when the first moment at which such a threat exists, or whether it is only when the plaintiff discovers or with reasonable diligence should have discovered such a state of affairs that time begins to run.[3] If it is the latter, the potential liability of the vendor, like that of the builder, architect or local authority, could continue for an almost indefinite period of time. On the one hand, it appears particularly harsh on the vendor, whose liability does not depend upon negligent building, design or inspection, but simply on knowledge, to have this threat (albeit unwittingly, most probably) hanging over him; on the other hand, if there is any point in imposing liability, it might be unfair on the purchaser to prevent him from suing for defects of whose existence he could not have been aware until it was too late. However, it may be argued that the liability under discussion, that of a vendor for dangerous defects of whose existence he is aware, will not often raise limitation problems as, if the defect's existence is known to the vendor, the purchaser is likely to discover them in turn well before the limitation period has expired.

1 For the position where both parties are aware of damage caused or about to be caused by subsidence, prior to the exchange of contract, see Street [1979] Conv 241.
2 See *Batty v Metropolitan Property Realisations Ltd* [1978] QB 554, [1978] 2 All ER 445.
3 However we have suggested in para 1.39, above that the latter represents the better test.

6.58 Uncertainties might still exist concerning the defects for which liability should be imposed: not all defects in premises constitute a threat to health or safety, and the dividing line might be difficult to draw. In addition it might not be clear whether liability should be imposed for a defect which might in the future, though not at present, threaten health or safety, for example woodworm in a floor, which might at some time in the future cause injury. Much would depend upon how 'imminent' was defined, but it is suggested that there is a strong case, if liability were to be imposed on a vendor, for restricting that liability in some way, whether by means of a clearly defined period of limitation or a strict definition of the type of defects and/or damage for which he would be responsible. A final point here concerns the persons to whom the duty should be owed. The Law Commission recommended that the duty be owed to all those who might reasonably be expected to be affected by the defects in question, thus extending beyond the purchaser to persons who might otherwise go remediless if, for example, the defect were one that could not reasonably have been discovered by the occupier (and this presumably, in an appropriate case, might include the person who bought from the purchaser).

6.59 Section 6(3) of the Defective Premises Act 1972 outlaws any attempt to exclude or restrict the operation of any of the Act's provisions. As regards negligence liability, section 2 of the Unfair Contract Terms Act, which would subject attempts to exclude such liability other than for death or personal injury, and if relating to business liability to a test of reasonableness, does not extend to any contract so far as it relates to the creation or transfer of an interest in land.[1] The effectiveness of Condition 4(2)(a) of the Law Society's General Conditions of Sale[2] fell to be examined in the context of a vendor's liability for defective work in *Hone v Benson*.[3] The condition provided: 'The purchaser shall buy with full notice of the actual state and condition of the property and shall take it as it stands, save where it is to be constructed or converted by the vendor.'[4] As we have seen[5] the court held that the purpose of the condition was to prevent a purchaser from calling off the sale or asking for an abatement in price, where defects were discovered between contract and conveyance. For negligence liability to be excluded, it must be set out in clear words in a contractual term, referring expressly to negligence. The prudent vendor will seek to include an appropriately worded exclusion in the conditions of sale, whether or not he fears that a court might impose liability for non-disclosure of defects of which he is aware, for it is suggested that a term excluding liability for negligence would be broad enough to cover both that potential liability and also *Hone v Benson* liability: positive acts of negligence and failure to disclose defects.

1 Unfair Contract Terms Act 1977, Sch 1, para 1(b).
2 1970 edn. The wording of s. 5(2)(a) in the 1980 edn is effectively the same.
3 (1978) 248 Estates Gazette 1013.
4 Condition 13(3) of the National Conditions of Sale (19th edn, 1976) is to similar effect.
5 See para 6.48, above.

6.60 Whether or not a court would impose liability on a vendor for failure to disclose known dangerous defects remains speculative. Despite the general expansion of liability for defective premises over the last decade, strong policy arguments can be made against allowing such expansion to undermine, however narrowly, the principle of *caveat emptor*. The desirability of encouraging the purchaser to commission a private survey and the undesirability of imposing a duty of care upon the vendor who is in no way responsible for the defect,[1] militate, amongst other factors, against the imposition of a duty of disclosure. On balance it is suggested that a court is unlikely to go beyond a duty of care in respect of physical defects caused by the defendant (as in *Hone v Benson*) to a duty of disclosure; the principle of *caveat emptor* is probably too entrenched for anybody other than Parliament to effect such a change, and Parliament has many more important priorities. But arguments in favour of the imposition of a duty have a stronger basis than they did ten years ago, and stand a better chance of success, and it would be unwise to assume that a sufficiently senior court would never contemplate such an expansion of liability.[2]

1 Though note the point made by the Law Commission (Law Com No 40, para 53) that it would be in the public interest if as the result of the imposition of a duty a vendor were persuaded to remedy defects rather than leave it to the purchaser to take remedial action after the sale.
2 See *Bowen v Paramount Builders (Hamilton) Ltd* [1977] 1 NZLR 394 at 415, per Richmond P, who was prepared to contemplate such an expansion of liability.

Chapter 7

Landlords

7.1 The liabilities of a landlord, especially those owed to his tenants, form a major aspect of the law concerning premises, and represent a complex area where the common law has moved forward rapidly in recent years, and has been further augmented by a considerable degree of statutory intervention, especially in the field of rented residential accommodation. It is in this area that the deficiencies of the original common law position appeared most clearly. However, this chapter does not confine its coverage to the landlord-private tenant relationship but covers the whole range of the civil liabilities of all landlords, whether of office blocks or bedsits, except in relation to agricultural tenancies.

7.2 The starting-point for any discussion of the landlord's liabilities in respect of defects in the premises which he lets must be the famous dictum of Erle CJ in *Robbins v Jones*,[1] where he stated, 'fraud apart, there is no law against letting a tumbledown house: and the tenant's remedy is upon his contract, if any'. This comment shows simultaneously a failure to allow a tortious remedy except in the unusual case where fraud may be proven and a failure to appreciate the shortcomings of the contractual approach at that stage, viz the problems (then, as now) of privity and, also, the problems of exclusion clauses, symptomatic of the then approach to freedom of contract, now to some extent eroded. This approach was confirmed by the House of Lords in *Cavalier v Pope*,[2] a case where a tenant's wife was injured as a result of the premises being in a dangerous state of dilapidation. Even though the landlord knew of the defect, and had promised to repair it, the wife was held unable to claim. Lord Atkinson, giving the principal judgment,[3] held that a landlord who let premises in a defective condition was not liable in respect of injuries suffered by the tenant, his servants, guests, customers or other invitees. This clear expression of the principle of *caveat emptor* in respect of tenancies has sounded through the subsequent years with great force, although, as will be seen, its force is now decreasing.

1 (1863) 15 CBNS 221 at 239.
2 [1906] AC 428.
3 Ibid at 432.

7.3 One aspect of the increasing duties now owed by the landlord which will not be dwelt upon at length in this chapter is the obvious fact that the range of duties now owed by the occupier generally will extend to many landlords; if they fall within the limited degree of control that has been held to amount to occupation,[1] then the full range of occupiers' liabilities, including particularly

231

those laid down by the Occupiers' Liability Act 1957, will be owed by them. However, the absentee landlord may be able to argue that he can escape these duties, and to reflect this, as well as to govern the respective responsibilities of landlord and tenant more clearly, the law has had to go further.

1 See paras 2.4 ff, above.

The landlord and his tenant

7.4 The first point to note is of course that this relationship is governed by a contract. It is naturally for the parties to agree to the precise terms of the contract, though the extent to which genuine negotiation about the terms will take place will vary. In most cases, the landlord will have the superior bargaining position, though in a case, for example, of the letting of a large office block for a considerable period, the sums involved will be more conducive to genuine discussion. A combination of the landlord's advantageous position with the traditional notions of *caveat emptor* does lead, however, to leases of premises normally containing a promise by the lessee that he will be responsible for the repair of premises, though care must be taken to ensure that the clause is appropriately drafted,[1] and its effectiveness is subject to what follows. The landlord may give effect to the tenant's obligation either by an express contractual stipulation allowing entry for the purposes of repair or by an action for damages as compensation for the property being in a state of disrepair, though the leave of the court is now required where a landlord seeks compensation from a tenant who resists the landlord's claim, where the tenancy has been granted for a term of seven or more years and at least three years of the period remain unexpired. Leave will only be granted where the court is satisfied that the appropriate procedures have been followed and that immediate action is needed to prevent substantial diminution in the value of the reversion and/or departure from statutory requirements. To obtain leave it is also possible to show that to remedy the breach will cost more later, or that there is a failure by the lessee to repair part of the premises which he is obliged to repair but does not occupy, if failure to repair is required in the interests of the occupier of that part of the premises, or that there are special circumstances which render it just and equitable to give leave.[2] In the case of a business tenancy, the tenant's failure to repair is a ground for refusing a new tenancy.[3]

1 For a detailed discussion on construction of covenants to repair, see Woodfall *Landlord and Tenant* paras 1.1429–1.1454.
2 Leasehold Property (Repairs) Act 1938, s. 1 as amended by the Landlord and Tenant Act 1954, s. 51(1).
3 Landlord and Tenant Act 1954, s. 30(1)(a).

7.5 There is nothing whatsoever to prevent the landlord ensuring that work be done (and to his standard) by reserving for himself a right to repair (and an associated right of entry), though the obligation to repair will not generally arise until the landlord has received notice that repair is needed.[1] The landlord can be compelled to carry out his promise by the award of a decree of specific performance against him in an appropriate case,[2] or by the award of damages.[3] However, the operation of law increasingly forces the landlord to accept greater responsibility, whether he contracts to that effect or not.

1 *Torrens v Walker* [1906] 2 Ch 166.
2 *Jeune v Queens Cross Properties Ltd* [1974] Ch 97, [1973] 3 All ER 97.
3 See Woodfall *Landlord and Tenant* para 1.1501.

7.6 Firstly, the common law has occasionally assisted the tenant with the insertion of implied terms into tenancy agreements, albeit on a restricted basis. As long ago as 1843, in *Smith v Marrable*,[1] it was conceded that there was an implied term as to the habitable condition of premises. This term however only arose at the commencement of the period of the agreement, and not later in its duration, and also only applied to furnished accommodation, a distinction confirmed subsequently in *Sleafer v Lambeth Metropolitan Borough Council*,[2] a case concerning furnished property. The term also appears to be confined to clear threats to the health of the tenant, such as infestation,[3] and the recent presence of infectious diseases.[4] The narrowness of this implied term has hindered its utility; on the other hand, it may be noted that there has been until recently a relative increase in the importance of furnished accommodation within the private rented sector.

1 (1843) 11 M & W 5.
2 [1960] 1 QB 43, [1959] 3 All ER 378.
3 *Smith v Marrable* (1843) 11 M & W 5.
4 *Collins v Hopkins* [1923] 2 KB 617.

7.7 A different and perhaps more significant approach to implied terms in landlord and tenant cases has recently been provided by the House of Lords in *Liverpool City Council v Irwin*.[1] This case concerned a large 'high-rise' block of municipal flats and was brought by certain tenants resident in upper storeys who had been withholding their rents as a protest against conditions in the block; the principal complaints related to the common parts of the block – the rarely functioning lifts, the unlit stairs, with unguarded holes providing additional hazards and frequent blockage of rubbish chutes. The local authority had failed to collect the rents due, and so began possession proceedings; the tenants counterclaimed for damages in respect of the defects in the premises. The contractual documents were silent as to the position concerning the matters complained of, and it was therefore held that terms should be implied to give full effect to the main tenancy agreement, and that a tenancy agreement for a flat in such a block could only be comprehensible with the addition of implied terms allowing the tenants an implied right to have the services to their flats maintained, e g the provision of adequate access and refuse disposal, and rendering the landlord liable for any failure to take reasonable care of the common parts of the flats. This is obviously a decision of potential significance, but it must be asked just how important this case will ultimately prove to be. *Liverpool City Council v Irwin* displays many of the features of an easily distinguishable decision. The House of Lords were able to take advantage of the total silence in the local authority's conditions of tenancy as to the matters complained of, and their decision is easily explicable in the light of the unique circumstances of a badly maintained (and heavily vandalised) multi-storey block of flats. On the other hand, an examination of the speeches in the case discloses an (apparently intentional) approach whereby the discussion of the landlord's liability in respect of the common parts is conducted at a general level, not solely applicable to municipal flats or 'high-rise' buildings, though this in turn may be counteracted by the admission that it is difficult to create such implied terms in the presence of specific terms covering the whole or part of the area covered by the implied terms that are claimed to exist. Thus, *Liverpool City Council v Irwin* is clearly an important case, though its ambit may be somewhat restricted; it will however undoubtedly be of assistance to tenants where their agreements are not fully comprehensive and will be of some assistance to anyone who is the

tenant of premises where access and services are in common with other premises, such as flats and offices in multi-occupied buildings.
1 [1977] AC 239, [1976] 2 All ER 39.

7.8 However, the attempts of the courts to imply terms into tenancy agreements fade by comparison with the efforts of Parliament to protect tenants, particularly in the residential sector. The principal enactment is section 32 of the Housing Act 1961, whereby a covenant is implied into leases of many dwelling houses. By section 32(5) 'lease' includes any other tenancy,[1] while section 33(1) limits the implied terms to insertion in agreements for less than seven years, or at least where an agreement is determinable by the lessor within seven years (section 33(2)). Additionally, by section 33(4) any agricultural holding does not come within the protection of section 32, and, by section 33(3), new tenancies which fall within Part II of the Landlord and Tenant Act 1954 (i e business or partly business tenancies) are also not covered by section 32.
1 See also *Brikom Investments Ltd v Seaford* [1981] 2 All ER 783, [1981] 1 WLR 863.

7.9 What then are the terms implied into leases by section 32? The lessor is taken as covenanting that he will keep in repair the structure and exterior of the dwelling house, including drains, gutters and external pipes, and will also keep in repair the key domestic installations for the supply of water, gas and electricity and for the provision of sanitation and water heating, and these implied terms will overcome any express promise of the lessee to the contrary. By section 32(2), it is provided that the lessor's duties do not extend to cover reconstruction of the premises after accidental damage, or to repairs which the tenant at common law should carry out as part of his duty to use the premises in a tenant-like manner,[1] nor does the duty extend to the maintenance of anything which the lessee is entitled to remove from the dwelling house. The duty is not an absolute one; by section 32(2) the standard of repair required by the implied term shall be assessed in the light of the age, character and prospective life of both the house in question and the area in which it is situated. A final aspect of the statutory package covers attempts to exclude the operation of section 32. No agreement, whether in a lease or a collateral agreement, will take effect to exclude or limit the terms implied by section 32.[2] However, an exception to this is provided whereby the county court may authorise a departure from the section 32 terms if the parties to the agreement consent, and it appears to the court that the proposed departure from the statutory provisions is a fair and reasonable one in the circumstances of the case.
1 See para 7.17, below.
2 Housing Act 1961, s. 33(7).

7.10 On paper, section 32 provides a clear, normally binding, protection for the tenant, clearly establishing the landlord's role in maintaining the premises and preventing him from making onerous demands on the tenant in the field of repair. Whether section 32 is as successful as this implies, however, is a more contentious issue, since the courts have tended to interpret the provisions restrictively.[1] Perhaps the most serious limitation is provided by the recent case of *Newham London Borough v Patel*.[2] In this case, the tenant of a house owned by the local authority in a redevelopment area complained, by way of counterclaim against possession proceedings, about the disrepair of the property. It was clear that his complaints, if proven, would amount to a clear breach of the section 32 implied terms, but nonetheless his action failed because of the intention to demolish the house imminently, and redevelop the area. In the words of Templeman LJ,[3] 'The prospective life of the dwelling-house affected the duty of the council under section 32 and they were not bound to carry out repairs which would be wholly useless.' It was additionally noted that the low rent charged to Mr Patel would negate any claim for damages, even had his action succeeded. In other words, in low rental, short-life property, the repairing covenant implied by section 32 appears almost worthless, in relation to properties where perhaps it is most needed.

1 See Hughes *Public Sector Housing Law* pp. 213–215.
2 [1979] JPL 303.
3 Ibid at 304.

7.11 A further limitation on the landlord's liability under section 32 exists in cases where major work needs to be done to the property which can be regarded as tantamount to replacement of the property rather than just repair of it. A recent case concerning a commercial letting illustrates the point clearly, viz *Ravenseft Properties Ltd v Davstone (Holdings) Ltd*.[1] In this case, expansion joints had to be inserted in a block of flats fifteen years after their initial construction. It was held that it was a question of degree whether works fell within the ambit of the covenant of repair, and the joints, representing as they did only a tiny fraction of the value of the whole building, fell within the covenant, and had in no way changed the character of the building. However, had the repair work involved major expenditure and ended with the landlord receiving at the end of the letting period a different, enhanced property, then this would be outside the ambit of the repairing covenant.[2] Once again, the statute fails to extend protection in cases which might otherwise be regarded as amongst the more serious breaches of section 32.

1 [1980] QB 12, [1979] 1 All ER 929.
2 *Pembery v Lamdin* [1940] 2 All ER 434.

7.12 A final question arises as to the precise scope of section 32. It will be recalled that the principal repairing covenant extends to the structure and exterior of the premises. Perhaps the leading case now is *Campden Hill Towers Ltd v Gardner*.[1] Here, it was held by the Court of Appeal that the scope of the covenant to repair would be interpreted widely; in the circumstances of the case, which concerned a third-floor flat, the section 32 obligations would extend to the exterior of the particular dwelling-unit in question, e g the outside of inner party walls and outside walls of the block which were also outside walls of the flat and the structural framework, whether demised or not. However the obligations in respect of domestic installations would only extend to installations within the physical confines of the flat itself. Other cases indicate that means of access to premises will only be counted as the 'exterior' thereof if they form essential means of access.[2] Overall, section 32 may be said to have established at least basic requirements that the landlord of private rented accommodation takes responsibility for repairs, but its actual utility has undoubtedly been impaired by recent court decisions. It has also been very slightly limited in scope by section 80 of the Housing Act 1980, whereby section 32 does not apply in the context of a lease granted after 3 October 1980, to certain educational institutions and housing associations, and local and central government.

1 [1977] QB 823, [1977] 1 All ER 739.
2 *Brown v Liverpool Corpn* [1969] 3 All ER 1345; *Hopwood v Cannock Chase District Council* [1975] 1 All ER 796, [1975] 1 WLR 373.

7.13 An additional statutory provision purports to protect tenants of low rental accommodation. This is in the form of section 6 of the Housing Act 1957 whereby an implied term of fitness for human habitation is inserted into contracts for letting houses at low rents (in the case of contracts made after 6 July 1957, defined as £52 per year, or £80 per year in London, except the Outer London boroughs prior to 1965). The shortcoming of this implied term is obvious; over and above the restrictive view again adopted by the courts,[1] few, if any, houses are still let at such low rentals; the implied term is therefore now of no practical importance and will so remain until (and if) the rental limits are raised to reflect over two decades of inflation.

1 See Hughes *Public Sector Housing Law* pp. 211–212.

7.14 One further statutory protection is granted to the tenant by section 125 of the Housing Act 1974. This assists the tenant of any dwelling which is part of a larger set of premises and amounts almost to a statutory circumvention of the doctrine of privity of contract, thus forming a seemingly useful link between the tenant's contractual and tortious remedies. The section permits a tenant to complain against a landlord who is in breach of his repairing covenant relating to a part of the premises other than that let to the tenant, and to obtain at the court's discretion an order of specific performance of that covenant, although he is not party to it. This is only applicable to private dwellings, and does not apply if the tenancy is even in part a business one.[1] However, it seems to cover any covenant by the landlord, whether express or implied. The precise ambit of the section is hard to determine; the section was designed to confirm the then controversial decision in *Jeune v Queens Cross Properties Ltd*[2] that specific performance was an appropriate method of enforcing a landlord's compliance with his repairing covenants, the defect arising in a balcony which had not been let to any of the tenants of the block of flats in question, but the wording adopted does appear to go further, and allows the tenant to claim specific performance of covenants to repair not only the common parts of the premises, but also ostensibly allows him to claim specific performance of covenants made by the landlord with other tenants. It is suggested that this liberal approach must be adopted, but that its widest implications may be limited either by the use of the court's discretion or perhaps by an assertion that the decree of specific performance only applies so as to enforce contracts and that it is therefore inappropriate in the absence of privity, thus limiting the wide terminology of the statutory provision in the light of the general law.

1 Housing Act 1974, s. 125(2).
2 [1974] Ch 97, [1973] 3 All ER 97.

7.15 One remaining aspect of the contractual rules governing the landlord-tenant relationship as regards defects in the premises falls to be discussed. It is always open to a tenant to withhold rents as a set-off against defects in the premises in an appropriate case,[1] but the decision of Goff J in *Lee-Parker v Izzet*[2] goes further in rediscovering what the judge saw as an ancient common law right, based on dicta in *Taylor v Beal*[3] almost four centuries ago, for tenants to recoup the cost of repairs which they themselves have undertaken when the landlord is in breach of his obligations, by withholding their rents until such time as their losses have been met. This right is limited only by a need for the landlord to be given due notice of his breach and by the need for the expenditure incurred to be regarded as proper in the circumstances, presumably this being evidenced by the provision of an independent estimate. It is fair to note that this remedy is not without its limitations. Quite apart from the restrictions inherent in Goff J's formulation, it may also be contradicted by a specific clause in the tenancy agreement excluding the operation of the right of set-off against future rents by absolving the landlord from any obligation to accept responsibility for repairs unilaterally initiated by the tenant.

1 See White [1981] LAG Bull 182.
2 [1971] 3 All ER 1099, [1971] 1 WLR 1688.
3 (1591) Cro Eliz 222.

7.16 Subsequent cases have given general approval to *Lee-Parker v Izzet.*[1] In particular, *Asco Developments Ltd v Gordon, Lowes and Lewis*[2] allowed the principle to be extended so as to allow rent arrears to be written off against the cost of repairs carried out by the tenant when the landlord was in breach of his repairing obligations, although normally such costs should be clearly quantified. The most recent case in the area is *British Anzani (Felixstowe) Ltd v International Marine Management (UK) Ltd*[3] where Forbes J endorsed the *Lee-Parker* decision, though slightly confining its scope once again to cover certain sums which the landlord would not be able genuinely to dispute; general principles of set-off might still be appropriate if other costs are being claimed by the tenant e g damage to property. It therefore now seems that there has been clearly established a right on the part of tenants to set at least the cost of necessary repairs off against rents due after adequate notice has been given, though the practical effect of this right may be more limited.[4]

1 [1971] 3 All ER 1099, [1971] 1 WLR 1688.
2 (1978) 248 Estates Gazette 683.
3 [1980] QB 137, [1979] 2 All ER 1063.
4 See Hughes *Public Sector Housing Law* p. 210.

7.17 In all cases it should be noted that the tenant has certain residual duties concerning repair; he must use the premises in a 'tenant-like manner'. This vague notion imposes a somewhat minimal duty upon tenants not to fall too far below the standards which might be expected from the tenant e g by not committing waste[1] or neglecting damage caused by himself or his guests, or taking care of minor jobs which it may be unreasonable to ignore.[2]

1 *Marsden v Edward Heyes Ltd* [1927] 2 QB 1.
2 *Warren v Keen* [1954] 1 QB 15, [1953] 2 All ER 1118.

7.18 As in so many other areas covered by this work, the law of contract is no longer the sole governor of the specific relationship discussed in this part of the chapter. Tortious principles have been refined so as to provide specific assistance to the tenant in disputes with his landlord. Firstly, there seems little, if any, doubt that the many recent decisions concerning the potential liabilities in negligence of the builder-vendor also are capable of easy extension to the builder-lessor; the clearest example is provided by the case of *Batty v Metropolitan Property Realisations*[1] where, after a house was threatened with subsidence, its builder and the development company, who let the property to the plaintiff on a long lease, were held liable in negligence. The wide-ranging side-effects of this decision are noted elsewhere,[2] but here it is merely suggested that any firm which arranges and establishes the construction of premises for letting may be held liable to tenants who suffer loss in consequence of a careless failure by the landlord to adequately check and prepare the land and choose appropriate parties to carry out the building work.

1 [1978] QB 554, [1978] 2 All ER 445.
2 See paras 3.92 ff, and paras 6.50 ff, above.

7.19 Whether the law will go further, however, and permit a tenant to complain via the medium of the law of negligence about the condition of older premises of which he becomes the tenant is more doubtful. Certainly such a claim would be novel and would be in danger of falling foul of two traditional taboos of the law of negligence. Firstly, the usual kind of claim might well be merely an allegation of nonfeasance, i e a failure to carry out repair work, on the part of the landlord. Secondly, and perhaps more seriously, unless actual physical damage has occurred any claim can only be in respect of purely qualitative defects which are not generally regarded as falling within the proper ambit of the rules of negligence. This view is supported by dicta in *Anns v London Borough of Merton*[1] by Lord Salmon;[2] 'the immunity of a landlord who sells or lets his house which is dangerous or unfit for habitation is deeply entrenched in our law'. On the other hand we know that the vendor of premises may conceivably be liable in negligence,[3] and if this attack on Lord Salmon's 'deeply entrenched' position may be taken as applying to the creation of leaseholds, as seems to be the case,[4] then it could be extended without any difficulties in logic to cover the creation of tenancies. This is not entirely speculative; one decision of the Court of Appeal, not officially reported,[5] does appear to hold a local authority liable in negligence for letting a flat to a tenant without having properly removed cockroaches from the premises through not covering certain space and ducts, and using discredited insecticide. It should be noted that this case appears to involve a misfeasance, rather than a nonfeasance, by the council in that, having undertaken the disinfection, they failed to carry it out adequately, providing a potential distinction in any future case where there may be a simple omission to maintain a property.

1 [1978] AC 728, [1977] 2 All ER 492.
2 Ibid at 768 and 512.
3 See paras 6.40 ff, above.
4 See Newsome [1980] Conv 287.
5 *Sharpe v Manchester Metropolitan Borough Council*, noted in *Social Welfare Law* (ed Pollard) paras C.7277–C.7254 (Noter-Up, April 1980).

7.20 Such speculations are to some extent academic, however; although the common law may be moving towards the position that the landlord is liable in negligence for letting an unfit property, in so doing it is only following the path already trodden by the legislature in its decision to promulgate the Defective Premises Act 1972, which gives the tenant a wide range of remedies against the landlord in certain circumstances. The Act offers three possible way forward for a tenant faced with defective premises and who is seeking redress from the landlord. Firstly, section 1 of the Act creates a strict duty[1] on anyone who takes on work in connection with the provision of a dwelling to ensure that the work is done in a workmanlike manner with proper materials so that the premises be fit for habitation; this duty is said to be owed to anyone who acquires a legal or equitable interest in the dwelling. This was seen as a great improvement on the then common law, but it does not unduly affect the landlord. Although a stricter duty is imposed by the Act than any duty perhaps imposed by the common law, it will only cover a landlord who has actually carried out work in connection with the provision of premises and also the duty only covers dwelling houses. Secondly, the tenant may look to section 3 of the Act for redress. This states that any duty of care owed by anyone carrying out work of construction, repair, maintenance or demolition is not abated by that person's subsequent disposal of the premises. In other words, if the landlord could be sued then his subsequent disposal of the premises, e g by creating a tenancy, will not affect his position, and the tenant can still take action; however, by section 3(2) this does not apply to cases where the relevant tenancy was entered into before the Act came into force, on 1 January 1974. The intention of this section was clearly to remove the immunity of vendors and anyone else who 'disposes' of premises (this is defined by section 6(1) as including a letting); the common law has arguably now also taken this step, but section 3 confirms the removal of the immunity. However, section 3 does not create a cause of action but only removes a possible defence; the tenant therefore still has to frame his action under another part of the Act or the common law. A third possible path for the tenant to follow in any action against his landlord is that provided by section 4 of the 1972 Act. This is considered in more detail later,[2] since it chiefly concerns the relationship between the landlord and third parties, but its scope is sufficiently wide to permit tenants themselves to take advantage of the tortious remedy thereby provided against the landlord for breaches of his obligations as to maintenance or repair. The remedy under section 4 may be particularly useful to the tenant since, by virtue of section 6(3), the landlord's duties under this and other sections of the 1972 Act may not be excluded by contractual terms. However, section 4 is not without its problems and restrictions,[3] and adds little to the tenant's own rights since it only provides a tortious remedy for breaches of obligations as to maintenance and repair already owed to the tenant by virtue of the tenancy agreement.

1 See para 3.104, above.
2 See paras 7.22 ff, below.
3 Ibid.

The landlord and the lawful visitor

7.21 So far we have been solely concerned with the predominantly contractual relationship between the landlord and his tenant. However, any defects in demised premises may well not only affect the tenant but may also cause harm to third parties, for example the tenant's guests and relatives lawfully visiting him, who, by reason of the doctrine of privity of contract, are unable to take advantage of the express or implied terms of the tenancy agreement. Fortunately, from the point of view of such lawful visitors to the premises, recent developments have come to their aid. Again it may be reiterated that if the landlord may properly be regarded as an occupier then the various duties of the occupier[1] will be owed by him and clearly the tenant's lawful visitors will be in the forefront of those protected. Particularly worthy of comment in this regard is section 3(1) of the Occupiers' Liability Act 1957[2] which is designed to circumvent any attempt by the occupier to avoid his obligations to persons who are strangers to a contract but nonetheless enter under its auspices. In our context, this covers any attempt by a landlord to stipulate in a tenancy agreement that he does not owe the common duty of care otherwise owed to visitors to the tenant's lawful visitors (whose lawful status is only gained by reason of the landlord-tenant agreement); the landlord has to offer these visitors the same standard of care as he does to his tenant, except where he can lower the level of duty by some means other than the tenancy agreement e g a non-contractual notice placed by the landlord at the entrance to premises, this of course being subject to the Unfair Contract Terms Act 1977, section 2.[3] Additionally, section 3(1) of the 1957 Act allows the tenant's visitors to claim the benefit of any more onerous obligations which the landlord accepts in the contract, unless otherwise stated.

1 See paras 2.20 ff, above.
2 See also para 2.35, above.
3 See para 2.29, above.

7.22 There are, however, additional rules which impose tortious liability upon all landlords. Here we must consider section 4 of the Defective Premises Act 1972; section 4(1) states:

> Where premises are let under a tenancy which puts on the landlord an obligation to the tenant for the maintenance or repair of the premises, the landlord owes to all persons who might reasonably be expected to be affected by defects in the state of the premises a duty to take such care as is reasonable in all the circumstances to see that they are reasonably safe from personal injury or from damage to their property caused by a relevant defect.

This provides a clear extension of the duties owed by the landlord to the tenant in respect of maintenance or repair to a wide range of third parties; obviously, the range of persons who might reasonably be affected by defects in the state of the premises will include the tenant's guests, statutory visitors and subsequent tenants, at least the relatively immediate successors to the tenancy. The mysterious phrase 'relevant defect' is explained by section 4(3) as covering only those defects which have been discovered at or after whichever is the earliest of the commencement of the tenancy, the entering into of the tenancy agreement or the time when possession is taken of the premises in contemplation of the letting, except in the case of pre-1974 tenancies, where the obligation arises in respect of defects existing on or after 1 January 1974; 'relevant defect' also is explained by section 4(3) as only including defects which would amount to a breach of the landlord's obligations to the tenant. These are obvious and uncontroversial minor limitations, likewise the provision in section 4(2) whereby the landlord's duty is only owed in respect of defects of which he has actual or constructive knowledge.

7.23 Generally, the scope of section 4 is otherwise wide-ranging; section 4(4) has the effect of deeming any power which the landlord has to undertake repairs (e g as a result of being notified of a defect when he has a contractual right of entry to carry out repairs, or where he learns that the tenant is in default of his own repairing obligations) to be an obligation on the part of the landlord so to act for the purposes of section 4, as far as third parties (but not the tenant himself) are concerned. Section 4(5) establishes clearly that the landlord's obligations as to repair and maintenance include statutorily imposed obligations and section 4(6) extends the already wide definition of 'tenancy' for the purposes of the Act[1] to include for the purposes of section 4 any right of occupation given by a contract or by statute, even though not otherwise a tenancy, thus benefiting those entering under contractual licences, in particular. It should also be remembered that section 6(3) of the 1972 Act does not permit any exclusion clause restricting the ambit of the Act's provisions.

1 Defective Premises Act 1972, s. 6(1).

7.24 This section of the Defective Premises Act 1972 must be counted as one of its more successful measures. It represents a clear improvement on the scope of its predecessor, section 4 of the Occupiers' Liability Act 1957, and operates in favour of a wide range of parties – visitors, neighbours, highway users, etc. The overall breadth of coverage does seem to outweigh the minor limitations on the section's ambit and the section is perhaps capable of greater use, especially in cases concerning non-resident landlords who may well not be regarded as occupiers. In the meantime, the dearth of cases utilising its provisions is harder to explain; perhaps the sums involved in a typical section 4 case, e g where minor injuries are caused by visitors falling on badly maintained stairways, are insufficient to provoke litigation.

7.25 A note must be made of the landlord's responsibility for nuisance. Notwithstanding that he has let the property to a tenant, he will still be liable if its condition at the time of the letting constituted a nuisance. In *Metropolitan Properties Ltd v Jones*,[1] the owner of a flat installed a noisy electric motor for the purposes of circulating hot water. This caused a nuisance to the tenant of the flat above, and he was held to be entitled to claim against the landlord, and not the tenant who was actually using the device. The landlord may also still be liable in nuisance if he is responsible for repairs during the tenancy.[2] The landlord will be held liable in public nuisance where this is caused by the condition of premises adjoining the public highway, unless the nuisance is caused by the intervention of a third party of which the landlord has no cause to be aware.[3]

1 [1939] 2 All ER 202.
2 *Pretty v Bickmore* (1873) LR 8 CP 401.
3 See, inter alia, *Mint v Good* [1951] 1 KB 517, [1950] 2 All ER 1159. For a fuller discussion in the context of the law of nuisance generally see para 2.47, above. See also Woodfall *Landlord and Tenant* para 1.1684.

7.26 Also meriting a brief comment is the fact that certain statutory duties normally cast upon the occupier are in certain circumstances additionally placed upon or alternatively transferred to the landlord.[1] For example, under the Factories Act 1961, it is the owner of a tenement factory (i e one which is associated with but is legally separate from a 'mother' plant nearby) or of a building, part of which only is let as a factory, who is responsible for securing compliance with the duties imposed by sections 48–52 of the Act in respect of fire precautions. It is also the responsibility of the owner, defined for the purposes of the Act by section 176(1) as the person in receipt of the rack-rent of the premises in question, of a tenement factory to secure compliance with other aspects of the Act e g as to sanitation and cleanliness, fencing and general safety of plant, etc., while the owner of a building part of which is let as a factory is responsible for the cleanliness, lighting and general s fety of the common parts. These liabilities are clearly established by sections 120–122 of the Factories Act 1961, three very detailed sections, and there seems no bar to injured employees bringing a civil action against the owner/landlord. Similarly, under the Offices, Shops and Railway Premises Act 1963, the owner of the premises, again defined by section 90(1) of the Act as being the person who at that time is receiving the rack-rent of the premises in question, or the relevant part thereof, is responsible for securing compliance with certain of the Act's provisions if the shop or office is part of a building wholly owned by him. Thus, by section 42, he is responsible for securing the cleanliness and lighting of the common parts, the provision of conveniences, and safe access within the common parts. By section 43, joint owners of the common parts of buildings in multi-ownership (as defined) which contain shops or offices are under similar duties. Again, it is submitted that any employee injured by a breach of these statutory duties may succeed in bringing an action based on breach of the statutory duties against the owner/landlord.

1 For a full discussion, see Woodfall *Landlord and Tenant*, paras 1.1687, 1.1700.

7.27 The general duties imposed by the Health and Safety at Work Act 1974, which with its associated regulations will in due course come to replace the foregoing provisions, also cover the landlord. By section 4, general duties commensurate with their actual degree of control are imposed on non-employers onto whose (non-domestic) premises persons come in the course of their work, to ensure that the premises, access thereto and the environment therein are safe and free from risks to health, while by section 5, further general duties are imposed upon those in control of premises to prevent the emission of noxious fumes into the atmosphere. However, no civil action exists at present for the breach of these statutory duties, under section 47 of the 1974 Act. Landlords, especially those retaining any degree of control of the premises, will nonetheless have to be careful of these provisions in due course.

7.28 A final general note in this section must be made in relation to the position of the landlord as far as exclusion clauses are concerned. By Schedule 1, para 1(b) of the Unfair Contract Terms Act 1977, sections 2–4 of that Act, which contain the principal controls on exclusion clauses in contracts other than for the sale of goods and related contracts, do not extend to 'any contract so far as it relates to the creation or transfer of an interest in land'. Clearly, for the purposes of the 1977 Act, the landlord is still free to impose exclusion clauses via the tenancy agreement, since any formal tenancy agreement must be regarded as creating and transferring an interest in land, though the creation of a contractual licence, e g by giving permission to enter, would not seem so to amount. However, it must be recalled that there are restrictions on the extent to which the provisions of the Housing Act 1961 (implied terms imposed as to repair) may be avoided, even by agreement[1] and the provisions of the Defective Premises Act are protected by section 6(3) thereof, which prevents the avoidance of liability under the Act by the use of contractual terms.

1 Housing Act 1961, s. 33(6) and (7), above.

7.29 It is clear that both the tenant and his guest are overall given far greater protection by the law today than has hitherto been the case. Both the principles of the law of contract and those of the law of tort now operate to impose more onerous liabilities on the landlord, and the old view that it was for the tenant to take care, not the landlord, now seems to a high degree discredited, particularly in the case of residential accommodation, where the statutorily implied terms play a crucial role and section 1 of the Defective Premises Act also operates. On the other hand, other parts of that Act, the common law rules of negligence and the extended rules of set-off apply to all premises whether let for residential or business purposes, and the lessor of business premises has also to be conscious of the statutory duties he owes to employees (not necessarily his own) who come onto premises in the course of employment by another. However, it is still true to say that these various rules, even in combination, have in no way totally eradicated defective demised premises, and it is debatable whether this is due to their 'patchwork' nature or whether it is because of their dependence on an individual taking legal advice, and often having to take formal legal action, to

obtain redress. In any event, it has been found necessary to supplement these
private law remedies by a further set of rules involving the intervention of the
local authority. These are considered separately.[1]

1 In ch 8, below.

Chapter 8

Public control of defective premises

8.1   This chapter is concerned with what may be regarded as a different form of civil liability for defective premises, where redress is obtained by some channel other than the action for damages based on a breach of some aspect or other of the rules of contract or those of tort, in particular through use of public law remedies stemming from specific statutory provisions. The chapter is also distinctive in that it does not concern itself with any one prospective defendant or group of defendants, but rather covers both the liabilities of those who are subject to the statutory controls under review, and the liability of those bodies entrusted to administer the statutory programmes if others are lacking in their response, the bodies in question being the local authorities.

Housing Act 1957 (Part II)

8.2   Part II of this Act represents the first major attempt at providing, via a comprehensive consolidation of preceding legislation, a clear delineation of the expected standard of housing. Although there is no specific definition of 'house', other than to mention that yards, gardens, outhouses, etc. are within the term, and that any separate unit of occupation (or one intended to be separate) should be treated as a house in its own right,[1] the Act clearly confines its attention to dwellings only. The particular subject for attack by this legislation is housing unfit for habitation, and this term is defined in section 4.

1 Housing Act 1957, s. 189(1).

8.3   By section 4(1):[1]

> In determining for any of the purposes of this Act whether a house is unfit for human habitation, regard shall be had to its condition in respect of the following matters, that is to say—
> - (a)   repair;
> - (b)   stability;
> - (c)   freedom from damp;
> - (cc) internal arrangement;
> - (d)   natural lighting;
> - (e)   ventilation;
> - (f)   water supply;
> - (g)   drainage and sanitary convenience;
> - (h)   facilities for preparation and cooking of food and for the disposal of waste water;

and the house shall be deemed to be unfit for habitation if and only if it is so far defective in one or more of the said matters that it is not reasonably suitable for occupation in that condition.

While this at first sight seems to be a helpful delineation of the areas which must be considered in assessing issues of unfitness, it must also be said that the concluding part of the section both limits the Act's impact and subjects its use to potentially great factual argument by its insistence on considering perhaps only one particular aspect in isolation and subjecting the aspect or aspects in question to detailed analysis. It must also be noted that the absence of certain features which, at the very least, might be regarded as highly desirable in a house, does not invoke the wrath of section 4; for example, houses can be lawfully inhabited notwithstanding the absence of a bathroom, inside toilet or washing facilities; a house can be legally habitable even though there is no safe method of supply of gas or electricity.

1 As amended by the Housing Act 1969, s. 71.

8.4 There is another type of omission in section 4, too. Nowhere does the section give an indication of precisely what standard the particular shortcomings of a property must attain before the house becomes uninhabitable. In the absence of such guidance, the position under the old law has to be examined, and this imposes a relatively minimal level of fitness for habitation, at least traditionally. In *Jones v Geen*,[1] it was stated that the standard imposed by the predecessors of the 1957 Act was 'naturally . . . a humble standard',[2] and that an obligation to keep a property in good and tenantable repair was far higher. Other cases perhaps show a somewhat different picture, e g a fall of plaster from a ceiling has been held to render a property unfit for human habitation[3] (however the fall had seriously injured a woman and all the ceilings appeared to be dangerous), while the House of Lords has held that broken window sash-cords can render at least a small house, with no other window but the defective one in one of the two bedrooms, uninhabitable;[4] here too injury was caused by the defect. The governmental view seems stricter; a MHLG circular[5] speaks of the need for serious inconvenience to its inhabitants to be caused before a house should be regarded as being unfit, and states that instability is only relevant where further movement is likely and would cause a threat to the occupants. Similarly, dampness must be a permanent health hazard before it becomes a reason for declaring a house to be unfit, in the official view. Overall, then, it is clear in most cases that a property must possess major defects before it will be deemed to be unfit for human habitation.

1 [1925] 1 KB 659.
2 Ibid at 668.
3 *Walker v Hobbs & Co* (1889) 23 QBD 458.
4 *Summers v Salford Corpn* [1943] AC 283, [1943] 1 All ER 68.
5 Circular No 69/67.

8.5 What now fall to be discussed are two interrelated issues viz who is liable under the Act and for what are they liable. Perhaps the best starting point is with the local authority. By section 193 of the Local Government Act 1972, it is the district authority which is responsible for housing matters. In fulfilling their functions in relation to unfit housing the local authority does not have to rely on the random reporting of such properties. Indeed, they cannot so do; by section 70 of the Housing Act 1969 it is the duty of the local authority to inspect their district so as to fulfil their Housing Act obligations. Since this is a

245

duty, any failure to perform it could be the subject of an action seeking an order of mandamus brought by an aggrieved citizen, with the necessary *locus standi* to bring such an action. Additionally, by section 157(2) of the 1957 Act itself, it is possible for any local magistrate to complain to the local medical officer of health in writing that a house is unfit for human habitation; he must then inspect and report on the house to the local authority stating his opinion on the issue of fitness. Although local authorities are no longer obliged to appoint a medical officer of health, this procedure is still extant and complaints should now be directed to another appropriate officer,[1] for example the Director of Housing. Having received the information, from whatever source, they must obviously then give consideration to it, and what action they actually take will depend on whether they feel the property in question is unfit for human habitation and, if so, on whether the property is reasonably repairable or not.[2]

1 Local Government Act 1972, Sch 29, para 4(a).
2 See Housing Act 1957, s. 39(1). See also *Ellis Copp & Co v Richmond upon Thames London Borough Council* (1976) 245 Estates Gazette 931 and *Dudlow Estates Ltd v Sefton Metropolitan Borough Council* (1978) 249 Estates Gazette 1271.

8.6 In the case of a house[1] which is capable of repair at a reasonable cost, section 9 of the 1957 Act governs the legal position. When the local authority have satisfied themselves that a house is unfit for human habitation but is capable of being brought back to the appropriate standard, they are under a duty to serve a notice upon the person having control of the house requiring him to execute works to bring the house up to the standard, detailing what works are in the authority's view needed and stating that these works will achieve the object of rendering the house again fit for human habitation. A reasonable period of at least twenty-one days has to be given for the execution of the works.

1 See Housing Act 1957, s. 9(3).

8.7 Thus a duty, established by statute, is placed upon the local authority to act upon information received and to issue notices requiring the execution of works. Similarly the statute imposes a duty on the person having control of the premises not to fall below the standard of fitness ordained and to carry out the works demanded by the local authority. Who then is the person in control of premises? By section 39(2) of the 1957 Act, this term is defined as the person who receives the rack-rent of a house, on his own account or as agent or trustee, or who would be entitled to receive it if the house were let. Thus, it may be the absentee landlord or owner of premises who is regarded as being in control of premises, rather than the tenant, although owner-occupiers will be liable in their own right. However, section 9(2) of the Act permits the local authority to serve a section 9 notice on any other person having an interest in the house, in addition to the person regarded as having control of the house.

8.8 Subsequent legislation has added to the coverage of the 1957 Act. By section 9(1A), added by virtue of section 72 of the Housing Act 1969, the local authority is granted additional powers whereby it can after due consideration also order repairs within a reasonable time exceeding twenty-one days to a property which, although not unfit for human habitation, is in need of substantial repair to bring it up to a reasonable standard, this being assessed with reference to the age and character of the property, and its locality, although this power does not extend to the ordering of internal decorative repair works. This merely gives an enabling power to the local authority but, if they decide to exercise it, again places a duty on the person having control of the house. By section 9(1B), added by virtue of section 149 of the Housing Act 1980, the local authority, if they receive representations from an occupying tenant (defined by section 9(1C) of the 1957 Act and section 104 of the Housing Act 1974 as a non-owner occupier, occupying by reason of a lease, tenancy or restricted contract provision), and if in consequence they feel that the property's condition is such as to interfere materially with the comfort of the occupying tenant, may again order repairs, again within a reasonable time of at least twenty-one days, and again not extending to internal decorative repair work. This power also applies irrespective of whether the property is fit for human habitation or not and both these new subsections go some way to ameliorating the rigorous definition of unfitness for human habitation.

8.9   It has been stated that these provisions put the person having control of the premises under a duty – how then is that duty enforced? It is section 10 of the Housing Act 1957 that provides the statutory framework. By section 10(1), the local authority may themselves carry out the work if the notice to repair has not been complied with in the stipulated time. This discretionary right is backed up by a range of ancillary provisions, including the following. By section 10(2) the local authority can give notice of its intention to proceed under section 10(1) either to the person having control of the house or its owner and if, after seven days have elapsed and work has commenced, the presence of anyone in receipt of the notice attempting to carry out any works himself will be deemed to be an obstruction of the local authority (a criminal offence) unless he shows a sudden urgent necessity to do the work because of danger to the occupants. Additionally, section 10(3) allows the local authority to claim the cost of the work, plus interest, from the defaulter, with certain limitations in the case of a claim against a mere agent or trustee, against whom a claim can only be made up to the total amount of money he has had given to him on account of repairs. Other subsections allow the local authority a choice of different forms of recovery e g via a debt action, in instalments or via the creation of a charge on the premises.

8.10   It is also possible for the person in control of the premises, or indeed any person aggrieved (though it is hard to see who else other than the person(s) in control of the premises might be aggrieved), to appeal by virtue of section 11(1) against either the notice of repair or a claim for expenses or their recovery after non-repair; such appeals must be brought within twenty-one days of the service of the notice, etc., and the appeal halts any action until the county court decides the case; this the court may do, by section 11(3), in a variety of ways, such as partly or fully upholding the notice, etc., and the court may, in a case where the appeal against a notice to repair is allowed, state whether the house is capable of repair at a reasonable cost or not. If it is held to be capable of economical repair, the local authority may, under section 12 of the 1957 Act compulsorily purchase it with ministerial authorisation, or purchase it in the ordinary manner. The authority is obliged to execute the works originally demanded if they effect a compulsory purchase of the property.

8.11   It should also be briefly noted that any tenant or lessee who has to carry out works as a result of the issue of a section 9 notice to repair is entitled to claim such proportion of his expenditure from his landlord/lessor as the court may feel just if it amounts to a default by the landlord/lessor under the agreement between the parties. The court is directed to have regard to the respective repair obligations, the length of the unexpired part of the lease, the rent payable and other relevant circumstances.

8.12　In the case of a house which in the view of the local authority is unfit for human habitation a separate set of rules is applicable. The keynote section here is section 16 which creates a different procedure whereby the local authority, having received information and in consequence satisfied themselves of the unfitness and economically unrepairable condition of the premises in question, is then under a duty to give notice of a meeting at least twenty-one days after the service of the notice to the person having control of the house, any other person who is an owner thereof and if reasonably ascertainable, every mortgagee thereof; these parties are then entitled to attend the meeting with the local authority to consider the future of the premises. By section 16(3) they may themselves undertake to carry out renovation; by section 16(4) it is for the local authority to decide whether to accept this offer, after consultation with any other interested parties at the meeting and they may accept an undertaking that the work will be done within a specified time, or alternatively that the premises will not be used for human habitation until appropriate works have been carried out.

8.13　If no acceptable undertaking is forthcoming or if an undertaking's terms are breached, further action must be taken by the local authority.[1] The most usual response is the issue of a demolition order; by section 21, this commands the evacuation of the premises within a stated period of at least twenty-eight days and the demolition of the premises normally within a six week period thereafter. A copy of the demolition order is sent to all the parties to whom notice is given under section 16.[2] The issue of a demolition order removes any Rent Acts protection the tenant might otherwise have enjoyed and is accompanied by what is in effect a possession order issued by the local authority, according to section 22 of the 1957 Act.

1　Housing Act 1957, s. 17.
2　Ibid, s. 19.

8.14　The demolition order obliges the owner of the premises to carry out the work of demolition and if he does not do so within the stated time limit, the obligation reverts to the local authority who must enter and demolish the premises and sell the materials, under section 23 of the 1957 Act; this section also permits the local authority to claim for the expense incurred in the demolition work though with due credit being given in respect of any profits made by the sale of materials, and any net surplus reverting to the owner or owners of the premises. The only alternative approach is for the owner to submit proposals to the local authority for reconstruction, enlargement or improvement of the property. According to section 24(1), the authority, if satisfied that this will mean that habitable houses will be provided, may extend the demolition period in order to allow the owner time to do the work; however, it has been held by the Court of Appeal that such an extension of time must not be unreasonable, and a seven-year extension would be so unreasonable.[1]

1　*Pocklington v Melksham UDC* [1964] 2 QB 673, [1964] 2 All ER 862.

8.15　In certain cases, a demolition order is inexpedient or inappropriate, and instead the local authority may make a less drastic order, the closing order.

There are three main instances where a closing order will be more appropriate. By the proviso to section 17(1) of the 1957 Act, the local authority may issue a closing order, where the effect of a demolition order would be to have an adverse effect on another building, e g the next house in a terrace. By section 17(3) of the same Act a closing order must be used in the case of any listed or other building of historic or architectural interest, while by section 18 a closing order has to be issued if the local authority wishes to take any action in respect of an unfit dwelling which is part of a building or a wholly or substantially underground room which is deemed to be unfit for human habitation by reason either of its height being less than 7 feet or its inadequate ventilation, lighting or hygiene. By section 26(1) of the Housing Act 1961, a closing order may be substituted for a demolition order when the owner of the premises makes an acceptable proposal for use of the premises for something other than human habitation.

8.16 It is a criminal offence to continue to use premises in contravention of a closing order, knowing that such an order has been made, by section 27(1) of the 1957 Act; naturally, Rent Act protection is removed where a closing order has been issued, according to section 27(5). Appeal can be made against both demolition[1] and closing orders[2] by any person aggrieved to the county court, and the judge has a wide discretion in relation to demolition orders, under section 20(3). No appeal may however be brought against either order by a person who is in occupation of the premises under a lease or agreement of which the unexpired term does not exceed three years, under sections 20(2) and 27(4) of the 1957 Act.

1 Housing Act 1957, s. 20(1).
2 Ibid, s. 27(3).

8.17 There is an alternative method of proceeding given to the local authority by section 17(2) of the Housing Act 1957; if the authority is of the view that the house is or could be made capable of being usable as short-term accommodation, they may purchase the house instead of making a demolition or closing order. Similar procedures are established; all the relevant parties have to be given advance notification of the decision to purchase under section 19; the rights of appeal against demolition orders also apply in relation to the decision to purchase, according to section 20. Care must be taken by the authority not to use this power to increase the size of its permanent housing stock, however; this was emphasised by the Court of Appeal in *Victoria Square Property Co v Southwark London Borough*.[1] By section 29 of the 1957 Act, the purchase may be effected either by agreement or, with ministerial consent, compulsorily. Compensation is payable under this section, and is assessed at cleared site value i e the site is regarded as a site which has been cleared and is available for development.

1 [1978] 2 All ER 281, [1978] 1 WLR 463.

8.18 These wide-ranging powers of demolition, closure and purchase may leave certain parties aggrieved, for example persons who have poured much money into a property in an attempt to keep it fit for human habitation, or sitting tenants who suddenly, and often through no fault of their own, find themselves without Rent Acts protection and indeed without a tenancy. Further provisions of the 1957 Act endeavour to cover these situations. Under section 30, compensation is normally payable by the local authority to anyone who claims within three months of the issue of a demolition or closing order or of a notice of intended purchase that the property has been well maintained, and that this is due at least in part to his own work – either landlords or tenants are able to bring claims under this section. A complex formula exists for the calculation of such payments.[1] By section 32 of the 1957 Act, the local authority may pay to any person displaced from a property as a result of the exercise of the foregoing powers a reasonable allowance towards removal expenses and an allowance towards lost trade if the person displaced was carrying on a business from the house in question.

1 Housing Act 1957, Sch 2, Pt 1, as substituted and amended.

8.19 The statutory control of unfit houses provided by Part II of the 1957 Housing Act is not simple, but it is hoped that the pattern has been made clear. Any person having control of premises is subject to duties to prevent them becoming unfit for human habitation if they are used for residential purposes; additionally, the new subsections interposed into section 9 provide extra duties even when the premises have not (yet) reached the statutory standard of unfitness. The local authority is also under extensive duties to investigate and to take action though their obligations to actually enforce the orders they make are more onerous in the case of an unfit house beyond economical repair. The principal deficiencies of the legislation are, it is suggested, the definition of unfitness in section 4 which both leaves too much to the discretion of the court in each case and is, overall, a somewhat restrictive definition, and also the great complexity of the legislation, which is hardly an incentive to employ it. An additional deficiency has recently been confirmed by the decision in *R v Cardiff City Council, ex parte Cross*.[1] In this first instance decision, the plaintiff was the tenant of a council-owned property in Cardiff which was agreed to be unfit for human habitation. However, it was held that he could not act against the landlord under the 1957 Act because it was imposssible for a local authority to apply the statutory formulations to its own houses; they could not serve on themselves notices of repair or to demolish. If the case is correct, which may be doubted, the 1957 Act therefore has no application to a local authority's own houses in its own area. However, it is fair to say that the 1957 legislation attempts to provide a uniform standard covering most of the basic expectations which might be had in relation to housing, and the fact that the basic duties and ancillary powers are placed in the hands of local authorities is an assistance to their enforcement.

1 [1981] RVR 155.

Public Health Act 1936 (Part III)

8.20 An entirely separate set of statutory rules in relation to defective premises is laid down by the Public Health Act 1936; this is concerned with what is undoubtedly a narrower range of premises, mainly those prejudicial to health. The key to the approach of the legislation is the term 'statutory nuisance'. Section 92(1) (a) includes within this term 'premises in such a state as to be prejudicial to health or a nuisance'. Section 343(1) explains that 'prejudicial to health' means 'injurious, or likely to cause injury, to health', and 'nuisance' would appear to have its usual common law meaning.[1] Other examples of statutory nuisance given by section 92 include accumulations or deposits, or workplaces (whether inadequately ventilated, uncleaned or overcrowded) which, in each case, are prejudicial to health. The crucial word 'health' goes undefined, and the cases which discuss the meaning of 'prejudicial to health or a nuisance' although tending not to distinguish between the two aspects, nevertheless ultimately give a clear picture. In *Coventry City Council v Cartwright*,[2] a case concerning an accumulation of building and household refuse on a vacant site in a residential area, it was held by Lord Widgery CJ in the Divisional Court that 'the underlying conception of the section is that that which is struck at is an accumulation of something which produces a threat to health in the sense of a threat of disease, vermin or the like'.[3] This is the clearest recent case, but previously, in *Galer v Morrissey*,[4] it had been held that a defendant's collection of noisy greyhounds was not for that reason alone to be regarded as a statutory nuisance, but could be so regarded in the light of the insanitary or similar consequences of their presence, and this case was explained in the *Coventry* case as justifying an overall view that the 1936 Act applies to any situation where there is a public health consequence, irrespective of the actual form taken by the threat to health. So any tangible manifestation of a threat to health will attract the attention of Part III of the Public Health Act 1936.

1 See paras 2.47 ff, above.
2 [1975] 2 All ER 99, [1975] 1 WLR 845.
3 Ibid at 102 and 849.
4 [1955] 1 All ER 380, [1955] 1 WLR 110.

8.21 How, then, does the Act endeavour to deal with statutory nuisances? Again local authority enforcement is the key, and an essential precursor of this is provided by section 91, which places the local authority (again the district council)[1] under a duty to ensure that their area is inspected, with a view to the detection of statutory nuisances. Whether through this inspection, or any other reason, when they are satisfied that there is in existence a statutory nuisance, they must, by virtue of section 93, serve an abatement notice on the 'person by whose act, fault or sufferance the nuisance arises or continues; or, if that person cannot be found, on the owner or occupier of the premises on which the nuisance arises'. This notice requires the abatement of the nuisance and commands the performance of such works as are necessary.

1 Local Government Act 1972, s. 180.

8.22 The section is not without its difficulties. Although the words of the section indicate that a local authority, on being satisfied of the existence of a statutory nuisance 'shall' serve an abatement notice, it has been held that the word 'shall' does not indicate a mandatory duty on the local authority. The authority for this unusual view is *Nottingham Corporation v Newton*,[1] where Lord Widgery CJ, in the Divisional Court, stated that the local authority is not bound to follow the section 93 procedure, but may invoke any other form of proceedings to deal with the problem, such as those laid down by the Housing Act 1957. It may at least be said, therefore, that the local authority are obliged by section 93 to act albeit that they are not under an obligation to follow the procedure established by that section. It now seems likely that the local authority can be forced by an order of mandamus to fulfil their obligations under the Act, the cause of previous objections having been removed, though it is debatable whether this remedy is of great assistance here given the wide range of options open to the local authority after the decision in the *Nottingham* case; mandamus may only be usable to force the authority to exercise their discretion as to which remedy to take.[2] The other noteworthy feature of section 93 is the huge range of persons against whom the local authority may take action; not only is anyone who may remotely be regarded as being in any way responsible for the nuisance (though apparently not beyond those held liable under the common law)[3] potentially liable, but if they cannot be found the owner[4] or occupier will be liable even though he might until the service of the notice have been unaware of the existence of the nuisance. However, two additional provisions of section 93 do limit the range of persons potentially affected by abatement notices. Firstly, where the statutory nuisance arises from any defect of a structural character, the notice shall be served on the owner of the premises and, secondly, where the actual person causing the nuisance cannot be found, and the owner or occupier cannot be regarded as personally responsible (by 'act, default or sufferance') for the nuisance, the local authority may, if it so wishes, proceed itself to deal with the problem.

1 [1974] 2 All ER 760, [1974] 1 WLR 923.
2 See *Social Welfare Law* (ed Pollard) paras 1151–1152.
3 See paras 2.47 ff, above.
4 See Public Health Act 1936, s. 343(1)

8.23 If the abatement notice does not succeed in its aim of removing the nuisance, or if there will, in the view of the local authority, be a likely recurrence of the nuisance, the local authority may then make a complaint to a justice of the peace;[1] a summons is then issued against the person in breach of the abatement notice. If the local authority's claim is substantiated,[2] the magistrates' court, under section 94(2) 'shall' issue a nuisance order. This is another potentially misleading use of the imperative, since once again the *Nottingham* case states that although the justices have no option but to make a nuisance order, there is a considerable scope for variation of the terms thereof e g as to the time to be given for compliance, or reflecting the actual level of danger (if any) created by the statutory nuisance. This is however quite appropriate in the light of the wording of section 94(2), which gives the justices wide powers to deal with the matter; the nuisance order may demand compliance with all or some of the stipulations of the abatement notice or abatement by some other means and the execution of works, but is silent as to how this end shall be achieved.

1 The local authority must take some action but is not confined to proceedings under the Public Health Act 1936; *Nottingham Corpn v Newton* [1974] 2 All ER 760, [1974] 1 WLR 923.
2 With regard to the facts existing at the date of the hearing; *Coventry City Council v Doyle* [1981] 2 All ER 184.

8.24 If the nuisance still exists (or is likely to recur) at the date when the abatement notice is served and when the complaint was made, the defendant will be ordered to pay the local authority's reasonable expenses, even though the nuisance no longer exists (or is unlikely to recur) at the date of the hearing, under section 94(3) of the Act.

8.25 The court's powers are not confined simply to the issue of a nuisance order and the associated items of ancillary relief. By section 94(6) the nuisance order may be addressed to and executed by the local authority if the person who causes the nuisance or the owner or occupier of the premises cannot be found. Section 94(2) permits the court additionally to prohibit the use of a building for human habitation if the nuisance renders the premises unfit for that purpose. By section 95 the court can fine persons who without reasonable excuse are in breach of a nuisance order made against them, and in cases such as this where a nuisance order has not been obeyed the local authority is permitted to abate the nuisance itself and, by section 96, may claim reasonable expenses.

8.26 The provisions can be widely applied. By virtue of section 98, a local authority may take action against a statutory nuisance perpetrated outside the authority's own area if their area is to some extent affected. Of far greater importance, however, is section 99 of the Act, which grants a right to any person aggrieved by a statutory nuisance to lay a complaint before the justices and this will activate the nuisance order proceedings before the magistrates' court; these will proceed in almost exactly the same fashion as if the complaint had been brought by the local authority itself. The main differences are that although the authority did not bring the complaint, they may nonetheless be commanded to abate the nuisance, though they may make representations to the court, and also the complainant may be paid his own reasonable expenses on the same basis as that established for payment of the local authorities' own expenses under section 94(3).[1]

1 *Coventry City Council v Doyle* [1981] 2 All ER 184.

8.27 A note is in order on the vexed question of the precise relationship of the 1936 and the 1957 legislation. They overlap with each other; in *Salford City Council v McNally*[1] it was held that compliance with Housing Act provisions was no defence to action under the 1936 Act. This is unsurprising, however, since the Acts are designed to deal with different situations; the 1957 Act seeks permanent change in the condition of (repairable) properties by ordaining the carrying out of works to rectify the situation, whereas the earlier legislation will only seek to remove the short-term nuisance, and may not seek to attack its underlying causes. Although a statutory nuisance may overall be a narrower concept than unfitness for human habitation, the Public Health Acts do seem to be more readily usable. The 1936 legislation may be used against a local authority itself responsible for a statutory nuisance, whereas as has been seen the 1957 Act obligations have been held not to extend to local authorities' own premises. Also, the 1936 legislation gives via section 99 a useful remedy whereby the individual aggrieved by a statutory nuisance may take action himself without recourse to the local authority; this is particularly important in cases where council tenants wish to take action against their landlords, and section 99 actions are increasingly now threatened in such cases. Also, it will be recalled that there now seems no bar in seeking an order of mandamus against a local authority in breach of its obligations under either code. Only the 1936 Act may be used in respect of non-residential premises.

1 [1976] AC 379, [1975] 2 All ER 860.

Other statutory provisions

8.28 The foregoing should in no way be regarded as representing the totality of statutory provisions providing for public control of defective premises. It may be observed that neither the 1936 nor the 1957 legislation provides an obvious answer to a dangerous structure in need of immediate repair or demolition, while the provisions are also cumbersome if it is sought to apply them to a whole group of dwelling units in need of attention.

1 DANGEROUS PREMISES AND EMERGENCY ACTION

8.29 The best starting-point here is with the Public Health Act 1936, section 58. This permits the district council to go to the magistrates' court and there apply for an order requiring the owner[1] of any dangerous or dilapidated building or structure either to execute works to render the building or structure safe or else to demolish either the whole structure or the dangerous parts thereof and remove the resultant rubble. The Public Health Act 1961, section 24, extended the coverage of the earlier Act, and the order may be granted whether the building is dangerous to its own occupants or to the occupants of neighbouring buildings or to passers-by. Non-compliance with an order made pursuant to section 58 permits the local authority to carry out the terms of the order themselves and to recover their reasonable expenses from the defaulting owner. It should be noted in this context that section 278 of the Public Health Act 1936 states that a local authority shall make full compensation to anyone who through no fault of their own sustains damage by reason of the local authority's exercise of any of the powers granted to it under the Act. The effect of this section is to negate any claim of statutory authority which the local authority may be minded to plead[2] in a civil action against it; it seems that the section would permit the payment of compensation to anyone in adjacent premises which were damaged by the local authority's exercise of its demolition powers under section 58, at least where that damage is an inevitable consequence of the exercise of the power.[3]

1 See Public Health Act 1936, s. 343(1).
2 *Lingké v Christchurch Corpn* [1912] 3 KB 595.
3 See also paras 5.61 ff, above.

8.30 An alternative method of dealing with certain dangerous buildings is provided by section 72 of the Housing Act 1957 which covers 'obstructive buildings', buildings which by reason of their contact with, or proximity to, other buildings, are dangerous or injurious to health, but not including properties owned by the local authority or (if not an office, dwelling or showroom) any statutory undertakers.[1] By section 72(1) the local authority may serve a notice on the owner or owners[2] of the building giving at least twenty-one days' notice of a meeting to consider whether the building should be demolished. If after due consideration the authority decides at this meeting to demolish the building as being obstructive, no more than two months shall be given to vacate the building, though persons aggrieved have twenty-one days in which to lodge an appeal to the county court. In many respects this section provides a remedy analogous to, and representing an extension of, the powers under section 16 of the same Act,[3] covering all buildings, if obstructive, and not just dwelling houses.

1 Housing Act 1957, s. 72(4) and (5).
2 Ibid, s. 189(1)
3 See para 8.12, above.

8.31 Additional methods of dealing with possibly dangerous structures are provided by the Public Health Act 1961. This, by section 25, permits emergency action by the local authority to deal with dangerous buildings and structures or parts thereof. These expedited procedures, as compared with section 58 of the 1936 Act, are to be used when the authority is of the view that immediate action should be taken to remove the danger, and may be employed without even giving notice to the owner and occupier of the building, if it is not reasonably practicable so to do (though this will presumably be a rare event in the case of the occupier). The section empowers the authority to take such steps as are necessary for the removal of the danger created by the premises – a blanket discretion. The local authority is also permitted to recover its expenses, if reasonably incurred. By section 25(8) the surveyor of a local authority may act on his own initiative, without being empowered so to do by his local authority.

8.32 The same Act, by section 26, also provides an expedited procedure for dealing with premises which are prejudicial to health or a nuisance, i e are in effect a statutory nuisance, but which cannot be satisfactorily dealt with under the procedures laid down by the 1936 Act in consequence of an unreasonable delay being caused by their use. If a local authority is satisfied that premises fall into this category they may, instead of serving an abatement notice, serve a notice stating that they themselves intend to remedy specified defects. Only nine days need then elapse before the authority can enter and execute the works in question, and also claim expenses reasonably incurred thereby. The recipient of the notice (normally the person responsible for the nuisance or the owner or occupier of the land on which it exists)[1] has seven days to serve a counter-notice stating that he will deal with the statutory nuisance himself; this will halt the local authority unless and until recommencement of the works is still unduly delayed or is being carried out at an unduly slow rate.[2] By section 26(6) these powers are subject to the presence of a building preservation order, while by section 26(7) they are in addition, and as an alternative, to the powers granted by the Housing Act 1957, section 9.[3]

1 Public Health Act 1936, s. 93. See para 8.22, above.
2 Public Health Act 1961, s. 26(3).
3 See paras 8.6 ff, above.

8.33 Also, section 27 of the 1961 Act provides additional powers, though in this instance in respect of buildings or structures which are in such a ruinous or dilapidated condition that they are seriously detrimental to the amenities of the neighbourhood. Such premises are dealt with by the local authority issuing a written[1] note to the owner of the premises, specifically[2] requiring him to execute repair or restoration work or to demolish the premises and clear the site, so as to enhance the amenity of the neighbourhood. A further additional power is created by the Local Government (Miscellaneous Provisions) Act 1976, section 8(1). Under this, a local authority (again the district council in most cases) may order the demolition of or the execution of other works on premises after only as little as forty-eight hours' notice to the owner, if the premises are unoccupied, and are the subject either of an undertaking that they will not be used for human habitation or a closing order, made by virtue of the Housing Act 1957. This power may be employed either to secure more effectively the premises against unauthorised entry or to prevent them being or becoming a danger to public health.

1 Public Health Act 1936, s. 283(1).
2 Public Health Act 1961, s. 27(3); Public Health Act 1936, s. 290.

2 PROPERTIES IN MULTI-OCCUPANCY
8.34 Separate powers exist in relation to properties in multi-occupancy i e premises where more than one dwelling-unit exists, such as a house split into flats or an old tenement building.[1] The current definition of a house in multi-occupancy is provided by the Housing Act 1969, section 58(1), whereby

the legislation on the topic is taken as covering houses which are occupied by persons who do not form a single household. This means that a house which is occupied by a large family is not covered by the legislation,[2] but a large communal grouping of people in a house may be covered. This latter point is confirmed by the decision of the House of Lords in *Simmons v Pizzey*,[3] which concerned a hostel for wives who had been violently treated by their husbands, with a large and fluctuating population of unrelated women, situated in an ordinary suburban house. The question of what constituted a 'household' was regarded as a question of fact, and consideration was given to the very large number of women in the house, the fact that there was nothing constant or permanent about either the number or the identities of the population and the inherently temporary nature of the accommodation provided by such a refuge.

1 But not a purpose-built block of self-contained flats. See Woodfall *Landlord and Tenant* para 1.1605.
2 *Wolkind v Ali* [1975] 1 All ER 193, [1975] 1 WLR 170.
3 [1979] AC 37, [1977] 2 All ER 432.

8.35 In cases of multi-occupancy, by section 12 of the Housing Act 1961 the local authority is empowered to apply a code of management to the property; this code follows the general principles set out in section 13(1) of the Housing Act 1961, covering such matters as sanitation, safe access and refuse disposal and covered in detail by the Housing (Management of Houses in Multiple Occupation) Order 1962.[1] This then imposes an obligation upon the owner or lessee of the property who receives the rents from the actual occupants to fulfil the management order; it is a criminal offence if it is knowingly contravened.[2] If, however, the condition of a house remains defective after this, in the view of the local authority, because of a neglect to comply with the regulations, the authority may issue a further notice to the owner or lessee of the property in receipt of the rents specifying the shortcomings of the property and requiring that they be made good within a stated period of at least twenty-one days.[3] By section 15 of the Housing Act 1961 a similar power is granted to the local authority whether a management order has been applied to the property or not, whereby the authority may require works to be carried out to remedy a situation where certain stated basic features of the property, e g lighting, ventilation, hygiene and sanitation, water supply and food storage and preparation arrangements, are inadequate in the light of the particular level of multi-occupancy. The notice will be satisfied by an adequate reduction in the level of multi-occupancy, according to section 15(2) of the Act. Additional provisions in the form of section 147 of the Housing Act 1980 (and Schedule 24 thereto) give the local authority power to require works to be carried out in multi-occupied houses to aid escape in the event of a fire.

1 SI 1962 No 668.
2 Housing Act 1961, s. 13(4).
3 Ibid, s. 14.

8.36 Under section 18 of the 1961 Act, the local authority is again empowered to carry out the work (and obtain reasonable compensation for its labours) if the requirements of the previous sections have not been complied with by the owner, etc. It is also a criminal offence if there is a wilful failure to comply with the notices to repair. On the other hand, a right of appeal is granted to the recipient of a notice, to the magistrates' court in a case under section 14, otherwise to the county court, on certain grounds covering both the reasoning behind and the form of the notice.¹

1 See Woodfall *Landlord and Tenant* para 1.1610.

8.37 An additional provision to be noted briefly is the Housing Act 1964, which by Part IV (sections 73–91) allows the local authority to make a control order in respect of any house in their locality either if an order made under section 12 of the 1961 Act is in force, or if a notice has been served by virtue of sections 14, 15 or 19 (the latter is an order to reduce overcrowding) or if any such order or notice could be made or served in view of the living conditions in the house under discussion. The control order permits the authority to enter the premises itself and take all such immediate steps as appear to be necessary to protect the safety, health or welfare of residents of the house; by section 74(1) the local authority is granted a right to possession of the premises, and effectively takes control of them, often for a long period.

3 AREA ACTION
8.38 Houses do not exist in isolation from each other; groups of them are usually constructed together. It is therefore often the case that defects in premises are shared by many adjacent properties and that the concentration of the law on remedying defects in individual houses may be seen as misplaced. Housing law has recognised these facts, and subjects certain areas to additional controls. The Housing Act 1969 created, by section 28, 'general improvement areas', areas of a predominantly residential character where the local authority is of the view that living conditions are in need of improvement. The Housing Act 1974 created 'housing action areas', areas where the physical state of the housing stock and the social conditions in the area are poor, but are capable of improvement over a period, and also created 'priority neighbourhoods', an area usually adjacent to one of the other types of area, and in any case a category no longer in existence.¹ In housing action areas, the local authority, by section 44, may with the consent of the Secretary of State, inter alia improve or repair houses in the area; they also have powers to purchase property in the area. In general improvement areas, the local authority's principal power is to provide assistance of a financial nature towards the carrying out of works on the premises.

1 Housing Act 1980, s. 109.

8.39 In both housing action areas and general improvement areas, under Part VIII of the Housing Act 1974, powers are given to the authority to raise the standard of accommodation by means of an insistence on the provision of 'standard amenities' viz a fixed bath or shower, washbasin and sink, in each case with hot and cold water supplied, and a water closet with the bath/shower normally in a bathroom and the water closet, if reasonably practicable, in the dwelling.¹ Where the authority finds a dwelling in an appropriate area which lacks one or more of the standard amenities, and which is capable at reasonable expense of improvement to the full standard or, failing that, to the reduced standard (these terms are explained below) and the dwelling was in existence before 3 October 1961, the authority may serve a notice, by virtue of section 85(1) on the person having control of the dwelling, specifying the works necessary for the improvement of the dwelling up to the appropriate standard, and giving a date for a meeting with interested parties at least twenty-one days in the future to decide on the works or any alternatives and related issues such as interim accommodation. The local authority may not, under section 85(3), serve a section 85 notice on an owner-occupier, unless they feel another dwelling cannot be improved without the owner-occupied property also being improved, while under section 99, the provisions do not extend to, inter alia, properties owned by local authorities and other public bodies.

1 Housing Act 1974, ss. 58, 84, 104 and Sch 6.

8.40 The full standard of housing is where the dwelling has all the standard amenities for the exclusive use of its own occupants, is in good repair with regard to age, locality etc., conforms with thermal insulation requirements, is fit for human habitation, and is likely to be usable as a dwelling for a period (normally) of fifteen years. A formal dispensation with any of these elements will mean that the property still has to attain the reduced standard, i e compliance with all those requirements in respect of which there has been no dispensation.[1]

1 Ibid, s. 103A, inserted by the Housing Act 1980, Sch 25.

8.41 The issue of a section 85 notice may be followed by a satisfactory undertaking by the person having control of the dwelling (or anyone else with an estate or interest therein) that he will undertake the work, and perform it within nine months; if no satisfactory undertaking is forthcoming, or if the works are not carried out or are unlikely to be fulfilled, the local authority may serve an improvement notice on the person having control of the dwelling.[1] By section 90 of the 1974 Act, this notice must specify the works required to improve the dwelling, giving an estimate of the cost, and require their performance within twelve months. If this period also elapses, and the work is still not done, or if this appears to be likely to be the case after due enquiry, the local authority may enter and do the work themselves, under section 93, and claim their reasonable expenses from the person having control of the dwelling, by virtue of section 94.

1 Housing Act 1974, ss. 87 and 88.

8.42 The recipient of the improvement notice may of course appeal against it; by section 91 an appeal lies to the county court by the person having the control of the dwelling or anyone else with an interest in it, including the tenant, on a wide range of grounds, relating to substance and form.[1] The notice becomes operative after this six week period has elapsed, unless there has been an appeal, under section 92(1) of the 1974 Act.

1 Ibid, s. 91(2).

8.43 In the event of an area being as a whole unfit for human habitation or being potentially dangerous or injurious to the inhabitants because of the narrowness or bad arrangement of the streets, more drastic measures are open to the local authority. If they are satisfied that demolition of the buildings in the area is appropriate (rather than rehabilitation), they may declare the area to be a clearance area by a resolution made by authority of section 42(1) of the Housing Act 1957, which insists that suitable accommodation be available for those displaced and that the authority has adequate resources. By section 43 (1)(b) it is a question for agreement between the parties as to how the clearance will then take place e g by compulsory purchase or an agreement that the owner will carry out the demolition. This is a complex area with much litigation and many ancillary provisions to confuse the picture.[1]

1 See Hughes *Public Sector Housing Law* pp. 251 ff.

4 OTHER POWERS AND DUTIES

8.44 Local authorities are granted a considerable range of further powers and duties in respect of premises, chiefly ensuring adequate standards of health or hygiene. The Public Health Act 1936, section 83 (as amended)[1] states that the local authority shall give notice to the owner or occupier of the premises requiring him to take (specified) steps to prevent the premises remaining in such a filthy or unwholesome condition as to be prejudicial to health; or from being verminous. Cleansing and disinfecting are the normal consequences of action under this section. Also, the Prevention of Damage by Pests Act 1949, section 2, states that, as far as is practicable, local authorities must keep their areas free from vermin i e rats and mice. The occupier is obliged to inform the authority of any vermin on his land; the local authority may then require their destruction, and the premises' continuing freedom from vermin.

1 By the Public Health Act 1961, s. 35.

8.45 More generally, the local authority has obligations concerning sewage and sanitation. The Public Health Act 1936[1] creates a duty to provide a sewage system, by section 14, and to maintain it, by section 23. These obligations are backed up by a duty[2] to require the owner of buildings to make adequate provision for drainage where none has been made or require the owner or occupier to carry out work of renewal, repair or cleansing where existing drainage facilities are inadequate; similar provisions exist in relation to buildings where the provision or standard of sanitary conveniences is inadequate.[3] The mandatory character of these obligations implies that an order of mandamus may be obtained as against a local authority in breach by anyone affected by that breach.[4] Also, section 322 of the 1936 Act entitles anyone to complain to the Minister that a local authority is in breach of its obligations under the Public Health legislation and the Minister may feel that an inquiry is appropriate to investigate the allegations. If this supports the claims against the authority, the Minister may direct them to act in accordance with the legislation; if default continues, the Minister may even transfer the relevant functions to himself.

1 On public health generally, see, inter alia, 37 *Halsbury's Law of England* (4th edn).
2 Public Health Act 1936, s. 39.
3 Ibid, ss. 44–47.
4 If they have appropriate *locus standi*.

5 LONDON

8.46 It is important to note that the Public Health Acts have only a limited application to London or, to be precise, to the inner London Boroughs and the City of London. In particular, section 58 of the 1936 Act, and sections 24, 25, and 27 of the 1961 Act do not apply, but a similar regime is established by Part VII of the London Building Acts (Amendment) Act 1939, as amended by the London County Council (General Powers) Act 1958.

8.47 The important public law controls on defective premises now form a major part of the law on the subject, and run hand in hand with the private law remedies discussed in the rest of this work. They usually do not rely on the individual taking action, though the discretionary nature of a large number of the obligations placed on local authorities does perhaps lessen their importance, especially in times which are difficult financially. However, they clearly still are highly significant in their effect on the responsibilities of both local authorities and owners and occupiers, and must not be ignored in the consideration of defective premises cases.

Chapter 9

Joint liability and contribution between parties

9.1 It will be apparent that many cases concerning defective premises involve more than two parties; many of the major decisions we have discussed have recurred in two or more chapters of this book for precisely that reason. Therefore, in many cases the owner or occupier of defective premises will be seeking redress from more than one defendant. As a result of this, it is important to see what legal rules govern such situations of joint liability, and if more than one person is found liable for any damage, what principles are employed to assess the proportion each should pay. In addition to coverage of these two legal issues, this chapter will also attempt to provide some more practical guidance, in cases where a multiplicity of potential defendants are involved in a defective premises case, by considering whether it might be advantageous to sue any particular party, and also by considering how, in cases where more than one person is liable, liability may be apportioned between the parties.

A Joint liability

9.2 In a defective premises case, the various potential parties may be liable either in contract or tort, and formerly separate and special rules applied to joint liability issues in the two forms of obligation. However, as will be seen, much of the complexity has been removed by recent legislation.

9.3 The common law position is that a plaintiff may sue any or all of a multiplicity of tortfeasors for the full amount of his loss,[1] irrespective of the actual degree of responsibility of the defendant or defendants chosen, as long as he or they in some way contributed to the same damage as the others. (Where tortfeasors are responsible for independent aspects of the damage suffered by the plaintiff, their liability is apportioned appropriately.) Thus, if A, an architect and B, a builder are both negligent in their work on C's house, C can sue either A or B, or take action against both, in each case for the full sum lost if they both contribute to the same damage.

1 *Clark v Newsam* (1847) 1 Exch 131 at 140.

9.4 In contract cases, construction of the contract will normally show that there is joint and equal liability imposed on two or more parties when they have agreed to perform a single contractual obligation for another, unless the contract clearly shows that this is not the intention. This may even be the case when not all the parties have themselves provided consideration, though the point is not as yet settled.[1] It is also a question of construction in most cases as to whether the contract is to be regarded as a joint contract or as a joint and several contract i e whether action has to be taken against all the promisors or against any or all. Where the plaintiff's loss has been caused by separate breaches of contract on the part of more than one contractor e g where C's premises are damaged by both A, his architect, and B, his builder, being in breach of their separate contracts with him, this is not as such a question of joint liability; C may sue either A or B for as much of his loss as he can prove is attributable to that defendant.

1 See *Coulls v Bagot's Executor and Trustee Co Ltd* [1967] ALR 385; *McEvoy v Belfast Banking Co Ltd* [1935] AC 24.

9.5 Where a plaintiff may be able to sue different wrongdoers in contract and in tort, e g where the plaintiff's property is damaged by both a builder's breach of contract and a local authority's negligent inspection, this again is not a case of joint liability, but is one where the court has to attempt to apportion the liability.

9.6 In many cases therefore, the plaintiff will have to take action against all those responsible for his loss; however, where there is a genuine case of joint liability in contract or in tort, the plaintiff may select only one of those liable and seek full redress from him, leaving the other party to claim a contribution from the others responsible.[1]

1 Below.

9.7 However, the complexity of the position will be eased by the fact that two or more persons may be joined together in one action as defendants where some common question of fact or law would arise in all the otherwise separate actions;[1] even if the plaintiff does not himself seek to join all the potential defendants, a defendant may himself try and lessen his liability by joining any other party from whom he can claim a contribution or indemnity by means of a third party notice.[2] Thus, it is normal that issues of apportionment of liability, and issues of contribution between those jointly liable, will both arise at the trial.

1 RSC Ord 15, r 4.
2 RSC Ord 16, r 1.

B Contribution – entitlement to claim

9.8 There are two ways in which an entitlement to claim contribution arises. Firstly, there is a statutory right to claim against others liable in respect of the same damage, in particular those jointly liable, under the Civil Liability (Contribution) Act 1978.[1] Secondly, a defendant may also claim a contribution from the plaintiff, if the plaintiff is contributorily negligent, under the Law Reform (Contributory Negligence) Act of 1945.

1 See Dugdale (1979) 40 MLR 182.

9.9 The Civil Liability (Contribution) Act 1978 is a major piece of legislation, representing an incorporation and a development of the previous legislation, section 6 of the Law Reform (Married Women and Tortfeasors) Act 1935, which was itself the first attempt to provide for contribution, as between joint tortfeasors only. The 1978 Act applies in respect of all damage occurring after 1 January 1979, unless the obligation in question was undertaken before that date.[1] The first major change made by the Act is by section 1(1), which permits any person liable in respect of damage suffered by another to claim a contribution from anyone else liable in respect of the same damage, this clearly including cases of joint liability.

1 Civil Liability (Contribution) Act 1978, ss. 10(2), 7(2).

9.10 The full significance of this is made clear by section 6(1), whereby 'a person is liable in respect of any damage for the purpose of this Act if the person who suffered it . . . is entitled to recover compensation from him in respect of that damage' (whatever the legal basis of his liability, whether tort, breach of contract, breach of trust or otherwise). Thus the architect who is being sued in tort may now, for the first time, proceed against the builder who is liable contractually to the plaintiff, and recover a contribution from him, though the phrase, 'entitled to recover compensation', is the source of some minor difficulty since it is an open question whether it will extend, for example, to a case where the builder is not held liable in damages, but rather 'compensates' the plaintiff by way of a predetermined sum agreed in the contract, or by forfeiting a bonus. It is submitted tentatively that since the effect of both these is to provide, directly or indirectly, some degree of recompense to the plaintiff, they should therefore be regarded as falling within the statutory formulation; this also has the advantage of rendering the 1978 Act more cogent and comprehensive in its scope.

9.11 It is the comprehensiveness of its coverage that is indeed the keynote of the 1978 Act. A further example is provided by section 1(4) which deals with the situation where one co-defendant has settled the claim made against him by the plaintiff, and now seeks to recover a contribution from another co-defendant. By section 1(4), anyone who either has made or has agreed to make a bona fide settlement of a claim against him shall be entitled to claim a contribution so long as he would have been liable on the assumption that the factual basis of the claim could be established. While this is an important extension of the former law, it should be borne in mind that it is not without restrictions; the settlement must have been a genuine one, and the settlement must, in the light of the wording of the subsection, be in the form of a payment (rather than, say, an agreement to carry out remedial work) before the right to claim a contribution arises. Also, the settlement must be one where there would have been liability had the factual basis of the claim been fully established in court; it is therefore essential that the settlement is based on a clear and accepted legal principle and is made simply because of difficulties of proof, and not because of doubts as to the law in the area. By section 1(2) of the 1978 Act, the fact that someone is no longer liable does not prevent him from claiming a contribution in any case, so long as he was liable at the stage when he made the payment in respect of which contribution is sought. Thus a subsequent judgment or a settlement or compromise within the relevant limitation period does not prevent a claim for contribution from being made. Similarly, section 1(3) makes the potential contributor liable even though he has now ceased to be liable in respect of the damage in question; his liability to contribute thus survives notwithstanding settlement, judgment or, in this case, the expiry of a limitation period, since this extinguishes only the remedy and not the right itself.[1] However, it should be borne in mind that the actual claim for contribution must be brought within two years from the accrual of the right to obtain contribution.[2]

1 *Winfield and Jolowicz on Tort* (11th edn) p. 694.
2 Limitation Act 1963, s. 4, as substituted by the Civil Liability (Contribution) Act 1978, s. 9(1), Sch 1, para 6.

9.12 A plaintiff may also make his own claim against one of those responsible for his losses notwithstanding that he has already recovered against another of those responsible for his losses, under section 3 of the 1978 Act. However, in the later actions his costs will not be met, unless the court is of the view that there was reasonable ground for bringing the action, thus preventing excessive or even vexatious litigation. On the other hand, by section 1(5) of the Act, a claim for contribution will be defeated if the claim by the plaintiff directly has not succeeded, even though the person seeking the contribution may be able to bring better evidence than the original plaintiff.

9.13 The 1978 Act therefore can be seen to be of considerable significance in many defective premises cases. The plaintiff, in seeking redress for the defective state of his premises, is now able to pick out one or more of those jointly liable, and gain full redress, leaving the unsuccessful defendant or defendants to attempt to spread the losses incurred by claiming a contribution from the other parties potentially involved irrespective of the forms of action involved.

9.14 Little needs to be said in relation to the other type of entitlement to contribution which exists viz under the Law Reform (Contributory Negligence) Act 1945. This Act replaces the former rule that contributory negligence by a plaintiff automatically defeated his claim, and inserted in its place the clear statement in section 1(1). This states, inter alia:

> Where any person suffers damage as the result partly of his own fault and partly of the fault of any other person or persons, a claim in respect of that damage shall not be defeated by reason of the fault of the person suffering the damage, but the damages recoverable in respect thereof shall be reduced . . .

This therefore means that after the plaintiff's damages have been assessed, a reduction is made; it is therefore not in literal terms an entitlement to receive a contribution, it is simply a deduction in respect of a notional contribution. Two further points should also be noted in respect of the ambit of these pieces of legislation. Firstly, the 1978 Act only applies to damages claims, and claims in respect of debts are still governed by the common law. Also, it should be borne in mind that the 1945 Act, unlike the 1978 Act, only applies to contributions as regards fault-based liabilities i e negligence cases or cases of a negligent breach of contract, and there is in consequence no provision for a deduction in respect of the plaintiff's own fault in most contract cases; whether the plaintiff's default affects the situation will be a question of causation only.

C Practical implications in defective premises cases

9.15 It is clear from the foregoing that in a defective premises case where several parties are prospectively involved it will be necessary or desirable for the plaintiff to 'select his victim', by choosing which, if not all, prospectively jointly liable defendants to proceed against, and similarly a defendant will have to have regard to the need to consider the claiming of a contribution from other prospective defendants. With this in mind, it is perhaps useful to consider some common features which militate in favour of (or against) pursuing a claim against a particular class of prospective parties to defective premises actions.

9.16   At first sight, the builder should be the obvious starting-point for an action in respect of defective premises; his recently imposed tortious liability, over and above his contractual liability, would tend to confirm this impression. However, it is necessary to sound a note of caution since many firms in the building trade are small firms. Figures compiled from 1969 statistics[1] show that 90.3 per cent of firms engaged in the construction trades were small firms (i e ones employing less than twenty-five); these firms were responsible for 22.7 per cent of the total work done in the construction trades. Unsurprisingly, the majority of the small firms were either general building contractors, or were engaged in such 'household' trades as plumbing, joining and painting. Thus, in a significant numbers of cases, the builder may not have the resources to meet a substantial claim against him.

1   Hillebrant 'Small Firms in the Construction Trade' (Research Report No 10 for Committee of Inquiry on Small Firms), p. 17.

9.17   Additionally, the level of bankruptcy in the construction trades is high, as more recent figures show.[1] Of all the liquidations notified that were either compulsory liquidations or creditors' voluntary liquidations, in 1978, 929 out of a total of 5,086 were in the construction trades; in 1979 the corresponding figures were 789 out of 4,537. While the number is of course small when set against the total number of firms engaged in the construction trades (now believed to be in the 60–70,000 range), it nonetheless represents a considerable problem in the enforcement of claims against builders, especially in tort cases where many years may have elapsed since the construction work took place. It may also be the case, though it cannot be proved, that the firms which go into liquidation may be among the less competent; indeed, it may be that the success of a large claim against a small building firm may be a significant cause of involuntary liquidation. Of course, the purchase of a house protected under the NHBC scheme, with its inbuilt guarantees, obviates this particular problem, at least while the guarantee period lasts.

1   *Companies in 1979* (pub. Department of Trade), Table 8a.

9.18   A further problem arises when a property is sold by a development company. Developers have not been treated separately in this work; they almost always sell the property which has been constructed under their aegis, but normally only have a minimal responsibility for much of the actual building work, as in *Batty v Metropolitan Property Realisations Ltd*.[1] Development companies are often created solely for the purpose of executing one particular development and when that is complete are then wound up; this is of considerable significance for prospective plaintiffs in subsequent years, who find their intended defendant no longer in existence and, legally, quite inaccessible, other than in the exceptional case where a court may permit the raising of the corporate veil, for example in some cases of fraud or similar wilful evasion of legal obligations.[2]

1   [1978] QB 554, [1978] 2 All ER 445.
2   *Gilford Motor Co v Horne* [1933] Ch 935.

9.19   Ordinary domestic vendors, at least, are clearly as yet not fully within the grasp of the law of negligence,[1] and any action against an ordinary vendor alone is unlikely to be successful, unless the vendor has some special knowledge (perhaps because he has done work on the premises) which might render him at fault if he sells without adequate disclosure or checking. In any case, the ordinary domestic vendor may find it difficult to meet a major claim concerning a property of which he had disposed. To a lesser extent, it is also suggested that action against the architect or professional adviser should not be contemplated lightly; while of course in some cases he will be clearly liable, in many others he will be able to create a smokescreen based on two closely related factors. Firstly, he will be able to point out in cases where inadequate supervision is alleged that he was, as is often the case, only intermittently on the site and could not be taken as being some kind of guarantor of their satisfactory standard. Secondly, and this may be of greater utility to an architect involved in a case concerning a claim of inadequate design, the architect is in a good position to raise issues of causation; a builder or specialist engineer will have constructed the property and it may be alleged that he either departed from the design, or alternatively was negligent in not noticing the defects therein, this amounting to a *novus actus interveniens*. It is not here suggested that such claims by an architect will succeed in every case; it is merely being noted that the architect's position in the chain of those responsible for defective premises may on some occasions render him less likely to be liable, rather than more likely. Also, it must be borne in mind that insurance by architects is by no means widespread (indeed, they often have difficulties in obtaining insurance), leaving them perhaps unable to meet a major claim. It is in addition now possible for architects to form themselves into limited liability companies.

1 See ch 6, above.

9.20 It is inevitable that many prospective plaintiffs in premises cases will end up casting covetous eyes at the local authority – a permanent body, unlikely to be wound up or declared bankrupt, with what at least are perceived as being ample resources to meet any claims. The recent expansion of local authorities' negligence liability will undoubtedly be seen by many as a real chance to gain redress in cases where perhaps the other parties are inaccessible. To some extent, this is a fair view; where the local authority has been involved in the provision of the premises, particularly in the exercise of its inspection functions, it is only to be expected that it will be joined to the action by the plaintiff and, if no other parties are available to be sued, the local authority, if jointly liable to any degree, will have to meet all the losses of the plaintiff. There are now some suggestions that the local authority will not be regarded as the guarantor of premises,[1] but it is as yet unclear whether this view will find expression by rendering the local authority not liable, or only liable to a small degree. This is crucial since, if the latter approach is taken, it will of course mean that the local authority, in the absence of other parties, will find itself liable for the full loss suffered by reason of its inability to extract a contribution from other parties, notwithstanding its small degree of blame.

1 See para 9.24, below.

D Contribution – assessment

9.21 Where issues of contribution arise under the Civil Liability (Contribution) Act 1978, section 2(1) governs the assessment of that contribution. This provides that in any proceedings for contribution payable by anyone liable shall be 'such as may be found by the court to be just and equitable having regard to the extent of that person's responsibility for the damage in question'. A similar formulation is adopted by section 1(1) of the Law Reform (Contributory

Negligence) Act 1945 which states that damages awarded to a plaintiff should be reduced in the light of his own contributory negligence 'to such extent as the court thinks just and equitable having regard to the claimant's share in the responsibility for the damage'.

9.22 Thus both Acts give very substantial discretions to the courts; inevitably most cases where these provisions are at issue will be decided on predominantly or entirely factual points. However, the law does provide a little guidance; the 1978 Act, by section 2(3), ensures that a contributor is not liable to pay any greater sum than was paid in damages in the principal action, where that sum has been lowered by reason of contributory negligence, or by a contractual or statutory stipulation, while by section 2(2) the court may exempt any person from any liability to make a contribution, if it is felt to be appropriate, subject to section 2(3). Under the 1945 Act, less assistance is given, but the reduction of damages in the light of a finding of contributory negligence appears to be mandatory.

9.23 The courts have, however, had an opportunity to consider questions arising from the 1945 Act and discussions of precisely how the vague discretion granted by the Act is to be interpreted seem equally relevant to the 1978 Act in view of the close similarity of the wording of the two provisions. Questions both of causation and of culpability will be relevant,[1] though at the end of the day the court will always be able to resort to the factual background of cases and take what they regard as a commonsense view.

1 *Stapley v Gypsum Mines Ltd* [1953] AC 663 at 682, [1953] 2 All ER 478 at 486, per Lord Reid.

9.24 In the specific context of defective premises, again factual considerations will ultimately determine the precise assessment of contribution. Nevertheless, some guidelines showing the courts' attitude to the various parties involved can be drawn from some of the recent cases. It seems clear that the local authority will in the ordinary case only be held responsible for a relatively small proportion of the losses, 20–30 percent being the proportion of the total loss for which they were held liable in *Eames London Estates Ltd v North Hertfordshire District Council*,[1] *Acrecrest Ltd v W S Hattrell & Partners Ltd*,[2] *Oxborrow v Tendring District Council*[3] and *Grice v Williams Jehu Ltd*,[4] all recent decisions at first instance. Various reasons are given for this level of proportion being chosen; factors noted include the relatively low level of qualification of building inspectors, in *Stewart v East Cambridgeshire District Council*[5] (where in fact the local authority were not held to be liable), and the correspondingly high level of the architect's duty to reach his decisions independently, not relying on the local authority, noted in *Acrecrest* and *Eames*. This seems a fair reflection of the proper responsibility of the local authority; in an unreported decision of Judge Fay QC,[6] he said that the building inspector was the policeman; it was the designer and builder who were the true transgressors. It should also be noted that the level of the local authority's responsibility will depend on which particular functions they have actually exercised in a particular case e g in the *Grice* case, Phillips J, having held the local authority 25 percent to blame in considering their negligence in inspecting the premises and in passing the plans, went on to say that were they only negligent in their inspection, they should be held only 10 percent liable.

1 (1980) 259 Estates Gażette 491. See para 4.83, above.
2 (1979) 252 Estates Gazette 1107.
3 (1980) unreported.

4   (1980) 16 May (unreported). See para 5.52, above. See also *Worlock v SAWS and Rushmor Borough Council* (1981) 131 NLJ 1084 (local authority held 40 per cent liable).
5   (1979) 252 Estates Gazette 1105.
6   *Brown and Martin v Walters and Surrey Heath Borough Council* (unreported).

9.25   It is perhaps harder to generalise when questions of contribution arise as between architect and builder, though in both *Eames* and *Oxborrow* they were held equally liable to the plaintiff, and generally they seem to share not dissimilar proportions of the blame in many cases. This is perhaps not surprising; it is suggested that in general the proper approach is to regard the architect and builder as having separate responsibilities (albeit that they overlap to some extent), making roughly equal division appropriate. The builder must be regarded as primarily responsible for the actual construction work, since the architect cannot provide continual supervision; similarly the architect must be primarily responsible for design defects, unless they are so glaring that an experienced builder would notice the shortcomings himself. So, for example, if a building is a novel design, the architect would probably have to bear an even greater share of the liability. It may also be relevant to consider the level of involvement of the architect; if the architect is responsible both for design and supervision, his share of the blame will be greater than if he is only bound to exercise one of those functions.

Index

[References are to paragraph numbers]

[References are to paragraph numbers]